the Unofficial Guide® to Selecting Wine

Felicia M. Sherbert

WILEY

Wiley Publishing, Inc.

To my family and friends who have encouraged me along the way, but especially to my husband, Frost, and our two favorite vintages, Alexandra (1990) and Teddy (1997). Without their constant support and understanding, this book could never have been written.

Acknowledgments

The part that I enjoy most about wine and the wine business is the people I meet and work closely with along the way.

Special thanks to Kevin Zraly, who was instrumental in helping me turn my passion for wine into a very rewarding career by taking a chance on a young writer.

To Marvin R. Shanken, my publisher at M. Shanken Communications, who with his standard for excellence opened the door to a wine world that I could have only dreamed.

To my friends and colleagues at M. Shanken Communications, whom I respect and admire and who are always helpful: Michael Moaba, vice chairman; Martin Leeds, senior vice president, creative services; Frank Walters, senior vice president, research; David L. Ross, managing editor, and Terri Allan, contributing editor, *Market Watch*; Michael and Ariane Batterberry, cofounding editors and associate publishers of *Food Arts*; Thomas Matthews, executive editor; Kim Marcus, managing editor; Bruce Sanderson, senior editor—all of *Wine Spectator*.

I wish to thank all of the winemakers, restaurateurs, hoteliers, fine-wine merchants, trade commissioners, and ambassadors who are always so generous with their time and are very open in sharing their inside view of wine and wine selection. Their willingness to speak so freely is a tribute to the relationship we have built over the past 15 years.

I thank all of the wine importers, producers, and distributors who so kindly supplied labels, samples, and whatever information I needed—and so quickly, too! Special thanks to Margaret Stern, president of Margaret Stern Communications, New York, and Riedel Crystal for supplying illustrations used in this guide.

It is impossible to list everyone who has helped make this book a reality, but there are some who always go above and beyond the call of duty including:

Rory Callahan, president of Wine & Food Associates, New York; Odila Galer-Noel, Frederick Wildman & Sons, Ltd., New York; Marsha Palanci, president of Cornerstone Communications, New York; Carol Sullivan, executive director of the German Wine Information Bureau, New York, for fact-checking the German chapter; Jean-Louis Carbonnier, director of the Champagne Wines Information Bureau, New York; Allen Shoup, president and CEO of Stimson Lane Vineyards and Estates in Woodinville, Washington, and Katie Sims, director of public relations for Stimson Lane; Phil di Belardino, vice president & director of the Vinum Division of Banfi Vintners, and Sharron McCarthy, director of wine education at Banfi Vintners, both from Old Brookville, New York; Cathleen Burke, vice president and director of marketing, her marketing assistant Michelle Quinn, and Jane McGrath, national accounts specialist for Kobrand Corporation, New York; John Gillespie, president of the Wine Market Council, Greenbrae, California; Michaela Rodeno, CEO of St. Supéry Vineyard & Winery; Stephanie Kane of Seagram Château & Estate Winery, New York; Mary Marshall, Media Relations Manager of Paterno Imports, Chicago; Jeffrey Pogash, media relations director at Schieffelin & Somerset Company, New York;

Kathleen Talbert, president of Kathleen Talbert Communications, New York; Rudi and Brent Wiest of Cellars International, Inc., Carlsbad, California; Terry Theise of Terry Theise Estate Selections, Jessup, Maryland; Al Ferrone, corporate director of food and beverage operations, Promus Hotels, Memphis; Charles Sonnenberg, owner of Frugal MacDoogal's fine-wine shop, Memphis; and Fred Tibbitts Jr., president of Fred Tibbitts and Associates, New York.

I thank the doctors and lawyers and other wine collectors whom I have had occasion to sit with at "serious" wine dinners as well as the many "occasional" wine drinkers I know who provide a constant reality check of the way "real" people select wine.

Thank you to my managing editor Brice Gosnell and development editor Amy Langston, who kept this book on track, as well as our panel of experts who provided valuable input along the way. Thank you to my agent, Bert Holtje.

Special thanks to Brian Zevnik who showed me the ropes.

To my parents, Murray and Lila Sherbert, and my in-laws, Ted and Martha Schroeder, for all their help and encouragement.

Above all, I thank my husband and unofficial editor, Frost Schroeder, a wine wizard himself who devoted even more time to our children, Alexandra and Teddy, so I could put in the long hours necessary to write this book.

Contents

The *Unofficial Guide* Reader's Bill of Rights ..xvii

About the Author..xxi

The *Unofficial Guide* Panel of Experts xxiii

Introduction xxv

I Wine for Every Occasion 1

1 Wine—What Are You Saving It For? 3

Two Camps of Wine Savers............................4

Gauge the Mood..5

"Old Faithful" Wines 5

Wine with Food 6
    Wine and Food Pairing 101 7
    For Every Food Action There Is a Wine
        Reaction 9
    Casual Family Dinner 12
    Barbeque...12
    Formal Dinner Party 13
    Dry Kosher Wines 14
    After-Dinner Options............................15

A Little Romance.......................................16

ABC Wines (Anything but Chardonnay) 17

Pick a Price Point.....................................19
    What Makes a Wine So Expensive or So
        Cheap? 19
    How You Can Find Value..........................21

Just the Facts...22

2 What's Your Style?...............................23

Red, White, or Rosé?................................23

Sparkling Options 24

Dry, Fruity, or Sweet?................................24

Varietals Versus Blends..............................26

Light-, Medium-, or Full-Bodied Wine...........29

Pick a Region 30

The Label: Information or Information
Overload?...37

Healthful Aspects of Wine............................43

Just the Facts...45

3 How to Taste Wine.................................47

Taste Sensations...48
  Sweet 49
  Sour..49
  Bitter..50
  Salt...50
  Umami: The New Taste Sensation 51
  Mouthfeel or Texture...............................51

Revelations of Color....................................51

The Five S's 52
  See 53
  Swirl...53
  Smell..54
  Sip 55
  Savor..55

What Does Wine Taste Like?.........................56
  Flavor Profiles of White Grapes 57
  Flavor Profiles of Red Grapes...................62

Expanding Your Wine Repertoire 67

Just the Facts...69

II A Glass of White Wine, Please?.........71

4 Classic French Whites 73

Importance of Appellation d'Origine Contrôlée
(AOC) 74

Alsace 75

Loire Valley 77

Bordeaux...79
  Graves..79
  Pessac-Léognan 80

Burgundy 81
  Chablis...82
  Mâcconais 85
  Côte de Beaune 86

Côte Châlonnaise *89*

Rhône Valley....................................*90*

Just the Facts....................................*91*

5 Noble German Whites 93

Land of Riesling *95*

Strict Controls....................................*98*

Tafelwein....................................*99*
Qualitätswein bestimmter Anbaugebiete.....*99*
Qualitätswein mit Prädikat *99*

Deciphering a Label *102*

Just the Facts *109*

6 American Whites 111

Wine, Wine Everywhere............................*111*

American Viticultural Areas (AVAs)—American
for AOC *113*

California *116*

North Coast....................................*117*
North Central Coast *118*
South Central Coast............................*119*
Central Valley *119*
Sierra Foothills *119*
Jug Wines....................................*119*
Varietals, California Style....................*120*
Chardonnay....................................*121*
Sauvignon Blanc *122*
Viognier....................................*123*
Gewürztraminer....................................*123*
Pinot Blanc....................................*124*
Riesling *124*

California Vintages....................................*124*

The Pacific Northwest....................................*125*

Washington State....................................*125*
Oregon *127*

New York State and Long Island................*128*

Just the Facts *130*

7 Old- and New-World Whites....................131

La Moda Italia....................................*132*

Spain Updates Its "Old-World" Ways *134*

Portugal Beyond Port 136

White Wines from the Outback..................137
   New South Wales *139*
   South Australia................................*140*
   Victoria *141*
   Western Australia *141*

Increasing Importance of Australian
Appellations 142
   White Varietals Down Under *143*
   Australian Vintages *145*

New Zealand's Best 145

South American Whites..........................147
   Chile..*148*
   Chilean Joint Ventures *149*
   Argentina *150*

South Africa 152

Just the Facts 154

III Warming Up to Reds....................155

8 The French "Red" Standard...................157

The Return to Reds 157

Red Burgundy Wines 159
   Beaujolais..*160*
   Côte d'Or *162*
   Best of the Burgundies.........................*165*
   Côte Châlonnaise.............................*171*

Bordeaux.....................................172
   Official Classification of 1855................*176*
   Cru Bourgeois Values...........................*179*
   Classified Buying Strategy....................*180*
   Top Graves *181*
   The Best of Pomerol and St.-Émilion........*182*

The Rhône Valley 185
   The Prestigious Northern Rhône *185*
   Southern Rhône *186*

Values from Southern France 189

Just the Facts 190

9 U.S. Reds...................................191

Easing into Reds, California Style..............192

Getting Your Arms Around California's
Regions...200
    North Coast...*203*
    North Central Coast *204*
    South Central Coast.............................*204*
    Central Valley *204*
    Sierra Foothills *205*
Meritage Wines...205
California Vintages....................................207
Pacific Northwest......................................207
    Washington State.................................*208*
    Oregon *210*
New York State and Long Island.................212
Just the Facts 213

10 Old- and New-World Reds 215
From Italy with Love.................................216
Quality Control, Italian Style 217
Tuscany..219
    Chianti...*219*
    Brunello di Montalcino *220*
    Vino Nobile di Montepulciano.................*221*
    Carmignano..*221*
Piedmont..222
Veneto: Land of Valpolicella, Bardolino, and
Amarone...224
Other Italian Reds 225
Olé for Spanish Reds 226
    Historic Rioja *227*
    Age Matters..*228*
    Ribera del Duero *229*
    Penedès...*230*
Portugal Sees Red......................................231
Australia 232
Chile..235
Argentina 237
South Africa 238
Just the Facts 239

IV All Blush and Bubbles 241

11 Rosé or Blush Wine 243
How and Where Rosés Are Made.................243
Sutter Home's "Overnight" Success.............245
French Rosé 248
  Loire Valley *249*
  Provence..*250*
  Languedoc-Roussillon *251*
  Rhône Valley (Tavel) *252*
Spanish Rosado 252
Italian Rosato 253
How to Select and Serve Pink Wines..........254
Just the Facts 255

12 Sparkle Plenty.....................................257
Champagne Versus Sparkling Wine.............258
How Champagne Is Made 259
What Determines Style?.............................264
How to Read a Champagne Label 265
How to Select Champagne..........................268
Sparkling Alternatives 270
  United States *271*
  Spain..*273*
  Italy *274*
  Australia...*275*
Storing and Serving Champagne.................276
How to Open Champagne and Sparkling
Wine..277
Just the Facts 277

13 After-Dinner Delights............................279
Port from Oporto 279
  Wood Port..*280*
  Vintage Port...*282*
  How to Decant Port *285*
  Port-Style Alternatives...........................*286*
Sauternes and Barsac 287
Other Dessert Wines from France...............291
Germany's Signature..................................291

Late Harvest Wines from the United States..294

Other Dessert Wine Options.......................297
    Australian "Stickies".............................*297*
    Italian Vin Santo *298*
    Hungarian Tokay *298*

Just the Facts 300

V Buying and Ordering Wine 301

14 Demystifying the Wine List....................303

A Note About Restaurant Markups 304

Different Types of Wine Lists 307
    The Extended Wine List *308*
    House Wine and Wines by the Glass.........*308*
    Flights..*309*

How to Read a Wine List 309
    Wine Lists by Region Versus Varietal........*310*
    Progressive Wine Lists *311*

How to Order Wine..................................313

Need Help Navigating the List?...................314
    Sommelier, Cellarmaster, or Server? *314*
    Flying Solo.......................................*316*
    The Most Basic Wine List Survival Technique
        for Safety *317*
    How the Wine Savvy Cut to the Chase......*318*

Getting a Grip on the Wine Ritual 319

When to Send Wine Back and
How to Do It 321

Just the Facts 322

15 How to Find a Good Wine Merchant.........323

What to Look For in the Store and in the
People 324

Building a Relationship with Your Wine
Merchant..326

Returning Bad Bottles 329

A Note About Retail Markups.....................330

Buying Strategies 333
    Cheaper by the Dozen *333*
    Wine Futures.....................................*333*
    The Pros and Cons of Buying Direct *334*

How to Start a Wine Collection 336
Buying at Auction................................337
   Auction Strategies..............................*338*
   Special Tips for Selling at Auction..........*341*
   Wine Auction Houses and Retailers..........*342*
Wine Advisers 343
Just the Facts 345

VI Entertaining with Wine 347

16 Crowd Pleasers 349

Business Entertaining...........................349
   Business Protocol for Wine....................*351*
   Price as a Consideration.......................*352*
Dinner Party 353
Brunch..354
Banquets: Weddings, Anniversaries, Bar
Mitzvahs and Bat Mitzvahs...................355
   Dealing with Banquet Directors...............*355*
   Catering Wine Options..........................*357*
   Wine Service at Banquets *359*
What to Buy for an Event and How Much 361
The Mechanics of Setting Up Wine Service
at Home...366
Entertaining Recipes 367
Organizing a Wine-Tasting Party.................370
Just the Facts 372

VII How to Serve and Store Wine..........375

17 Essential Tools and Tricks 377

Extracting the Cork 378
   Double-Winged Opener *378*
   Waiter's Corkscrew *379*
   Pulltap's...*380*
   Screwpull..*380*
   Ah-So...*381*
   Troubleshooting Cork Catastrophes *382*
Serving Temperature.............................383
Proper Stemware.................................386

How to Decant Wine 389

Break Open the Bubbly..........................390

How to Save Leftovers...........................391
    Vacu-Vin *392*
    Private Preserve *393*
    Cruvinet...*393*
    Le Verre de Vin *393*

Storing Wine at Home 394

Just the Facts 397

A Glossary...**399**

B Resource Guide....................................**429**

C Recommended Reading **453**

**D Entertainment Wine Service
Cheat Sheets** **457**

E Wine on the Web...................................**469**

The *Unofficial Guide* Reader's Bill of Rights

We Give You More Than the Official Line

Welcome to the Unofficial Guide series of Lifestyles titles—books that deliver critical, unbiased information that other books can't or won't reveal—the inside scoop. Our goal is to provide you with the most accessible, useful information and advice possible. The recommendations we offer in these pages are not influenced by the corporate line of any organization or industry; we give you the hard facts whether those institutions like them or not. If something is ill-advised or will cause a loss of time and/or money, we'll give you ample warning. If it's a worthwhile option, we'll let you know that, too.

Armed and Ready

Our handpicked authors confidently and critically report on a wide range of topics that matter to smart readers like you. Our authors are passionate about their subjects, but they have distanced themselves enough from them to help you be armed and protected and to help you make educated decisions as you go through the process. It is our intent that, having read this book, you will avoid the pitfalls everyone else falls into and get it right the first time.

Don't be fooled by cheap imitations; this is the genuine article *Unofficial Guide* series from IDG Books. You may be familiar with our proven track record of the travel *Unofficial Guides*, which have more than three million copies in print. Each year, thousands of travelers—new and old—are armed with a brand-new, fully updated edition of the flagship *Unofficial Guide to Walt Disney World* by Bob Sehlinger. It is our intent here to provide you with the same level of objective authority that Mr. Sehlinger does in his brainchild.

The Unofficial Panel of Experts

Every Lifestyle *Unofficial Guide* is intensively inspected by a team of three top professionals in their fields. These experts review the manuscript for factual accuracy, comprehensiveness, and an insider's determination as to whether the manuscript fulfills the credo in this Reader's Bill of rights. In other words, our Panel ensures that you are, in fact, getting the inside scoop.

Our Pledge

The authors, the editorial staff, and the Unofficial Panel of Experts assembled for *Unofficial Guides* are determined to lay out the most valuable alternatives available for our readers. This dictum means that our writers must be explicit, prescriptive, and above all, direct. We strive to be thorough and complete, but our goal is not necessarily to have the "most" or "all" of the information on a topic; this is not, after all, an encyclopedia. Our objective is to help you narrow down your options to the best of what is available, unbiased by affiliation with any industry or organization.

In each *Unofficial Guide*, we give you:

- Comprehensive coverage of necessary and vital information
- Authoritative data, rigidly fact-checked
- The most up-to-date insights into trends
- Savvy, sophisticated writing that's also readable
- Sensible, applicable facts and secrets that only an insider knows

Special Features

Every book in our series offers the following six special sidebars in the margins. They were devised to help you get things done cheaply, efficiently, and smartly.

1. **Timesaver**—tips and shortcuts that save you time
2. **Moneysaver**—tips and shortcuts that save you money
3. **Watch out!**—more serious cautions and warnings
4. **Bright Idea**—general tips and shortcuts to help you find an easier or smarter way to do something
5. **Quote**—statements from real people that are intended to be prescriptive and valuable to you
6. **Unofficially…**—an insider's fact or anecdote

We also recognize your need to have quick information at your fingertips. We therefore have provided the following comprehensive sections at the back of the book:

1. **Glossary**—definitions of complicated terminology and jargon

2. **Resource Guide**—lists of relevant agencies, associations, institutions, and so on

3. **Recommended Reading List**—suggested titles that can help you get more in-depth information about related topics

4. **Important Documents**—"official" pieces of information to which you need to refer

5. **Web Sites**—places to visit on the Internet with the most up-to-date information

6. **Index**

Letters, Comments, Questions from Readers

We strive to continually improve the *Unofficial* series, and input from our readers is a valuable way for us to do that.

Many people who have used the *Unofficial Guide* travel books write to the authors to ask questions, to make comments, or to share their own discoveries and lessons. For Lifestyle *Unofficial Guides*, we also would appreciate all such correspondence—both positive and critical—and we will make our best efforts to incorporate appropriate reader feedback and comments in revised editions of this work.

How to write us:
Unofficial Guides
Lifestyle Guides
IDG Books
1633 Broadway
New York, NY 10019
Attention: Reader's Comments

About the Author

Felicia M. Sherbert can tell you everything you need to know about selecting wine. Felicia is a journalist who has specialized in wine for more than 15 years. She wrote and edited the best-selling *Windows on the World Complete Wine Course* (Sterling Publishing Co., 1985) with wine director Kevin Zraly and recently completed a major revision of the book, the *Windows on the World Complete Wine Course Millennium Edition* (Sterling Publishing Co., 1999). Since the book's debut in 1985, it has sold more than one million copies, making it the top-selling wine book in the United States.

Before launching her own company in 1997, Felicia was a senior editor at M. Shanken Communications, Inc., the publisher of *Wine Spectator*, *Food Arts*, and *Market Watch*, a magazine specializing in wine and spirits trends. She continues to contribute to these and other publications, she writes a regular column called "At the Bar," in *Market Watch* magazine, and she is a frequent guest speaker about wine, restaurant, and retail trends. Felicia also is a founding member of the International Food & Beverage Forum, a think tank composed of food and beverage professionals.

When she is not writing, Felicia enjoys sharing a glass of wine with her husband, Frost Schroeder, playing with their two children, Alexandra and Teddy, and entertaining family and friends.

The *Unofficial Guide* Panel of Experts

The *Unofficial* editorial team recognizes that you've purchased this book with the expectation of getting the most authoritative, carefully inspected information currently available. To that end, for each and every title in this series, we have selected a minimum of two "official" experts for the Unofficial Panel who painstakingly review the manuscripts to ensure the following: factual accuracy of all data; inclusion of the most up-to-date and relevant information; and that, from an insider's perspective, the authors have armed you with all the necessary facts you need—but that the institutions don't want you to know.

For *The Unofficial Guide to Selecting Wine*, we are proud to introduce the following panel of experts:

Rory Callahan is the president of Wine & Food Associates, a New York City market development firm which was founded in 1987. Its clients are New Zealand, Wines from Spain including the regions of Ribera del Duero, Rias Baixas, Cava, and several regional U.S. winery associations among others. Mr. Callahan was trained in enology at the University of California at Davis and gained experience as a winemaker before moving to New York City where he was a cofounder of the International Wine Center in 1981. He established the East Coast offices for the Wine Institute (of California) in 1985 prior to opening Wine & Food Associates.

Abigail Sawyer is the former editor of *Wine Business Monthly* magazine and a freelance writer on wine, food, and related indulgences. Her work has appeared in a number of magazines and Websites. Ms. Sawyer is also the director of content development for YumYuk.com, an information site for the grocery-store–wine consumer, and is at work compiling an anthology of wine literature. She lives in San Francisco.

Bo Thompson has worked with wine professionally for almost 20 years as a manager and wine buyer for many highly acclaimed San Francisco restaurants including Greens, Buckeye Roadhouse, Fog City Diner, and Gordon's House of Fine Eats. He is a passionate advocate of improving wine service and wine product knowledge within the restaurant industry. Presently, Mr. Thompson is a wine buyer for Wine.com (formerly Virtual Vineyards) in the Napa Valley and lives in Tiburon, California.

Introduction

Why is it so important to know how to select wine? Wine has been a part of civilization since biblical times. It sits on the table in Europe as part of the meal just as we set our table with salt and pepper. Gradually, wine is gaining wider acceptance in the United States, and it has even become a part of our United States Department of Agriculture (USDA) accepted dietary guidelines. More and more medical evidence attests to wine's benefits to one's health, especially in preventing heart disease, when used in moderation.

Wine consumption is growing gradually in the United States, and it is expected to continue growing well into the 21st Century due to the following trends:

- Wine has health benefits. We continue to hear good news about wine's role in keeping you healthy as long as you don't overdo it.

- Our population is aging. As people mature, they drink more wine. Typically, Americans drink more beer and spirits when they first hit the legal drinking age. Then they gradually switch over to wine.

- Organizations such as Wine Brats are making wine more appealing and hip to the 21- to 34-year-old market. Wine Brats includes the younger generation of winemakers like Jeff Bundschu (Gundlach-Bundschu Winery), Michael Sangiacomo (Sangiacomo Vineyards), and Jon Sebastiani (Viansa Winery) who have started reasonably priced Wine Raves that go along with rock fashion shows as a hip alternative to stuffy and expensive wine tastings.

- Wine is the perfect "sharing" beverage. Unlike beer or spirits that are skewed to a male or female audience, both men and women enjoy wine equally. Interestingly enough, more women are buying wine at retail, perhaps because it is so accessible in many supermarkets and because women still do most of the grocery shopping.

- Wine is more accessible. Over the past several years, wine has become more accessible in restaurants thanks to wine-by-the-glass programs. And instead of being saddled with a glass of ordinary plonk, you often can choose from many different quality wines.

Removing the Mystery, Not the Magic

Despite these encouraging trends, historically in the U.S., wine has been put on a pedestal for the rich and famous, and this is unfortunate. Michael Mondavi, president of the Robert Mondavi Winery in Napa, California, is the first to say, "My father's generation made wine elitist." Ironically, his father, Robert Mondavi, the eighty-something-year-young founder of the winery, is an icon of the wine world. He is known for bringing wine down to earth and encouraging people of all generations to make it a part of their daily lifestyle.

The whole pomp and circumstance surrounding wine selection and wine service shrouded it in mystery, made it intimidating, and effectively put it in the "special occasion" category. Many people, even today, are just as happy if that special occasion doesn't come, and if it does, they're content to have someone else do the dirty deed of wine selecting. You have to remember that there are only 9 million wine drinkers out of a country of 142.6 million legal-aged adults, and they account for 75 percent of the total wine consumption in the United States. This means that a lot of people are at best only occasional wine drinkers. When pressed, people who are not regular wine drinkers might opt for "a glass of red," "white," or "blush" wine. They might even venture to the next level and order "a glass of Cabernet," "Chardonnay" or "White Zinfandel." This is a step in the right direction.

Even more seasoned wine drinkers fall into the rut that is their comfort zone by sticking with what they know. For instance, plenty of old-timers will drink French wine because that was what was considered "good" and "sophisticated" when they came of age in the 1940s or '50s. Other people stick to California Chardonnay because that's what they know. This book will help you comfortably expand your repertoire of wines.

Wine Independence

There's an old saying, "Give a man a fish and he eats for one day. Teach him how to fish and he eats for a lifetime."

In this book, we don't tell you that you must go out and buy a specific wine from a specific vintage. This can be very frustrating if you can't find that particular wine at your wine shop or restaurant. We do something better: We teach you how to fish. The tools are here for you to make your selection depending on your personal taste and budget. Though we don't give you specific wines, we do make recommendations of specific producers. These are very important throughout the wine world because these key players have earned a reputation for reliability and consistency. This helps you hedge your bets when you are selecting wine.

In terms of the actual selection process, if you know, for example, that you enjoy and usually drink California Chardonnay, we may recommend that you try a white Burgundy from France because this wine also is made from Chardonnay. If you enjoy Sangiovese, perhaps you'd like a tasty Chianti or a Chianti Riserva from Italy. You say you have a taste for Bordeaux but you're not currently on a Bordeaux budget? Try a Cabernet Sauvignon from Chile, the Bordeaux of the Southern Hemisphere, for a fraction of the price. These are just a few ways you can broaden your wine horizons.

Value

Seeking value in wine does not necessarily mean you should buy the cheapest wine on the retail shelf or the restaurant wine list. In fact, you are practically guaranteed to select a poor value because you get what you pay for. Value is getting the best quality for the least amount of money. Our mission is to show you how to get the biggest bang for your wine buck whenever possible. If we can make wine drinking an affordable pleasure, we figure we've done our share to remove wine from your "special occasion" category and move it closer to your daily life.

The best way to find a wine value is to:

1. Select a grape variety that is less popular such as Sauvignon Blanc instead of Chardonnay in white wines.

2. Select a wine from a lesser-known region. Instead of Napa or Sonoma Valley, for example, look for a wine from California's Central Coast.

3. Try a blend. Some good winemakers are producing very tasty blends either by using one grape variety, such as Chardonnay, sourced from different wine regions (where the land is cheaper) or by mixing varieties. The most common blends are Sémillon with Chardonnay for white and Cabernet Sauvignon with Shiraz for red, but now you can even find a white made from Chardonnay blended with Pinot Grigio. It makes for an interesting quaff, and it usually saves you money because the winemaker is not using 100 percent of his most expensive grapes. The two blends mentioned here caught on in Australia, but they are beginning to show up in other wine regions as well.

If you are seeking a good wine value, it makes sense to pay careful attention to where in the world the most important wine regions are located. Even if you cringe at the thought of high school geography, you'd be surprised at the wine discoveries you'll make if you recognize the little village off the beaten path of a famous, high-priced vineyard.

A Note on Ratings

Most wine publications rate the wine they taste.

Ratings can be as effective as a restaurant review because they give you an idea of what to expect before you plunk down your hard-earned cash for a bottle. It works like a dream if you know from experience that your taste in wine is similar to that of the person or panel doing the tasting. On the flip side of the equation, if you find that you rarely agree with the consensus, stop chasing rainbows and go with your own taste buds. People often ask, What makes a wine good? The answer is simple: A good wine is one you like. If you don't like it, it's not good.

If you follow wine ratings the way some people track the movement of the stock market, keep in mind that it might be difficult to find the exact wine that earned the 90 points. This is especially true if you are not located in a major market such as New York, Chicago, or Los Angeles, for example, where the wine distribution is best as compared to a smaller market like Albuquerque. We're not trying to discourage you from looking for these wines, but we do urge you to either use a little commonsense wine logic or tips from this book or have the confidence to ask your retailer for a good alternative. Of course, when a wine receives a high rating, it becomes hard to get as soon as the numbers hit the stands. Read publications for the trends, not the numbers.

A Note About Vintages

Speaking of numbers, we don't get hung up on vintages. In this book, where appropriate, we highlight some of the better recent vintages. Some wine wizards might disagree with our view of vintages, but we know that most wine purchased at a wine shop or a grocery store today is going to be consumed within three days of the purchase. In most cases, no cellaring is involved. The closest you might get to this is to stock your wine rack as you would your pantry as a matter of convenience so you can grab a bottle to open with dinner.

Getting the Most Out of This Book

Part I takes you through the thought process of selecting wine and matching the appropriateness of the wine to your mood and the occasion. You also will learn how to taste wine like a professional.

Part II begins with the major white-wine regions. White wines are covered first because they are lighter in style, beginning with the classic French regions and working our way to the New World, which includes Australia, New Zealand, South America, and South Africa.

In Part III, we move into the bigger flavors with red wines, tracing the renaissance of red wines and covering the major red-wine areas. Again, we begin with the classics from France and work our way into the New World.

You'll get the complete lowdown on the difference between Champagne and sparkling wine in Part IV as well as an inside look at how blush wine like white Zinfandel is made. For anyone who enjoys this pink beauty from California, there are plenty of other rosé wines from which to choose if you are looking for a welcome change of pace. Also in Part IV, you'll learn how to select the perfect Port or dessert wine to satisfy your sweet tooth at the end of the meal.

In Part V, we get down to the brass tacks of buying wine at retail or at a restaurant. There's no need to make yourself crazy poring over a laundry list of wines if you can narrow down your selection in the most basic sense. At a restaurant, for example, you may decide you're in the mood for a red wine, and you might prefer an Italian wine because you're having dinner at an Italian restaurant. You've just cut the wine list in half or even more, and you can better focus on what you want without wasting time.

If you're thinking about entertaining with wine at home, go directly to Part VI and Part VII. These sections cover every conceivable party situation from dealing with banquet directors and caterers to knowing how much wine you'll need to serve at a party. In fact, we ran all the numbers to create special Wine Entertainment Cheat Sheets (located in Appendix D) that will come in handy when you need to know how much wine to buy—whether you're having a few friends over for dinner or throwing a lavish wedding.

Selecting wine can be fun and easy when you have some inside information at your fingertips.

One of the best things about wine is that it is constantly changing. There are so many world-class wine regions, truly from all over the world, that produce so many different and interesting styles of wine.

As Auntie Mame used to say, "The world's a banquet and look at all those poor sons of bitches who are starving." Fortunately, when it comes to selecting wine, there's a feast ripe for the picking.

Select a bottle to have with dinner this evening. Be daring and try something a little different. Chances are, you'll be glad you did. Sit back with a glass, relax, and enjoy!

Wine for Every Occasion

PART I

GET THE SCOOP ON...

How a few Americans drink all our wine ▪ How
your mood determines your wine selection ▪
How food factors into wine selection ▪ Adding
festivity to the occasion ▪ How much you need
to spend ▪ Finding the best wine values

Wine—What Are You Saving It For?

Chapter 1

A mericans make a big deal about wine. They
often are so afraid of making a mistake
in selecting, opening, or serving wine that
they decide the easiest thing to do is to have a glass
of something else.

I suspect that this happens quite often, and there
are statistics that confirm this. Recent research from
the Wine Market Council, a California group whose
mission it is to get more people to drink wine, shows
that out of an adult population of 142.6 million people aged 21–59, there are only 15.7 million core
wine drinkers.

Of this group of wine drinkers, 8.6 million could
be considered serious consumers. These people
drink wine more like the Europeans—several times
a week or daily. The other 7.1 million core consumers drink wine weekly. The bottom line? These
15.7 million core wine devotees who amount to 11
percent of the legal adult population drink 88 percent of the table wine consumed in the United
States.

Another 25.7 million Americans are considered marginal wine consumers. These are people who save wine for a special occasion such as a celebratory dinner out or for entertaining guests. They drink wine less often than weekly but at least as often as every two to three months. Another 42.8 million people choose not to drink alcohol of any kind, and the remaining 15.6 million enjoy beer or a cocktail but do not drink wine.

Two camps of wine savers

As I see it—and this isn't part of the research—there are two groups of wine "savers." One group is the marginal wine drinkers who would drink more regularly if they felt more comfortable with it. These people save wine for special occasions such as events that require strapping into a fashionable but uncomfortable suit.

The other group of wine savers might enjoy a glass every day (and chances are you might be one of them), but they still save wines, too. For instance, do you have a tendency to put your better wines aside for a special occasion? I'm not talking about wine lovers who have good storage conditions at home and truly collect. I'm talking about people who squirrel away that bottle of Dom Pérignon or Château Very Expensive that was received as a housewarming gift years ago. These are the bottles that are put in the wine rack or at the back of the closet to collect dust in a warm apartment. Inevitably, the bottle gets broken before you get a chance to open it. Or, you might finally find a reason to celebrate and pull the cork with great anticipation, only to be disappointed when the wine seems as if it would taste better as part of your salad dressing. Been there, done that.

When it comes to enjoying wine, my attitude is, "What are you saving it for?"

Gauge the mood

Mood has everything to do with the kind of wine you want to have. What are you in the mood for? Are you looking to quench a thirst, relax on the porch and admire the sunset, accompany your dinner, or just celebrate? Are you winding down after a long day by yourself, catching up with your significant other, or mellowing out with some friends? Are you in the mood for adventure? Or would you prefer to drink something as comfortable as your perfectly worn pair of jeans?

Sometimes you select a wine because you want to create a mood. Looking for an instantly festive atmosphere? Break out the champagne or, as a guest, bring a bottle to the host of the party. Another way to liven the party is to serve wine from oversized bottles. Magnums, the equivalent of two regular-size bottles or 1.5 liters, and double magnums, the equivalent of four regular bottles or 3 liters, add to the drama. Big bottles are available in both popular-priced varietals and more expensive wines from California, Bordeaux, Champagne, and other wine regions.

"Old Faithful" wines

After a long day, I look forward to a having a glass of wine just to relax for a few minutes. The type of wine I'm talking about here is something you might adopt as your personal "house wine." It can be red, white, or rosé (blush) depending on your preference, and it usually is inexpensive. Whatever you select, it should be noncerebral, meaning you don't have to think about it. You can just go to your fridge or your wine rack, pull out the bottle, and pour yourself a glass. Recork the bottle tightly and place it back in your fridge for later or tomorrow. You should even refrigerate red wine because reds that have been opened maintain their freshness best in the refrigerator. It's that easy.

When I go to my in-laws' house, at the end of the day, they take a 1.5 liter bottle of Robert Mondavi Woodbridge Sauvignon Blanc out and pour everyone a glass of wine to have with a few munchies. The wine is pleasant, versatile, easy to drink, and easy on the pocketbook. You can get a 1.5 liter on sale for under $10. It's a great buy, and it definitely fits into the "kick back and quaff" category.

In warmer months, I almost always keep a simple bottle of white wine in the fridge. When it's cooler out, there's usually a warming red at the ready. I'm not loyal to one brand as my in-laws are, but that's because I like to experiment with different wines made from different grape varietals and from different wine regions.

Wine with food

Years ago, when I worked with a chef on a wine-and-food book, he made a point that has stuck with me ever since. He said that wine is like a spice used to enhance food. It doesn't sound like rocket science to me now, but it makes more sense than I first imagined.

First of all, wine tastes one way when you drink it by itself. If you then take a bite of food, you'll have a different taste experience because of the way the flavors marry. That's why, in the wine business, they say, "Buy on apples; sell on cheese." Typically, the acid in the apple exposes the flaws in a wine, but a good piece of cheese such as brie or cabrales covers a multitude of sins because the protein and the fat interact with the wine to actually make it taste better. Under these conditions, the reasoning goes, if you like the wine with the apple, the wine must be very, very good. Why do you think they call them "wine and cheese" parties? The better wine and food pairings will make your food taste better.

Chefs, by their training and experience, have an affinity for what spice goes with what food. Rosemary and thyme are naturals with roasted chicken; dill is so often used with salmon; garlic and basil are staples in many tomato sauces. In each of these tried-and-true combinations, the food and the spice interact to create a harmonious flavor. But does this mean that these are the only spices and flavors to be had? No.

The same is true for wine. Some basic food and wine pairings are considered to be as classic as peanut butter and jelly because they are known to work so well together. Take, for instance, Chablis with oysters; red Bordeaux, California Cabernet Sauvignon, or Australian Shiraz with rack of lamb; Sauternes with Roquefort cheese; or Port with Stilton cheese and walnuts. There are many more classic combinations, but the most important wine and food combinations are the ones you enjoy.

Wine and food pairing 101

The most basic and best-known general wine and food pairing rule in winedom is this: red wine with meat, white wine with fish or fowl. In recent years, we've gotten bold and said it's okay to have Pinot Noir, which is a light red wine, or even Merlot with salmon. This is good for starters, but I believe it is more important to have lighter-bodied wines with lighter foods and fuller-bodied wines with heavier foods. Lighter-bodied wine generally means white, though there are lighter-bodied reds such as Pinot Noir, Merlot, Gamay (Beaujolais), and Dolcetto.

To keep things simple, here's a list of grape varietals, or styles of wine, in order from the lightest to the most full-bodied. It's not absolute because there are so many variables in winemaking, but it will help you make an informed wine selection:

TABLE 1.1: WINE WEIGHT— FROM LIGHT TO FULL-BODIED

White Wines (Grapes)	Red Wines (Grapes)
	Champagne or sparkling wine
	Gamay
White Zinfandel	Dolcetto
Riesling	Barbera
Pinot Grigio	Pinot Noir
Sauvignon Blanc (also known as Fumé Blanc)	Tempranillo
Chenin Blanc	Cabernet Franc
Pinot Blanc	Grenache/Garnacha
Gewürztraminer	Malbec
Sémillon	Sangiovese
Viognier	Merlot
Chardonnay	Syrah
	Cabernet Sauvignon
	Zinfandel
	Nebbiolo

When you get into how the food is made—the style of cooking used (grilled, roasted, fried, and so on), the spices used in the preparation, and the sauces—these general wine and food pairing suggestions just aren't good enough. The sauce, like a lemon beurre blanc, for instance, lends a different flavor profile to chicken than a tomatoey pizzaiola sauce. In this case, you'll most likely want to select your wine based on the lemon-butter or tomato-based sauce in order to come up with a good match.

At this juncture, you have two choices. You're welcome to stay with whatever wine you find most comfortable, regardless of the way it does or does not go with the food according to the "experts" who are not eating your dinner. After all, look at how many people always have bottled water or a soft drink with their meal. Your other option is to learn the basics of what types of foods work best with different types of wine and experiment for yourself. You might ask, how does wine work with food to make your dinner taste better? Read on.

For every food action there is a wine reaction

When I was growing up, I remember that my grandfather used to sprinkle salt on his cantaloupe and grapefruit. It always seemed rather odd to me, but when I asked him why he did it, he explained that the salt made the fruit taste sweeter. The salt neutralized the bitterness and sourness of the fruit and accentuated the sweetness.

Take this a step further and consider what happens when you have salty food with wine. The saltiness of the food will actually make your wine seem sweeter the same way it made my grandfather's cantaloupe and grapefruit taste sweeter.

Here are some basic reactions between food flavors and wine styles that will make it easier for you to select a wine that enhances your meal.

1. **Sweet Foods.** You might think that you eat sweet foods only during dessert, but the truth is that there is a fair amount of sweetness in many dishes such as Italian tomato sauce, Japanese teriyaki, honey-mustard glazes, and the cocktail sauce you enjoy with shrimp

cocktail. The sweetness in the food makes your wine seem drier than it really is, so you might want to go with an off-dry wine to balance out the flavor. Dry wines do not go well with sweet food. Good balancing acts for sweet foods include:

White Zinfandel

Chenin Blanc

Riesling (an off-dry style)

2. **Foods High in Acid.** These might include salads with a balsamic vinaigrette dressing, a main course such as fish served with a fresh squeeze of lemon (the acid ingredient), or a dish made with soy sauce. The acid in the food or the sauce needs a wine high in acid to balance the flavors. There are several ways you can go to make a good match, depending on your personal preference. Good balancing acts for foods high in acid include:

White Zinfandel

Sauvignon Blanc

Pinot Grigio

Dry Riesling

Muscadet

Pinot Noir

3. **Bitter Foods.** If you love tri-colore salads made with endive, radicchio, and arugula, if you can't get enough of the Greek kalamata olives, or if you prefer your meat charbroiled, you enjoy bitter tastes. The only challenge is that bitter foods, in general, will accentuate a wine's bitterness. To counteract the bitterness in your food, look to these wines for balance:

Cabernet Sauvignon

Sauvignon Blanc

Pinot Noir

4. **Astringent Foods.** Take a handful of nuts such as walnuts or pecans, throw them in your mouth, and chew. What does it feel like? As you chew the nuts, they act like a squeegee in your mouth and leave you with a dry, astringent feeling. The same is true for the smoked salmon and decadent chocolates you love so much. The best way to handle these foods is to meet them head-on with more tannic wines, which primarily are red, to break down these specially textured foods. To counteract the astringency in your food, try these wines for balance:

Merlot

Cabernet Sauvignon

Syrah

Côte du Rhône wines

Nebbiolo

If you're having a big juicy steak, the best wine suggestion I can offer is a big, tannic red wine. The fat in the steak will tone down the tannin in the wine and will make it rounder, smoother, and easier to drink. The same strategy can be used when you have a soft-ripened Roquefort or bleu cheese.

In case you're not clear about what tannin is, try drinking a plain cup of hot, strong-brewed tea. It makes your mouth pucker, doesn't it? Now add a splash of milk and taste the difference. It should be smoother and easier to drink. The milk serves to break down the tannin that made your mouth pucker in the first place.

Unofficially...
Wine gets tannin from the skins, seeds, and stems and sometimes from the wooden barrels in which it is fermented and/or aged. Tannin most often is found in red wines, and it gives off the sensation of astringency or drying of the mouth. Tannin is the element that helps a wine age gracefully.

Casual family dinner

Whether you are assembling a rotisserie chicken dinner with a little help from your local supermarket's deli section (or "Home Meal Replacement Center"), picking up some Chinese food on the way home from work, or slaving over a hot stove, wine will make your dinner taste better.

Depending on your mood, you can either reach for the "house" white or red that you keep on hand or buy something to go with your meal. Consider what you're going to eat, the way it is prepared, and whether any special spices or sauces are used. For dishes that you know might be on the salty side or that have an element of sweetness, acidity, bitterness, or astringency, remember the basic principles of how food and wine interact with each other.

Barbeque

Beer and barbecue go hand in hand, but there's no reason why you can't serve wine alongside beer at a cookout. Whether you're having hamburgers and hot dogs, grilled vegetables, salmon, or a whole chicken, I would go for a wine with a little fruitiness to complement the grilled flavors. This is another instance when you can treat the occasion as a "no-brainer" and reach for your house red, white, or blush wine. If you don't already buy the magnum size (1.5 liter), which is equivalent to two regular-size bottles, for your regular house wine, it is perfect for barbecues. If you want to get a little more creative, you can select from an assortment of varietals bottled in handsome-looking magnums from virtually every wine-producing country. Many of these can be found at an excellent price ($10–$20), depending on the varietal and the producer.

A few wine producers make wine in a bag-in-the-box package, which is very convenient for barbecues. There are two available sizes that I know of—3 liters and 5 liters. Except for the convenience these offer for barbecues and picnics, for wine quality, you are better off with the bigger bottles of varietal wines.

Formal dinner party

The wines you serve at a dinner party set the tone and send a message to your guests. You take great care in putting together a group of people to create a lively party. You plan your menu meticulously from hors d'oeuvres to pastry. This is the perfect opportunity to wow your guests with your wine selections.

For a formal dinner party, I always begin with champagne or a top-notch sparkling wine. Again, it sets the tone and is festive, which is what I want from a good dinner party. Depending on your personal preference, you probably will offer your dinner in courses: appetizer, salad, entrée, and dessert, which might include a cheese plate, fresh fruit, and nuts.

Select a wine to go with each course, taking into consideration what you are serving, how it is prepared, and the sauces used. Don't be afraid to make your wine selections personal because that's part of what makes them interesting. If you have a favorite wine you enjoyed while visiting a winery, or if you merely want to share your latest wine discovery, the wine becomes a conversation piece.

To be on the safe side, I like to offer a choice of both red and white to go with the main course. Inevitably, you'll have at least one person who is a "white-wine drinker" or a "red-wine drinker," and you'll want them to feel at home. As a general rule, your food courses will progress from lighter style to

Bright Idea
The magnum size (1.5 liter) of your favorite varietal is the perfect size to have on hand for cookouts.

heavier and so will the wines. You wouldn't want to serve a big red wine like a Cabernet Sauvignon or a Barbaresco with delicate canapés to start off the evening and then follow with a Sancerre or Fumé Blanc with a seafood salad appetizer. You'd have palate fatigue before the main course arrived, and you wouldn't appreciate the delicate flavors in the appetizer course.

Dry kosher wines

The word "dry" is not traditionally associated with Kosher wines, but this is slowly changing because more wineries have decided that an important niche market exists. A generation of Jewish Baby Boomers is returning to its traditional roots and keeping a kosher home, but they could do without the cloying sweet Kosher wine made from Concord grapes. In response, Kosher winemakers now produce varietal wines such as Chardonnay and Cabernet Sauvignon in California using state-of-the-art winemaking technology. They are importing kosher wines from Bordeaux and champagnes from France, Soaves and Chianti Classicos from Italy, and Riojas from Spain.

What makes a wine kosher? A kosher wine cannot contain gelatin, lactose, glycerin, corn products, nonwine yeasts, or most chemical additives. In addition, kosher wines must be produced by Sabbath-observing Jews under direct rabbinic supervision from the crush to the bottling. Only 100 percent kosher materials can be used in the winemaking, maturation, and bottling process. This is not unlike the special kosher kitchens used in some hotels exclusively for the preparation of food for a kosher banquet. In cases where the hotel has only one kitchen, a rabbi is brought in with a full

Sabbath-observing Jewish crew to ritually clean the kitchen and all of the utensils within by extensive boiling and blowtorching if necessary.

Some reliable kosher wines to look for include:

- Hagafen Cellars
- Baron Herzog
- Gan Eden
- Yarden
- Gamla
- Golan
- Carmel
- Fortant de France
- Reserve St. Martin Val d'Orbieu
- Baron Phillipe de Rothschild
- Mt. Madrona

After-dinner options

This is the time and place to linger at the end of a good meal with a sweet wine. Like any dessert, it will give you the satisfaction of being pleasantly full.

The most popular dessert wine of the moment is Port. To many people, this must mean vintage Port, which is very special and is going to set you back a pretty penny. The fact is, however, it doesn't have to be an expensive experience because there are several different types of Port that will fit into your menu and lifestyle. For instance, you might try a simple Ruby Port or a Tawny with some age on it. For more details about how to select Port, see Chapter 13, "After-Dinner Delights."

If you're looking for a classic dessert wine, you can't do much better than a Sauternes from France, a Trockenbeerenauslese from Germany, or a late harvest wine from California. These wines can be so rich that you might prefer to savor them on their own and forego the crème brulée. Yet another popular after-dinner option is Vin Santo, a dessert wine from Italy. I personally enjoy a small glass with a few plain Italian biscotti on the side and an espresso.

The good thing about all these after-dinner options is that they often are available at better wine shops in a half-bottle (375 ml) size. It's the perfect size for two people, you don't have to be concerned with leftovers, and it's a little cheaper than buying the full bottle. In a restaurant situation, you have the convenience of being able to get a glass of dessert wine without investing in the bottle, plus you have even more choices. One person can have a glass of Port and the other a glass of Vin Santo without a worry.

A little romance

In my book, Champagne and romance are synonymous. For an extra-special evening, it's got to be rosé Champagne. I love to look at the tiny bubbles bursting through the salmon-colored wine. In fact, it only gets better with smoked salmon canapés.

Champagne might not be for everyone, but when romance is on the menu, it's time to pull out all the stops and break out whatever wine is special to you. If you drink a popular brand of White Zinfandel day in and day out, why not splurge on a pricier blush wine or try a racier rosé such as a Tavel from France? The European rosé wines are drier than most White Zinfandels, but you'll never know if you like them until you pop the cork.

For me, the next best thing to rosé Champagne is a special bottle of Burgundy, preferably from the top-rated village of Chambolle-Musigny and from

> **"** [The perfect Valentine's day dinner] would be in a private bungalow in Kona, Hawaii. We'd sit on the terrace, overlooking a lagoon stocked with exotic tropical fish, and drink Champagne and eat peaches, lobster, garlic-mashed potatoes, and strawberries and cream.
> —Jackie Collins, best-selling romance novelist **"**

one of the top producers such as Groffier, Louis Jadot, Joseph Drouhin, or J. Faiveley. I don't drink this wine on a daily or even weekly basis, so I look forward to it as part of a romantic evening.

Though I believe that selecting a special wine helps set the mood for romance, it doesn't mean that you must spend $50, $100, or more on a single bottle of wine. Stick with a style that you know you enjoy and with which you are comfortable and trade up to the next price point. If you buy $5 wines, look at a $10 bottle; if you normally buy $10 wines, look at the $15 range or even the $20s. You will notice the difference and will enjoy sharing it with that special someone.

ABC wines (anything but Chardonnay)

Members of the wine press grew weary of Chardonnay a long time ago. Mind you, we still drank tons of it, but we were in a rut. We were feeling, as celebrated recording artist Peggy Lee sang, "Is that all there is?"

The battle cry became "Anything but Chardonnay," hence the acronym ABC wines. The expression ABC was even expanded to include the red "C" wine, Cabernet Sauvignon. In time, the consuming public also grew weary but continued to drink tons of Chardonnay and Cabernet Sauvignon. Then something happened. I can't put my finger on exactly when, but suffice it to say that, within the past five to ten years, people became more attuned to the varietal grape names.

Mind you, we always have leaned that way in California, but this new awareness and curiosity about varietals have encouraged people to select wines primarily by their grape variety. Where the wine was made is less of a concern today. That's a major step because, not too long ago, traditional wine consumers looked to the French section in the wine store. Period. Today, they are more likely to look for a Syrah, and they don't necessarily care if it came from the Rhône Valley in France, the Napa Valley in California, or the Columbia Valley in Washington State.

There's a full rundown of grape varietals and their taste profiles (meaning how the wine should taste) in Chapter 3, "How to Taste Wine." It seems, however, that people now have a greater comfort level seeking out new and different grape varieties. Some of the trends I've been seeing, based on regular discussions I have with wine merchants, restaurateurs, winemakers, and wine marketers from around the world, include:

- Rhône varieties are in. In white wine, this means Viognier and might include grapes used in Rhône blends such as Marsanne. For red Rhône wine, it means Syrah and often is a blend of the other grapes such as Mourvèdre.

- Pinot Grigio from Italy is hot. It's easy to drink, and customers and waitstaff know how to pronounce it. Perhaps as an offshoot of Pinot Grigio, there is some activity on Pinot Blanc, which really tastes closer to Chardonnay in style. Pinot Gris from France is also beginning to gain a bit in popularity.

- There's a spike of interest in the Italian red variety, Sangiovese, but the true darlings in the ABC category are Merlot, Syrah (mentioned previously), and Malbec, an up-and-comer that you'll hear more about in Chapter 10, "Old- and New-World Reds," when I cover Argentina.

It boils down to this: Experimentation is really part of the fun of enjoying wine.

Pick a price point

Today, I consider myself lucky if I can find a good house wine for $6.99 in the 750 ml (regular bottle) size from my local wine merchant, though I know I can get a good well-known brand in a 1.5 liter size at the nearby warehouse club for about $10. Take that as the price of entry and consider what you want to spend and are comfortable spending on wine. Realistically for my husband and me, who consider wine to be part of our lifestyle, $10 is what we typically spend on a 750 ml bottle of everyday wine. We'll spend more for a special occasion and less if we can catch a good sale.

Even if you make most of your purchases in the lower end of the price scale, I urge you to create some occasions to spend a little more. You will be surprised at the difference between a $10 and a $15 bottle of wine. It could make all the difference in how you enjoy wine. Don't worry. In Chapter 15, "How to Find a Good Wine Merchant," I'm going to share some strategies for getting the best value for your dollar so it will be possible to trade up.

What makes a wine so expensive or so cheap?

This whole discussion of how much you are willing to spend on wine brings us to an issue that is a mystery to many people: What makes a wine so expensive or so cheap?

It starts with the real estate. Let's assume we're talking about the best places in the world to grow certain grapes. The best wine-growing areas are delimited by law as to how much wine they can produce per acre. This means there is a finite supply.

Add to that the cost of planting the vines. For your information, in round numbers it costs $6,000 per acre to plant vines in the Napa Valley. If you're not going to own your own vineyards and prefer to buy the grapes, the average going price for Chardonnay is $1,200 per ton; the best Chardonnay grapes can easily fetch over $2,000. So if you can see the difference between varietals, consider that Sauvignon Blanc costs an average of $700 per ton.

Now factor in the methods of production. You'll see what makes champagne so expensive when you get to Chapter 12, "Sparkle Plenty." Just the methods for picking the grapes can add to the equation. In Germany, for example, the hillsides are so steep that producers cannot use mechanical harvesting; they must rely on workers to pick the grapes by hand. There also are special dessert wines made in which the grapes are left on the vines longer. This means the workers have to sweep through the vineyards several times to pick grapes as they are ready. The winemaker takes a risk by leaving the grapes on the vine beyond the regular harvest because, if the weather doesn't cooperate, the entire crop can be lost.

In the actual production and fermentation, you get into the issue of wood aging. A new French oak barrel costs about $600. Some winemakers try to save on the cost by buying used oak barrels so they can still age their wine in wood but not in brand-new barrels. Others cheap out and throw wood chips into the fermentation tank so the end product will have wood flavors, but it's just not the same.

Finally, there is the good old-fashioned economic law of supply and demand. If all of a sudden there is a virtual wine lake of Chardonnay from a certain area, the price of Chardonnay will drop. In recent years, we saw this when Merlot-mania hit and vineyard owners scrambled to plant Merlot. Four years later, when the vines reached fruition, there was an overabundance of this variety. Consumers quickly learned, however, that there is good Merlot and there is stuff that can be called Merlot that tastes nothing like the "better ones."

In many parts of the world, there are laws that govern how long a wine must be aged before it is released. The better-quality producers generally age wines longer, even longer than the law requires, because their mission is to release the best-possible product into the marketplace. Deep down, they know that Americans have little patience and usually are not willing to lay wines down to age for any significant amount of time. The extra time spent aging and not on the market takes away from potential cash flow, which inevitably adds to the price tag.

How you can find value

The general consensus in wine buying is that the price goes up with the quality of the wine. This is basically true, but there are strategies you can use to get a better buy.

1. Look for a wine made from a lesser-known varietal. Instead of Chardonnay, try a Pinot Blanc or something altogether different such as Sauvignon Blanc or Riesling. At the same time, understand that curiosities such as Cal-Ital wines made in California from Italian grapes or Rhône-style wines made in California such as Viognier probably will command a premium due to the law of supply and demand.

2. Look for a wine made by a major winery. The biggest wineries such as Gallo, Mondavi, Chateau Ste. Michelle, and others produce

wine on such a grand scale that they can afford to market it for less money than smaller (boutique) wineries.

3. Look for wine produced in lesser-known regions. You're going to find some major values in the Foothills of California compared to Napa or Sonoma. The same goes for the Languedoc-Rouisillon in France as opposed to Burgundy or Bordeaux.

Just the facts

- Selecting and enjoying wine is no big deal.

- You can pick your wine by the mood you're in, just like everything else you do.

- You can find a basic wine that you like and make it your own, or you can take a gourmet approach and dissect the flavors—but you don't have to.

- Food changes the way wine tastes, but it's most important to start out with a wine you like.

- You can get the best value by selecting a wine made by a mass producer from a lesser-known grape variety and winegrowing area.

GET THE SCOOP ON...
Figuring out what kind of wine you like
▪ Varietal wines and blends ▪ What type of wine
to expect from different countries ▪ What you
need to know from a wine label

What's Your Style?

chapter 2

What kind of wine do you like? This isn't a trick question, and it isn't a test. Yet it makes some wine drinkers feel uncomfortable as if they are being put on the spot to express their personal preference about wine. I hazard to guess that it also contributes to the reasons why America's 25.7 million "marginal wine drinkers" only consume wine every two or three months. Many nonwine drinkers simply don't want the hassle.

Yet if you ask practically anyone what type of milk they drink, they will matter-of-factly reply "Skim," "One percent," "Soy," "Lactaid," and so on. There's no thoughtful pause or hesitation because virtually no one would let someone else influence his or her ideas about what type of milk to drink. So why do so many people let others influence the type of wine they drink or think they should be drinking?

Red, white, or rosé?

Let's start with the different colors of wine. A lot of people begin with white or rosé wines because they like their drinks cold. White wines and rosés, also known as blush wines, are always served chilled. You can even throw in a few ice cubes if you want.

Most red wines, on the other hand, are served at room temperature. A stronger flavor profile is involved with red wines. They taste stronger than white and rosé wines, and for people unaccustomed to drinking red wine, it is an acquired taste.

Sparkling options

Do you like bubbles? If you do, many different sparkling wine and Champagne options are available to you in many different styles and price points. It's worth mulling over this option rather than leapfrogging over it. Then you can continue to the next set of criteria for your consideration.

Dry, fruity, or sweet?

After you decide on a color and determine whether you prefer a table wine or a sparkler, the next decision to make is whether you would like a dry, fruity, or sweet wine. Many people say they like a dry wine, probably because they believe this is what you are supposed to like. In fact, they might really prefer a fruity or even a sweet style.

Here are some basic definitions:

- **Dry**—This is the descriptive term used to convey the opposite of sweet. If you do not perceive sweetness when you taste a wine, you say it is dry.

- **Fruity**—In its most simple form, a wine can be described as fruity if you smell and taste fruit flavors. These flavors are most common in young wines and in wines that are fermented in stainless steel tanks as opposed to wooden barrels, which impart woody flavors. You also will find fruit in older, balanced wine but not to the same fresh, fruity degree. Some examples of fruit flavors you might find in Chardonnay and other white wines, for example, include apples, pineapples, and citrus. In Cabernet Sauvignon and other reds, you might find black cherries, strawberries, and plums, among other flavors. Wine tasters also will describe a wine as fruity if it expresses the varietal character of the grape from which it is made. When you drink a Chardonnay, for example, you expect to taste the fruit of a Chardonnay grape. For a complete list of grape varietals and their typical taste profiles, see Chapter 3, "How to Taste Wine."

■ **Sweet**—There are few people who don't know what sweet tastes like. In a wine, sweetness is associated with residual sugar that is left over when the fermentation stops.

The fermentation process is the process by which grape juice is turned into wine. It works like this:

Natural Sugar from the Grape Juice + Yeast = Alcohol (Wine) + Carbon Dioxide (CO_2)

When all the sugar from the grape juice is converted to alcohol, the fermentation process is over. If the grapes are very ripe and contain lots of natural sugar, however, the alcohol level of the wine might reach 15 percent, which kills the yeast and stops the fermentation instantly. Without the yeast, the rest of the natural sugar in the grape juice cannot ferment. This leaves residual sugar that makes the wine naturally sweet. The CO_2 naturally dissipates in the process.

Watch Out!
"But I really wanted a fruity wine...." Because most people are reluctant to ask for a sweet wine (aside from dessert wine) or something "on the sweet side," it's become more common to find sweet wines marketed as *fruity*.

- **Off-Dry**—This is another way to describe a wine that has at least a hint of sweetness. I would include wines such as White Zinfandel, Riesling, Chenin Blanc, German Kabinett wines, and even some Gewürztraminer in this category.

Varietals versus blends

Varietals are wines named for the grape variety from which the wine is made. California started this trend, and it is how wines are commonly labeled in the United States and even in other parts of the world to appeal to the American market. If a wine is labeled with the varietal in California, at least 75 percent of the wine must come from the so-named grape. In Washington State, the percentage is 90 percent. Truth be told, however, a lot of varietal wines are made from 100 percent of the grape named on the label.

Blends are wines made from a blend of different grapes. Historically in California, wine producers blended together a mixture of inexpensive grapes to produce jug wines. Blends did not have a very good connotation in California until the 1980s when winemakers started to emulate some of the finer wines from France, particularly Bordeaux, where they traditionally blend Cabernet Sauvignon, Merlot, Cabernet Franc, and Malbec to produce some of the best wines in the world. Through experimentation, some wineries now produce their top-of-the line wine from red blends and even from some white wines that are comparable to their Bordeaux counterparts.

Being Californians, however, whose greatest tradition is to challenge winemaking tradition and push the envelope, these winemakers are still actively experimenting with different blends. They have taken grapes native to Italy such as the Sangiovese, Nebbiolo, and Barbera and have begun to mix different wines that have become know as Cal-Ital wines. In addition to making Italian blends, winemakers also are using some of the Italian grapes, notably Sangiovese, to produce a varietal wine labeled "Sangiovese."

Before the Italian wave, a handful of Californians started playing with different Rhône Valley varietals. These Rhône Rangers, as the winemakers became known (including Randall Graham of Bonny Doon and Joe Phelps of Joseph Phelps Vineyards), created different Rhône-style blends made with grapes native to the Rhône. They planted red grapes such as Grenache, Syrah, Mourvèdre, Cinsault, and Carignan as well as the white grape Viognier. Again, they produced some very interesting blends but also some good varietals made from the red grape Syrah and the white grape Viognier. Both Cal-Ital and Rhône-style blends from California are emerging categories. The winemakers are fine-tuning their styles, and more wine drinkers are willing to try new varietals and styles, especially in a restaurant setting where they can buy them by the glass.

Let's face it. Wine drinkers are becoming more sophisticated. They are getting acquainted with more grape varietals, and they know the difference between a cheap blend and a stylish blend. This has became very apparent to me as I've observed the exploding coffee craze. Customers go into a coffee bar and ask for coffee produced from a specific-quality bean (Arabica), from a specific area (Kona, Hawaii), roasted in a particular style (dark roast) that was even roasted on a particular date. In the case of coffee, they're looking for the most recent vintage available (meaning roasted yesterday) so they can grind and brew it immediately for maximum freshness. The other day when I stopped into a Starbucks for a cup of coffee, I couldn't believe that the construction worker behind me asked specifically for the Sunset Sonata Blend.

Another interesting occurrence is taking place with wine blends. I'm beginning to see some of the better wine producers release some very drinkable everyday wines produced by skillful blending. For me, it is a refreshing change from Chardonnay or Cabernet Sauvignon, and the wine is reasonably priced. One of my most recent discoveries is a refreshing Bianco, a simple white wine blend from filmmaker Francis Ford Coppola's family wine line of Niebaum-Coppola Estate. It just goes to show that you can find some good "house wines" made from blends by top-quality wine producers.

Outside Bordeaux or the Rhône Valley, where blends are a way of life and the wine is named for the place from which it came such as Bordeaux, Château So-and-So, or Côtes du Rhône, American blends usually go by a made-up name. The most famous of these high-end labels is Opus One, a Bordeaux-style blend that came out of the partnership between Robert Mondavi of California and the Baron Philippe de Rothschild, owner of Château Mouton. Many others since then carry what is known as a proprietary or brand name on their label such as Trilogy (Flora Springs), Rubicon (Niebaum-Coppola Estate), and Conundrum (a white blend by Caymus Vineyards).

Light-, medium-, or full-bodied wine?

Wine is one of the few things in life in which you truly get to choose your body. The body of a wine is the perceived sense of richness it has on your palate. What makes a wine light-, medium-, or full-bodied? And how can you tell? The answer is in the alcohol content.

Alcohol content in table wines ranges from about 8.5 percent to 15 percent. For fortified wines, such as Port and Sherry, it can be anywhere from 15 percent to 24 percent. Wines that are lower in alcohol are light-bodied. As the alcohol content increases, so does the body of the wine. One way to anticipate whether a wine is going to be light- or full-bodied is to look at the alcohol content on the label.

Another way is to look at the grape varietal. Certain grapes produce lighter-style wines or heavier-style wines than others. In white wines, for example, Sauvignon Blanc is generally lighter than Chardonnay. In reds, Pinot Noir is lighter than Cabernet Sauvignon. For more information about how varietals rank in their weight class, go back to the section "Wine and Food Pairing 101" in Chapter 1. It will give you a better idea of what to expect.

Yet another way is to look at where the wine is from. Wines that come from the hotter wine-growing regions, such as the Rhône Valley, Italy, and parts of California and Australia, have a tendency to be higher in alcohol because the grapes get very ripe from the long growing season. Conversely, areas with cooler growing seasons such as Germany, Champagne, and Washington State will produce wines with a lower alcohol content.

If you're tasting the wine blind, meaning without seeing the alcohol content on the label and without knowing what grape variety is used or even where the wine is from, you can still tell if it is light-, medium-, or full-bodied. Taste the wine. Roll it in your mouth before swallowing it. How does it feel in your mouth? When you taste a light-bodied wine, you take a sip, you get a little flavor, you swallow, and it's gone. With a medium-bodied wine, you get a little more flavor and a sense of viscosity in your mouth. After you swallow, you get a brief, pleasant aftertaste. A full-bodied wine gives you a definite texture in the mouth. You can practically chew it. After you swallow, the better full-bodied wines leave a lingering finish of all the wonderful flavors that mingled to make the wine so special.

Pick a region

Although it's true that more wine drinkers today are selecting wine by the grape varietal, I still maintain that people are creatures of habit and go back to the region they know the best. If you have been drinking wine since before the 1980s and you live on the East Coast, chances are you are a French-wine drinker. If you're from the West Coast, you probably cut your teeth on California wine and remain chauvinistically loyal.

Things have changed drastically in the last 20 to 25 years. Like the rest of the world, winemaking has gone global, and wine drinkers are well aware of it. Many Americans are traveling more, and in their travels, they are visiting wine country more than ever before in California, Washington State, Oregon, New York, France, Italy, Spain, and as far away as Australia, New Zealand, and South America. At the same time, successful winemakers are getting out of the fields and participating in world tours to host winemaker dinners and other elaborate tastings. In addition to selling their wine, they take home mental notes from consumers they meet along the way.

After you've tasted enough wines from different countries, you start to realize that each country has its own style. Some you will like, and others you could live without.

Because of the globalization of the wine industry and the ease with which people can travel from one part of the world to another, new wine styles are emerging. You don't just find Sangiovese and Nebbiolo in Italy. Now you find it in California as well. The same is true for the Syrah, Viognier, and other Rhône Valley grape varietals. You will now find them in California and Washington state.

On the other hand, California has done a lot to create Chardonnay and Cabernet Sauvignon consumers. Yet countries that are not really known for these grapes, such as Italy and Spain, are planting vines to get in on the marketing frenzy.

The list goes on and on. It is possible to get top-quality sparkling wine outside the Champagne region of France, even though the wine might not be labeled as Champagne. Ditto for Port.

The point is that practically every winemaking region in the world makes many different types of wine. Like a good restaurant, however, each one creates its signature dish, or wine in this case, for which it is best known. When I go to a restaurant to which I have never been, I ask the server what the house specialty is and what he or she recommends. I don't want to hear that everything's good—even if it is— unless the server will also highlight one or two dishes that the chef does really well. I take the same approach to wine.

Unofficially...
Move over, Disneyland! More than 5 million visitors flock to the Napa Valley each year.

Here's a rundown of the most important wine regions in the world and the types of wines for which they are best known. In regions, particularly France, where you select wines by the specific wine regions and more specifically by the communes and vineyards, I have included some buzzwords to put you on the right track. In these cases, there are many other wines from which to choose. The idea here is to help you group together in your mind the main wine regions and the best wines you'll find in each area.

For complete details about how to select wine from each wine area, including recommendations of reliable producers, go to the chapters that cover the individual regions.

TABLE 2.1: THE WINES OF FRANCE

Region	White Wines	Red Wines
Alsace	Riesling (dry)	
	Gewürztraminer	
	Pinot Gris	
	Pinot Blanc	
	Muscat	
Loire Valley	Pouilly-Fumé	
	Sancerre	
	Vouvray (can be sweeter)	
	Muscadet (can be sweeter)	
Bordeaux	White Bordeaux	Médoc
	Graves	Graves
	Pessac-Léognan	Pessac-Léognan
	Sauternes	Pomerol (dessert wine)
	Barsac	St.-Émilion
Burgundy	White Burgundy or Bourgogne Blanc	Red Burgundy or Bourgogne Rouge
	Chablis (all white wine)	Beaujolais

Region	White Wines	Red Wines
	Côte de Beaune	Côte de Beaune
	Côte Chalonnaise	Côte Chalonnaise
	Mâconais	Côte de Nuits
Rhône Valley	Côtes-du-Rhône	Côtes-du-Rhône
Champagne	White Champagne	Rosé Champagne*

*This is a pink Champagne made from red grapes, but it is treated like a white wine and served chilled.

TABLE 2.2: POPULAR "BUZZWORD" FRENCH WINES BY REGION

Region	White Wines	Red Wines
Côte de Beaune (Burgundy)	Meursault	Beaune
	Chassagne-Montrachet	Aloxe-Corton
	Puligny-Montrachet	Pommard±
Côte Chalonnaise (Burgundy)	Rully	Mercurey
	Montagny	Givry
	Mercurey	
Côte de Nuits± (Burgundy)		Gevrey-Chambertin
Mâconais (Burgundy/ Mâcon-Vire)		Chambolle-Musigny Nuits Saint George
	Mâcon-Lugny	
	Mâcon-St.-Verán	
Beaujolais	Beaujolais Blanc†	Brouilly Chiroubles
		Fleurie
Rhône Valley	Hermitage Blanc	Côte-Rôtie
	Châteauneuf-du-Pape Blanc†	
	Beaumes-de- Venise‡	Hermitage
		Crozes-Hermitage St.-Joseph Cornas Châteauneuf-du-Pape
		Gigondas _continues_

continued

Region	White Wines	Red Wines
		Lirac
		Vacqueyras
Médoc (Bordeaux)	Graves	Margaux
	Pessac Léognan	Haut-Médoc
	Sauternes (dessert)	St.-Estèphe
	Barsac (dessert)	Pauillac
		St.-Julien
		Listrac
		Moulis
		Graves
		Pessac-Leognan
		Pomerol
		St.-Émilion
Languedoc-Roussillon (Southern France)		Corbières
		Minervois

± Please see the full list in Chapter 8.
† Rarely found in the United States.
‡ This rich wine is commonly thought of as a dessert wine in the United States, though Europeans also enjoy it as an aperitif.

Germany's most notable white wine is Riesling, which is made in all styles from dry "trocken" to delectably sweet dessert wines. Unlike some other European winemaking countries like France, where it's helpful to make the association between a popular wine like Mersault and the Côte de Beaune area of Burgundy, in Germany you are best served to know the "buzzwords" of style that will appear on the label. It helps a great deal to become familiar with the better-quality producers, many of which are listed in Chapter 5. Some popular "buzzword" wines that express the style of the wine, from light- to full-bodied, are:

- Kabinett
- Spätlese

- Auslese (can be dessert wine, but not always)
- Beerenauslese (dessert)
- Trockenbeerenauslese (dessert)
- Eiswein (dessert)

TABLE 2.3: THE WINES OF THE UNITED STATES

Region	White Wines	Red Wines
California	Chardonnay	Cabernet Sauvignon
	Sauvignon Blanc (Fumé Blanc)	Merlot
	Chenin Blanc	Zinfandel
	"Late Harvest" (dessert wines)	Syrah
	Sparkling	
	White Zinfandel*	
	White Grenache*	
Washington state	Chardonnay	Merlot
	Riesling	Cabernet Sauvignon
	Gewürztraminer	Syrah
	Sauvignon Blanc (Fumé Blanc)	
	Sémillon	
	Chenin Blanc	
	Sparkling	
Oregon	Chardonnay	Pinot Noir
	Pinot Gris	
	Riesling	
	Gewürztraminer	
New York (including Long Island)	Chardonnay	Merlot
	Riesling	Cabernet Sauvignon
	Pinot Blanc	
	Gewürztraminer	

*"Blush" wine, which is a white wine made from red grapes.

TABLE 2.4: THE WINES OF AUSTRALIA AND NEW ZEALAND

Region	White Wines	Red Wines
Australia	Chardonnay	Shiraz (Syrah)
	Sémillon	Cabernet Sauvignon
	Riesling	
	Sem/Chard (blend of Sémillon and Chardonnay)	
New Zealand	Sauvignon Blanc	

TABLE 2.5: THE WINES OF SOUTH AMERICA

Region	White Wines	Red Wines
Chile	Chardonnay	Cabernet Sauvignon
	Sauvignon Blanc	Merlot
Argentina	Chardonnay	Malbec
	Sauvignon Blanc	Cabernet Sauvignon

TABLE 2.5: THE WINES OF ITALY, SPAIN, AND PORTUGAL

Region	White Wines	Red Wines
Italy	Soave	Barbera
	Pinot Grigio	Dolcetto
	Gavi	Gattinara
	Friuli	Bardolino
		Valpolicella
		Chianti
		Chianti Classico
		Barbaresco
		Barolo
		Vino Nobile de Montepulciano
		Carmignano Rosso
		Brunello di Montalcino
Spain	Rías Baixas (Albariño grape)	Rioja
	Sparkling (Cava)	Penedès

Region	White Wines	Red Wines
	*Ribera del Duero	
	*Navarra	
Portugal	Vinho Verde (literally "green wine" due to its youthfulness)	
	Alvarinho (in Vinho Verde region)	

*"Blush" wine, which is a white wine made from red grapes.

TABLE 2.6: THE WINES OF SOUTH AFRICA

White Wines	Red Wines
Steen (Chenin Blanc)	Pinotage
Chardonnay	Cabernet Sauvignon

The label: information or information overload?

Wine has been around since biblical times, but winemakers only started to label the contents of the bottle in the mid-1800s. Since then, the amount of information that appears on wine labels has become mind-boggling. Between the labeling information mandated by the Bureau of Alcohol, Tobacco, and Firearms (the agency that regulates the United States' wine industry) and international standards combined with the wine producer's desire to break through the clutter on the shelf, it helps if you know how to cherry-pick the information you need to know to make your wine selection.

Required information on wine labels includes:

■ **Type of Wine:** Among the designations you'll see are "Table Wine," "Dessert Wine," "Appellation d'Origine Contrôlée" from France, "Qualiätswein mit Prädikat" from Germany, and so on.

- **Geographical Origin:** You'll see the name of the country or, more specifically, the state, the village, the vineyard, or in the United States, a specially designated winegrowing area known as an American Viticultural Area (AVA). Again, in France, you'll often find the specific area as part of the "Appellation d'Origine Contrôlée" or "Vin de Pays" along with the name of the area.

- **Bottle Size or Volume of Wine in the Bottle:** The standard-size bottle will be labeled 750 ml, a magnum will be labeled 1.5 liters, and so on.

- **Alcoholic Strength by Volume:** The amount of alcohol in the wine usually is expressed as a percentage such as "12.5 percent alcohol by volume."

- **Vintage Year:** Most wines except the low-end generic jug wines and nonvintage Champagne carry a vintage year, which is the year of the harvest. If a wine carries a vintage year, in California at least 75 percent of the wine should be a product of the year named on the label. The actual percentage varies from region to region.

- **Name and Address of Wine Producer:** You'll usually find this information at the bottom of the label.

- **Specific Bottling Information:** This tells you where the wine was bottled. For example, a wine bottled by the winery that produced it will be labeled "produced and bottled by," "vinted and bottled by," "estate bottled," or in French, "mis en bouteille au château."

- **Government Warning:** All wines produced or imported to the United States must carry

Watch Out!
Do not rely on the name and the address of the wine producer to gauge the wine's quality because they can be misleading. Some wine producers today buy grapes or bulk wine from less expensive regions such as California's Central Valley or parts of South America, then finish the wine at a custom crush facility in a more desirable location so they can put a well-known winery name and address on the label.

government health warnings pertaining to pregnant women, the link between alcohol and one's ability to drive a car vehicle or operate machinery, and general health (just for good measure).

■ **"Contains Sulfites":** This is an additional warning that all wines produced or imported to the United States must carry somewhere on their label.

When the government first mandated this warning, it made many people wonder why wine contained sulfites. It reminds me of how kids sometime tease each other when they point and say, "Your epidermis is showing." The accused does everything to hide it, not knowing that the epidermis is his or her skin.

Sulfites are a natural by-product of wine, and virtually all wines contain sulfites. This warning appears, however, for the same reason the government banned peanuts on airlines—there are a few people in the world who suffer from allergies that are triggered by sulfites. What I don't understand is that, if this is such a concern, why doesn't the government insist on sulfites warnings on other household products, such as fruit juice, that contain a higher amount of sulfites than wine.

Recently, I read one winery's back label that addressed the issue of sulfites in an honest and creative way. Instead of rubber-stamping the phrase "Contains Sulfites," this winery said "Sulfites Naturally Contained in This Wine."

In Champagne, the government requires that the producer use codes alongside the registered number of the bottler. You'll find these codes in the Champagne chapter (Chapter 12, "Sparkle Plenty"), but for your information, they are:

NM—négociant-manipulant (shipper, a Champagne house)

CM—coopérative de manipulation (a cooperative of growers)

RM—récoltant-manipulant (a grower who independently produces Champagne wines with his or her own grapes)

RC—récoltant-cooperateur (a grower who produces Champagne with the help of a cooperative)

MA—marque d'acheteur (when the brand is owned by a third party who is not a producer)

In Germany, the government requires that wine producers include the wine's official testing number. This code begins with the letters "A.P.-Nr" and is followed by a serial code that proves the wine was tasted by the government panel.

Now that you know the important elements to look for on a wine label, here are two basic types of wine labels you will see on the market. The Paul Jaboulet Parallèle "45" Côtes du Rhône is typical of the "Old World" European wine labels that place emphasis on *where* the wine is from. In this case, it is the Côte du Rhône region of France. The Robert Mondavi Cabernet Sauvignon Reserve wine label, which emphasizes *grape variety,* is more typical of wines from the United States as well as other "New World" countries like Australia, New Zealand, South America, and South Africa. In fact, some European wine producers now include the name of the grape variety on their labels in addition to the place name.

Some of the more useful information that I look for on labels includes:

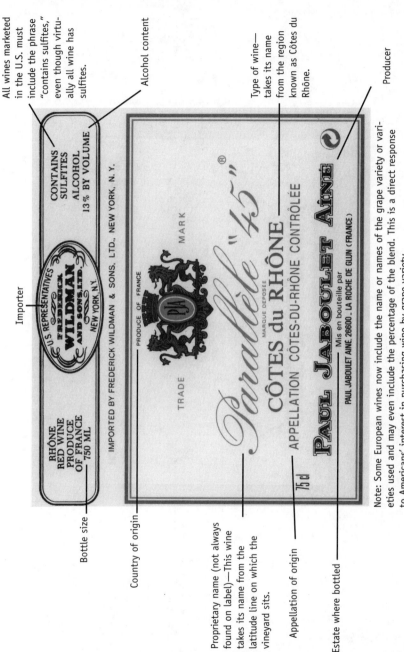

All wines marketed in the U.S. must include the phrase "contains sulfites," even though virtually all wine has sulfites.

Alcohol content

Importer

Type of wine—takes its name from the region known as Côtes du Rhône.

Producer

Bottle size

Country of origin

Proprietary name (not always found on label)—This wine takes its name from the latitude line on which the vineyard sits.

Appellation of origin

Estate where bottled

Note: Some European wines now include the name or names of the grape variety or varieties used and may even include the percentage of the blend. This is a direct response to Americans' interest in purchasing wine by grape variety.

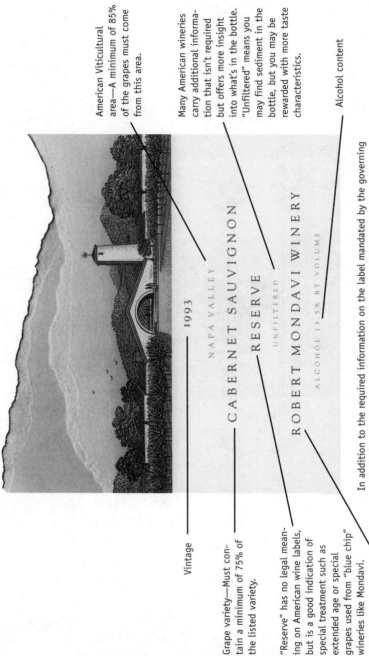

American Viticultural area—A minimum of 85% of the grapes must come from this area.

Many American wineries carry additional information that isn't required but offers more insight into what's in the bottle. "Unfiltered" means you may find sediment in the bottle, but you may be rewarded with more taste characteristics.

Alcohol content

1993

NAPA VALLEY

CABERNET SAUVIGNON

RESERVE

UNFILTERED

ROBERT MONDAVI WINERY

ALCOHOL 13.5% BY VOLUME

Vintage

Grape variety—Must contain a minimum of 75% of the listed variety.

"Reserve" has no legal meaning on American wine labels, but is a good indication of special treatment such as extended age or special grapes used from "blue chip" wineries like Mondavi.

Producer

In addition to the required information on the label mandated by the governing bodies, you'll find a host of other information on the front and back labels. Some of it is useful; some of it is just fluffy marketing that tells you how great the wine is.

- The blend of the grape varieties used.

- Serving suggestions.

- Suggested wine and food pairings.

- The winemaker's tasting notes. These usually give you an idea of the style of the wine and the sweetness level. It's then up to you to taste the wine and come to your own decision.

- Whether the wine was aged in oak barrels or aged on its lees. This information lets you know to expect a fuller-bodied wine.

Healthful aspects of wine

Doctors have known for years that moderate consumption of wine can help prevent heart disease. Before the Puritanical neo-Prohibition movement of the late 1980s and part of the 1990s, it was not uncommon for a doctor to informally "prescribe" a glass of wine to a patient for this purpose or even to stimulate the appetite. All of a sudden, however, it became big news when the link between wine and a healthy heart hit the airwaves of the CBS news magazine show *60 Minutes*. If nothing more, it gave people an excuse to raise a glass on a regular basis.

In terms of the link between alcohol and breast cancer, many studies show that heavy drinkers have a notably higher risk than nondrinkers. As for moderate drinkers, it depends on which study you read and on what day. For every study that links breast cancer to women who have even one glass of wine a day, there are other studies that maintain there is no relationship between moderate wine consumption and breast cancer.

Dr. Curtis Ellison, director of the Institute on Lifestyle & Health at Boston University, recently completed a study of women who consumed wine,

Watch Out!
Wine producers sometimes adorn their label with medals or hype that the wine won such-and-such Gold Medal. Don't make your buying decision based on these claims unless you are familiar with the competition. You're better off taking a recommendation from a friend or a knowledgeable wine merchant instead.

spirits, or beer and their risk of breast cancer. His team followed the health of more than 5,000 women for 25 to 45 years. They found that the group of women who never consumed alcoholic beverages throughout their lives was at the same risk of breast cancer as that which consumed any type of alcohol.

One day you hear that something is good for you, and the next day you hear that it's detrimental to your health. Only you and your doctor can decide what is best for you, especially if you have a family history of heart disease, breast cancer, or another condition that you believe might be hindered or helped by having a few glasses of wine.

I can't help but look around at some of the people I have known who have lived to a ripe old age simply by following the rules of common sense that include, as Benjamin Franklin advised, "moderation in everything."

As a result of all this scientific evidence stacking up in favor of the healthful benefits of moderate wine consumption, the U.S. government has finally come around to making a place for wine in the U.S. Dietary Guidelines.

As a result, American winemakers are trying to get equal time on the wine label to balance out the negative warnings they are required to include. Recently, the BATF approved two labels that refer to the potential health effects of moderate wine consumption. Carmenet Winery from the Napa Valley, part of the Chalone Wine Group, was one of the first U.S. wineries to include the new message that reads: "The proud people who made this wine encourage you to consult your family doctor about the health effects of wine consumption."

> **"**
> ...Alcoholic beverages have been used to enhance the enjoyment of meals by many societies throughout human history ...Current evidence suggests that moderate drinking...is associated with a lower risk for coronary heart disease in some individuals.
> —An excerpt from the U.S. Dietary Guidelines, 1995
> **"**

U.S. Senator Strom Thurmond (R-SC), the author of the health hazard warnings on wine labels, does not want to see any encouraging words on the label. He has managed to get the BATF to take a second look before approving any more labels with these positive health messages. Mind you, the labels are not permitted to make outright health claims, but it's better than nothing. As you can see, wine labels in the United States are still evolving. Stay tuned for more!

Just the facts

- You are the best judge of whether a wine is good.
- If you prefer sweet over dry, let your wine merchant or restaurant server know so you will get a wine you will enjoy.
- Alcohol content is what makes a wine light-, medium-, or full-bodied.
- Wine regions around the world now make a garden variety of wines, but they still produce one or more specialties that their wine country is known for.
- Wine labels can give you the complete low-down on a wine—if you know how to read them correctly.
- Even the U.S. government has become friendlier to wine by adding it to the nation's official dietary guidelines.
- Only you and your doctor can decide what is best for you, especially if you have a family history of certain medical conditions.

How to Taste Wine

Y ou eat. You drink. You taste things every day. So what's so special about tasting wine, and why is there a whole chapter dedicated to explaining how to do it?

First of all, there is a difference between drinking wine and tasting wine. If you're a person who enjoys and appreciates good food and wine (and it doesn't have to be anything extravagant like Champagne and sushi) as opposed to someone who looks at food and drink merely as fuel to keep the body going, you probably know what I mean.

Many of my friends who are not in the wine business enjoy wine, and they usually have at least one favorite. They don't, however, know how to express what it tastes like or why they like it. This wouldn't be such a terrible thing except that it limits their ability to select wines intelligently. Instead of making a choice based on tastes they know they like, these casual consumers are more likely to stumble upon new wines. They might, for example, discover that they liked what they were served at a dinner party.

My point is that you probably know what you like, but it will be much easier to put your finger on it if you take a little quiet time with a glass of wine to get to know your taste buds. You then can run through the five S's of tasting to get a glimpse of how professionals and serious wine consumers taste and evaluate wine.

Taste sensations

Taste sensations begin with, but are not exclusively formulated by, your mouth. You've probably heard the expression that people "eat with their eyes." The same could be said for drinking wine. Wouldn't you prefer a beautifully chilled glass of golden Chardonnay served in a stemmed goblet rather than a yellow-brown Chardonnay that looks like it's been sitting around for a while in a juice glass? I know I would.

Assuming you selected the goblet of chilled Chardonnay, you'd be no better off if you had a head cold and temporarily lost your sense of smell. Without it, you can't taste. This is why smell is so important to the wine-tasting process, which I'll discuss in further detail later on.

For now, we're assuming you are tasting wine by itself, with only some bottled water and some plain crackers or bread within reach to cleanse your palate. As soon as you put a bite of food in your mouth, you change the taste of the wine. It's like adding a spice to your meal that will change the flavor and hopefully enhance it.

Still, taste does begin in your mouth, specifically on your tongue. You've got thousands of taste buds on your tongue, yet they register only these four basic taste sensations:

Unofficially...
Some food scientists and wine geeks wax poetic about a fifth taste sensation called *umami*, a flavor sensation associated most with Asian cuisine, (though the trained palate can spot it in other foods as well). Don't make yourself crazy if you can't pick it out.

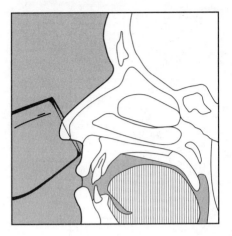

Figure 3.1
Your nose and
mouth act in
concert to con-
trol your taste
sensations.

Sweet

Sour

Bitter

Salt

These terms are important to know when you are trying to describe the way a wine tastes and how it interacts with food. When in balance, these components blend to provide a wine in perfect harmony for your enjoyment.

Sweet

You detect sweetness on the tip of your tongue, so if you taste a sweet wine, you'll know the moment you take a sip. Fruitiness is different, though it sometimes is confused with sweetness. You'll actually smell the fruit flavor in the wine.

Sour

Sour or, in wine terms, acidity, is detected on the side of the tongue. Think of what your mouth feels like after you've had too much orange juice, and you'll get an idea of what acid in a wine is like.

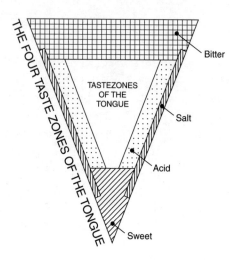

Bitter

Bitterness is detected on the back of your tongue. This sensation is associated with tannin in a wine, particularly in reds.

Tannin comes from the grape skins, stems, and seeds. When winemakers press red grapes to make red wine, they keep the juice in contact with the skins for a longer period of time to extract the red color. For white wines and even rosés, the grape skins are discarded immediately or soon after the grapes are crushed so that the resulting wine does not pick up the red color. If you've ever had strong tea without milk, you can relate to the drying sensation that tannin creates in your mouth.

Salt

Rarely, if ever, do you pick up a salty flavor in wine. If you did, however, you would detect salt on the front edges of your tongue. In wine, sugar or acid usually overpowers any trace of salt that you might detect.

Umami: the new taste sensation

Umami actually was discovered by a Japanese scientist in the early 1900s. Not surprisingly, umami is associated more with Asian cuisine. The "sweet" taste associated with many shellfish actually is the taste of umami. It also is found in caviar, oyster sauce, fish sauce, and different Asian broths as well as in Worcestershire sauce. For people who are somewhat fanatical about creating the perfect wine and food match, a little bit of knowledge about umami will go a long way.

Mouthfeel or texture

Part of the whole tasting experience includes how a wine feels in your mouth. What is the texture like? After you take a sip of the wine, draw in a little air and roll the wine around in your mouth. Chew on it for a few seconds. What is the texture like? To answer this question, think to yourself: Is it like water? Is there a little more body to it like, say, skim milk? Or is it fuller, going up the scale like 1%, 2%, whole milk, or even a milk shake? I think it's fair to say that, if you are a person who drinks skim milk, you'll probably be more comfortable drinking a lighter-style wine. If you prefer whole milk, on the other hand, it might take a fuller-style wine to ignite your taste buds.

Revelations of color

Whether you are drinking red or white, the color of the wine gives you some important clues about what to expect in the glass. For example:

- You can get an idea of whether a wine is older or younger by looking at the color. White wines generally become darker in color as they age, while red wines fade in color. In either case, if you see a brownish tinge around the edge of the wine in the glass, you know the wine is older and may be past its prime.

- The color could tip you off to what grape variety was used to make the wine. In white wines, Sauvignon Blanc most likely will be lighter in color than Chardonnay. For reds, Pinot Noir most certainly will be lighter than Cabernet Sauvignon. You can check out the complete list of white and red grape profiles later in this chapter; they are listed from the lightest to the fullest-bodied.

- A deeper-color white or red wine also could signify that the wine spent some time in wood. The oak aging imparts more depth of color than that of wines which do not undergo any wood aging.

The five S's

Now that you know more about what you are looking for, you can follow these simple steps for how to taste wine like an expert. In a professional wine-tasting setting, I'll sit in a quiet room at a table set with a white tablecloth, usually with a paper place mat or circle sheet that has a circle for each wine I am going to taste. This helps keep the wines from getting mixed up. There should be a pitcher of water and a few crackers within reach to cleanse the palate, and a wine bucket can be used as a spittoon. True wine tasters do not swallow the wine; they literally taste a sample and spit out the rest.

Consider this as my warning label: This wine-tasting exercise is okay for you to do to get a better understanding of how to taste and to help you find out what you like. I wouldn't suggest, however, that you sit down to taste all your wine this way because you'd be missing out on the true pleasure of the complete package—the company of good friends and good food.

I divide the wine-tasting process into five S's to make it easy to remember:

1. See

2. Swirl

3. Smell

4. Sip

5. Savor

See

See the wine. Look at it. Check out the color. The best way to do this is to pick up a piece of white paper or to tilt the glass against the white tablecloth and use it as a neutral background against which you can examine the true color. If you're tasting white wine, ask yourself: What shade of white is it? Is it a pale straw? Is it golden like honey or bright like the sun? The same goes for red. Is it a deep-grapey red, garnet, ruby, or even a brick red with a hint of brown? If you are in a situation in which you are tasting the same wines side by side with other people, don't be surprised if you see crimson red and your neighbor sees purple. It's not unusual. Just wait until you get to the third "S"—smell. In a crowded room of tasters, sheer pandemonium breaks out! The bottom line is that there are no "right" answers in wine tasting; beauty is in the eye and taste of the beholder.

Swirl

Begin with a stemmed wine glass that holds 6 to 8 ounces. Fill the glass one-third to one-half full. Pick

Unofficially...
Your wine glass
should be filled
no more than
halfway to give
you room to
swirl the wine.
The proper way
to pick up a
glass is by the
stem, not the
bowl. Handling
the bowl with
your hand raises
the temperature
of the wine and
doesn't allow you
to see what the
wine looks like.

up the glass by the stem and gently swirl the wine by making a small circular motion with your wrist. Take special care not to get overzealous or you will wear the wine on the front of your clothing. If you want to get technical, righties should swirl counter-clockwise, and lefties should swirl in a clockwise motion.

The first time you swirl your wine, you might feel a little self-conscious, but rest assured, there's a good reason to swirl. The motion allows oxygen to mingle with the wine and releases the aroma or bouquet of the wine.

Smell

After you have swirled the wine to release the aroma, the next thing you do is stick your nose right in the glass and take a whiff. Breathe deeply through your nose to get a good whiff of the wine. If I had to choose the single most important aspect of tasting, smelling the wine would be it.

Your sense of smell is uncanny. Over the years, you collect thousands upon thousands of different smells that you keep in your memory bank. As a result, you have the ability to identify about 10,000 different smells. In wines, you will come across smells that range from raspberry to tropical fruit, chocolate, vanilla, honey, bell peppers, and down-right earthiness. And that's just the tip of the olfactory lobe. The words you use to describe what you smell in the wine are referred to as the "nose." As you become more experienced, many times you'll be able to detect the grape variety used to make the wine. Different grapes do smell differently, as you will see when we get to their flavor profiles in a few moments.

A particular smell can take you back to a gentler time and place. Think about how you feel when you smell freshly baked chocolate chip cookies, a roaring fireplace, or the familiar scent of that special person in your life. The smell of a wine can take you back to that fabulous vacation you spent on a little beach on the coast of Portugal drinking vino verdhe, the youthful white wine for which the Portuguese are known. The wine is nothing extraordinary, but the smell brings back the whole memory of pleasure in a way that nothing else will.

Sip

Finally, it is time to actually taste the wine. By this point, you've earned it. Pick up the glass—by the stem—bring it to your lips and take a sip. In wine tasting, the trick is not to swallow right away. You want to roll the wine around in your mouth, not quite like gargling but enough to let it coat the inside of your mouth. If you want to get every last nuance out of the wine while you have that sip in your mouth, suck in a little bit of air and slurp. It enhances your ability in a formal tasting, but I frankly wouldn't recommend this at a dinner party if you care to be invited back.

Savor

Close your eyes and think about what you tasted. Did you get any sweetness on the tip of your tongue? Do you feel the acid on the side of your mouth? Are you experiencing any bitterness—that feeling of your mouth drying out from the tannin? Now swallow.

Take another sip and reevaluate your initial impressions from your first sip. This time, think about how long the flavor lasts in your mouth. The best wines will have a long, lingering finish, even moments after you swallow a taste. More ordinary wines stop short on flavor immediately after you swallow.

Now that you've gone through the exercise, the $64,000 question is "Did you like the wine?" That's all that really matters.

What does wine taste like?

If a person were to ask you, "What does Coca-Cola/ a Granny Smith apple/Prime rib taste like?" you would probably reply in this order: Coke, apple, and steak. There is a common reference point to which most people can relate, even, for instance, if the apple you are talking about is a Red Delicious or a Macintosh.

This common reference point does not exist with wine, which makes it all the more challenging to give a simple answer to this question. Many factors go into the taste of the wine. The most important factor is the raw ingredients—the grapes. Even within the grapes, there are many different types, each with its own flavor profile.

To make life more interesting, winemakers sometimes use blends of the grapes, and they also use different winemaking or vinification techniques. They might elect to ferment the wine in stainless steel to yield a lighter, fruitier style, or they might opt for some barrel aging, which will alter the taste of the grapes and make a fuller-bodied wine. It's not worth going into the minutiae here because it will just make your eyes glaze over. The best thing to do is to get a handle on the flavor profiles of the different grape varieties, or varietals as we sometimes refer to them. No matter what the winemaker does with them, they should always exhibit inherent qualities.

Flavor profiles of white grapes

To help you select a white wine, here is a list of the major white grapes you will encounter along the way. There are others, mind you, but these are the most important.

- **Albariño** (al-ba-REE-nyo)—This white wine grape from Galicia in Spain produces crisp, light-bodied wines. In Portugal, it is known as Alvarinho and it produces a similar style.

- **Chardonnay** (shar-doe-NAY)—Known as the king of white-wine grapes, Chardonnay has become so synonymous with "a glass of white wine" for many wine drinkers that some people think it is a brand. Fruit flavors such as pineapple, grapefruit, apple, lemon, peach, pear, melon, and ripe figs are commonly found in Chardonnay grapes as are butter, butterscotch, and honey, depending on the style of the wine. Chardonnay is a grape that might be produced in that fruity style or one that is kissed with oak.

  The white wines of Burgundy are made from 100 percent Chardonnay grapes, yet it was California that put the grape on the map and on the lips of the American public. Australian Chardonnay is known to emphasize wood over fruit, making some big, full-bodied wines.

  Chardonnay is one of those grapes that is pretty prolific, so you'll see it planted all over the world. Even in places such as Italy where Chardonnay is not considered to be one of the major grapes, you'll see more Italian Chardonnays on the market in an obvious attempt to capitalize on its popularity here in

Watch Out!
Though you can
certainly find
Chardonnay bar-
gains on the
market—the
$5.99 specials in
the 750 ml bot-
tles or the $9.99
1.5 liter size—be
advised that in
many cases the
grapes are not
from the best
vineyards, and
the yield per
acre of grapes is
typically higher,
which means the
fruit is less
intense. Still, for
the price, you
might discover
your next house
wine. Remember,
you get what you
pay for.

the United States. Even though Chardonnay is
a prolific grape, it also is an expensive one.
This means that the better-quality Chardonnays
are made from the best grapes and cost the
most money.

■ **Chenin Blanc** (SHEN-in blahnk)—This grape
produces a lighter-style wine marked by melon,
citrus fruits, and peaches. The best examples
are seen in the Loire Valley, which produces
the famous Vouvray. In California, Chenin
Blanc is either blended to produce generic
wines or marketed as a 100 percent varietal.
Compared to Chardonnay and Sauvignon
Blanc from California, Chenin Blanc is
semi-sweet. In South Africa, Chenin Blanc
abounds but it is known as Steen.

■ **French Colombard** (kohl-um-BARD)—This
workhorse white grape is responsible for the
white jug wines made in California that you
might still see labeled as Chablis. This grape
has nothing to do with the true Chablis from
France, however, which is made from 100 percent Chardonnay.

■ **Fumé Blanc** (FOO-may blahnk)—This is the
name given to Sauvignon Blanc by Robert
Mondavi years ago to make the wine sound
more sexy to Americans. It worked. Taste characteristics are generally crisp, clean, and
refreshing with an herbal, grassy quality. For
more information, see Sauvignon Blanc on
page 60.

■ **Gewürztraminer** (geh-VERTZ-tra-ME-ner)—
"Gewürz" means spicy in German and is an
appropriate description for this grape's flavor
profile. It gives off a distinct aroma and flavor

marked by floral characteristics, and it usually
is dry in style. It can, however, be made from
late harvest grapes to yield a dessert wine. Best
known for flavor-packed Gewürztraminer is
Alsace, France. California and the Pacific
Northwest produce Gewürztraminer, but it is
tame by comparison. Some other areas where
you will find Gewürztraminer are Germany,
Italy, and New Zealand.

▪ **Marsanne** (mahr-SAN)—Found in the Rhône
Valley, wines made from Marsanne are fuller-
bodied. Flavors can range from nutty to zingy
with citrus. This grape also is being used in
California by winemakers who produce Rhône-
style wines. (These winemakers are known as
Rhône Rangers.) Marsanne also shows up in
Australia.

▪ **Muscat** (MUSS-cat)—You never know where
Muscat is going to turn up. This grape goes by
many different aliases depending on where it is
grown. Vines are planted in southern France,
the Rhône Valley, Alsace, Italy (known as
Moscato), Spain and Portugal (known as
Moscatel), California, Australia, and elsewhere.
Muscat yields a wine that can range from the
famous dessert wine made in the Rhône Valley
called Muscat de Beaumes-de-Venise to a bone-
dry Muscat d'Alsace and even a sparkling Asti
Spumante. Muscat's general flavor can be
described as floral, and well, musky.

▪ **Pinot Blanc** (PEE-no blahnk)—This shows
good fruit when young, similar to but not with
the same amount of depth as a good
Chardonnay. Good examples of Pinot Blanc
come from the Alsace region of France and

Germany (Weissburgunder) as well as Italy (Pinot Bianco), Burgundy, and California.

■ **Pinot Grigio/Pinot Gris** (PEE-no GREE-ji-o/ PEE-no GREE)—At its best, this grape produces dry, crisp white wines from Italy. At its worst, it's something white and wet to fill a wine glass. It is best to find a reliable producer whose product you enjoy and grab a glass. Though most people today are most familiar with the Italian variety, the French grape is known as Pinot Gris, and it produces some very tasty wines from Alsace (where it's also known as Tokay d'Alsace), Germany (Ruländer), and even Oregon.

■ **Riesling** (REECE-ling)—This floral grape goes hand in hand with its native Germany and gets a bum rap as always producing sweet wines. It doesn't, but it certainly has the wherewithal to produce knockout dessert wines. Riesling is one of the most versatile, food-friendly grapes you'll ever meet if you give it a chance. Excellent dry-styled Rieslings are found in Alsace, Washington State, Oregon, and California, where they sometimes are known as White Riesling. Australia also does a good job with Riesling.

■ **Sauvignon Blanc** (SO-VEE-nyon blahnk)— Famous wine auctioneer and wine personality Michael Broadbent ruined it for me when he presided over a grand tasting of top Sauvignon Blanc wines and described the "nose" or aroma as "cat's piss." It took me a while to get past that to truly enjoy Sauvignon Blanc for its many good qualities. When I come across one that is particularly strong-smelling, however, I

still think about that unusual descriptor.
Sauvignon Blanc is a gutsy grape that cuts
through the clutter with its acid combined with
its herbal flavor. Grassy and vegetal are two
commonly used descriptors. Sometimes you'll
even see a late harvest version that makes for a
more complex dessert wine. When not used as
a 100 percent varietal, Sauvignon Blanc is traditionally blended with Sémillon, but you'll
sometimes see a bit of Chardonnay added by
some winemakers.

The Loire Valley, especially Pouilly-Fumé
and Sancerre as well as Bordeaux, is definitely
Sauvignon Blanc country. Still, you'll be quite
pleased if you pick up a bottle from New
Zealand, Australia, or California. Robert
Mondavi created new demand for the grape
when he dubbed it "Fumé Blanc" on his label.
(See Fumé Blanc on page 58 for more information.) Sauvignon Blanc is generally less
expensive than Chardonnay.

- **Sémillon** (SEM-ee-yon)—When blended with
  Sauvignon Blanc to make dry white Bordeaux,
  especially in Graves and Pessac-Leognan,
  Sémillon acts as a softening agent to tone
  down the assertive Sauvignon Blanc grape. On
  its own, Sémillon is not considered to be a
  fruity grape or one that is rich in acid, but it
  does have character. Late harvest Sémillon that
  is used to make sweet dessert wines in
  Sauternes, France, has a richer, fuller, more
  honey-like flavor profile.

In addition to Bordeaux and Sauternes,
France, Sémillon is a staple in white wines—
often blended with Sauvignon Blanc or

Watch Out!
Some winemakers
produce
Sauvignon Blancs
to taste more
like a
Chardonnay by
using some of
the same wine-
making tech-
niques to add
complexity. Hint:
If you see "barrel
fermented" on
the label, you
know that the
wine is intended
to be a "poor
man's
Chardonnay."

Chardonnay—in Australia and Chile. On occasion, you will see a Sémillon varietal made from 100 percent Sémillon grapes, but it is underwhelming for the most part. Sémillon also is found in California and Washington state.

- **Trebbiano/Ugni Blanc** (treb-ee-AH-no/ OO-nyee Blahnk)—This prolific white-wine grape is widely planted in Italy and yields a dry white wine that is high in acid. You'll find it under its own name, "Trebbiano," or blended in some other popular Italian whites such as Orvieto and Soave. In Italy, some winemakers still blend some Trebbiano into their red Chianti and Vino Nobile di Montepulciano.

   In France, this grape is called Ugni Blanc. It is sometimes blended into a simple Rhône white or is used in wines from Provence. Sometimes called St.-Émilion, this grape also is distilled to make Armagnac and Cognac.

- **Viognier** (VEE-oh-nyeh)—This distinctive grape, with its mix of spice, peaches, and apricots, is native to the Rhône Valley. California winemakers are producing some Viogniers, but they are nothing like those of the Rhône Valley. It's a difficult grape to grow, and it will take a little more time for California to get a grip on this grape.

Flavor profiles of red grapes

Again, this is not a list of every red grape known, but it covers the most important ones you will find.

- **Barbera** (bar-BEAR-uh)—This deep-ruby–colored grape thrives in Piedmont, Italy, and yields wines with berry flavors that are low in tannin but high in acid. There is some Barbera in California, but it's nothing to write home about.

- **Brunello** (brew-NELL-oh)—A long-lost cousin of the Sangiovese grape, Brunello produces one of the most intense, concentrated wines marked by luscious black cherry and berries. The only wine this grape makes is the full-bodied Brunello di Montalcino and a younger version called Rosso di Montalcino.

- **Cabernet Franc** (cab-er-NAY Frahnk)—This red grape plays second fiddle to Cabernet Sauvignon and Merlot when it is blended for the wines of Bordeaux. On its own, however, it tastes like a lighter-styled Cabernet Sauvignon. The taste is of berries and currants. In addition to Bordeaux, the Loire Valley produces some very tasty, good-value reds such as Chinon and the popular rosé called Cabernet d'Anjou. It's been around in California for many years but is first gaining some interest for its role in California's Bordeaux blends that are sometimes referred to as Meritage (rhymes with "heritage"). Good examples of Cabernet Franc, both as 100 percent varietals and as blending wines, come from Argentina, Italy, Long Island, New Zealand and Washington State.

- **Cabernet Sauvignon** (cab-er-NAY so-vee-NYON)—Still king of the red grapes in popularity, Cabernet Sauvignon is the backbone of fine red Bordeaux wines. California wines made from 100 percent Cabernet Sauvignon as well as blends in which Cabernet is the main ingredient are collectibles when produced by the best winemakers in optimum vintages. Cabernet Sauvignon is flavor-packed with tastes that range from spicy to jammy or that remind you of black currants or even chocolate.

Other parts of the world that produce good Cabernet Sauvignon are Argentina, Australia, Chile, Italy, Long Island, the Pacific Northwest, and South Africa.

- **Carignan** (kar-EE-nyon)—This red grape, found mainly in an area of southern France known as the Languedoc-Roussillon, has a high level of tannin. This makes it best-suited for blending with other varieties to produce pleasant, easy-drinking reds. Carignan is also popular in Spain.

- **Dolcetto** (dole-CHET-toe)—Grown in Italy, Dolcetto produces some of the most pleasant, light, fruity reds you'll find outside of the Gamay grape, which is used to make French Beaujolais.

- **Gamay** (gam-MAY)—This is the grape that produces the light, fruity-style wines of Beaujolais. California grows its version of Gamay that is called Gamay Beaujolais.

- **Grenache** (gre-NOSH)—When made as a red wine, this grape from the Rhône Valley produces a medium- to full-bodied wine with good fruit and spicy overtones that is commonly used as part of a blend. A rosé version presents a fruitier, less spicy style. These wines also are made in California, Australia, and Spain, where the Spanish know the grape as Garnacha.

- **Malbec** (MAHL-beck)—This is a blending grape used in Bordeaux and sometimes in California to help round out a wine. You're likely to see more Malbec, both as blends and as 100 percent varietals, in Argentina. Malbec's flavors include those of plums and cherries.

- **Merlot** (mare-LOW)—Traditionally used to make Bordeaux blends, Merlot has struck out on its own as a solo act and has won rave reviews. This red grape appeals to wine drinkers across the board for its pleasant fruit flavors, easy approachability, and versatility with food.

  Outside France, Merlot is popping up everywhere on vines in California, Washington State, Italy, Argentina, and Chile.

- **Mourvèdre** (more-VAY-druh)—This red grape is primarily found in the Rhône Valley, in Provence, and in the Languedoc-Rouisillon, where it produces a spicy wine with some black-cherry flavors. Spain produces wines made from Mourvèdre as do winemakers known as the Rhône Rangers in California.

- **Nebbiolo** (NEH-bee-yo-low)—This is a full-bodied red grape from Italy that produces wines worthy of aging such as Barbaresco and Barolo. California produces some Nebbiolo, but the wines are considerably lighter in style.

- **Petite Sirah** (pe-TEET see-RAH)—Expect a little pepper and spice from this red grape, which is grown primarily in California. It is a long-lost cousin of the Rhône grape, Syrah. Argentina makes some good examples of Petite Sirah as well.

- **Pinot Noir** (PEE-no nwar)—The classic grape of Burgundy and Champagne, Pinot Noir is understated elegance in a bottle. A well-made wine made from Pinot Noir, whether it's from Burgundy, California, or Oregon, will entice you with the soft sell of berry flavors contained within. Unlike red grapes such as Cabernet Sauvignon or Zinfandel, Pinot Noir does not knock you over the head to get your attention. It doesn't have to.

- **Sangiovese** (SAN-gee-o-VAY-see)—A true paisan from Italy, Sangiovese packs a medium- to full-bodied punch and contains flavors of spice, anisette, and black cherry. California wine-makers are working more with Sangiovese to create their own style known as Cal-Ital wines.

- **Syrah/Shiraz** (see-RAH/shee-RAHZ)—The latest red darlings to hit America's tastebuds since Merlot, Syrah comes from the Rhône Valley and from Australia where it is known as Shiraz. Both grapes have the ability to produce some of the longest-lived, wonderfully spicy, peppery reds that are balanced out by block-buster black cherry and currant flavors. Although Syrah produces some heavy hitters that wine collectors vie for, the grape is good for some youthful, easy-drinking wines (which was a big part of Merlot's mass appeal). Because of the new interest in Syrah, vines are popping up everywhere in California, Washington State, and other winemaking regions.

- **Tempranillo** (tem-pra-KNEE-yo)—You get ruby-red, full-flavored wines from this grape from Spain.

- **Zinfandel** (ZIN-fan-del)—First of all, yes, Zinfandel is a red grape. It is used to make the popular semi-sweet white Zinfandel. (For the complete scoop on white Zinfandel, see Chapter 11, "Rosé or Blush Wine") Until recently, Zinfandel was thought to be of North American origin. However, DNA fingerprinting and other ampelographic research now point to the grape's European origin. Flavor profiles vary widely for Zinfandel from a light-bodied, fruity style to a late harvest Port variety, depending on the producer. If there were such a thing as a baseline flavor profile for Zinfandel, it would be spicy, robust, and marked by the taste of rich mixed berries.

Expanding your wine repertoire

When you find something you like, it's easy to fall into a rut and have it over and over again. Many of us do this with food, and I venture to say it's more common with wine because most Americans do not drink wine with dinner every evening or even every week. So you stick with what you know.

Deep down, I'm sure you'd welcome the opportunity to try something different. You willingly drink what is served at a dinner party, but what about when you are the one making the selection?

If you'd like to drink outside the box and expand what I like to call your "wine repertoire," take a look at the following list of possibilities. If you consider yourself to be a California Chardonnay drinker, for example, consider a classic white Burgundy, which happens to be made from 100 percent Chardonnay. It's that simple.

For white-wine drinkers:

TABLE 3.1: EXPAND YOUR WHITE-WINE HORIZONS

If You Like...	Try...
California Chardonnay	White Burgundy wines such as those from Mâcon, Pouilly-Fuissé, Meursault, Chablis, Puligny-Montrachet, Chassagne-Montrachet, Rully, or Montagny; Australian Chardonnays; Pinot Blanc from Burgundy, Alsace, Germany, California, and Italy
California Sauvignon Blanc	Loire Valley wines such as Fumé Blanc, Pouilly-Fumé and Sancerre; white Bordeaux such as Graves and Pessac-Léognan; New Zealand Sauvignon Blancs; Chilean Sauvignon Blancs
Pinot Grigio (from Italy)	Pinot Gris from Burgundy and Oregon; Tokay d'Alsace from Alsace; Rülander from Germany; Soave and Verdicchio from Italy
Riesling (from Germany)	Riesling from Alsace, Washington State, and New York State (all areas make all styles from dry to dessert wines)
Gewürztraminer (from Alsace)	Gewürztraminer from Germany, California, Washington State, and Oregon
Sémillon (Bordeaux)	Sauternes from France; Sémillon from Australia and Chile
Viognier (from Rhône Valley)	Viognier from California

For red-wine drinkers:

TABLE 3.2: EXPAND YOUR RED-WINE HORIZONS

If You Like...	Try...
California Cabernet Sauvignon	Bordeaux; Cabernet Sauvignon from Chile
California Merlot	Bordeaux (especially from Pomerol and St.-Émilion); Merlot from Washington State and Chile
California Pinot Noir	French Burgundy; Oregon Pinot Noir; Beaujolais
Syrah/Shiraz	Rhône Valley Syrah; Australian Shiraz
Sangiovese (from Italy)	California Sangiovese
California Zinfandel	Petite Sirah from California; Rhône wines
French Bordeaux	Meritage (Bordeaux blends) from California, Rioja from Spain

Just the facts

- Your sense of smell is your most valuable taste sensation.

- You need the right tools to taste wine correctly—proper stemware and a white background to look at the wine.

- The color of a wine can tell you about its age.

- Different wine grapes have distinctly different taste profiles. There really is a difference between Chardonnay and Sauvignon Blanc.

- You can venture outside your accustomed wine world by trying your favorite wine varietal, such as Chardonnay, from a different part of the world.

A Glass of White Wine, Please?

PART II

GET THE SCOOP ON...
The difference between AOC and table wines ▪
The importance of geography ▪ The gamut of
styles and price ranges available ▪ How to read
a wine label ▪ Why shippers are so important

Classic French Whites

Now that we're getting into specific wine regions, why begin with France? It's simple. For one thing, the French continue to be the biggest wine consumers in the world, drinking an average of 16 gallons per person per year. To put that into perspective, Americans consume only about two gallons of wine per person each year. Though wine consumption in the United States is on the rise, we have a long way to go before we become a true wine-drinking nation.

In addition to being the number one wine-consuming country, France also is one of the top wine producers in the world in terms of both quantity and quality. Long before world-class wines were produced on American soil, at least two of our forefathers, Thomas Jefferson and Benjamin Franklin, both Francophiles, were known to have a regular supply of French wine shipped across the Atlantic to stock their personal cellars. To this day, winemakers from around the world still look to French wines as a benchmark of quality.

Chapter 4

Unofficially...
You could say
that the French
drink wine like
water. Americans
consume about
11 gallons of
bottled water per
person annually,
far less than the
amount of wine
the French drink.

Importance of Appellation d'Origine Contrôlée (AOC)

For all of the wonderful wine produced in France, there also is plenty that is downright ordinary. Because the French are pretty laid back about wine, it is not unusual for them to pick up a jug at the supermarket the way we would grab a container of milk. The big decision? Red or white. The French can do this without the hassle of complicated labels because these everyday wines carry minimal labeling.

Despite the very casual *joie de vivre* attitude attached to wine drinking in France, the French are very serious about the quality of their wines. This is reflected in the Appellation d'Origine Contrôlée (AOC) laws that were created in France in 1935 to protect the integrity of their wine.

The Appellation d'Origine Contrôlée laws protect the integrity of the wine by regulating or monitoring the following:

- Where the grapes are grown.

- The grape varieties used.

- Vineyard yield (how many grapes can be grown per acre). Generally speaking, vineyard owners who strictly control grape yields will be rewarded with the riper, more intense fruit that is typical of the finest wines. Those who permit overproduction inevitably wind up with less-flavorful grapes.

- The minimum amount of alcohol the wine must contain.

- Other winemaking practices that must conform to the traditional methods of the wine region.

These laws apply to four different categories of wine, listed here from highest to lowest rank:

1. Appellation d'Origine Contrôlée—The specific region or sometimes even the name of the vineyard appears on the label. A wine made in the Chablis region, for example, will be labeled "Appellation Chablis Contrôlée."

2. Vins Délimités de Qualité Supérieure (VDQS)—One short rung below an A.O.C wine.

3. Vins de Pays—Known as country wines, these labels also include the name of the place of origin, though the area is considerably broader. You might find a Sauvignon Blanc or a Chardonnay labeled "Vins de Pays D'Oc," for example, which could have been produced in the Rhône Valley, Provence, or the southwest region of Languedoc-Roussillon.

4. Vins de Table—Your basic simple table wine. This merely carries the label "Vins de Table Francais" to show that it's from France. You won't find a grape variety on the label, nor will you find a vintage.

Alsace

If you are interested in finding some of the most delightful white wines from France that happen to be a good value, you needn't look further than Alsace. This region produces some of the tastiest wines made from the widely planted Riesling, Gewürztraminer, Pinot Gris (also known as Tokay d'Alsace), and Pinot Blanc grapes as well as other grape varietals.

Here is where geography becomes important in the wine world. If you were to look at a map, you

Timesaver
A quick way to size up a French wine is to check out the label for its ranking. Expect to pay more for the top-ranking Appellation Contrôlée wines and VDQS selections. Vins de Pays wines offer some interesting alternatives and are a good value for the flavor. Vins de Tables from reliable producers make perfect everyday wines.

would notice that Alsace is just across the Rhine River from Germany. In fact, for many years, Alsace was a part of Germany until the French reclaimed it after World War I. Because of Alsace's history and the region's geographical proximity to Germany, most people automatically assume that the wines from Alsace are sweet like the wines of Germany. This could not be further from the truth. In Chapter 5, "Noble German Whites," I will further dispel the myth that all German wines are sweet.

Except for the fact that Alsatian wine producers bottle their wines in the same tapered green bottles as those from the Mosel region of Germany, Alsace produces an entirely different style of wine. True to their French roots, the wines from Alsace are fermented completely dry.

In terms of quality, all Alsatian wines carry the AOC designation. If you're looking for something more special and, of course, more pricey, try a Grand Cru. This term on an Alsatian wine label tells you that the wine came from a single top-rated vineyard and was made from a single vintage as opposed to a blend. More than 50 vineyards now qualify as Grand Crus.

A Grand Cru from Alsace can be produced legally from one of the four following varieties and must contain 100 percent of the grape named on the label:

- Riesling

- Gewürztraminer

- Pinot Gris

- Muscat

Alsace is the first French wine region to include the grape variety on its labels.

Basic Alsatian wines begin in the $10 to $15 range at most wine stores, perhaps a little less at a discount operation. Grand Crus start at about $20 and go well over $50 for the top-of-the-line varieties.

A major factor in the selection of most wines is the reputation of the producer. Here are some reputable names to look for on the label:

- Leon Beyer
- Marcel Deiss
- Hugel
- Josmeyer
- Pierre Sparr
- F.E. Trimbach
- Domaine Weinbach
- Zind-Humbrecht

Some of the better vintages on the market are 1990, 1994, 1995, 1996, 1997, and 1998.

Loire Valley

Along one of France's longest rivers you will find another major white wine region, the Loire Valley. Though this region produces an assortment of reds and rosés, including the popular Rosé d'Anjou, the Loire Valley is best-known for its white wines.

The best-known white wines from the Loire Valley come from these famous villages for which they are named:

- Pouilly-Fumé
- Sancerre
- Vouvray
- Muscadet

Both Pouilly-Fumé and Sancerre are made from 100 percent Sauvignon Blanc grapes, which means

Watch Out!
Do not automatically be impressed by the terms "Grande Reserve" or "Réserve Personnelle." They mean nothing unless you see either of these terms on the bottle of a reliable producer.

Watch Out!
You may have seen Pouilly-Fumé and Pouilly Fuissé on a wine list somewhere and suspected that the two must be related. Right? Wrong. Pouilly-Fumé comes from the Loire Valley and is made from 100 percent Sauvignon Blanc grapes. Pouilly-Fuissé comes from the Mâconnais region of Burgundy and is made from 100 percent Chardonnay grapes.

you're going to get a dry, crisp wine. In fact, many of these wines have a fresh, grassy, herbal quality, though Pouilly-Fumé generally is more full-bodied. Vouvray, made from 100 percent Chenin Blanc, can produce wines that range from dry to fruity and even honeysuckle sweet. Muscadet, made from 100 percent Melon grape, produces a lighter-style, dry white wine that is easy to drink.

Loire Valley white wines are extremely versatile. They make for some of the best summer sippers, but they also are excellent as aperitifs year round. In terms of wine/food combinations, just look at the region's proximity to the sea—both the Atlantic Ocean and, of course, the Loire River. This should tip you off that Loire Valley wines are a natural with shellfish and other seafood. Historically, wines were made to go with the food of the region.

Once you narrow down your area of interest in the Loire Valley, here are the names of some reputable producers to look for.

Pouilly-Fumé:

- de Ladoucette
- Michel Redde
- Didier Dagueneau
- Guyot

Sancerre:

- Domaine Lucien Crochet
- Château de Sancerre (Marnier-Lapostolle)
- Pascal Jolivet
- Henri Bourgeois

Vouvray:

- Hüet
- Jean-Claude Bougrier

- Marc Brédif
- Robert Michele

Muscadet:

- Marquis de Goulaine
- Sauvion & Fils
- Louis Métaireau
- Domaine de la Pépière

Wines from the Loire Valley are best when consumed young, though the sweeter-style Vouvrays develop nicely with five or more years of age. You can get a basic Pouilly-Fumé or Sancerre in the $10 to $15 range at retail, though a producer's special bottlings or cuvée can run more like $25 to $50, depending on the market. The best deal remains in Muscadet where, for $6 and certainly less than $10, you'll enjoy some of the true flavors of the Loire.

For Muscadet wines in particular, the younger the better. The 1998 vintage would be just fine. Other recent good vintages of the Loire Valley are 1995 and 1996.

Bordeaux

When you think of Bordeaux, chances are you are thinking about red wine. Though Bordeaux is best known for its famous classic reds—first growths such as Château Lafite and Château Latour—this winemaking region produces some excellent dry white wine from Graves and world-class white dessert wines from Sauternes. We will concentrate on the dry white wines of the Graves area in this chapter, and we will talk more about Sauternes in Chapter 13, "After-Dinner Delights."

Graves

Graves is the French word for gravel, which refers to the soil where the grapes are grown. The primary grape varieties used to make white Graves wines are Sauvignon Blanc and Sémillon. Most Graves are made in the true French style—that is, a blend of the two grapes. The Sémillon typically smooth the edges on the more assertive Sauvignon Blanc and gives the wine more depth. You will find a range in styles of Graves wines from winery to winery for a number of reasons, but one reason in particular is the "recipe" a winemaker uses.

The winemaker at top-rated Château Haut-Brion Blanc, for example, might use about a 50/50 blend of Sauvignon Blanc and Sémillon during one vintage, while a winemaker at Château La Louvière might opt for a 70 percent Sauvignon Blanc/30 percent Sémillon blend. Still others take the "purist" approach, popularized in California, where 100 percent of a grape is often used. In this case, it is more common to find a Graves made from 100 percent Sauvignon Blanc rather than 100 percent Sémillon.

Your basic Graves wines, which happen to offer good value as everyday drinking wines, simply carry the Graves appellation on the label.

Moneysaver
Just across the Garonne River in the village of Entre-Deux-Mers, you can find great values in dry white Bordeaux.

Pessac-Léognan

One way to spot the better-quality wines from Graves is to look for the name Pessac-Léognan on the label. This actually is an area within the northern part of the Graves region, closer to Bordeaux, where the finest Graves properties happen to be located. Another way is to look for the name of a specific château. The wineries were rated and classified by the French government in 1959, so if you're looking for the best, here are the top château wines from Graves:

- Château Bouscaut
- Château Carbonnieux

- Domaine de Chevalier
- Château Couhins, now known as Château Couhins-Lurton
- Château La Louvière
- Château La Tour Martillac
- Château Laville-Haut-Brion
- Château Malartic-Lagravière
- Château Olivier

Burgundy

As with Bordeaux, people have a tendency to associate the Burgundy region with red wine. After all, when we describe something as Burgundy in color, we are talking about red. For now, forget about the reds. If you consider yourself a Chardonnay drinker, you will want to know about the many different styles available in Burgundy. That's because, with very few exceptions, all white Burgundy is made from 100 percent Chardonnay.

Burgundy is a famous wine region located in the eastern part of France. The most important wine-growing regions within Burgundy, listed from north to south, are:

- Chablis
- Côte de Nuits
- Côte de Beaune
- Côte Châllonnaise
- Mâcconnais
- Beaujolais

All of Burgundy's main wine regions produce white wine, though Beaujolais and the Côte de Nuits make so little that you will rarely find it at a wine shop or restaurant.

Unofficially...
Château Haut-Brion from Graves is noticeably missing from this illustrious list of classified châteaux. Why? Château Haut-Brion was the only Graves wine included in the prestigious Bordeaux Classification of 1855, and its owners did not want to be included in the Graves classification.

Unofficially...
Together, the Côte de Nuits and Côte de Beaune are part of a bigger wine-growing area within Burgundy called the Côte d'Or, which means "golden slope" in French.

Even though Chardonnay is the grape used to make white Burgundy wines, you'll be amazed by the broad spectrum of styles. A lot of this has to do with where the grapes are grown. The cooler, northerly climate of Chablis, for example, is going to produce grapes that are higher in acidity than those of the more southerly Mâcconnais, where the wines typically are riper and fruitier. Also, winemakers use different vinification techniques to make their wine. The most pronounced flavor difference will depend on whether the wine was aged in wooden barrels. Traditionally, wine has been fermented in oak barrels, which impart a woody flavor marked by vanilla and butterscotch as the wine ages, especially in the better wines. Wines fermented in stainless steel tanks have a tendency to be crisper, fresher, and fruitier. In the case of Burgundy wines, both styles are dry.

Generally speaking, better-quality white Burgundies ("better-quality" is the code word for more expensive) are more likely to spend some time in oak. If you are unsure, check the back label on the bottle. Along with some taste description, the winemaker's notes usually include whether the wine was fermented or aged in wood.

Chablis

Before the buzzword for a glass of white wine became "Chardonnay," Americans almost always asked for a glass of Chablis. It reached the point where practically any white swill was labeled as Chablis, and it didn't matter what types of grapes were used as long as they were white.

The reason I'm making such a big deal out of this is that true Chablis comes from a village of the same name in France's Burgundy region. It is a little over 100 miles southeast of Paris and is quite separate from the rest of Burgundy. It actually is located closer to the Champagne region, which will be discussed in Chapter 12, "Sparkle Plenty."

Wines from Chablis typically are clean, and crisp, and have a mineral flavor from the soil, or "terroir" as the French like call it. There are three basic quality levels of Chablis, translating into three different price categories. From the most ordinary and least expensive to the more special and most expensive, they are:

- **Chablis**—This basic or "village" Chablis can be produced anywhere within the region. On the label, you will simply see the word "Chablis" and the name of the producer.

- **Chablis Premier Cru**—This Chablis must come from one of the specially designated premier cru vineyards. The wine is labeled "Chablis Premier Cru" and includes the name of the actual vineyard where the grapes were grown. Sometimes the word "Premier" is abbreviated on the label as "1er."

- **Chablis Grand Cru**—In Chablis, you can't get any better than these seven specially designated vineyards. The wine is labeled "Chablis Grand Cru" and includes the name of the vineyard where the grapes were grown.

The price of entry in the Chablis market is in the $15 range for a village wine, $20 to $40 for Chablis Premier Cru, and $40 to $60 for the crème de la crème. Basic Chablis wines are intended to be consumed young—within about two years of the vintage. Chablis Premier Cru and Grand Cru vineyards, on the other hand, could use three to five years and may age gracefully for 10 to 15 years.

For people who want to cut to the chase and buy the best, here is a list of the seven Chablis Grand Cru vineyards:

- Blachots
- Bougros
- Grenouilles
- Les Clos
- Preuses
- Valmur
- Vaudésir

Some of the best values can be found from the premier cru vineyards of Chablis. Here are some of the better-known vineyards that you are likely to find in your local wine shop or when you dine out:

- Côte de Léchet
- Forêt
- Fourchaume
- Mont de Milieu
- Montmains
- Montée de Tonnerre
- Vaillons
- Vaulorent

Whether you opt for a Chablis Grand Cru or a basic village wine, it always is best to look for the most reliable producers including:

- Albert Pic & Fils
- A. Regnard & Fils
- Domaine Laroche
- Joseph Drouhin
- J. Moreau et Fils
- Francois Raveneau

- René & Vincent Dauvissat
- Jean Dauvissat
- Vocoret & Fils
- Pascal Bouchard
- William Fèvre
- Louis Latour

Finally, in Chablis, hedge your bets by selecting a good vintage. In the northern part of Burgundy, where the cooler weather and frosts can be more challenging for the winemaker to deal with, the vintage is more important than in other wine-growing areas where the weather is more even. Some of the better recent vintages are 1995, 1996, and 1997.

Mâcconais

The Mâconnais happens to be one of my favorite white-wine–producing areas because I know that, no matter the quality level of the wine I choose to buy, I am going to get excellent value. Practically all the wine produced in the Mâconnais area is white.

The most basic wines from the Mâconnais are simply labeled "Mâcon," and a small step up is labeled "Mâcon Supérieur." As the quality level increases, so does the information given on the wine label. At the next level, "Mâcon-Villages," which is still in the $10 range in many markets, the wine carries the name of one of the 43 villages permitted to use this appellation.

A sampling of reliable Mâcon-Village wines to look for include:

- Mâcon-Viré
- Mâcon-Lugny
- Mâcon-Chardonnay
- Mâcon-St.-Véran

Though there is no classification in the Mâcconais as there is in Chablis and other wine-growing areas of France, the designer Mâcons are Pouilly-Vinzelles and especially Pouilly-Fuissé, which are named for the villages from which they are produced. These wines are more full-bodied than the other Mâcon wines and come with a hefty price tag ($15 to $20) compared to others in the Mâconnais region because of their trendiness.

In fact, some Pouilly-Fuissé producers are raising the envelope and the price by producing single-vineyard Pouilly-Fuissés and aging the wine in oak as they do in other parts of Burgundy. As the name implies, single-vineyard wines are those made from one particular vineyard that the winemaker believes produces the best grapes. These fuller-styled wines run in the $20 to $40 range.

Côte de Beaune

Within the Côte d'Or, there is the Côte de Beaune where only about 30 percent of the wine produced is white. Size in this case does not matter one bit because these wines are considered to be the gold standard of Chardonnay. We're talking about the classics from the following three main communes:

- Meursault
- Chassagne-Montrachet
- Puligny-Montrachet

Due to the law of supply and demand, expect to pay dearly for these wines at all three quality levels.

- **Level 1—Village Wine.** A simple village wine will set you back $30 to $35. As the name implies, you will see the name of the village such as Chassagne-Montrachet on the label.

- **Level 2—Premier Cru.** A premier cru fetches about $75 per bottle. In addition to the name of the village, you also will see the name of the specific vineyard from which the wine came such as Les Ruchottes.

- **Level 3—Grand Cru.** The top-of-the-line varieties start at about $100 and can compete with your car payment at over $350. A grand cru Chassagne-Montrachet carries the name of the grand cru vineyard from which it came, such as Bâtard-Montrachet.

You don't need to be a wine wizard to select one of these silky Chardonnays. Go back to the three main villages and look for the following better-known, top-rated vineyards. The grand crus (the crème de la crème) are noted by an asterisk.

In the village of Meursault, look for:

- Les Perrières
- Les Genevrières
- Les Charmes
- Le Poruzot
- Blagny

In the village of Chassagne-Montrachet, look for:

- Les Ruchottes
- Morgeot
- Le Montrachet*
- Bâtard-Montrachet*
- Criots-Bâtard-Montrachet*

In the village of Puligny-Montrachet, look for:

- Les Caillerets
- Les Combettes
- Les Pucelles

- Les Clavoillon
- Les Referts
- Bâtard-Montrachet*
- Bienvenue-Bâtard-Montrachet*
- Chevalier-Montrachet*
- Le Montrachet*

Other excellent vineyards to look for in addition to the "big three" villages previously described include Corton-Charlemagne and Le Charlemagne, both grand crus in the village of Aloxe-Corton, and Clos des Mouches, a premier crus vineyard in the village of Beaune.

In the Côte de Beaune, it is not uncommon for several producers to own vineyards and produce wines within one of these top-rated appellations. This means they have the right to market their wine under the prestigious name. That's why it is still important to look for wines from producers with a strong track record, especially if you are willing to shell out big bucks. Look for reputable producers such as:

- Louis Jadot
- Joseph Drouhin
- Louis Latour
- Bouchard Père & Fils
- Domaine Leflaive
- Domaine Ètienne Sauzet
- Prosper Maufoux
- Olivier Leflaive Frèrer
- Domaine des Comtes Lafon
- Labouré-Roi

If you're looking to stock your cellar, buy the 1995, 1996, and 1997 vintages. Village wines are best when consumed within three to five years of the vintage date. Premier crus are enhanced by five to 10 years, but the grand crus really need at least 10 years to show what they're made of. (Be sure to stock your cellar with plenty of Mâcon wines to drink while you patiently wait for the big boys to blossom.)

Côte Châlonnaise

Sandwiched between the high-rent district of Côte de Beaune and the versatile values of the Mâconnais is a lesser-known wine region called the Côte Châlonnaise. Because the Côte Châlonnaise is not on the tip of everyone's tongue, you're going to find good values here.

Two other areas that, although better known for their reds, also produce some excellent whites are Mercurey and Givry.

If you look at a map, you'll notice that Rully and Mercurey are awfully close to the Côte de Beaune. Some wines produced in these northern villages of the Côte Châllonaise could have qualities similar but not equal to the Montrachets of Beaune. Considering that you're going to pay somewhere between $10 and $25 for a Côte Châllonaise compared to $30 for a basic Côte de Beaune, it's a bargain.

As in other parts of Burgundy, vintages are important. In the Côte Châllonaise, 1995 and 1996 are the best recent vintages followed by 1997, which wasn't as generous.

Along with the vintage, look for these reliable producers:

- Olivier Leflaive Frères
- Louis Jadot

- Louis Latour
- Antonin Rodet
- Michel Juillot
- Joseph Drouhin

Rhône Valley

If you are one of the people whose taste buds occasionally grow weary of Chardonnay, perhaps you have ventured to try Viognier. Some California winemakers started producing white wines from this grape in the early 1990s and hyped Viognier as the next Chardonnay. Truth be told, this wine has been around for many years in the northern Rhône Valley, where it is called Condrieu.

Condrieu, which is made from 100 percent Viognier, is a dry white wine with a distinctive perfume flavor and a rich body. Within Condrieu, there is a separate small appellation called Château-Grillet. They both are meant to be consumed young—within a few years after the vintage. Look for 1995, 1996, and 1997.

Other Rhône Valley whites include:

- **Hermitage Blanc**—Made in the northern region of Hermitage, this wine typically is delightfully dry and full-bodied. Two grape varietals, Marsanne and Roussanne, are blended together to create this wine, a fact that might be mentioned on the wine's back label. On the front, you'll simply see the name "Hermitage Blanc" and the name of the producer. You might enjoy the freshness of a recent vintage, or if you have the patience, lay one down for 10 to 15 years and then savor it. Excellent older vintages, if you can find them, are 1988, 1989, and 1990. More recent good years are 1991, 1994, 1995, 1996, and 1997.

- **Châteauneuf-du-Pape Blanc**—Extremely small quantities of white wine are made in this village in the Rhône region. Like the better-known red, Châteauneuf-du-Pape, the whites are made from a blend of many grapes including Grenache Blanc, Roussanne, and Clairette. One of the main differences between different Châteauneuf-de-Pape Blanc styles is in the recipe or blend of the grapes used. Look for the same vintages as recommended for Hermitage Blanc plus the 1993.

- **Beaume-de-Venise**—This appellation within the Rhône Valley produces sweet and rich dessert wines made from the Muscat grape. It is discussed further in Chapter 13, "After-Dinner Delights."

Moneysaver
Because only about 3 percent of the Rhône Valley's total wine production is white, bargains are hard to come by. They do exist, however. Look for wines from the Côtes du Ventoux and the Côtes du Luberon for some easy-drinking whites. They usually can be found for under $10.

Just the facts

- France offers a complete range of white wine styles for every taste and budget.

- Most French wines are labeled by the region from which they originate, not the grape variety.

- If you like Chardonnay, go straight to Burgundy. Do not pass go.

- The wine label provides a wealth of information including the quality level, the vintage, the alcohol content, and sometimes the actual vineyard where the grapes were grown.

- Vintages are important, but as an insurance policy, you should always seek out reliable producers.

GET THE SCOOP ON...
Obsessive precision in winemaking and labeling
■ The truth about Riesling ■ Deciphering
a German wine label ■ The best German wine
producers

Noble German Whites

Chapter 5

Offer someone a German wine and, more often than not, they'll tell you, "It's too sweet for me. I prefer a dry wine." Few people, outside of the more serious wine consumers, know that Germany produces some excellent dry white wines.

Even when it comes to the fruitier or sweeter white wines, Germany has the Midas touch. Through many years of experience and fine winemaking techniques, the Germans know how to produce a wine in which the sugar in the grapes is harmoniously balanced with the natural fruity acid, which renders a lively three-dimensional wine. It is not cloying or sickeningly sweet, as many people who are not familiar with German wines might assume.

Regardless of the style, most German wines you'll see in the U.S. market are white because white grapes grow best in Germany's cool northern climate.

The two major white grapes used to make German wine are:

- Riesling

- Müller-Thurgau

Germany also makes some very good wine from the following five other white grapes, though their plantings are scarce compared to Riesling:

- Silvaner

- Gewürztraminer

- Scheurebe

- Pinot Gris

- Pinot Blanc

Riesling is the white star of Germany, and it recently edged out Müller-Thurgau in terms of acreage planted. Müller-Thurgau, however, is still considered to be the workhorse grape you often find blended in many of Germany's white bulk wines, which are, of course, the least expensive. Silvaner also is commonly used to make a white wine blend.

Gewürztraminer produces the aromatic, spicy-style wine that is so well-known in Alsace (See Chapter 4, "Classic French Whites," for more information.) Though less than 1 percent of Germany's plantings are Gewürztraminer, it is still very possible to find an enjoyable wine.

Scheurebe, a lesser-known grape, is actually a cross between a Riesling and a Silvaner, which is capable of producing a well-crafted wine in the hands of an able winemaker.

Pinot Gris and Pinot Blanc account for only 2.5 percent and 2.1 percent of Germany's vineyard plantings respectively, but they, too, contribute to crisp, light wines.

Though Germany produces some red wines, they only amount to about 22 percent of the country's

total wine production. Most of the reds are consumed at home in Germany.

I've done some extensive tasting of German
wines over the past year, and even though I've been
in the business for some 15 years, my recent encoun-
ters with German wines and their producers have
been a real eye-opener for me. If you have never
considered Germany to be part of your regular
repertoire of wines, I would urge you to explore and
reconsider.

Land of Riesling

Germany is best known for its Rieslings, and the
Riesling grape is the most widely planted in the
country. Riesling is so synonymous with Germany
that, again, the tendency for the uninitiated is to
believe that Rieslings are always sweet. They aren't.

Wine experts who know of the Riesling's track
record for producing great wines and its potential
to produce a whole lot more now and in the future
consider it to be a "noble grape." It is in good company along with other noble grape varieties such as
America's white and red darlings, Chardonnay and
Cabernet Sauvignon, respectively.

Interestingly enough, at the turn of the century
(and I'm referring to the early 1900s), top Rieslings
from the Rheingau and Mosel regions often were
selling at two or three times the price of first-growth
Bordeaux. Even in the early 1960s, a Riesling from
Bernkasteler Doctor Spaetlese fetched as much as
50 percent more than first-growth Bordeaux including the famous Château Pétrus.

Typically, Riesling wines have a pleasant, fra-
grant aroma, and they can range in style from
a light, crisp easy-drinking wine to a medium-bodied
wine that is able to complement more complex

dishes to an out-an-out rich, full-bodied, intensely concentrated elixir.

Dry Rieslings offer perhaps the most versatile style of wine to pair with most main courses, and they make an especially good match with spicy Asian dishes and the funky fusion cuisine so popular today. Late harvest Rieslings can be enjoyed with dessert but are even better savored after dinner on their own.

What determines whether your Riesling or any other wine will be dry or sweet? It's all in the basic fermentation process during which the grape juice is turned into wine. The magic formula is as follows:

Natural Sugar from the Grape Juice + Yeast =
Alcohol + Carbon Dioxide (CO_2)

The sugar is converted to alcohol; therefore, the riper or sweeter the grapes, the higher the alcohol content of the wine.

When all of the sugar is converted to alcohol, the fermentation process is over. In cases where the grapes are very ripe and very high in natural sugar, the alcohol level can reach about 15 percent at which time the alcohol kills the yeast; this automatically stops the fermentation and leaves the wine-maker with a wine that has some residual sugar or sweetness. The better German wine producers who want to make a sweeter-style wine will stop the fermentation manually by lowering the temperature and filtering out the remaining yeast before all the sugar has had the opportunity to turn into alcohol.

During the fermentation process, the carbon dioxide dissipates. The exceptions are Champagne and other sparkling wines, which get special handling.

Unlike other winemaking regions of the world such as Burgundy, France, where white wine means

Chardonnay, in Germany, grape growers have the choice of planting Riesling or any other white grapes they want in any one of the country's 13 wine-growing regions. The regions are, in descending order of size:

1. Rheinhessen*
2. Pfalz*
3. Baden
4. Mosel-Saar-Ruwer*
5. Württemberg
6. Franken
7. Nahe*
8. Rheingau*
9. Mittelrhein
10. Ahr
11. Hessische Bergstrasse
12. Saale-Unstrut
13. Sachsen

You'll want to better acquaint yourself with the five regions with an asterisk because these are the regions that produce the best wines that are imported into the United States.

If you have the opportunity to tour German wine country, you might want to make a special effort to sample some Silvaners from Franken and Baden. In Germany, these two areas are considered key wine-making regions even though you will not find their wines to be as available in the United States. If you get the opportunity, be sure to sample some of Germany's red wines made from the Pinot Noir grape, known locally as Spätburgunder.

Strict controls

For a country that has made its beer so accessible to Americans, it's amazing to me that German wine producers, as a whole, have not made it easier to select a German wine with confidence. The government took a step toward simplifying German wines by passing the German Wine Law of 1971. Unlike the Appellation Contrôlée laws of France that designate quality levels of that country's wine based on the appellation (or more specifically, where the grapes are grown), the German government decided that the ripeness of the grapes when harvested should determine the level of quality. After all, with Germany's colder climate, the number one challenge is producing the ripest grapes possible.

German wine producers and importers are quick to cry foul because they maintain that the sugar level in the grapes at the time of picking is not responsible for quality and that there are many other factors involved in producing top-quality wine, namely the skill of the winemaker. Although this is absolutely true, winemakers worldwide will tell you that a great wine begins with great fruit, meaning the grapes. In the interest of facilitating your selection, let's begin with the ripeness levels. You're going to see them on the label, so you need to know what they mean.

Basically, German wine falls within these major categories:

- Tafelwein, or "table wine"
- Qualitätswein bestimmter Anbaugebiete, or "quality wine"
- Qualitätswein mit Prädikat, or "quality wine with distinction"

Tafelwein

These wines occupy the lowest rung of the German wine ladder. You needn't bother with them.

Qualitätswein bestimmter Anbaugebiete

Qualitätswein bestimmter Anbaugebiete, or "quality wine," is a comfortable rung above Tafelwein.

When necessary, usually in a poorer vintage when the grapes do not ripen fully, winemakers are permitted to add a little beet or cane sugar to their Tafelwein and QbA wines before fermentation in order to raise the alcohol level needed to make a wine.

This addition of sugar is known as chaptalization. The sugar they use is not what you use to sweeten your coffee.

Qualitätswein mit Prädikat

Qualitätswein mit Prädikat, or "quality wine with distinction," is the best German wine. On the label, look for this phrase or the abbreviation QmP. Winemakers are not permitted to chaptalize QmP wines, but they can use unfermented grape juice called Süss-Reserve to add some residual sugar. For example, in a year in which the harvest yields grapes with higher acidity, the wine may need some added sweetness to balance the wine. In many cases, the addition of Süss-Reserve is a style decision made by the winemaker.

The better German wine producers use grape juice from the same grape variety, the same vineyard, and the same ripeness level; the bulk producers do not. If you're looking for a basic QbA wine, this is just one more reason to select your wine from a producer with a reputation for quality.

So you now know to look for a QmP wine from a top quality producer—probably a Riesling. You're halfway there. Your next consideration is style, which goes back to what you're in the mood for.

Here's where the grapes' level of ripeness at the time of harvest comes in. These levels, from the lowest to the highest level of ripeness, also reflect the weight of the grape juice (also called "must"). They are designated by the following terms:

- **Kabinett**—This is the lightest and least expensive style of German wine you will encounter. The wines generally are crisp, elegant, and easy to drink because they are low in alcohol. Their alcohol level is only 8.5 to 10 percent as compared to wines from other parts of the world, not including dessert wines, that average around 12 percent. The low alcohol content makes Kabinett a good "lunchtime" wine for people who enjoy a glass in the middle of the afternoon but need to go back to work!

Unofficially...
"Trocken" (dry) German wines can be made through the Auslese level, which is fuller bodied.

- **Spätlese**—In German, spätlese means "late picking," which is precisely what these grapes are all about. They are picked at least a week after the regular harvest begins. Because the grapes are a little riper, they are naturally sweeter than the average grapes and therefore have the potential to produce a more full-bodied wine than a Kabinett. A Spätlese can be produced in a dry style, which usually will be indicated on the label by the German term "trocken." This style of wine is extremely food-friendly. Spätlese also can be made in a sweeter but well-balanced style.

- **Auslese**—Beginning with the Auslese level of ripeness, it's safe to say that you're going to get a sweeter and more expensive bottle of wine. Bunches of grapes that were left on the vines later in the harvest are picked to make Auslese wines.

- **Beerenauslese**—Individual grapes, or "beeren" in German for "berries," are picked off of the vines still later in the harvest. The extra time spent on the vine means that these overripe grapes yield some of the most luscious wines that taste of honeyed fruit. Vintages in which Beerenauslese can be made come about only a few times in a decade, which is why these dessert wines are expensive.

- **Trockenbeerenauslese**—Not only are these grapes given extra time on the vine, they also begin to dry (hence the term "trocken"). The shriveled raisinated grapes produce an even more intense, richer, fuller wine that often is referred to as TBA by those in the know. TBAs are not made very often—maybe once every 10 years if the weather cooperates and the winemaker plays his cards right. As a result, TBAs command top dollar.

- **Eiswein**—The word literally means "ice wine" in German. As the name indicates, grapes are left on the vine to freeze and then are pressed immediately after being picked. If you've ever eaten a frozen grape, which happens to be a tasty snack (keep a few in the freezer), you're familiar with the sweet, concentrated flavor. According to German wine law, the grapes used to produce Eiswein must be of at least Beerenauslese quality.

To make life more interesting, a winemaker might produce two, three, or four different wines from the same vineyard using the same grape—usually Riesling. What could be the difference? You

Unofficially...
Under certain climatic conditions, a mold called Botrytis cinerea might attack the grapes and actually enhance the flavor of the wine. This "noble rot" that helps make the great French dessert wine, Sauternes, does the same for the luscious Beerenauslese and Trockenbeerenauslese and is known by its German name, Edelfäule.

might ask. It's in the level of ripeness of the grapes when they are picked (the six terms just explained). According to German law, this must be noted on the label.

As you will see, there is absolutely nothing arbitrary or capricious about German winemaking. You will see this as we take a closer look at the wine label.

Deciphering a label

A new generation of German wine producers is doing its best to shake the old, sweet, stodgy image that German wines have and replace it with a more hip style. In addition to the younger winemakers' renewed emphasis on quality winemaking, they also are trying to simplify the labeling to encourage more people to drink German wines.

Although the trend is to market German wines with more contemporary, consumer-friendly labels, you're still going to see plenty of Gothic script in your pursuit of Riesling. Here's a label whose design has not changed since the year 1900. Like all German wine labels, it gives you an enormous amount of information.

These elements might appear on the wine label, but they are not required by German law:

1. **Dryness Level:** Two terms you might come across on a German wine label are "trocken," which means "dry," and "halb-trocken," which means "semi-dry." Winemakers are not required to include this information on the label, but those who do help make your selection easier.

Producer

Address of producer—insignificant; look at the region, which is very important.

Region of origin

Vintage (Note: The Germans add the suffix "er" to describe what year it is from.)

Grape Variety—must contain at least 85% of that grape.

Quality level

Alcohol content

Village and vineyard

Bottle size

The A.P. number is the wine's internal I.D. number. The last two numbers tell you that is was tasted and approved by the government in 1998.

"Estate" where bottled

THEO MINGES
MINGES
D-76835 FLEMLINGEN A.D. WEINSTR.
Pfalz

Produce of Germany   alc. 10% by vol
1997er Gleisweiler Hölle
Riesling Spätlese   750 ml e
Qualitätswein mit Prädikat   A. P. Nr. 5 025 066 29 98
Erzeugerabfüllung Weingut Theo Minges, D-76835 Flemlingen

2. **Gold Star (optional):** Sometimes you'll see one, two, or three stars next to the name of a German wine. The star reflects the wine's level of ripeness compared to others in its class, according to the winemaker. Because there is such a broad spectrum of ripeness, beginning with the Ausleses, the star system gives you a better idea of what to expect in the bottle.

Unofficially...
As a small aside, grape growers in Germany take on great importance because one famous vineyard such as Piesporter Goldtröpfchen has 350 different owners. This means there are some 350 different wines being produced that use this prestigious name.

3. **V.D.P.:** If you see the initials V.D.P., usually on the wine neck's label of a German wine, you'll know that a panel of top grape growers and their peers tasted the wine and gave it their seal of approval. This is one more shortcut you can use to your benefit in search of quality producers.

The only way you can distinguish the best wines from Piesporter Goldtröpfchen is to know who really made the wine. Again, this goes back to the importance of the producer.

Imagine if every ice cream was permitted to be called Ben & Jerry's! How would you pick out your favorite? Here again, you would have to be familiar with the producer. Thankfully, with trademark laws in the United States, this is not an issue.

Remember the following tips for selecting white German wines:

▪ Stick to Riesling. This is what Germany does best.

▪ Look for the name of one of Germany's top-five wine regions: Mosel-Saar-Ruwer, Rheingau, Nahe, Rheinhessen, and Pfalz.

▪ Always buy from a reliable producer.

▪ If money is no object, seek out the best vineyards. (Their names will appear on the label.)

- Select a wine from a good vintage. In recent years, this has not been a major issue.

- For the best values, look for Rieslings on the lower end of the ripeness scale—that is, a basic Qualitätswein or a Qualitätswein mit Prädikat, specifically those labeled Kabinett or Spätlese. Look for one of the single vineyards recommended at the end of the chapter or consult your wine merchant. Your most basic Rieslings should start at about $10. Staying within these parameters, you should get a good bottle for under $20.

- When you do not see or do not recognize the name of a single vineyard on the label, make sure the wine is from a reputable producer. Some of the better-known German wine producers who produce good-quality Rieslings from many vineyards simply label them Riesling with the broader name of the region such as Riesling Rheingau.

Already you know that a good Riesling starts at about $10. If you're in a wine shop and spot a bargain-basement German wine labeled with a famous village, think again. Chances are, the wine comes from a "Grosslage," or "larger site." Grosslagen are permitted to use the names of some of the top villages if the wine is made anywhere in that region. In essence, these producers are riding the coattails of the reputation of the well-established single vineyards. I'm sure there are some very pleasant Grosslage wines, but they should in no way be confused with the top vineyards from Germany's finest winemaking villages.

Timesaver
To quickly gauge how dry a German wine might be, look at the level of ripeness and check the alcohol level. Wines up to the Spätlese level with lower alcohol, say 8 to 10 percent, tend to be fruitier. Those with higher alcohol, such as 11 to 12 percent, are more likely to be dry.

There are many Grosslagen in Germany's top winemaking regions. The following lists provide a sampling.

From the Mosel-Saar-Ruwer region:

- Zeller Schwarze Katz
- Bernkasteler Badstube
- Bernkasteler Kurfürstlay
- Piesporter Michelsberg

From the Rheinhessen:

- Niersteiner Gutes Domtal
- Oppenheimer Krötenbrunnen

When it comes to selecting German wines, you usually need to look carefully at the vintage because the weather typically is uneven and can make or break a harvest. Having said that, however, with the unusual global weather patterns we've been experiencing lately, Germany has lucked out and has managed to produce a string of good vintages over the last decade.

You really can't go wrong if you buy a German wine from one of the last 10 vintage years, but the most recent good vintages on the market are 1994, 1995, 1996, 1997, and 1998.

German's dessert wines are considered to be world-class. Many of these, most commonly at the Beerenauslese and Trockenbeerenauslese levels, have enormous aging potential. For people with deep pockets or good "wine" friends, seek out these great older vintages: 1971, 1975, and 1976. Other very good vintages are 1970, 1979, 1983, 1988, and 1989.

Look to the following top regions and note their basic style for the best Rieslings and the most reputable producers within. They are listed from north to south.

Mosel-Saar-Ruwer (light and fruity with lively acid):

- Deinhard
- Fritz Haag
- Reinhold Haart
- Heribert Kerpen
- Dr. Loosen
- von Kesselstatt
- Egon Müller
- J.J. Prüm
- Schloss Saarstein
- Willi Schaefer
- Selbach-Oster
- Dr. F. Weins-Prüm

Famous vineyards within the Mosel-Saar-Ruwer region include:

- Bernkasteler Doctor
- Goldtröpfchen (from the village of Piesport)
- Scharzhofberg
- Sonnenuhr (from the village of Wehlen)

Rheingau (more powerful, fuller-bodied, and elegant):

- Georg Breuer
- H.H. Eser
- Freiherr zu Knyphausen
- Franz Künstler
- Josef Leitz
- Robert Weil
- Balthasar Ress

Timesaver
You don't even have to read the label to tell the difference between a Mosel and a Rhein wine. Mosels come in green bottles; Rheins are packaged in brown ones. The chances are good that both are made from Riesling.

Famous vineyards within the Rheingau region include:

- Erbacher Marcobrunn
- Kiedricher Gräfenberg
- Happenheimer Wisselbrunnen
- Hochheimer Kirchenstück
- Hochheimer Domdechaney
- Hölle
- Rüdesheimer Berg Rottland
- Rüdesheimer Berg Schlossberg
- Rauenthaler Baiken
- Schloss Johannisberg
- Schloss Vollrads
- Steinberg

Nahe (style is between those of the Mosel and the Rheingau):

- Hans Crusius & Sohn
- H. Dönnhoff
- Kruger-Rumpf
- Schlossgut Diel

Rheinhessen (soft and delicate and sometimes smoky):

- Gunderloch
- Heyl zu Herrnsheim
- Georg Albrecht Schneider
- J.U.H.A. Strub
- Wittmann

Pfalz (rich, fruity, fuller-bodied, and earthy):

- Dr. von Bassermann-Jordan
- Dr. Bürklin-Wolf

- Fritz-Ritter
- Kurt Darting
- Lingenfelder
- Muller-Catoir
- Pfeffingen
- Theo Minges
- Von Buhl

Just the facts

- The Riesling grape makes the best white wine in Germany.
- Germany is best known for its world-class dessert wines, but it makes some delicious dry wines, too.
- Compared to wines from other countries, Germany's white wines are lower in alcohol.
- Dry and fruity Reislings make excellent food companions.
- It's extremely important to look for top-name wine producers when selecting German wine.

GET THE SCOOP ON...
The proliferation of wine in America ▪ What is
an AVA? ▪ Why are AVAs important in wine
selection? ▪ Chardonnay and other great grapes
▪ How white wine styles vary ▪ Jugs ▪ How to
select a wonderful white wine

American Whites

Chapter 6

T he United States often is called a melting
pot because of the diversity of people and
cultures who live here. The melting pot
spills over into wine. Early winemaking in America
relied on a Native American grape variety known as
Vitis labrusca. Though Vitis labrusca grapes were
popular in part because of their hardiness and their
natural ability to thrive even under extreme winter
conditions, they produced wines that tasted like
Welch's grape juice.

Fortunately, when the early Europeans came
to America, they introduced the grapes of their
homeland, known as Vitis vinifera. Through trial
and error, they figured out how to grow the
European grape varieties on American soil. It's a
good thing they did because these are the grapes
that make the wines Americans are accustomed to
drinking today—Chardonnay, Sauvignon Blanc,
Chenin Blanc, and others.

Wine, wine everywhere

Many people don't realize that grapes are grown to
produce wine in 48 out of the 50 states of America.

I've actually had some rather pleasant white wine made from pineapples in Hawaii, I've had Chardonnay from Pennsylvania, and I've had some unbelievably good sparkling wine from New Mexico. Admittedly, these are off the beaten track, but they are fun discoveries for anyone who enjoys trying different wines.

Despite the proliferation of winemaking that goes on throughout the country in small batches, the top five wine-producing states are, in order of quantity produced:

1. California
2. New York
3. Washington
4. Oregon
5. Texas

To put it in perspective, California produces the lion's share of wine made in the United States, about 90 percent. The number two wine producer, New York, contributes about 6 percent to America's total wine production. This is why the bulk of the American chapters, both red and white, concentrate on California.

In some ways, the Californians make things so easy, and in other ways, they don't. There are interesting points worth mentioning here. Unlike the classical European winemaking areas where you know, for instance, that Chardonnay is the main white grape of Burgundy and Pinot Noir is the red, in America, particularly in California, an assortment of different red and white grapes might grow in one area. Chardonnay vines, for example, are planted all over the state of California. There are top areas and vineyards that are known to produce excellent and more expensive Chardonnay, and there are other areas that produce decent Chardonnay used for lower-priced bottlings.

Here's an interesting twist of fate. Ever since the California wine industry's early years (and I'm only going back to the 1950s and 1960s), American winemakers have borrowed some popular French winemaking place names such as Chablis, Champagne, and Burgundy, and they have used them on their own labels, often to market generic plonk, much to the chagrin of the French. Traditionally in France, the label features the name of the place where the wine is produced. According to French law, only a wine made in the region of Chablis can carry the name Chablis on its labels to protect the integrity of the wine.

Now, years later, the California winemakers have developed such a special relationship with their grape varietals that they prominently feature the name of the grape, such as Chardonnay or Sauvignon Blanc, on the label. If you consider the fact that most Americans who drink wine drink California wine, you will begin to understand why Americans are more comfortable with varietal wines. California wines that carry the varietal name must by law contain at least 75 percent of that varietal grape. The truth is that many wineries that use the varietal name use 100 percent of the varietal.

American Viticultural Areas (AVAs)— American for AOC

Some Europeans picked up on this phenomenon about 10 years ago and started to include the varietal name on their wine labels along with its geographical appellation of origin. Even though the practice went against the traditional grain of some

European winemakers, many producers who added varietal labeling noticed the immediate benefits of this marketing technique. Suddenly, consumers had a foolproof way to make the connection between a white Burgundy and a French Chardonnay.

Ironically, as American winemakers pinpoint specific areas right down to the vineyards where certain grape varietals grow best (which is an ongoing process), the place names become as important as they are in France. Some of these areas are considered to be so special that they have gained status as an American Viticultural Area (AVA). If a wine is labeled with the name of an official AVA, a minimum of 85 percent of the grapes must come from that AVA.

AVAs become more important as you move up the ladder of quality wines made by reliable produ-cers, but it isn't as much a guarantee of quality control in the United States as it is in France for two reasons:

1. The AVA system does not dictate which grapes can be planted where.

2. The AVA system does not set limits on the maximum yield per acre.

Still, if you enjoy a wine from a certain producer—Kendall-Jackson Chardonnay, for example—you might be interested in trading up from the Vintner's Reserve, produced in one area of California and retailing for about $15 to a Kendall-Jackson Chardonnay Arroyo Seco Paradise Vineyard, which is from a designated AVA that retails for about $20.

The Kendall-Jackson Chardonnay Arroyo Seco Paradise Vineyard is not only located in the North Central Coast, it is more specifically in Monterey

County. Within this county, the label takes you one step further and points you to a specific vineyard—the Arroyo Seco Paradise Vineyard. Arroyo Seco actually is a special designation within the American Viticultural Areas.

There are more than 100 AVAs in this country and 70 of them are in California. The following are some of the more popular AVAs in California, along with the grape varieties for which they are known and a sampling of some wineries in parentheses that are representative of the area. This will give you a better point of reference because you're probably familiar with many of the wineries listed. Note that many of the wineries listed produce both white and red wines. I've omitted some that produce red wines exclusively because you will come across them in Chapter 9, "U.S. Reds."

> **Napa Valley**—Chardonnay, Sauvignon Blanc, also known as Fumé Blanc in California, and Riesling do well as do Cabernet Sauvignon and Merlot.
>
> **Sonoma Valley**—Chardonnay does especially well in the southern part of the Valley as does Pinot Noir. Cabernet Sauvignon and Zinfandel generally do well in Sonoma (Arrowood, Château St. Jean, Kendall-Jackson, Sebastiani, Laurel Glen, Landmark, and Kenwood).
>
> **Russian River Valley**—This AVA within Sonoma produces good Chardonnay, Sauvignon Blanc, and Pinot Noir (Sonoma-Cutrer Vineyards, De Loach Vineyards, and Chalk Hill).
>
> **Alexander Valley**—This popular AVA within Sonoma is known for full-bodied Chardonnay

Unofficially...
Remember, in California, as in France, the general rule is that the more specific the name of the place on the label, the better the wine and the more expensive it will be.

and Cabernet Sauvignon (Jordan, Simi, Chateau Souverain, Murphy-Goode, Stonestreet).

Dry Creek Valley—This key AVA within Sonoma is known for crisp Sauvignon Blanc as well as good Zinfandel and Cabernet Sauvignon (Dry Creek Vineyard, Ferrari-Carano).

Edna Valley—Known for buttery, rich Chardonnay (Edna Valley Vineyards, Meridian Vineyards, Sanford Winery, Zaca Mesa Winery).

Los Carneros—This important AVA that straddles Napa and Sonoma is known for Burgundian-style Chardonnay and Pinot Noir (Acacia, Saintsbury, Carneros Creek, and Bouchaine).

Mount Veeder—This AVA within Napa is known for Chardonnay, Sauvignon Blanc, and Cabernet Sauvignon (Hess Collection, Diamond Creek, Mount Veeder Winery, and Mayacamas Vineyards).

Temelcula—This southern California AVA is known for Chardonnay and Sauvignon Blanc as well as Cabernet Sauvignon and Zinfandel (Callaway Vineyard and Winery).

California

Selecting California wine used to be so easy. If you wanted a bottle of white, you looked for a Chardonnay from Napa Valley or Sonoma; if red was your color, you'd probably go for a Cabernet Sauvignon from the same two most-popular wine-making regions. Though Napa and Sonoma remain

Watch Out!
You won't find the term "AVA" on the label the way you see "AOC" on a French label. Perhaps one day this will change. Until then, when you taste a wine you like, make a mental note of exactly where it is made.

well-known for making world-class wines, only about 10 percent of California's wines come from these two regions. Over the past 15 to 20 years, wine country has literally branched out, and there are other important winemaking areas you need to know about when you're selecting California wines.

It can be a bit tricky, but when equipped with some basics of geography it will all begin to make sense to you.

California wine country can be divided into these major appellations:

- North Coast
- North Central Coast
- South Central Coast
- Central Valley, also known as the San Joaquin Valley
- Sierra Foothills

North Coast

Along the coast of California, north of San Francisco, you'll find these main regions:

- **Napa Valley**—Most if not all of the major grapes grow well in this highly-coveted wine region—Chardonnay, Cabernet Sauvignon, Merlot, Sauvignon Blanc (also known as Fumé Blanc), and others. (Many of the old-time vineyards are here such as Charles Krug, Schramsberg, Beringer, Inglenook Vineyards, and Beaulieu in addition to famous "newcomers" like Niebaum-Coppola Estate (which sits on the old Inglenook property), William Hill, and Sutter Home.)

- **Sonoma Valley**—Sauvignon Blanc, Chardonnay, and Cabernet Sauvignon (Alexander Valley Vineyards, Belvedere

Timesaver
You want a good white wine from Napa Valley, and you don't want to think about it. Cut to the chase and select from one of these vineyards for Chardonnay: Beringer, Far Niente, Grgich Hills, Raymond, Trefethen. For Sauvignon Blanc, choose from Cakebread, Frog's Leap, Robert Mondavi, Robert Pepi, and Sterling. For Riesling, choose from Joseph Phelps and Château Montelena.

Winery, Buena Vista, Chalk Hill, Château
St. Jean, Ferrari-Carano, Gundlach-Bundschu,
Grand Cru, Jordan Vineyard & Winery,
Kenwood, Matanzas Creek, Sebastiani,
Sonoma-Cutrer, Stone Creek).

- **Mendocino County**—Known for a variety of
  grapes including Chardonnay, Sauvignon
  Blanc, Gerwürztraminer, and Riesling in addi-
  tion to Cabernet Sauvignon, Merlot, Pinot
  Noir, and Zinfandel (Fetzer Vineyards,
  Handley Cellars, Navarro Vineyards, Parducci
  Wine Cellars).

- **Lake County**—Similar to Mendocino, Lake
  County is known for Chardonnay, Sauvignon
  Blanc, Gerwürztraminer, and Riesling as well as
  Cabernet Sauvignon, Merlot, Pinot Noir, and
  Zinfandel (Guenoc, Dunnewood).

North Central Coast

Along the North Central Coast, you'll find these
main regions:

- **Monterey County**—Known for Pinot Blanc and
  Chardonnay as well as Cabernet Sauvignon and
  Pinot Noir (Bernadus Vineyards and Winery
  and David Bruce Winery).

- **Livermore Valley**—Known for Chardonnay,
  Sémillon, and Sauvignon Blanc as well as
  Cabernet Sauvignon and Zinfandel (Wente,
  J. Lohr, Mirassou Vineyards).

- **Santa Clara County**—Similar to Monterey
  County, which is known for Pinot Blanc and
  Chardonnay as well as Cabernet Sauvignon and
  Pinot Noir (Calera Wine Co.).

South Central Coast

Along the South Central Coast, you'll find these two main regions:

- **San Luis Obispo County**—Known for Chardonnay (Edna Valley, Corbett Canyon, and Meridian Vineyards).

- **Santa Barbara County**—Known for Chardonnay (Fess Parker Winery and Zaca Mesa).

Central Valley

Within the Central Valley, which is located inland, between Lodi and Bakersfield, lies the San Joaquin Valley. Historically, the San Joaquin Valley has been known for producing inexpensive white grapes such as French Colombard, Chenin Blanc, and Grenache to produce bulk jug-wine blends. Today, you'll also find wineries like E. & J. Gallo, R.H. Phillips, and Robert Mondavi, producing inexpensive varietal wines like Chardonnay and Sauvignon Blanc (Fumé Blanc). The wine trade refers to these inexpensive entry-level wines as "fighting varietals." Robert Mondavi produces his popular-priced Woodbridge line of varietals in an area within the valley known as Lodi-Woodbridge.

Sierra Foothills

The Sierra Foothills contain the Amador County region, which is known for big Zinfandels and other robust red varieties that will be discussed in Chapter 9, "U.S. Reds."

Jug wines

Before the varietal craze, California was known for jug wines. These typically were blends of white grapes labeled as Chablis or red grapes labeled as

Moneysaver
Like anywhere else, the lesser-known wine regions outside the high-rent districts of Napa and Sonoma will offer the best values. You just have to look!

Burgundy that were bottled in large jugs and were appropriately inexpensive. Almaden, Inglenook, Gallo, and Sebastiani are among the better-known jug-wine producers. Although some jug wines are still produced, most of California's major players now emphasize quality, even at the low end of the market. Winemaking techniques have improved so much, even over the past 10 years, that you can find excellent values in varietal wines marketed in the 1.5 liter size that is slowly phasing out the generic jug business.

Gallo, the wine company created when two brothers, Ernest and Julio, made wine from a recipe they found in a library book, has been working hard to leave the jug image behind. Though the company still leads the world in jug-wine production and offers a full line of popular-priced wines such as Turning Leaf, Gossamer Bay, and Ecco Domani, the family is reaching higher. The quest for top-quality wines worthy of a price tag of up to $50 began with Ernest and Julio and is now being driven by the grandchildren—Gina Gallo, the winemaker, and her brother, Matt, the marketer. For those of us who grew up with jug wines, this younger generation is certainly changing the way you look at Gallo.

Varietals, California style

Some 50 different major white-wine grapes are planted around the world. California has the rare combination of climate, cutting-edge farming and winemaking techniques, and spirit of adventure that allows the state to grow half of them. Still, the more popular white varietals that you will find in wine shops and restaurants are:

- Chardonnay
- Sauvignon Blanc

- Viognier

- Gewürztraminer

- Pinot Blanc

- Riesling

The styles of each varietal wine can vary with the winemaker and the region from which the grapes are grown. Here are the basic styles in a nutshell, along with some buzzwords you need to know to look for on the label whenever possible, to understand what to expect in the bottle.

Chardonnay

You can get a mouthful of fruit on one end of the spectrum and a mouthful of toothpicks on the other, depending on the style of the winemaker and what style is considered "in" at the time of winemaking. In the mid-1980s, for example, barrel fermentation and oak aging were so popular that many Chardonnays overpowered most food. Today, California is producing much more elegantly balanced Chardonnays that mingle with the taste buds and don't necessarily take over.

Though it is California's answer to white Burgundy, the American version of Chardonnay offers a decided burst in flavor. The actual flavors? You'll find fruits such as pineapples and other tropical fruit in some versions, juicy apples or lemony citrus flavors in others. When wood comes into play, either through barrel fermentation or oak aging or sur lie aging, it adds complexity to the wine and brings out flavors of oak, vanilla, and butterscotch.

Because the winemaker went out of his or her way to produce a Chardonnay with some depth (the way a skilled chef would prepare a special dish), the information usually is noted on the label. If you like your Chardonnay with a little more complexity, read the back label for a description of the wine or look for these terms on the label:

- Barrel-fermented

- Sur lie

- Oak-aged

Chardonnay is the most expensive mainstream white-grape varietal. (Viognier, a more trendy grape at the moment, is more expensive because there are fewer plantings.) The ones made with the use of wood—not with wood chips, which is a cheaper method—will make the wine more pricey but definitely worth it.

The top turf for Chardonnay is Napa County, Monterey County, and Sonoma County. Lately, however, the coastal appellations, both North Central Coast and South Central Coast, have been doing quite well with Chardonnay as well.

Sauvignon Blanc

California took a page out of the French play book here and emulated the style of the Loire Valley wines where Sauvignon Blanc (also known as Fumé Blanc) is the main grape. Consequently, the common flavor profile here is grassy, herbal, and crisp-tasting because of the high acid content. If you get fruit flavors, it can be a whisper of peach, but usually it is more along the citrus lines, specifically lemon or grapefruit.

If you look at your wine shop or a wine list, you'll notice that Sauvignon Blanc is decidedly cheaper than Chardonnay. It simply hasn't reached that point of popularity yet. Robert Mondavi used a little marketing savvy to make Sauvignon more sexy to wine drinkers by calling it Fumé Blanc, and many other California wineries followed suit with some success. Other winemakers decided to take a different approach and use Chardonnay techniques such as oak aging, barrel fermentation, and sur lie fermentation to produce a "poor man's Chardonnay." How do you know? You don't always, but a good tip-off is if you see the same buzzwords on a Sauvignon Blanc label that you would expect to find on Chardonnay labels: barrel-fermented, oak aged, and sur lie fermentation.

The top turf for Sauvignon Blanc/Fumé Blanc is Napa Valley, Sonoma Valley, Livermore Valley, Santa Barbara, Central Coast, North Coast, Russian River Valley, Alexander Valley, and Temecula.

Viognier

California's "Rhône Rangers" is a group of wineries that have taken an interest in producing wines made from grapes grown in the Rhône Valley of France. Touted as a good alternative for people who tire of Chardonnay, Viognier provides an interesting combination of fruit and spice.

The top turf for Viognier is Napa Valley, Santa Cruz, Monterey, and Paso Robles.

Gewürztraminer

"Gewürz" means spicy in German, and it perfectly describes the main flavor profile of Gewürztraminer. In California, two distinct styles of Gewürztraminer are made. The first is a crisp, dry or off-dry wine with a distinct perfume that pairs well with Pacific Rim cuisine and spicy foods in general. The other is a late harvest dessert wine that is definitely more complex. Most late harvest wines are bottled in 375 ml bottles, include the words "late harvest" on the label, and are considerably more expensive than the "regular" Gewürztraminer, which is a table wine.

The top turf for Gewürztraminer is Napa, Sonoma, Carneros, the Russian River Valley, Mendocino County (especially in the Anderson Valley), and Central Coast.

Pinot Blanc

As prices creep up on varietals like Chardonnay, you will see less-expensive varietals such as Pinot Blanc at your wine shop or on a wine list to give you a decent wine at a lower cost. Pinot Blanc is similar in taste to Chardonnay; in fact, the better ones could fulfill your taste for a good crisp and fruity white.

The top turf for Pinot Blanc is Napa Valley, Santa Cruz Mountains, Mendocino County, and Sonoma County.

Riesling

Like Gewürztraminer, California produces two distinctly different Riesling, or White Riesling, styles. One is dry and pairs well with Pacific Rim and spicy foods. The other is a sweet dessert wine.

The top turf for Riesling is Mendocino County (especially in the Anderson Valley), Sonoma (especially in the Russian River Valley), Napa Valley, Monterey County, and Santa Barbara County.

California vintages

The combination of consistent good weather and the ability to make some adjustments in the event of less-than-good weather makes vintages less of an issue in California than in other wine-growing regions. Still, you can't go wrong if you look for these recent white-wine vintages: 1994, 1995, 1996, and 1997.

The Pacific Northwest

Depending on where you shop for wine or what wine list you are perusing, you might see an area designated for Pacific Northwest Wines. The tendency is to group Washington State and Oregon together because they are from the same geographic region. When you taste their wines, however, you immediately know that they are distinctly different.

Washington State

Washington might be the third-largest wine-producing state, but it is number two behind California in producing the Vitis vinifera European varietal grapes. Chateau Ste. Michelle, the state's biggest winery, put Washington State wines on the map when its Johannisberg Riesling blew others away in a major blind tasting in the early 1970s. Convinced that there were more good wines to be made in the state, Chateau Ste. Michelle hasn't looked back and has had notable success with Chardonnay and other whites as well as Merlot, which is considered to be its specialty in reds.

The most important white grapes planted in Washington are:

- Chardonnay
- Riesling
- Chenin Blanc
- Sauvignon Blanc
- Semillon
- Gewürztraminer

Washington's growing season, which typically features long sunny days and cooler nights, helps create grapes that yield a clean, crisp white wine with good fruit. Washington can be divided into three major winemaking regions, which also happen to be federally recognized AVAs:

- **Columbia Valley**—More than 50 percent of the state's vineyards are located in this winemaking region, which actually is an irrigated desert.

- **Yakima Valley**—The second largest winemaking region in the state.

- **Walla Walla Valley**—The smallest viticultural area in Washington state.

The last two regions technically are part of the Columbia Valley, but they can carry their own special designation.

Top Washington State white-wine labels to look for are:

Unofficially...
Chateau Ste. Michelle alone produces 50 percent of all of Washington State wines.

- Chateau Ste. Michelle

- Columbia Crest Winery (sister winery of Chateau Ste. Michelle)

- Covey Run Vintners

- The Hogue Cellars

- Leonetti

- Preston Wine Cellars

- Staton Hills Winery

- Snoqualmie Winery

- Paul Thomas Winery

- Columbia Winery

- L'Ecole #41

- Gordon Brothers

- Kiona

- Waterbrook Winery

- Woodward Canyon

From a quality standpoint, Leonetti is worth mentioning, but it is available in only a few restaurants nationwide and by mail. There's even a waiting list to get onto Leonetti's mailing list!

Oregon

Oregon is an American winegrowing region that has come very far very fast. There has only been renewed interest in this state as a winegrowing region since the 1970s. The wine world took serious notice in the 1980s when Robert Drouhin, a famous wine negociant from Burgundy, France, bought land to produce a Burgundian-style Pinot Noir, which has since helped put Oregon on the global wine map (more on that in Chapter 9, "U.S. Reds").

Firmly in the spotlight for reds, Oregon then had the opportunity to show what the state could do with white wines.

The most important white grapes grown in Oregon are:

- Chardonnay
- Pinot Gris
- Riesling
- Gewürztraminer

Oregon's main winegrowing regions, which also happen to be recognized AVAs, include:

- Willamette Valley
- Umpqua Valley
- Rogue River Valley

Top white-wine labels to look for from Oregon include:

- Amity
- Ponzi Vineyards
- Rex Hill

- Sokol Blosser Winery
- Tualatin
- Elk Cove
- Eyrie Vineyards
- Chehalem Vineyards
- Cooper Mountain Vineyards
- Cristom Vineyards
- Eola Hills
- Knudsen-Erath Vineyards
- Bridgeview
- Kramer Vineyards
- Henry Estate
- Lange
- Laurel Ridge
- Montinore Vineyards
- Willamette Valley Vineyards

New York State and Long Island

How many times have you heard the story of the native New Yorker who has never been to the Statue of Liberty? New York's wine country is taken for granted as well and is not really explored for much the same reason.

There are four major winegrowing areas in New York:

1. Finger Lakes
2. Lake Erie
3. Hudson River Valley
4. Long Island

New York has an intensely rich winemaking history. It is home to the Brotherhood Winery, established in the Hudson Valley in 1839, the oldest continually operating winery in America. (Brotherhood Winery suffered extreme fire damage in 1998, but it is undergoing restoration.) History alone, however, has not been enough to put New York wine on the lips of consumers outside the region.

Long Island stands out as *the* New York wine region for European grapes. The eastern end of Long Island has two of its own specially designated AVAs:

- The Hamptons
- North Fork of Long Island

Chardonnay and Riesling do well on Long Island as does Sauvignon Blanc, which doesn't ripen as well in the other areas of New York. In terms of red grapes, Merlot is the darling here and Cabernet Sauvignon grows nicely, but we'll get into that in Chapter 9.

Today, some 90 different vineyards in New York grow Vitis vinifera grapes. Some reliable labels to look for in each region are:

- **Finger Lakes**—Dr. Konstantin Frank, Glenora Wine Cellars, Herman, Lamoreaux Landing, Hunt Country Vineyards, Knapp Vineyards, Hermann J. Wiemer Vineyard, and Wagner Vineyards
- **Hudson River Valley**—Millbrook Winery
- **Long Island**—Gristina, Lenz, Hargrave Vineyard, Pellegrini Vineyards, Pindar Vineyards, Palmer Vineyards, and Sagpond Vineyards

Just the facts

- Vitis vinifera grapes, also known as European grape varieties such as Chardonnay, make mainstream wines that wine drinkers prefer.

- The first thing you need to do to select a white wine is name your grape variety.

- For a sure thing, select a wine from one of the better-known wine regions.

- The more specific the area on a wine label, the better the wine and the more expensive it will be.

- If you're looking for value and are willing to take a gamble, select a wine from a lesser-known region.

- Even California's lower-end wines have made quantum leaps in quality. Many are good to keep in the fridge as a "house wine."

GET THE SCOOP ON...

The difference between "Old-World" and "New-World" wines ▪ Italy's trendy Tri-Veneto ▪ Fashionable Albariño from Spain ▪ Portuguese green wine that's really white ▪ What's good Down Under ▪ Killer Sauvignon Blancs from New Zealand ▪ South American style ▪ A sea change in South Africa

Old- and New-World Whites

I never really thought about wine being "Old World" or "New World" until recently when it became clear that wine drinkers will go to a restaurant and order wines from areas that traditionally were not perceived by Americans as fine wine-growing areas. This is more remarkable in restaurants even though it's happening at retail stores as well because, when people go out to eat, they typically want to impress others with the labels they drink.

The old-school attitude about "Old-World" wines was that, if the wine wasn't from Europe, it couldn't be any good. California, itself part of the "New World," became the supreme exception to the rule. Napa and Sonoma single-handedly crashed down the "Old-World" wine barriers with their focus on grape varietals as opposed to where the wine came from and with California's scientific and innovative approach to winemaking.

In a nutshell, wine from Europe is considered to be "Old World." Everything else is considered to be "New World." France and the United States are covered in their own chapters in this book, so for the purposes of this chapter, here's how it breaks down:

TABLE 7.1: OLD AND NEW WORLDS

Old World	New World
Italy	Australia
Spain	New Zealand
Portugal	Chile
	Argentina
	South Africa

Ironically, as the wine world becomes more global, we're beginning to see a lot of cross-pollination of "New World" science with "Old World" tradition. Some "New World" winemaking regions are applying centuries-old methods to their winemaking, while some "Old World" countries are paying closer attention to individual grape varietals. In Italy, for example, where Chianti is as old as the hills and where it has always been made with the Sangiovese grape, some Italian winemakers are now beginning to release 100 percent Sangiovese wines. The line between "Old World" and "New World" is quickly blurring.

La moda Italia

Italy is a virtual wine machine in that it produces so much wine and so many different types—white, red, rosato (rosé), and spumante (sparkling). The country is best known for its amazing red wines, but when I am looking for an easy-drinking, crisp, dry white wine that's easy on the pocket, I often turn to Italy.

You most likely are familiar with the wines from these regions, which are better known for their white wines:

- Veneto—home of Soave

- Umbria—home of Orvieto

- Latium—home of Frascati (near Rome)

- The Marches—home of Verdicchio

- Sicily—home of Corvo

There's no need to memorize the areas as you would with French wine because the geography is not as important to selecting these simple wines. I can't imagine going into a wine store and telling the clerk that I'm interested in a nice little dry wine from Veneto if all I'm looking for is Soave.

I consider these wines to be the "bread and olive oil" staples from Italy. They are consistently good and basic. If you want to get into some of the better whites from Italy, however, check out the following regions in the northeast part of the boot. In this case, you'll want to look on the label for the name of the region or ask your wine merchant about a nice, dry white wine from Friuli. These regions, sometimes referred to collectively as the Tri-Veneto area, include:

- Trentino

- Alto-Adige

- Friuli

There are a number of grapes that Italian winemakers use to produce their white wines. Among the more popular are:

- Pinot Grigio (also known as Pinot Gris)

- Pinot Bianco (also known as Pinot Blanc)

Watch Out!
One thing that can be tricky about selecting an Italian wine, whether white or red, is that the wine is sometimes named for the grape variety, such as Pinot Grigio, the place it is from, such as Frascati, or it carries a brand name, such as Tignanello.

- Tocai Friulano
- Malvasia
- Verduzzo
- Verdicchio
- Trebbiano

In addition, wineries are stepping up their plantings of internationally known popular varietals such as Chardonnay and Sauvignon Blanc. You can find some good ones on the market, and you might want to sample one from any of the following producers listed. It's still a work in progress, however, so your best bet is to stick with Italy's thirst-quenching whites until they get a better handle on the newer varietals.

Some reliable producers of white Italian wines are:

- Anselmi
- Antinori
- Bolla
- Bollini
- Casa Girelli
- Folonari
- Fontana Candida
- Pighin

Because you want to drink these wines while they are crisp and refreshing, look for the most recent available vintage. These are wines to buy and drink, not to hold.

Spain updates its "Old-World" ways

Spain is another wine region in which I am most likely to turn to a robust red wine, which often is a good value as well. Traditionally, the white wines were dull and tired, having spent too much time in oak barrels, not to mention the oxidation factor. In

Timesaver
When you're unsure about an Italian wine, you might want to look for the initials DOC or DOCG. They are the Italian government's quality-assurance equivalent of the French AOC, except the acronyms stand for Denominazione di Origine Controllata. The additional "G" goes a step beyond by saying the quality is "Garantita." See Chapter 10, "Old- and New-World Reds," for more details about DOC.

recent years, however, there has been a whole new fresh and vibrant side to Spain's white wines, particularly those coming from the Rías Baixas area from the northwest region of Galicia.

Spain's better white wines come from the following regions and grapes:

TABLE 7.2: SPAIN'S WHITES

Region	Grape(s)
Rías Baixas	Albariño
Rueda	Verdejo
Rioja	Viura (also known as Macabeo)
	Malvasia
Penedés	Parellada
	Chardonnay
	Sauvignon Blanc

Reliable producers of Spanish white wine include:

TABLE 7.3: SPANISH REGIONS AND SOME TOP PRODUCERS

Region	Wine Producer
Rías Baixas	Martín Códax
Rueda	Marqués de Riscal
Rioja	Marqués de Cáceres
	CUNE
	Conde de Valdemar
Penedés	Torres

If you are not familiar with the producer of a Spanish wine, theoretically you should be able to look for the letters "DO" on the label, standing for Denominación de Origen. This is the Spanish government's version of the French AOC concept. For a while, however, the government was giving out DO

Unofficially...
Albariño from Rías Baixas produces one of the trendiest white wines from Spain today. Navarra, better known for its tasty rosé wines, produces some good Chardonnays as well.

status like gumdrops to wine-growing areas until it lost its significance to a degree. To rectify the situation, the Spanish government, like the Italians, created a higher status that took effect in the early 1990s called DOCa, for Denominación de Origen Calificada. The Rioja region was the first in Spain to earn this special quality designation. See Chapter 11 for more details about DO and DOCa.

As with Italian wines, for the best vintages, I look to the most recent when I want a good, crisp, easy-drinking, Spanish white wine.

Portugal beyond Port

Portugal has won the world over with its rich, luscious dessert wines, called Port, but it also produces some great red and white wine values.

Portugal's main white wine areas and grapes are:

TABLE 7.4: PORTUGAL'S WHITES

Region	Grape(s)
Vinho Verde	Loureiro, Alvarhino
Bucelas	Arinto
Ribatejo	Fernaño Pires

To zero in on your selection, head straight for Vinho Verde. Portugal's white wine begins and ends with Vinho Verde, which translates as "green wine." It is so-named because it is meant to be consumed young. The wine typically is crisp, dry, and tangy; it's low in alcohol (only 8 to 9 percent); and it often has a fun little petulance or sparkle to it. You'll often detect some lemony citrus flavors, which make this wine so good with light seafood. As in other parts of the world, the wine was produced to go with the local food. Vinho Verde comes from the north-western region of Portugal on the Atlantic Coast, and the fish/Vinho Verde pairing is a natural.

If you see a vintage on the label, remember that "verde," or young and green, is the watchword. Some good producers of white Portuguese wines, especially Vinho Verde, include:

- Quinta de Aveleda

- Sogrape

- J. P. Vinhos

- Adega Cooperativa Regional de Monçaño

White wines from the Outback

Outside of California, one of the first "New-World" wine countries that was embraced with open arms by the American public was Australia.

America's love affair with Australia goes way back, and it's an intangible that has had a positive impact on Australian wine sales. Americans are infatuated with this continent halfway around the world, and they admire the friendliness and free-spirited attitude of the people. In Americans' eyes, Aussies throw some shrimp on the "barbie" and wrestle a few crocodiles in the afternoon. Their whole attitude about wine is refreshing.

To be sure, there is a certain mystique about Australia that pulls like a magnet. The British used to export their criminals to this land filled with koalas and kangaroos. There's a bit of the Wild West left in this large country that is long since gone in the United States and, quite frankly, we miss it.

Politically, Australia is peaceful. Aussies mind their own business—eat, drink, and be merry. In addition to Len Evans, who likes to "whop down" his wine, Australians love their wine more than any other English-speaking country—almost 5 gallons per person annually as compared to 3.5 gallons per

> **❝**
> I like to whop it down.
> —Len Evans, the unofficial ambassador of Australian wines and chairman of The Rothbury Estate Ltd. to a roomful of wine connoisseurs
> **❞**

Unofficially...
Australia's wine exports have tripled to the United States in the past five years. The Aussies expect exports to double again in the next five.

person in England and almost 2 gallons per person in the United States.

From a practical standpoint, Australian wines are easy to learn, love, and afford. There is no language barrier, and as in California, Australian wines are identified on the label by grape varietal. Practically every international grape grown in other famous winemaking regions thrives in Australia but especially Shiraz, which is known as Syrah in France as well as other countries. Like the people, Australian wines typically are friendly but assertive with a lot of forward fruit.

In addition to making the wines approachable to drink, Australian wineries offer an extensive array of wines, beginning at the entry-level $10-and-under price segment. As your tastes develop and mature, Australia produces wines of increasing complexity including some world-class wines that are sure to satisfy more experienced wine drinkers. Regardless of the price, the wines provide an excellent price/ value relationship.

People look for well-known brands such as Lindemans, Penfolds, and Rosemount. When it comes down to it, however, most wine drinkers don't know or care if the wine comes from Coonawarra or Mudgee as long as it tastes good and the price is right. This is slowly changing as people start to travel to wine country more and as they become more sophisticated about making their wine selections.

As in California, anything goes in terms of where Australians plant different grape varieties. For example, you will find Chardonnay widely planted throughout the five states of Australia where grapes are grown. Certain areas within Australia, of course, will have better luck in growing the best Chardonnay by virtue of their microclimates.

Here are the four major wine-producing states and the most important appellations within each state. Where appropriate, the specialty of the appellation is listed.

New South Wales

One of the main wine-growing areas of Australia is concentrated in the southeastern part of the country in the state of New South Wales. Here are the more important wine districts you need to know about.

- **Hunter Valley**—Hunter Valley, the top premium wine producer in the state, is actually comprised of two distinct areas: Lower and Upper Hunter Valley. While they both produce some excellent white wines, the Lower Hunter Valley is especially known for its Chardonnay, Sémillon, and in the reds, Shiraz.

- **Mudgee**—Mudgee is the Aboriginal name for "Nest in the Hills," which is how this region was first described by the early natives. This area produces some very good Chardonnay, though it has an excellent reputation for robust reds.

- **Riverina**—Also known interchangeably as Griffith and Murrumbidgee Irrigation Area, Riverina specializes in Botrytis Sémillon and late harvest varietals (see Chapter 13, "After-Dinner Delights"). It is also a prolific area, with over half of the state's total wine production coming from this region.

- **Murray Darling**—Located in the southwestern part of New South Wales, Murray Darling runs along the Murray River, which means it straddles two states: New South Wales and Victoria, located to the south. The use of new state-of-the-art technology has helped Murray Darling gain its reputation for Chardonnay, which spearheads the white varieties, and Shiraz and Cabernet Sauvignon in the reds.

South Australia

At one time South Australia was responsible for 75 percent of Australia's total wine production. As the wine industry has blossomed in other regions of Australia, the state of South Australia, located in the mid-south part of the country, still accounts for about 50 percent of all Australian wine produced. Not only is South Australia known for its quantity of wine produced, but also its quality. Key regions in South Australia are:

- **Barossa Valley**—Perhaps one of Australia's best-known regions, the Barossa Valley built its reputation on its Shiraz, which is considered a world-class red wine. However, the Barossa Valley also makes very good Riesling, Sémillon, and Chardonnay.

- **McLaren Vale**—This fashionable wine region overlooking the ocean produces a full portfolio of white and red grape varieties and styles, though Chardonnay and Sauvignon Blanc are best bets for the whites.

- **Coonawarra**—Some of Australia's most pricey vineyard real estate is here due to the region's terra rosa soil, which is responsible for its rich, full-bodied wines, including Chardonnay.

- **Clare Valley**—With its continental climate, Clare Valley is known for Australia's finest dry Riesling wines.

- **Padthaway**—Located just north of Coonawarra, which is better known for its red wines, Padthaway is carving out its niche as a fast-growing region known for top-quality Chardonnay.

Victoria

The most important wine-producing regions in Victoria are:

- **Goulburn Valley**—While other regions have jumped on the Chardonnay bandwagon, Goulburn Valley specializes in the Marsanne grape, a white Rhône varietal.

- **Yarra Valley**—Over the years, the Yarra Valley has gained its reputation for sparkling wines and Pinot Noir, as well as long-lived Chardonnay.

- **Rutherglen**—Full-bodied white wines and specialties like rich, fortified Muscats and Tokays come from this region.

- **Murray Darling**—As mentioned before in the section of New South Wales, the region of Murray Darling runs across two states. The region is making better and better Chardonnay.

Western Australia

It seems ironic to me that the first winery was established in this remote part of Australia in 1829, since modern day winemaking is so heavily concentrated in New South Wales, Victoria, and the southeastern section of South Australia. Still, there are some notable wine regions in Western Australia that are producing some of the country's finest wines. They are:

Unofficially...
A lesser-known wine region in Victoria called Gippsland has a climate similar to that of the Loire Valley or Burgundy, both in France.

- **Margaret River**—One of Australia's most prized wine regions. With its cool climate from its location along the Indian Ocean, Margaret River produces elegant, almost European-style reds and whites. In white wines, look for Margaret River Chardonnay, Sauvignon Blanc, and Sémillon.

- **Pemberton**—With a cooler climate than Margaret River, Pemberton is most successful with Chardonnay. This area enjoyed rapid growth in the 1990s and is definitely a region on the move.

- **Swan District**—This is the warmest wine region in Australia, marked by a hot Mediterranean climate. It is home to the state's largest winery, Houghton. Like many other Australian wine regions, you will find good Chardonnay here, but Chenin Blanc is the specialty. Aside from the varietal wines, the Swan District makes some interesting blends worth trying.

Increasing importance of Australian appellations

In the 1980s, Australian Chardonnays were a major discovery for wine consumers looking for good value as wine prices began to creep up in California and France. Some of the bigger Australian wineries like Lindemans, Rosemount Estate, Hardy's, and others made a commitment to selling their wines to the U.S. market and it paid off for them in a big way.

At first, consumers knew merely to look for Australian Chardonnay. As they became more acquainted with Australian wines, consumers would look for the familiar diamond label that has become synonymous with Rosemount Estate, or the Bin number, such as Lindemans Bin 65 Chardonnay, to be assured of a certain level of quality.

Here we are some 20 years later and the wine public is becoming more sophisticated. Many people are traveling to wine country and becoming familiar with the geography of the land. At the same time, Australian viticulturalists are constantly experimenting with different grape varieties in different parts of the country to see exactly where they grow the best. The idea is to find the most desirable location to grow various grape varieties. The same process is currently going on in California and it is a natural part of winemaking evolution.

This is why appellations will become more important in selecting Australian wine over the next several years. Already, the following are considered to be some of Australia's top-quality appellations:

■ Barossa Valley

■ Coonawarra

■ Hunter Valley

■ Margaret River

Conversely, if you see a bargain bottle with the appellation "South Eastern Australia," don't be too impressed. This dust-catching appellation usually is a blend of wines from South Australia, New South Wales, and Victoria. You might find it to be a drinkable white, but it won't be extraordinary.

White varietals Down Under

You've seen these white grape varieties in California as well as in many fine European wine regions, but Australia prides itself on producing its own style.

■ **Chardonnay**—This is the grape that started the Australian invasion of American wine retail shelves and major wine lists across the country.

Australian Chardonnay typically is fruit-driven, but depending on the winery, you might come across a wine that is full of pineapple and mixed tropical fruit flavors, or you could get a rich, buttery wine that melts in your mouth.

- **Sémillon**—This is often blended with Chardonnay or Sauvignon Blanc to round out the wine. Judicious blending, especially with the more expensive Chardonnay grape, keeps the cost of producing the wine down and translates into good value for wine drinkers.

- **Riesling**—Australians like their Riesling, and most of it is consumed at home (in the Outback). Like Germany or Alsace, Riesling styles in Australia run the gamut from bone dry to late harvest sweet.

- **Sauvignon Blanc**—This grassy, herbal grape is nowhere near as popular as Chardonnay, but that just mirrors the reality in California. Expect to see more coming from the Outback over the next few years. When Chardonnay prices begin to escalate, this is where you'll find your bargains along with skillful blends.

Wines that are labeled with their varietal name may contain 100 percent of the named grape or at least be made mostly from it. Special blends like Sémillon-Chardonnay, sometimes referred to as "SemChards," are fairly common in Australia. Usually, the grape variety mentioned first on the label accounts for the larger percentage of the blend. A Sémillon-Chardonnay, for example, will contain more Sémillon.

Top wineries from Australia's different wine-growing regions include:

TABLE 7.5: SOME TOP AUSTRALIAN WINERIES BY REGION

South Australia	New South Wales	Victoria	Western Australia
Hardy's	Black Opal	Seppelt	Goundrey
Jacob's Creek	McWilliams	Yellowglen	Leeuwin
Lindeman's	Rosemount		
Orlando	Rothbury Estate		
Parker Estate	Tyrell's		
Penfolds	Wyndham Estate		
Petaluma			
Peter Lehmann			
Seppelt			
Wolf Blass			
Yalumba			

Australian vintages

In Australia, it's hard to go wrong with vintages. Like California, Australia enjoys consistently good grape-growing weather. If there's a blip on the screen for any reason, the Australians are quick to compensate with cutting-edge technology. They are on top of the latest vineyard management and vinification techniques, they have the curiosity to experiment, and they are driven to innovate to put Australia on the world wine map.

New Zealand's best

New Zealand, located a little more than 1,000 miles south of Australia, produces only a fraction of the amount of wine Australia does, but the New Zealanders have quickly become known for their crisply delicious Sauvignon Blancs. This is one wine-growing area that I specifically seek out for its Sauvignon Blanc. Incidentally, Sauvignon Blanc is the most widely planted grape in the country, though Chardonnay is not far behind.

Two other popular white varieties planted in New Zealand are Müller-Thurgau and Riesling. To a lesser degree, you'll see other white grapes from New Zealand such as Pinot Gris, Chenin Blanc, and Gewürztraminer.

The country consists of two neighboring islands in the South Pacific. The main white-wine–growing areas, in descending order from the largest to the smallest, are:

1. **Marlborough**—Marlborough has become the largest wine region in terms of vineyards planted, and it also happens to be the primo place for Sauvignon Blanc. This region also does a good job with Chardonnay.

2. **Hawkes Bay**—Sauvignon Blanc plays second fiddle to the Chardonnays from this area. The area's true specialty is Cabernet Sauvignon, though I consider all of New Zealand's reds to be a work in progress. They spoiled me with their Sauvignon Blanc.

3. **Gisborne**—Chardonnay is the top white wine from this region, though German-style wines such as Müller-Thurgau Riesling, and Gewürztraminer do well.

4. **Martinborough**—This area is known for high-quality, boutique-style Pinot Noir, though you'll also find Sauvignon Blanc, Riesling, and some Pinot Gris (boutique grapes for a boutique area).

5. **Nelson**—Chardonnay is tops in Nelson, though you'll also find Sauvignon Blanc and Riesling here.

The number of wineries in New Zealand has grown from 131 in 1990 to 304 in 1999, and this is amazing. There are many good wines coming out of this country of luscious green rolling hills, but the wines are only slowly finding their way to restaurant wine lists and retail shelves across the country. Look for some of these reliable producers or, by all means, consult with your wine merchant for a recommendation. Top New Zealand white wine producers to look for (especially for their Sauvignon Blanc and Chardonnay) include:

- Cloudy Bay (especially the Sauvignon Blanc)
- Stoneleigh
- Brancott
- Hunters
- Morton Estate
- Nautilus
- Highfield
- Longridge
- De Redcliffe
- Villa Maria
- Grove Mill

South American whites

Of all the countries in South America, Chile and Argentina have shown themselves to be on the forefront of winemaking. Some of the most famous names in the wine world have forged new joint ventures in Chile and Argentina such as Rothschild, Mondavi, and Kendall-Jackson. They bring to the table both the know-how and the scientific techniques, but just as important, they bring the financial backing to create a modern wine industry practically from the ground up.

Both Chile and Argentina are building their reputations as world-class winemakers based on their red wines, but they still make some solidly good, everyday white wines that I would keep in my fridge anytime—plus a few outstanding ones.

Chile

Chile's wine industry started way back in the 1850s when some wealthy, world-traveled Chileans bought some property and sought to re-create their own little Bordeaux-style wineries near Santiago. They planted traditional French grape varieties, including the white grapes Sémillon and Sauvignon Blanc, and they even imported a French winemaker.

The desire to make good French-style wines was there, but no real action was taken to create a wine industry until the 1980s when the Rothschild family, owners of the first-growth Bordeaux Château Lafite Rothschild, made an investment in a Chilean winery. They plowed a small fortune into upgrading the winery, which became known as Los Vascos, and sent Lafite's own winemaker to oversee the winemaking process in Chile. Because of Chile's location in the Southern Hemisphere and its opposite seasons, it's possible to have a European winemaking team work both harvests.

The main wine regions of Chile (and their specialties where applicable) are:

- **Aconcagua Valley**—This northernmost region specializes in Chardonnay and Sauvignon Blanc.

- **Casablanca Valley**—Technically a subregion of Aconcagua, Casablanca is known for its Chardonnay and Sauvignon Blanc.

- **Maipo Valley**—Known for Sémillon and Sauvignon Blanc as well as Cabernet Sauvignon.

- **Rapel Valley**—Known better for red wines such as Merlot, this area does well with Sémillon

- **Colchagua**——This subregion of Rapel is also better known for reds, but also produces good Sémillon and Sémillon/Chardonnay blends.

- **Maule Valley**—Known for Sémillon, Sauvignon Blanc, and the red Cabernet Sauvignon.

- **Curicó Valley**—An area within Maule that also produces reliable Sémillon, Sauvignon Blanc, as well as some white blends made from these grapes.

Chilean joint ventures

To see what's happening in the quick evolution of Chile's wine industry, all you have to do is follow the money:

TABLE 7.6: FOREIGN-OWNED WINERIES IN CHILE

Winery	Chilean Winery Venture
Domaine Rothschild (of Lafite Rothschild)	Los Vascos
Miguel Torres (of Spain)	Torres Winery/Chile
Bruno Prats of Château Cos d'Estournel and Paul Pontallier of Château Margaux	Bruno Paul Estate
Robert Mondavi Winery of California and Errazuiz Winery of Chile	Caliterra and Seña
Marnier-Lapostolle Family of France (makers of Grand Marnier) and Rabat family of Chile	Casa Lapostolle
Franciscan Estates of California	Veramonte
Kendall-Jackson of California	Calina and Viña Calina

Chilean regions where some of the big-named wineries produce their wine include:

TABLE 7.7: CHILEAN REGIONS AND A SAMPLING OF THEIR WINES

Casablanca	Maipo Valley	Rapel	Curicó
Concha y Toro	Cousiño-Macul	Los Vascos	Miguel Torres
Walnut Crest	Bruno Paul	Santa Rita	
Franciscan (Veramonte)	Unduragga	Montes	

Other top-quality wineries from Chile are:

- Viña Santa Carolina
- Viña Carta Vieja
- Canepa
- Carmen
- Viña San Pedro
- Sergio Traverso
- Stonelake

Chile's white wines are quite food friendly, easy to drink, and easy on the wallet. Between the recent technological infusion and Chile's natural resources—the soil, the sunshine, and the ample water supply from snow melting off the Andes Mountains—vintages are virtually hassle-free. Get yourself a recent vintage, open the bottle, and pour yourself a glass.

Argentina

It's ironic that Argentina produces twice as much wine as Chile, yet it has taken longer for Argentina to enter the global wine arena. The country, which is the fifth largest wine producer in the world, is likened to a sleeping giant. Like Chile, Argentina is building its reputation on its red wines, particularly those made from the Malbec grape.

You can, however, find some excellent white wine values made from Chardonnay and Sauvignon Blanc in the $10 and under category. Higher-priced bottlings in the $20 range and up are noticeably better, but they do not necessarily provide the same value for the money spent. If Chile's progress is any indication, this also could change quickly as Argentina continues to evolve aggressively.

Argentina's main wine-growing regions are:

- **Mendoza**—This is the biggest and most important wine region in all of Argentina that accounts for the lion's share of the country's total wine production.

- **Tupungato**—Within Mendoza, the area of Tupungato has a cooler microclimate that is perfect for white wine production.

- **Río Negro**—Its cool climate, chalky soil, and long growing season make this region perfect for Chardonnay, Sauvignon Blanc, and Sémillon.

- **Salta**—Microclimates within this region allow Salta to produce white wines with great depth and balance.

Look for these white wine producers from Argentina:

- Bodegas Esmerelda
- Catena
- Finca Flichman
- Navarro Correas
- Santa Julia

Unofficially...
Already we're beginning to see Argentina follow in Chile's footsteps of development. Kendall-Jackson Winery of California invested in Argentina's Mendoza region to create two new wine brands: Mariposa and Tapiz. Another well-known inexpensive wine, Marcus James, is now made in Argentina. It used to be made in Brazil.

- Trapiche (Fond de Cave and Medalla are two other wines in the line)
- Trumpeter

South Africa

Even though the country has a long history of wine-making, South Africa is a new discovery for even the most worldly American wine drinkers now that the political climate has warmed. The wines are slowly making their way onto wine lists and retail shelves as part of the "New-World" offerings. The white wines are absolutely refreshing and are a pleasant departure from the garden variety Chardonnay that is popping up in vineyards all over the world.

The three main white grapes used in South African wines are:

- Steen (what they call Chenin Blanc)
- Chardonnay
- Sauvignon Blanc

Other important white grapes are Riesling, Sémillon, Ugni Blanc, Gewürztraminer, and Muscat of Alexandria (called Hanepoot).

According to the government, varietal wines must contain at least 75 percent of the grape named on the label, and at least 75 percent of the wine must come from the current harvest.

The main wine-growing regions of South Africa are:

- **Stellenbosch**—Produces some excellent Chardonnays and Sauvignon Blancs, though it's probably better known for its reds. Many of South Africa's top wineries are located here.

- **Constantia**—Well-known for Sauvignon Blanc and Chardonnay as well as the red Cabernet Sauvignon.

- **Paarl**—South Africa's better late harvest wines are made in this warmer region as well as some good Sauvignon Blanc, Sémillon, and Chardonnay.

- **Robertson**—Mostly whites are produced here including Chardonnays, Sauvignon Blancs, and the German varieties.

- **Walker Bay**—Produces Burgundian style Chardonnay and other red grape varietals.

- **Elgin**—Up-and-coming area for Sauvignon Blanc.

South African labels to look for include (by region):

TABLE 7.8: SOUTH AFRICAN REGIONS AND THEIR WINES

Stellen-bosch	Con-stantia	Paarl	Robert-son	Walker Bay	Elgin
Fleur du Cap	Groot Constantia Estate	Backsberg Estate	DeWetshof	Cape Bay	Neil Ellis
Lievland Estate	Klein Constantia Estate	Boschendal Estate		Hamilton Russel Vineyards	
Louisvale		Glen Carlou			
Meerlust Estate			Nederburg Estate		
Mulderbosch Vineyards		Villiera Estate			
Overgaauw Estate					
Rustenberg Estate					
Simonsig Estate					
Thelema Mountain Vineyards					
Warwick Estates					
Zonnenbloem					

Just the facts

- "Old-World" wines rely more on *terroir* and tradition; "New-World" wines are more driven by varietal and technology.

- Spain and Chile, in particular, have modernized their winemaking technology to produce crisper, fresher, and fruitier white wines.

- Australian wines typically emphasize the fruit of the grape.

- New Zealand's Sauvignon Blancs rival the world's best including the classics such as Sancerre and Pouilly Fumé from the Loire Valley in France.

- Foreign investment has catapulted South America into the global wine arena.

- There is a treasure-trove of excellent wine values to be discovered in both "Old-World" and "New-World" white wines.

Warming Up to Reds

PART III

GET THE SCOOP ON...
Why Americans are seeing red ▪ A new taste
dimension ▪ Why some doctors recommend
red wine ▪ Red classics that never go out
of style ▪ How to select vin rouge for your
taste and budget

The French "Red" Standard

I can remember not too long ago when it seemed that most people who drank wine preferred white. "A glass of white wine" was the mantra with the exception of a serious core of wine drinkers who generally preferred red except perhaps during the dog days of summer.

Ironically, if you go back 30 or more years, you'll find that red was the color of choice. That's what people were drinking. The pendulum made a full swing from red wine to white, and is headed now back into "red" territory. So why the sudden red renaissance?

The return to reds

There are a number of reasons why Americans are warming up to red wines. In the early 1990s, salsa dethroned ketchup as America's favorite condiment, paving the way for the emergence of chilies and exotic spices on menus from coast to coast. People are looking for bolder flavors in the foods they eat, and this explains the increasing popularity of spicy Tex-Mex, Asian cuisine, and steak. This also has caused a change in the libations people drink, supporting the movement to single-malt Scotch, specialty beers, and in the wine world, more complex and robust reds.

Demographics also are shifting. With the graying of the Baby Boomers and the aging population at large, more Americans are fitting into the 35-to-49 and 50-plus age categories that tend to drink more wine than they did in their younger years.

Wine received another shot in the arm when the government released revised U.S. Dietary Guidelines that now include the moderate use of alcohol. The closest thing to an endorsement, however, came when the highly rated television program *60 Minutes* aired a special report about the French paradox.

According to a Danish study, the French have a lower rate of heart disease than Americans do, even though they eat a diet richer in fat. The reason? The French commonly drink wine with their meals as part of their lifestyle; Americans do not. According to the report, something in the skin of red grapes is beneficial to keeping a check on cholesterol. To gain the health benefits, the study recommended the moderate use of alcohol, which it defined as three to five glasses daily. Though "The French Paradox" first aired in 1991, its message lingers. *60 Minutes* has revisited the topic several times since the original broadcast, and each time, retailers and restaurateurs report a surge in red wine sales.

Though there was practically an overnight interest in red wines, many people didn't know what kind of red wine to select. The better wine merchants and more knowledgeable restaurant servers questioned

these new wine customers about their taste prefer-
ences to help them make a selection.

If you want to get into red wine, you can start
with any red-wine–producing country, but I recommend beginning with France. It is a classic region
that will never go out of style, and it has a range of
styles and prices.

The major red-wine–producing areas in France
are:

- Burgundy (which includes Beaujolais)
- Bordeaux
- Rhône Valley

An up-and-coming region for good value wines,
especially in reds, is the Languedoc-Roussillon in
southern France. This region is sometimes referred
to as the Midi.

Red Burgundy wines

When I think about red Burgundy, I think about
some of the most memorable wine experiences I
have had. The region is dotted with some of the very
best vineyards in the world, but my mind races
straight to Chambolle-Musigny in the Côte de Nuits.
For me, it is a personal favorite with its rare combination of velvet and fruit that dances on the tongue.

With the exception of Beaujolais, where wine is
made from 100 percent Gamay grapes, Burgundy
produces its red wines from 100 percent Pinot Noir.
Many other parts of the world have tried to duplicate the success of Burgundy's Pinot Noir, notably in
Oregon and California. Some are making good
progress, but no one does it better than the
Bourgogne.

Bright Idea!
In addition to
being a fun
drink, Beaujolais
Nouveau can be
used like a barrel
sample, meaning
that a taste of
the young wine
in winter will
give you an idea
of what the
winemaker's reg-
ular Beaujolais
will taste like
when it is
released the
following spring.

Beaujolais

If you normally stick to white wine or white Zinfandel and you want to add red to your repertoire, or if you just enjoy a good, versatile wine, I highly recommend Beaujolais. It is light, fruity, and easy to drink. In fact, it is better if you chill the bottle down a little. For the most basic Beaujolais, I even drop in an ice cube or two. No fuss, no muss, and it's easy on your pocketbook. Have I sold you yet?

There are four different quality levels of Beaujolais. From the most basic and least expensive to the highest quality and most expensive, they are listed on the following table.

TABLE 8.1: QUALITY LEVELS OF BEAUJOLAIS

Quality	Wine	Description
Nouveau	Beaujolais Nouveau	Literally translated as "new Beaujolais," the grapes are practically harvested and crushed as they enter the front door and bottled as the young wine goes out the back door. Beaujolais Nouveau is released to the world market on the third Thursday in November amidst great hoopla in the spirit of fun as retailers and restaurateurs all vie to be the first to serve the new wine of the harvest. It's great with turkey and makes an excellent wine alternative to beer if you're sitting around watching football. Beaujolais Nouveau has a short shelf life. It is intended to be consumed young, ideally within six months of its release.

Quality	Wine	Description
Basic	Beaujolais	Your basic Beaujolais will be labeled simply "Beaujolais" and will include the name of the producer. It's best when consumed within a year of the vintage date.
Better	Beaujolais-Village	As the next step up the ladder of quality, this wine comes from one of the 39 better-quality villages (sometimes referred to interchangeably as communes) within the Beaujolais region. It is labeled "Beaujolais-Village" with the name of the producer. Village wines are best when consumed within two years of the harvest.
Best	Cru Beaujolais	The highest level of Beaujolais comes from one of the region's most distinctive 10 villages. Unlike the other quality levels of Beaujolais that carry the name of the region, you won't even see the word "Beaujolais" on the label, only the name of the cru and the producer. Area winemakers do not want their top-of-the-line Beaujolais confused in any way with the simpler wines of the region.

Because these wines have more depth and are more Burgundian in style, they can age longer. As a general rule, your Cru Beaujolais will taste best when consumed within three years of the harvest, though the top producers in the best vintages can produce a wine that can last a decade or more.

From the lightest-style Cru Beaujolais to the fullest-bodied, they are listed below.

TABLE 8.2: CRU BEAUJOLAIS

Light	Régnié
	Brouilly
	Chiroubles
	Côte de Brouilly
	Fleurie
	Saint Amour
	Morgon
	Moulin-à-Vent
	Chénas
Full-Bodied	Juliénas

The majority of Beaujolais wines are best when consumed young. Some better recent vintages to buy are 1997, 1998, and 1999.

Top Beaujolais producers to look for are:

- Georges Duboeuf
- Louis Jadot
- Robert Drouhin
- Bouchard
- Mommessin
- Henry Fessy
- Prosper Maufoux

Côte d'Or

This is the heart of classic red Burgundy country, comprised of two main regions (from north to south):

1. Côte de Nuits
2. Côte de Beaune

The entire Côte d'Or is only about one-tenth the size of Bordeaux and physically a little bigger than the Napa Valley in California, yet it has a larger-than-life reputation for producing the greatest red wines of Burgundy. Winemakers in other parts of the world commonly refer to Pinot Noir as the "headache" grape because it is so difficult to grow. In the Côte d'Or, however, the climate, the location of the vineyard, the soil in which the grapes are grown, and the skill of the winemaker come together to make a very distinct wine. The French refer to this winning combination of factors as "terroir," the French word for soil. You'll hear the term thrown around a lot in wine circles.

As in other parts of France, the government classifies the different quality levels of wine from the Côte d'Or. In general, the more specific the information on the label about where the grapes were grown, the better the wine and the more expensive it will be. They are listed from the lowest- to highest-quality levels in the following table.

TABLE 8.3: FRENCH WINE QUALITY CLASSIFICATIONS

Quality	Wine	Description
Basic	Regional	You might select a simple everyday Burgundy to get a flavor for Pinot Noir. The region, "Red Burgundy" or "Bourgogne Rouge," will be noted on the label along with the name of the producer. A basic Bourgogne Rouge will begin at about $10.
Good	Village	A step up in quality and specificity from a Regional wine, the Village wine features the name of the village on the label along with the name of the producer. Expect to pay $20 and up for a good Village wine.
Better	Premier Cru	You're getting into the good stuff here that comes from one of Burgundy's top-rated vineyards. There are roughly 420 of them that produce red wines. Because they have something

continues

continued

Quality	Wine	Description
		to crow about, the label includes both the village and the vineyard name along with the name of the producer. You're going to have to dig a little deeper for these wines, which generally begin in the $35 range and easily go up to $75.
Best	Grand Cru	Only 25 vineyards in Burgundy are permitted to call themselves "Grand Cru." These names are so well-known in the wine world and have such snob appeal that the only name that appears on the label is the vineyard. In case you have any doubts, since 1990, the French government has mandated that all Grand Cru Burgundies include the phrase "Grand Cru" on the label. Of course, on any bottle of wine you will see the name of the producer, but believe me, when there is a prestigious vineyard involved, the vineyard gets absolute top billing. In terms of price, depending on the producer, you're looking at $60 or more, and the sky is the limit due to the laws of supply and demand.

Another way to illustrate the classification of Burgundies is to picture a pyramid in your mind, if you will.

The most basic or "regional appellations" are at the bottom of the totem pole, but they account for 65 percent of all French Burgundy (both red and white).

One level above, the "village appellations" comprise 23 percent of the wines made in Burgundy. Again, they really do offer you a good flavor for the style.

A little higher and you jump up to "premier cru" level. Now you see that these 420 or so vineyards only produce about 11 percent of Burgundy's wines. This explains why you're going to pay more.

At the very top tier, or the tip of the pyramid, are the "grand crus." Demand always outstrips the supply from these 25 red wine vineyards, which account for only about 1 percent of Burgundy's total wines.

Best of the Burgundies

I am not a fan of memorization by rote. I prefer to offer you tips for how to select wine by using a logical process, as I did in explaining the basic differences in quality levels of Burgundy wines. This is not always possible, however. The problem with this in Burgundy, and later as you'll see in Bordeaux, is that these special wines have built their entire reputation on the pedigree of location. The French are especially particular about their turf. If the wines do not come from the "right" place, they will not have the distinction of being known as a premier cru or a grand cru. It's that simple.

I'm going to bend my own rule and give you a list of the Burgundy buzzwords—the important names, the key villages in the Côte d'Or, the premier cru vineyards, and the grand cru vineyards, which I will denote with an asterisk like this *.

TABLE 8.4: CÔTE DE NUITS BURGUNDIES

Key Villages	Top Vineyards
Fixin	Clos de la Perrière
	Clos du Chapitre
	Les Arvelets
	Les Hervelets
Gevrey-Chambertin	Chambertin*
	Clos de Bèze*

continues

continued

Key Villages	Top Vineyards
	Latricières-Chambertin*
	Mazis-Chambertin*
	Charmes-Chambertin*
	Griotte-Chambertin*
	Ruchottes-Chambertin*
	Chapelle-Chambertin*
	Clos Saint Jacques
	Les Varoilles
	Combe aux Moines
	Cazetiers
Morey-Saint-Denis	Bonnes Mares*
	Clos de Tart*
	Clos de la Roche*
	Clos Saint-Denis*
	Clos des Lambrays*
	Clos Bussière
Chambolle-Musigny	Musigny*
	Bonnes Mares*
	Les Amoureuses
	Les Charmes
	Combe d'Orveau
	Les Cras
Vougeot	Clos de Vougeot*
	Vougeot
Flagey-Échézeaux	Grands Échézeaux*
	Les Échézeaux*
Vosne-Romanée	Romanée-Conti*
	La Tâche*
	Romanée Saint-Vivant*
	Richebourg*
	La Romanée*
	La Grande Rue*
	Les Gaudichots
	Aux Brulées
	Clos des Réas

Key Villages	Top Vineyards
Nuits Saint-George	Les Saint-Georges
	Les Cailles
	Clos des Corvées
	Les Vaucrains
	Les Pruliers
	Les Porrets
	Aux Thorey
	Aux Boudots
	Aux Cras
	Aux Murgers
	La Richemone
	La Perrière
	Aux Perdrix
	Clos des Argilières
	Clos Arlot
	Clos de la Maréchale

TABLE 8.5: CÔTE DE BEAUNE BURGUNDIES

Key Villages	Top Vineyards
Aloxe-Corton	Le Corton*
	Corton Bressandes*
	Corton Clos du Roi*
	Corton Renardes*
	Corton Perrières*
	Corton Maréchaudes*
	Corton Les Pougets*
	Les Chaillots
	Les Fourniéres
	Les Valoziéres
Pernand-Vergelesses	Ile des Vergelesses
	Les Vergelesses
Savigny Les Beaune	Les Vergelesses
	Les Laviéres
	Les Marconnets

Unofficially...
All of the Grand Cru Cortons listed in the village of Aloxe-Corton can elect to use the name "Le Corton" on their label. It's very well-known and very prestigious.

continues

continued

Key Villages	Top Vineyards
Beaune	Grèves
	Fèves
	Bressandes
	Clos des Mouches
	Les Cent-Vignes
	Aux Cras
	Champimonts
	Boucherottes
	Marconnets
	Clos de la Mousse
	Les Avaux
	Aigrots
	Clos du Roi
	Les Toussaints
	Les Teurns
Pommard	Rugiens
	Épenots
	Clos Blanc
	Pézerolles
	Petits-Epenots
	Chaponnières
	Boucherottes
	Platière
	Jarollières
	Argillières
	Arvelets
	Clos de la Commaraine
Volnay	Clos des Ducs
	Caillerets
	Champans
	Frèmiets
	Santenots
	Les Angles
	Bousse d'Or
	Clos de Chênes

Key Villages	Top Vineyards
Auxey	Les Duresses
Monthélie	Les Champs Fulliot
Chassagne-Montrachet	La Boudriotte
	Clos St. Jean
	La Maltroie
Santenay	Les Gravières
	La Comme

One village I didn't mention here is Marsannay, which is located at the furthest point north in the Côte de Nuits. Marsannay makes some good red, white, and rosé wines, but there are no premier cru or grand cru vineyards here. As a result, you will find some of your red Burgundy bargains here. In a good year like 1996, for example, you also can get good values from these red appellations:

- Beaune

- Monthélie

- Savigny les Beaune

To make life easier, just think about what you're in the mood for. If you want a more assertive, robust, and hearty Burgundy (and I don't mean the jug wine from California), consider the wines from one of these appellations or villages:

- Corton

- Gevrey-Chambertin

- Nuits-Saint-Georges

- Pommard

- Vougeot

If understated elegance and finesse is more your style, you might prefer red Burgundy from one of the following villages:

Timesaver
The most popular grand crus vineyards that produce red Burgundy are Le Chambertin, Clos de Vougeot, Le Musigny, Richebourg, and Domaine Romané-Conti (shortened to DRC by wine geeks). Top premiers crus include Beaune Clos des Mouches (which also does white), Beaune Les Grèvres, Chambolle-Musigny Les Amoureuses, Chambolle-Musigny Les Charmes, Gevrey-Chambertin le Cazetiers, Pommard Les Epenots, Volnay Clos de Ducs, and Vosne-Romanée Les Suchots.

- Chambolle-Musigny

- Volnay

- Vosne-Romanepé

Regardless of the wine you select, you will want to know about these shippers and producers because their names go hand in and with quality Burgundy. Reliable producers and shippers to seek out when you are buying red Burgundy include but are not limited to:

- Bouchard Père et Fils

- Joseph Drouhin

- J. Faiveley

- Jaffelin

- Louis Jadot

- Louis Latour

- Labouré-Roi

- Domaine de la Romané-Conti

- Domaine Leroy

- Domaine Marquis d'Angerville

- Denis Mortet

- Domaine Georges Roumier

- Domaine Jean Grivot

- Domaine Dujac

- Maillard Pere & Fils

- Prosper Maufoux

- Sérafin Pere & Fils

An added benefit to seeking out reputable ship-pers is that, if you want a really good bottle of Burgundy but you don't want to deplete all your cash reserves, you can buy a basic bottle of Burgundy that will taste more like a village wine, a village wine that will taste more like a premier cru, and a premier cru that will give a grand cru a good run for its money.

Most recent red Burgundy vintages to look for in the Côte d'Or are 1993, 1995, 1996, and 1997. The most basic Burgundy wines are made to be drunk upon release, and most red Burgundy is best when consumed within 10 years of the vintage. The exceptions are the premier cru and grand cru vineyards. Being made in better vintages, these will continue to develop over time.

Côte Châlonnaise

Physically sandwiched between the Côte d'Or and Beaujolais, the Côte Châlonnaise produces some great little red Burgundies, which again means 100 percent Pinot Noir, from the following communes:

- Mercurey
- Givry
- Rully

The village of Montagny is part of the Côte Châlonnaise, but it is strictly a white-wine–producing region. (See Chapter 4, "Classic French Whites.")

Part of what makes these wines so appealing is that you get good value. Compared to the big-name wines from the Côte d'Or (which, remember, includes the Côte de Beaune and the Côte de Nuits), the Burgundies from Mercurey, Givry, and Rully are a good deal, especially if you plan to drink them now or in the near future. Even the best wines from the Côte Châlonnaise are rarely more expensive than the well-known village wines from the très expensive Côte d'Or. The only downside for people who consider themselves to be collectors is that the red wines of the Côte Châlonnaise do not age as well as their fuller-bodied brethren. For this reason, it's best to look for more recent vintages such as 1995, 1996, and 1997.

Look for these reliable producers from the Côte Châlonnaise:

- Maison Faiveley (Mercurey)
- Domaine de Suremain (Mercurey)
- Domaine Michel Juillot (Mercurey)
- Domaine DeLaunay (Mercurey)
- Domaine Thenard (Givry)
- Louis Latour (Givry)
- Antonin Rodet (Rully)
- Louis Jadot (Rully)

Bordeaux

Another classic French red-wine–growing region, Bordeaux conjures up regal images of grandiose châteaux and lush, rolling vineyards. There is a certain amount of truth to the fairy-tale quality in this land that is home to the most famous estates that include Château Lafite-Rothschild, Château Latour, Château Margaux, and Château Mouton.

A closer look at Bordeaux, however, reveals that the highest-rated châteaux account for a very limited amount of wine produced. In fact, of all the wine regions in France, Bordeaux turns out the largest percentage of AOC wines. About one out of every four bottles of French wine is worthy of AOC designation, which is the French government's nod to quality. By all accounts, Bordeaux is red wine country. After all, about 75 percent of its production is red.

Although the trend in many wine-growing regions is to create wines using 100 percent of a grape variety, as they do in Burgundy with 100 percent Pinot Noir, the wines of Bordeaux are still primarily created from blends. The major red grapes used in this area are:

- Cabernet Sauvignon

- Merlot

- Cabernet Franc

- Petit Verdot

- Malbec

Traditionally, Cabernet Sauvignon has been the winemaker's grape of choice that is used to create the heart of red Bordeaux wines. Cabernet Sauvignon gives the wine backbone and the solid structure that allows the finest wines of Bordeaux to develop and that makes them worthy of cellaring. The other varieties, which soften the wine and give it soul, are added in varying degrees according to the winemaker's style and the quality of the grapes harvested. Two or more grape varieties may be blended to produce Bordeaux, and you will sometimes get a rough idea of the winemaker's recipe if he or she includes the information on the back label. The recipe itself usually varies from vintage to vintage, depending on the quality of the harvest.

Over the past five years, however, Americans have discovered Merlot and its easy drinkability. This has led to nothing less than Merlot mania. As a result, in Bordeaux, Merlot has overtaken Cabernet Sauvignon in terms of acreage, and it now accounts for more than 56 percent of red grapes planted. This marks a three-fold increase in Merlot since the 1970s, which is unbelievable.

Winemakers have taken notice of this taste trend and are using more Merlot in their blends, particularly in the lower- and mid-priced wines. They see Merlot flying off the shelves, and they want their wines to be a part of this frenzy. With a blend heavier in Merlot, they can make wines that do not need to be cellared to be appreciated. For the most part, they are ready and easy to drink.

The top red-wine–growing regions in Bordeaux are:

- Médoc
- Graves/Pessac-Léognan (which also produces whites, see Chapter 4)
- Pomerol
- St.-Émilion

I've listed the regions in this order for an important reason. The first two—Médoc and Graves/Pessac-Léognan—are situated on what is known as the Left Bank of the Dordogne River. They share soil characteristics and some elements of style. This is Cabernet Sauvignon country, which means that these wines generally taste better with a little, and preferably a lot, of age. The wines are typically tannic and can be downright austere in their youth. But oh, when they blossom, they are absolutely worth the wait.

The second two regions—Pomerol and St.-Émilion—are situated on the Right Bank of the Dordogne River. Again, they share soil characteristics and certain elements. Among these characteristics is that most of these wines are made primarily from the Merlot grape. See where this is headed? If you have an A-type personality and hate to wait, these are the regions for you to explore because the wines are more approachable earlier. They are softer, rounder, fruitier, and extremely food friendly.

Within the Médoc, which is considered to be the most important appellation in Bordeaux, consider these village names as buzzwords to help you select quality Bordeaux. From north to south, they are:

- Haut-Médoc
- St.-Estèphe
- Pauillac
- St.-Julien
- Listrac
- Moulis
- Margaux

I've mentioned before that pedigree is important to the French. In Bordeaux, it's not who you know but where you're from. Typically, the more specific the name on the wine's label, the better the wine and the higher the price. The following is how Bordeaux is categorized by quality, beginning with the most basic and ranging to the world-class château wines.

Unofficially...
Wines made in the Médoc area, but not necessarily within one of the chi-chi appellations, can carry the appellation "Haut-Médoc" on their label to distinguish themselves from wines made in the more northern part of Médoc, which is considered to be less desirable.

TABLE 8.6: BORDEAUX PEDIGREES

Quality	Wine	Description
Good	Proprietary or "Brand Name Wines"	These entry-level Bordeaux feature a brand name such as Maître d'Estournel or Mouton Cadet that has nothing to do with the vineyards. These are names used for marketing purposes like Coca-Cola or Kleenex. If you are a person who examines labels, you'll notice that the wine comes from Bordeaux. This is nice to know, but more than likely, you're attracted by the brand name and the reasonable price. The better producers create consistently tasty wines under $10 that are great for everyday consumption. Drink now.

continues

continued

Quality	Wine	Description
Better	Regional Wines	The second tier of quality in Bordeaux is found in wines that are labeled with the name of the region from which they originate. On the label you will see the name of the region, such as Margaux, along with the name of the producer. You know that the wine was made somewhere in the special appellation of Margaux, but when you're paying $10 to $15 for a regional wine, you've got to know that this quaff is a far cry from the legendary Château Margaux. These are best when consumed within a few years of the vintage date on the label.
Best	Château or "Vineyard" Wines	The finest wines in Bordeaux carry the name of the specific château or vineyard from which they originate. The French singled out many but not all of these vineyards in 1855 in an attempt to categorize the quality levels of the area's top vineyards. (See the full listing of the Classification of 1855 that follows.) These top-dollar wines are intended to be laid down for aging so they can develop fully. The price range of château wines begins at about $25 per bottle and can easily hit $100 for the very best estates. They are best enjoyed with at least 10 years of age, and the finest château will last much longer when stored properly.

Timesaver
To make sure you are selecting the very finest Bordeaux, you don't even have to remember the name of the vineyard. Look for the words "Grand Cru Classé" or "Premier Grand Cru Classé." Sometimes "Premier" is abbreviated as "1er."

Official Classification of 1855

The easiest way to get to the heart of the best wines in Bordeaux is to take a look at the famous Classification of 1855. According to the story, wine merchants were asked to rank the top wines of the

Médoc and Graves regions in preparation for showing off the country's finest wines at a Paris Exposition. Off the top of their heads, they sketched out a list of names, which they considered to be nothing more than an unofficial list. Despite their intent, the Classification of 1855 remains a sacred cow in wine that has only been revised once. The revision took place in 1973 when the Baron Philippe de Rothschild succeeded in having his Château Mouton-Rothschild elevated to "first-growth" status.

> **66**
> First, I am. Second, I was. But Mouton does not change.
> —Baron Philippe de Rothschild, after spending more than 50 years attempting to get his wine added to the A-list of first growths
> **99**

TABLE 8.7: THE OFFICIAL CLASSIFICATION OF 1855 FOR THE MÉDOC

Vineyard	Commune (Modern Name)
First Growths—"Premier Crus"	
Château Lafite-Rothschild	Pauillac
Château Latour	Pauillac
Château Margaux	Margaux
Château Haut-Brion	Pessac, Graves (Pessac-Leognan)
Château Mouton-Rothschild	Pauillac
Second Growths—"Deuxièmes Crus"	
Château Rausan-Ségla	Margaux
Château Rausan-Gassies	Margaux
Château Léoville-Las Cases	St.-Julien
Château Léoville-Poyferré	St.-Julien
Château Léoville-Barton	St.-Julien
Château Durfort-Vivens	Margaux
Château Gruard-Larose	St.-Julien
Château Lascombes	Margaux
Château Brane-Cantenac	Cantenac-Margaux (Margaux)
Château Pichon-Longueville-Baron	Pauillac
Château Pichon-Longueville, Comtesse de Lalande	Pauillac
Château Ducru-Beaucaillou	St.-Julien

continues

continued

Timesaver
Overachievers to
look for in the
second-growths
category are
Château Cos
d'Estournel,
Château Ducru-
Beaucaillou, and
Château Léoville-
Las Cases.

Second Growths—"Deuxièmes Crus"

Château Cos d'Estournel	St.-Estèphe
Château Montrose	St.-Estèphe

Third Growths—"Troisièmes Crus"

Château Kirwan	Cantenac-Margaux (Margaux)
Château d'Issan	Cantenac-Margaux (Margaux)
Château Lagrange	St.-Julien
Château Langoa Barton	St.-Julien
Château Giscours	Labarde-Margaux (Margaux)
Château Malescot-St.-Exupéry	Margaux
Château Cantenac-Brown	Cantenac-Margaux (Margaux)
Château Boyd-Cantenac	Margaux
Château Palmer	Cantenac-Margaux (Margaux)
Château La Lagune	Ludon (Haut-Médoc)
Château Desmirail	Margaux
Château Calon-Ségur	St.-Estèphe
Château Ferrière	Margaux
Château Marquis d'Alesme Becker	Margaux

Fourth Growths—"Quatrièmes Crus"

Château St.-Pierre	St.-Julien
Château Talbot	St.-Julien
Château Branaire-Ducru	St.-Julien
Château Duhart-Milon-Rothschild	Pauillac
Château Pouget	Cantenac-Margaux (Margaux)
Château La Tour Carnet	St.-Laurent
Château Lafon-Rochet	St.-Estèphe
Château Beychevelle	St.-Julien
Château Prieuré-Lichine	Cantenac-Margaux (Margaux)
Château Marquis de Terme	Margaux

Fifth Growths—"Cinquièmes Crus"

Château Pontet-Canet	Pauillac
Château Batailley	Pauillac
Château Haut-Batailley	Pauillac

Fifth Growths—"Cinquièmes Crus"	
Château Grand-Puy-Lacoste	Pauillac
Château Grand-Puy-Ducasse	Pauillac
Château Lynch-Bages	Pauillac
Château Lynch-Moussas	Pauillac
Château Dauzac	Labarde (Margaux)
Château Mouton-Baronne-Philippe (known as Château d'Armailhac since 1989)	Pauillac
Château du Tertre	Arsac (Margaux)
Château Haut-Bages Libéral	Pauillac
Château Pédesclaux	Pauillac
Château Belgrave	St.-Laurent (Haut-Médoc)
Château Camensac	St.-Laurent (Haut-Médoc)
Château Cos Labory	St.-Estèphe
Château Clerc-Milon	Pauillac
Château Croizet Bages	Pauillac
Château Cantemerle	Macau (Haut-Médoc)

A popular, beautifully crafted wine that is not included in the Classification of 1855 because it wasn't in existence at the time is Château Gloria from St.-Julien. In terms of quality, it rates right up there with the classified growths.

The Classification of 1855 includes a ranking of Sauternes and Barsac, which are sweet white dessert wines. This ranking can be found in Chapter 13, "After-Dinner Delights."

Cru Bourgeois values

A notch below the classified growths of the Médoc, you can find some great values in a group of wines known as "Crus Bourgeois." This classification originally was done in 1920 and has been revised periodically, most recently in 1978.

Because there is such a broad spectrum of quality between the very best Cru Bourgeois and the worst in a laundry list of some 400 wines, look for these Crus Bourgeois that I consider among the better ones, especially in a good vintage:

- Château d'Angludet
- Château La Cardonne
- Château Chasse-Spleen
- Château Coufran
- Château Fourcas-Hosten
- Château Forcas-Dupré
- Château Greysac
- Château Haut-Marbuzet
- Château Lafon
- Château Larose-Trintaudon
- Château Les Ormes-de-Pez
- Château Les Ormes-Sorbet
- Château Marbuzet
- Château Meyney
- Château Phélan-Segur
- Château Pontensac
- Château Poujeaux
- Château Sociando Mallet

Classified buying strategy

You can put the Official Classification of 1855 to work for you to help make an informed wine selection. This is especially helpful for people with Champagne tastes on a beer budget.

You've heard a lot about Château Margaux, and you'd really like to try it, but you hesitate to plunk down $300 or more for a bottle. What do you do? Follow these steps, which work particularly well in a good vintage:

1. Take a look at the Official Classification of 1855. You see that Château Margaux is a first growth, also known as a premier cru, and it comes from the commune of Margaux.

2. Scan the Official Classification of 1855 for other château wines that come from Margaux. You might also include the communes of Cantenac-Margaux, Labarde-Margaux, or Arsac, which today carry the modern name Margaux on their labels as well.

3. Keep a mental note in your mind that the further down you go in the classification, the less expensive the wine should be in comparison to the first growth.

4. If you come across a fifth growth from the region you are interested in, but you still find it too rich for your blood, drop down a notch and consider a crus bourgeois from Margaux. As a last resort, you might try a regional wine from that area.

Remember that you will not duplicate the first growth experience, but you will get a taste for the style of Margaux.

Top Graves

The Graves region, which includes Graves' designer subregion of Pessac-Léognan in the north, was officially classified in 1953 and was revised in 1959. As you now know, Château Haut-Brion, its most famous red estate, was the only Graves wine to crack the exclusive Classification of 1855.

Here is a list of the other top-rated reds from the Graves region that are worthy of cru classé status:

- Château Bouscaut
- Château Carbonnieux

- Domaine de Chevalier
- Château Fieuzal
- Château Haut-Bailly
- Château Malartic-Lagravière
- Château La Mission Haut-Brion
- Château Olivier
- Château Pape Clément
- Château Smith Haut Lafitte
- Château La Tour-Martillac
- Château La Tour Haut-Brion

The best of Pomerol and St.-Émilion

I previously explained that Pomerol and St.-Émilion both come from the Right Bank of the river, which means they are heavy-handed with Merlot. Although it's true that many of these wines are easy drinking compared to those from the Left Bank (Médoc and Graves), they are no slouches.

The star of Pomerol, Château Pétrus, for example, is one of the most sought after wines in all of Bordeaux. It costs more than the highly coveted premier crus of the Médoc. This is interesting because Pomerol, unlike the Médoc and other famous French appellations, does not have an official classification. Château Pétrus is in a class by itself. You will find that the best wines from Pomerol are expensive, mostly because Pomerol is the smallest red wine commune in Bordeaux. Demand simply outstrips supply.

Top Pomerol estates include:

- Château Pétrus
- Château Beauregard
- Château Le Bon Pasteur

Unofficially...
Christian Moueix, manager and co-owner of Château Pétrus recently purchased Château Certan Giraud, a neighboring vineyard. He will rename the estate and plans to renovate the cellar and vineyard. Under his patronage, Château Certan Giraud will be one to watch.

- Château Certan-de-May
- Château Certan Giraud
- Château Clinet
- Château La Conseillante
- Château La Pointe
- Château Gazin
- Château Latour à Pomerol
- Château l'Evangile
- Château Lafleur
- Château Le Pin
- Château Nénin
- Château Trotanoy
- Vieux Château Certan

In neighboring St.-Émilion, which is considerably larger than Pomerol, Merlot is still the main grape, but you're going to find more blends heavier in Cabernet Franc, Malbec, and even Cabernet Sauvignon. It took a while, but the wines of St.-Émilion were officially classified by the French government in 1955 and were revised in 1985.

The first-growth wines carry the distinction "Premier Grand Cru Classé" or "1er Grand Cru Classé" on their labels. They are:

- Château Ausone
- Château Cheval-Blanc
- Château Beauséjour
- Château Belair
- Château Canon
- Clos Fourtet
- Château Figeac
- Château La Gaffeliére

Unofficially...
Quality varies
between the
vineyards in St.-
Émilion. Two
châteaux that
stand head and
shoulders above
the rest and are
even on par with
the premier crus
of the Médoc are
Château Ausone
and Château
Cheval-Blanc.

- Château Magdelaine
- Château Pavie
- Château Trottevieille

A notch below the Premier Grand Cru Classés is wine from St.-Émilion that is entitled to be labeled "Grand Cru Classé." Some of the better wines in this category include:

- Château L'Angélus
- Château L'Arrosée
- Château Balestard La Tonnelle
- Château Berliquet
- Château Canon La Gaffelière
- Château Dassault
- Château La Dominique
- Château Fonplegade
- Château Franc-Mayne
- Château Larmande
- Château La Tour-Figeac
- Château La Tour du Pin-Figeac

Because of their tremendous potential for aging and cellaring, their salability as a "future" like other commodities, and the likelihood that you will one day find them at auction, vintage years are a big deal in Bordeaux.

Bordeaux aficionados look for these memorable past and great recent vintages: 1961, 1966, 1970, 1975, 1978, 1982, 1983, 1985, 1986, 1988, 1989, 1990, 1994, 1995, and 1996.

Some other good but not great Bordeaux vintages are: 1962, 1964, 1967, 1971, 1973, 1979, 1981, and 1993.

The Rhône Valley

For true price quality in robust reds, I look to the Rhône Valley. I love the fact that I can get a really good bottle of wine for under $10 that I know will go with whatever I'm grilling. What makes this region even more appealing to me is that, if you decide that you enjoy Rhône-style wines, you can explore the next level, and then the next, and so on. Each level from the different "crus" or winemaking regions within the Rhône offers more layers of complexity in their flavors, and this will be reflected in the price you pay.

As I previously mentioned, prices for your basic Rhône Valley reds begin at under $10 and can go to about $80 for the most celebrated vineyards. At the $15 to $20 levels, you will find an appreciable difference in quality. Many times, I would much rather pay more and know I'm getting a great red Rhône wine than settle for a lesser Burgundy or Bordeaux in the same price range.

This vast region has two distinct climates and covers so much territory from north to south that it is best understood if you divide it into the northern and southern Rhône.

The prestigious northern Rhône

The major red-wine–growing regions of the celebrated northern Côtes du Rhône are:

- Côte-Rôtie
- Hermitage
- Crozes-Hermitage
- St.-Joseph
- Cornas

They all produce the Syrah grape. Similar to Merlot mania, Syrah has become so trendy that it seems as if wine producers all over the world can't plant it quickly enough. The real McCoy, it should be noted, comes from the Rhône Valley. Having said that, the better producers from Côte-Rôtie and Hermitage make some very good wine that is worthy of laying down in your wine cellar and that will give the designer Burgundies and Bordeaux a good run for their money.

Wines from St.-Joseph and Crozes-Hermitage are generally more approachable if you give them five years of age, though some better ones will still give you pleasure at 8 or 10 years. Côte-Rôtie, Hermitage, and Cornas produce more blockbusters that really need 15-plus years to do the Syrah justice.

Southern Rhône

Compared to the Northern Rhône that is so well-known for quality, the southern Rhône is a virtual wine lake. About 80 percent of the ordinary Côtes-du-Rhône wines come from the south. Still, this area boasts one of the most famous regions in the Rhône Valley—Châteauneuf-du-Pape.

Red-wine–growing regions of the southern Rhône are:

- Châteauneuf-du-Pape
- Lirac
- Gigondas
- Vacqueyras

Because of the Mediterranean climate in the south, the grapes get lots of sun, which means they are extremely ripe. The high sugar content in the grapes creates a wine that is higher in alcohol (about 13 to 14 percent compared to an average of 12 percent for many table wines).

Unlike the northern Rhône, which uses the Syrah grape exclusively to produce its wines, the southern Rhône relies on blends. This is another reason for the big style difference between north and south. In fact, Châteauneuf-du-Pape is technically allowed to use a blend of 13 different grapes. The most important grape varieties of the southern Rhône are:

- Grenache
- Syrah
- Mourvèdre
- Cinsault
- Carignan

Although there is no formal classification system to help you gauge the quality of a Rhône Valley wine, there are levels of quality you can look for on the label. From the ordinary to the more interesting, they are listed in the following table.

TABLE 8.8: RHÔNE VALLEY QUALITY WINES

Quality	Wine	Description
Basic	Regional Côtes-du-Rhône	This most basic wine can come from anywhere in the Rhône Valley, though chances are it is from the south where quantity overrides quality.
Good	Côtes-du-Rhône Villages	A distinct step up in quality and value, a wine labeled Côtes-du-Rhône Villages might come from specific villages within the region. In fact, the wine might be a blend of wine from two different villages.
Better	Côtes-du-Rhône Villages (with the actual name of the village)	Unlike the regular Côtes-du-Rhône Villages, this wine label carries the name of a specific village within the Rhône Valley that is known for better-quality wines.

Timesaver
Look for these villages for some of the best values in the Rhône: Carianne, Rasteau, Sablet, and Séguret. Other appellations to look for that offer good value include the Côtes du Ventoux and the Côtes du Luberon.

continues

continued

Quality	Wine	Description
Best	Côtes-du-Rhône Crus	These are the best-quality wines from the Côtes-du-Rhône that are labeled with the name of one of the Rhône's top 13 wine-growing areas. Nine of these 13 crus are best known for their reds:
		Châteauneuf-du-Pape
		Cornas
		Côte-Rôtie
		Crozes-Hermitage
		Gigondas
		Hermitage
		Lirac
		St.-Joseph
		Vacqueyras

When you select a wine from the Rhône Valley, you can't go wrong if you see the name of one of these producers on the label:

- Paul Jaboulet Aîné
- M. Chapoutier
- E. Guigal
- Vidal-Fleury
- Jean-Louis Chave
- Albert Belle
- Château de Beaucastel (Châteauneuf-du-Pape)
- Domaine du Vieux Télégraphe (Châteauneuf-du-Pape)
- Château Mont-Reddon

Remember, because there is a big difference in climate between the northern and southern Rhône, vintage quality might vary.

Good recent vintages to look for in the north (Côte-Rôtie, Hermitage, Crozes-Hermitage, St.-Joseph, and Cornas) include 1989, 1990, 1991, 1994, 1995, 1996, 1997, 1998, and 1999.

In the south (Châteauneuf-du-Pape, Lirac, Gigondas, Vacqueyras), look for 1989, 1990, 1994, 1995, 1998, and 1999 .

Values from southern France

As wine prices creep up in the more established wine regions of France and elsewhere, I'm always on the lookout for an easy-drinking wine under $10 and preferably more like $7 or $8. The answer, these days, is in southern France and more specifically the Languedoc-Roussillon.

The Languedoc-Roussillon is a crescent-shaped region that hugs the Mediterranean coastline and borders on Spain.

Ordinarily, it would bother me that the majority of the wine here is considered only Vin de Pays d'Oc, a level below the Appellation d'Origine Contrôlée (AOC), which is so synonymous with quality in France. It doesn't in this case because there has been a great deal of investment in this wine region over the past 10 years to modernize its winemaking and to improve its quality.

Two major producers immediately come to mind that have produced a full line of wines (both red and white) and have priced them right— Fortant de France and Réserve St.-Martin. To make their wines even more user-friendly, they feature the grape varietal on the label. As a result, you'll see some very pleasant Cabernet Sauvignons, Merlots, and Syrahs from these makers.

In addition to these "newer" varietals to the area, you'll find wines from the Langedoc-Roussillon made from these traditional grapes:

- Grenache
- Syrah
- Cinsault
- Mourvèdre

There's no need to belabor the pros and cons of the individual villages, but two helpful names to know are Corbières and Minervois. They are two of the more popular villages in this region. If nothing more, you'll know to connect these two names to the Languedoc.

Just the facts

- Red wine in moderation can be heart-healthy.
- Beaujolais is the perfect stepping stone to reds, and it tastes great chilled.
- The more specific the region on the label, the better the quality and the higher the price.
- A little geography goes a long way in finding values in both Burgundy and Bordeaux.
- Some of the best red values in France can be found in the Rhône Valley and the Languedoc-Roussillon.

U.S. Reds

It amazes me to think that, at one time, practically all the American vineyards—at least those in California—were covered with red grapes. That's because when I came of age in the 1970s I started drinking white wine. I didn't know much about it except that it tasted good and was easy to drink. Most people around me were drinking white wine, too, well into the '80s.

What I didn't realize until I began to study wine was that most immigrants who came to America brought their red grapes to the party because that's what they were accustomed to at home. They were used to the more robust flavors. After all, these were the same people who drank Schlivowitz and Schnapps in Eastern Europe and Grappa, also known as "fire water," in Italy, so what do you expect?

As people became more Americanized, their tastes changed. It was a gradual process, of course, but it was very obvious in the 1980s when most Americans became obsessed with health and fitness. Steak and potatoes were "out." Fish, chicken, and grilled vegetables were "in." There seemed to be

Chapter 9

something lighter and more healthful about white wine, or so we thought until the report about the French paradox hit the airwaves on *60 Minutes* in 1991. (Refer to Chapter 8, "The French 'Red' Standard," for more information.) The whole idea that a couple glasses of red wine a day could potentially help prevent heart attacks made many Americans do a 180-degree turn to red. The French paradox even added a brand new group of beginning wine drinkers who wanted to learn to become red wine drinkers out of deference to their health.

Easing into reds, California style

Whether you consider yourself to be a red wine drinker or you are trying to find a red wine you will enjoy, you need to know about the flavor profiles of the grapes. Although Cabernet Sauvignon is the king of red grapes in California just by the sheer number of vines planted, I'm listing the following red grapes in order from the lightest style to the most robust. Because of the many variables involved in winemaking styles, you're always going to find a few exceptions, but this is a good general guide to follow.

Keep in mind that even though you will find Cabernet Sauvignon in other parts of the world such as Bordeaux and Chile—and they might share a similar taste profile—Cabernet Sauvignon from California will have its own distinct taste. This is partly due to the differences in the climate and the soil (what the French like to call "terroir") and, again, the individual style of the winemaker.

Without further ado, here is a quick rundown of the main grapes you will find in California, where they grow best, and a list of reliable producers where appropriate.

TABLE 9.1: CALIFORNIA WINES

Wine	Top Turf	Labels to Look For
Gamay Beaujolais California's answer to the French Beaujolais produces a lighter, fruitier style of wine that tastes better when served chilled. For someone who is just starting to drink reds, this is a great stepping stone from white or blush wine.	Napa Valley	Beringer
Pinot Noir Through trial and error, and fierce perseverance, California wine-makers have worked hard to create Burgundian style reds. Well-made examples offer a soft sell of berry flavors combined with velvety richness. Although some California winemakers have unlocked the secret to Pinot Noir, the famous French Burgundy negociant Robert Drouhin put Oregon on the wine map for its elegant French-styled Burgundies. Pinot Noir can be an excellent stepping stone to red wines for the uninitiated, yet it offers all the complexity and elegance that a serious wine drinker savors.	Carneros	Acacia Au Bon Climat Calera Cambria Winery Carneros Creek Corbett Canyon Vineyards Creston Vineyards David Bruce Winery Davis Bynum Winery Dehlinger Winery Étude Fiddlehead Cellars Gary Farell Wines Kistler Vineyards Robert Mondavi Rochioli Vineyards Saintsbury Sanford Winery Williams & Selyem Winery

continues

continued

Wine	Top Turf	Labels to Look For
Sangiovese California wine-makers are experimenting to come up with their own Cal-Ital style for this grape. It's on the tannic side, at least the California version is, but it packs a medium- to full-bodied punch and flavors of spice, anisette, and black-cherry.	Napa Valley Sonoma County San Luis Obispo County Sierra Foothills	Atlas Peak Seghesio Winery Louis Martini
Merlot Once upon a time not too long ago, Merlot was used almost exclusively to make Bordeaux blends. It still is to a degree in California. Some California winemakers come along, however, who decide to find out what a varietal can do on its own. In this case, they hit pay dirt. Merlot mania spread when people discovered how good and easy-to-drink Merlot is with its pleasant fruit flavors and its versatility with food. Only problem with all this popularity is that some of the brands you know and love, like the best-selling Columbia Crest Merlot from Washington state, can be	Napa Valley Sonoma County	Alexander Valley Vineyards Château Souverain Clos du Val Davis Bynum Winery Duckhorn Ferrari-Carano Forest Glen Franciscan Vineyards Geyser Peak Winery Merryvale Vineyards St. Francis Winery Silverado Vineyards Smith & Hook Winery

Wine	Top Turf	Labels to Look For
more challenging to find due to the increased demand. To fill the demand, many grape growers all over the state of California started to plant Merlot in their vineyards.		
Barbera California wine-makers are actively experimenting with this deep-ruby–colored Italian grape. Barbera yields wines with berry flavors that are low in tannin but high in acid. Consider this Cal-Ital grape to be a work in progress.	Central Valley (also known as San Joaquin Valley)	
Nebbiolo Though this red grape produces full-bodied wines in its native Italy that are worthy of laying down to age, the Cal-Ital version is somewhat lighter in style.	Central Valley	
Grenache Though this is a red grape, you're more likely to find it as a varietal made in a fruity rosé style called "White Grenache." (See Chapter 11, "Rosé or Blush Wine," for more information.) When used as a red wine, Grenache in California often is blended to produce inexpensive bulk red wines.	Central Valley Mendocino County	

continues

Watch Out!
As a buyer, you might be tempted to select any old wine that labeled as Merlot, especially if it's cheaper. That's fine if you discover one you enjoy, but be advised that, once a grape varietal "takes off," grape growers naturally try to cash in, and some of the grapes simply aren't as good.

continued

Wine	Top Turf	Labels to Look For
Malbec This grape produces wine with plummy, cherry-tasting flavors, and it commonly is used by California winemakers as a blending grape.	Napa Valley	
Petit Verdot This grape produces full-bodied, deep-red wine, and it sometimes is used by California winemakers as a blending grape in Bordeaux-style blends.	Napa Valley	
Zinfandel First of all, yes, Zinfandel is a red grape. Though it is used to make the popular semi-sweet White Zinfandel (see Chapter 11, "Rosé or Blush Wine"), if you like robust reds by the fireplace, you'll like Zinfandel. Until recently, wine wizards thought that Zinfandel was a Native American variety. Recent DNA fingerprinting now points to the grape's European origin. Still in my book, California does the best job with Zinfandel. The only problem I have with Zinfandel when recommending it to someone as a	Dry Creek in Sonoma Shenandoah Valley in Amador County Paso Robles in San Luis Obispo County Napa Valley	Burgess Cellars Château Montelena Château Souverain Cline Cellars Davis Bynum Winery De Loach Vineyards Dry Creek Vineyards Frog's Leap Winery Guenoc Winery Gundlach-Bundschu Winery Kendall-Jackson Vineyards Kenwood Vineyards Marietta Cellars Niebaum-Coppola Estate Parducci Wine Cellars Preston Vineyards Ravenswood Ridge Vineyards Rosenblum Cellars Seghesio Winery Willians Selyem Winery Storybook Winery Sonoma County Joseph Swan Vineyards

Wine	Top Turf	Labels to Look For
category is that several different styles are made. Depending on the producer, you could get a light-bodied, almost fruity Beaujolais style, a big wine that will leave you warm and fuzzy on a cold winter night, or a sweet Port-like, after-dinner variety. The best way to know what you're getting, if you're not already familiar with the producer, is to ask your wine merchant. If there were such a thing as a baseline flavor profile for Zinfandel, it would be spicy, robust, and bursting with ripe mixed berries.		
Cabernet Franc Californians some-times bottle Cabernet Franc as a varietal that tastes like a lighter-style Cabernet Sauvignon with flavors of berries and currants. Lately, there seems to be a movement in California toward more Bordeaux-style blends in which a small amount of Cabernet Franc is added to Cabernet Sauvignon to soften the wine and to make it more pleasant to	Napa Valley	

continues

continued

Wine	Top Turf	Labels to Look For
drink. These Bordeaux blends in California are sometimes categorized as "Meritage" wines (rhymes with "heritage"). They are labeled with proprietary brand names such as Opus One.		

Cabernet Sauvignon

Wine	Top Turf	Labels to Look For
California's reputation for world-class red wines was built by Cabernet Sauvignon. Though it creates the backbone of fine red Bordeaux wines and many Bordeaux-style blends in California, California also makes some 100 percent Cabernet Sauvignons that have become highly coveted collectibles. Cabernet Sauvignon is bursting with flavors that range from spicy and jammy with black currants and other berries to vegetal qualities like peppers and artichokes to even chocolate. It all depends on the winemaker and where the grapes are from.	Napa Valley Sonoma County	Alexander Valley Vineyards Arrowood Vineyards Beaulieu Vineyards (also known as BV) Beringer Vineyards Cakebread Cellars Caymus Vineyard Chappellet Château Montelena Château Souverain Clos du Bois Clos du Val Dalla Valle Dry Creek Vineyards Duckhorn Dunn Vineyards Far Niente Fetzer Vineyards Firestone Vineyard Frog's Leap Winery Groth Vineyards Gundlach-Bundschu Winery Heitz Vineyards (especially Martha's Vineyard or Bella Oaks Vineyard) Hess Collection Winery J. Lohr Winery Jekel Vineyards Jordan Vineyard Kathryn Kennedy Winery Kenwood Vineyards La Jota Vineyard Laurel Glen Marietta Cellars

Wine	Top Turf	Labels to Look For
		Markham Vineyards
		Mayacamas Vineyards
		Robert Mondavi (look for the "Reserves")
		Pine Ridge Winery
		Raymond Vineyard
		Ridge Vineyards
		Rodney Strong Vineyards
		Sequoia Grove
		St. Supery Vineyards
		Shafer Vineyards
		Silver Oak Cellars
		Silverado Vineyards
		Simi Winery
		Spottswoode Winery
		Stag's Leap Wine Cellars
		Sterling Vineyards
Syrah As the latest red darling to hit America's tastebuds since Merlot mania, Syrah has the ability to produce wonderfully spicy, peppery reds that are balanced out by blockbuster black cherry and currant flavors. Although Syrah produces some heavy hitters that wine collectors vie for, the grape is good for some youthful, easy-drinking wines (which was a big part of Merlot's mass appeal). Grape growers in California and State cannot plant Syrah fast enough to keep up with current demand.	Mendocino Sonoma County Napa Valley Monterey County	Arrowood Cline Cellars Dehlinger Fess Parker Winery Geyser Peak McDowell Meridian Vineyards Joseph Phelps Qupé Cellars Rabbit Ridge Sebastiani Zaca Mesa

Watch Out!
Don't automatically be impressed by the phrases "Reserve," "Special Reserve," "Special Selection," or "Proprietor's Reserve" on a wine label. These terms have no legal meaning, but they do carry clout when used by old reliables such as Mondavi, Beaulieu, and other reputable producers who actually try to make a distinction of quality on the label.

continues

continues

Unofficially...
Though we appear to be in the midst of a new lovefest with the Syrah as a varietal, some California winemakers, notably Randall Graham of Bonny Doon and Joe Phelps of Phelps Vineyards, have led the charge experimenting with Rhône varietals and blends like those of France. Labels to look for include Joseph Phelps Vin du Mistral, Bonny Doon's Le Cigare Volant, Old Telegram, and Clos de Gilroy.

Wine	Top Turf	Labels to Look For
Petite Sirah		
Expect a little pepper and spice from this red grape, grown primarily in California, that is a long-lost cousin of the Rhône variety, Syrah. Among other things, the actual berries of Petite Sirah are smaller petite compared to Syrah.	Mendocino Sonoma County Napa Valley Monterey County	Bogle Concannon Vineyard Foppiano Vineyards Hidden Cellars Markham Mirassou Parducci Wine Cellars Turley

An interesting point worth noting is that grapes come in and go out of fashion like everything else. Cabernet Sauvignon has had such a long run that it is considered a classic that will never go out of style. More recently, however, there has been Merlot mania, a Zinfandel renaissance, and a Syrah surge. Vineyards cannot turn on a dime. After a vine is planted, it takes five years until that vine can bear grapes that can be used to produce wine. So if you think European clothing designers need to think ahead, consider the American grape growers!

Getting your arms around California's regions

I've never been a great fan of geography or map reading, but I find it much easier to select wines if I can visualize the regions and know where certain grapes thrive. Cabernet Sauvignon, for example, thrives in the warm, sunny climate throughout Napa and Sonoma. The more fragile red grape, Pinot Noir, grows much better in the decidedly cooler conditions available in certain microclimates within

Napa and Sonoma, specifically in the Carneros and Russian River Valley districts. Microclimates are small areas within a region with weather that differs from the surrounding countryside. You can have a wine-growing region with a warm climate, but within the region is a pocket where the growing conditions are much cooler. You also can have cool regions with warmer microclimates. It's really a climate within a climate.

You're already familiar with the concept of American Viticultural Areas (AVAs) from Chapter 6, "American Whites." It's the same story with reds. American winemakers are still figuring out where their red grapes grow best. Here are some of the more popular California AVAs along with the grape varieties for which they are known and a sampling of wineries in parentheses that are representative of the area. One good shortcut to selecting a good red wine is to look for one of these AVAs:

- **Napa Valley**—Cabernet Sauvignon and Merlot as well as Chardonnay, Sauvignon Blanc (also known as Fumé Blanc in California), and Riesling do well here.

- **Sonoma Valley**—Pinot Noir does especially well in the southern part of the Valley. This area also is known for Cabernet Sauvignon, Merlot, and Zinfandel. In whites, look for Chardonnay. (Arrowood, Château St. Jean, Sebastiani, Laurel Glen, Landmark, Kenwood)

- **Howell Mountain**—This area is known for flavor-packed Cabernets and Zinfandels. (Dunn)

- **Los Carneros**—This area is known for Burgundian-style Pinot Noir and Chardonnay. (Acacia, Saintsbury, Carneros Creek, Bouchaine)

Unofficially...
Some top
Cabernet
Sauvignons made
in Napa Valley
come from an
area unofficially
known as the
"Rutherford
Bench." This
three-mile
stretch of land
runs from
Rutherford down
to Oakville and
includes vine-
yards that
belong to Heitz
Cellars (Martha's
Vineyard and
Bella Oaks),
Beaulieu,
Freemark Abbey,
Robert Mondavi,
Niebaum-Coppola
(formerly
Inglenook), Far
Niente, Joseph
Phelps, and
others.

- **Mount Veeder**—This area is known for rich Cabernet Sauvignon as well as Chardonnay and Sauvignon Blanc. (Diamond Creek, Hess Collection, Mount Veeder Winery, Mayacamas Vineyards)

- **Stags Leap**—This area is known for Bordeaux-style Cabernet Sauvignons. (Stags Leap Wine Cellars, Chimney Rock, Pine Ridge, Shafer)

- **Russian River Valley**—This area is known for Pinot Noir as well as Chardonnay and Sauvignon Blanc. (Sonoma-Cutrer Vineyards, De Loach Vineyards, Chalk Hill)

- **Alexander Valley**—This area is known for full-bodied Cabernet Sauvignon and Chardonnay. (Jordan, Simi, Chateau Souverain, Murphy-Goode, Stonestreet)

- **Dry Creek Valley**—This area is known for excellent Zinfandel and Cabernet Sauvignon as well as crisp Sauvignon Blanc. (Dry Creek Vineyard, Ferrari-Carano)

- **Paso Robles**—This area is known for Zinfandel and Cabernet Sauvignon. (Ridge)

- **Arroyo Seco**—This area is known for Cabernet Sauvignon as well as Chardonnay, Sauvignon Blanc, and Johannisberg Riesling. (Kendall-Jackson)

Another way to select a good red is to get a grip on the geography. It's most manageable if you take another look at California's five major wine-growing regions.

Here's a look at the regions along with the major grapes for which they are known and a sampling of the wineries that are representative of the area. I find this to be a good reference point when I'm selecting wine.

North Coast

Along the coast of California north of San Francisco lie some of the state's most famous premium wine-producing regions:

- **Napa Valley**—This is traditional Cabernet Sauvignon country, but it also produces top wines from Merlot, Pinot Noir, and Zinfandel as well as white varieties such as Chardonnay and Sauvignon Blanc, which is sometimes known as Fumé Blanc in California. (Many of the old-time vineyards are here such as Charles Krug, Schramsberg, Beringer, Inglenook Vineyards, and Beaulieu in addition to famous "newcomers" like Niebaum-Coppola Estate, William Hill, and Sutter Home.)

- **Sonoma Valley**—This area is known for Cabernet Sauvignon and Pinot Noir as well as Sauvignon Blanc and Chardonnay. (Alexander Valley Vineyards, Belvedere Winery, Chalk Hill, Château St. Jean, Gundlach-Bundschu, Grand Cru, Jordan Vineyard & Winery, Kenwood, Matanzas Creek, Sebastiani, Stone Creek)

- **Mendocino County**—This area is known for a variety of grapes including Cabernet Sauvignon, Merlot, Pinot Noir, and Zinfandel as well as Chardonnay, Sauvignon Blanc, Gerwürztraminer and Riesling. (Fetzer Vineyards, Handley Cellars, Navarro Vineyards, Parducci Wine Cellars)

- **Lake County**—Similar to Mendocino, Lake County is known for Cabernet Sauvignon, Merlot, Pinot Noir, and Zinfandel as well as Chardonnay, Sauvignon Blanc, Gerwürztraminer, and Riesling. (Guenoc, Dunnewood)

Timesaver
You want a guaranteed good red wine from Napa Valley, and you don't want to make yourself crazy looking. Look to these vineyards for Cabernet Sauvignon: Beaulieu Vineyard, Caymus, Clos Du Val, Château Montelena, Freemark Abbey, Heitz, Inglenook, Louis Martini, Mayacamas, Robert Mondavi Reserve, Shafer, Silver Oak, Stag's Leap Wine Cellars, and Sterling. For Merlot, look to Duckhorn and Rutherford Hill. For Pinot Noir, look to Acacia and Saintsbury.

North Central Coast

The North Central Coast begins south of San
Francisco and includes these main regions:

- **Monterey County**—This area is known for
  Cabernet Sauvignon and Pinot Noir as well as
  Pinot Blanc and Chardonnay. (Bernadus
  Vineyards and Winery, Jekel Vineyards,
  Chalone)

- **Livermore Valley**—This area is home to top
  Zinfandels and Cabernet Sauvignon as well as
  Chardonnay, Sémillon, and Sauvignon Blanc.
  (Ridge, Rosenblum, Wente, Concannon)

- **Santa Clara County**—This area is known for
  Cabernet Sauvignon, Merlot, Petite Sirah, and
  Pinot Noir as well as Pinot Blanc and
  Chardonnay. (Mirassou Vineyards)

South Central Coast

Further down the coast but more inland, you'll find
the South Central Coast, which includes these main
regions:

- **San Luis Obispo County**—This area is known
  for Chardonnay and Pinot Noir. (Edna Valley,
  Corbett Canyon Meridian Vineyards)

- **Santa Barbara County**—This area is known for
  Pinot Noir and Syrah as well as Chardonnay.
  (Zaca Mesa and Qupé Wine Cellars)

Central Valley

Within the Central Valley (located inland between
Lodi and Bakersfield), you'll find the San Joaquin
Valley, which is known for producing inexpensive
red grapes such as Barbera, Carigane, and
Grenache, and Zinfandel to produce bulk jug
wine blends, as well as other grapes used for varietal

bottlings. (Delicato Vineyards, E. & J. Gallo Winery, R. H. Phillips Vineyard)

Although the San Joaquin Valley used to be known primarily for quantity, some large producers like Gallo, Robert Mondavi and R. H. Phillips have pushed the envelope on quality and are using many of the grapes grown there to produce their inexpensive varietal lines. Mondavi, for instance, has spearheaded development in the Lodi-Woodbridge area where the company's entry-level Woodbridge wines are produced.

An up-and-coming winery from the Central Valley is Bogle. It's been producing wine for many years but recently has received some good press for its Petite Sirah. Its Merlot is pretty tasty, too. Because it is produced in the southern winemaking region that traditionally has been known for quantity and not quality, Bogle is a discovery wine that offers good value at $10.

Sierra Foothills

East of Sacramento on the edge of the Central Valley, the Sierra Foothills begin and extend up into the mountains. Here you will find Amador County, an area known for big Zinfandels and Cabernet Sauvignon and other robust red varieties. (Amador Foothill Winery, Stevenot Winery)

Meritage wines

Remember that all California wines labeled by varietal must contain at least 75 percent of the grape named on the label. Though it's very common to find varietals made from 100 percent of the grape named on the label, there is a trend toward more blending of top-quality grapes and experimentation to make more expensive wines. A separate category was created for these Bordeaux-style blends, called "Meritage" wines, that carry a proprietary brand name on the label. To be called "Meritage," a winery must be a member of the Meritage Association and use all of the following traditional Bordeaux red grapes in its wines:

- Cabernet Sauvignon
- Merlot
- Cabernet Franc
- Malbec
- Petit Verdot

By definition, Meritage wines are supposed to be the winery's crème-de-la-crème.

"Meritage," as a category (not the wines themselves), has received a lukewarm reception. Some wineries have no desire to belong to yet another association, but they still produce excellent Bordeaux-style blends nonetheless. Whether or not the wine you select is an official "Meritage" wine, if you read the fine print on the front or back label, you often will see the grapes used and sometimes even the percentage of each grape variety.

Some Meritage wines to look for at your wine shop or on a wine list include:

- **Dominus**—made by Christian Moueix, the same winemaker who makes Château Pétrus in Bordeaux, France
- **Insignia**—made by Phelps Vineyards
- **Marlstone**—made by Clos du Bois
- **Opus One**—made by Robert Mondavi Vineyards in partnership with the Baroness Philippine de Rothschild of Château Mouton-Rothschild, a first growth Bordeaux from France

- **Rubicon**—made by Niebaum-Coppola Estate, which is owned by filmmaker Francis Ford Coppola

Other excellent Bordeaux blends include:

- **Trilogy**—made by Flora Springs
- **Cain Five**—a blend of five Bordeaux varieties made by Cain Cellars
- **Cask 23**—a Cabernet Sauvignon blend made by Stag's Leap Wine Cellars
- **Pickberry**—made by Ravenswood, a winery well-known for its Zinfandel wines

California vintages

Vintages do not vary as much in California as they do in other parts of the world, but they do become more important when you are dealing with potential collectibles such as California Cabernets.

TABLE 9.2: RECENT QUALITY VINTAGES

Cabernet Sauvignon	Pinot Noir	Merlot	Zinfandel
1990			
1991			
1992			
1993			
1994		1994	1994
1995	1995	1995	1995
1996	1996	1996	1996
1997	1997	1997	1997
1998	1998	1998	1998

Pacific Northwest

Red wine selection is much easier in the Pacific Northwest because wineries in Washington State and Oregon, unlike those in California, focus on one or two main red grapes. Period. In Washington State, the main red grapes are Merlot and Cabernet Sauvignon. Syrah is just beginning to catch on in popularity, and plantings are on the increase. Oregon, meanwhile, has been developing its reputation of Pinot Noir.

Washington State

Here's a quick review of the geography. Washington State can be divided into three major winemaking regions, which also happen to be federally recognized AVAs:

- **Columbia Valley**—More than 50 percent of the state's vineyards are located in this winemaking region, which is actually an irrigated dessert.

- **Yakima Valley**—This is the second largest winemaking region in the state.

- **Walla Walla Valley**—This is the smallest viticultural area in Washington state and one of the fastest-growing wine areas in the country.

Unofficially...
Chateau Ste. Michelle is Washington state's oldest winery. It was founded in 1934 right after the Repeal of Prohibition. To this day, it remains the largest winery and accounts for about 50 percent of Washington's total wine production.

Although the last two regions are technically part of the Columbia Valley, they are federally-recognized American Viticultural Areas (AVAs) because they are especially good grape growing areas.

Washington State entered the big leagues of wine in 1974 when Chateau Ste. Michelle's Johannisberg Riesling was the top pick at the now-famous *Los Angeles Times* blind tasting. This Washington State Johannisberg Riesling beat out more expensive Rieslings from Germany, Australia, and other parts of the United States.

In no time, Washington State winemakers stepped up their efforts to produce top-quality wines from what they considered to be more marketable grapes: Chardonnay, Sauvignon Blanc, and Sémillon in the whites and Merlot and Cabernet Sauvignon in the reds.

Washington State has done well with Cabernet Sauvignon, but it catapulted to world prominence with its Merlot. In fact, Chateau Ste. Michelle Merlot is one of the best-selling Merlots in the United States. Allen Shoup, CEO of Chateau Ste. Michelle, expects that Syrah will follow in Merlot's footsteps. There are some good Washington State Syrahs on the market now, but Shoup adds that they can't plant quickly enough to keep up with demand. Only time will tell if Syrah turns out to be the next Merlot. Stay tuned.

The top Washington State red wine labels to look for are:

- Chateau Ste. Michelle
- Columbia Crest Winery (sister winery of Chateau Ste. Michelle)
- Chinook Wines (Merlot)
- Covey Run Vintners
- The Hogue Cellars
- Leonetti Cellars
- Pepperbridge
- Preston Wine Cellars
- Staton Hills Winery
- Snoqualmie Winery
- Paul Thomas Winery
- L'Ecole #41
- Gordon Brothers
- Kiona

- Waterbrook Winery
- Woodward Canyon

Good recent vintages to look for in Washington State reds are 1993, 1994, 1995, 1996, 1997, and 1998.

The incredible thing about Washington State is that the majority of the state's more than 100 wineries did not come on the scene until the early 1980s. Since that time, the Washington wine industry has made quantum leaps, as evidenced by its worldwide acceptance as a major top-quality Merlot producer. Not to be outdone by California, another feather in Washington's cap is the recent partnership between Italian winemaker Piero Antinori and Chateau Ste. Michelle, led by the winery's charismatic president, Allen Shoup. The wine, called Col Solare, is made at Chateau Ste. Michelle under the supervision of the winemakers from each winery. The blend may include Cabernet Sauvignon, Merlot, and Syrah. The first vintage, 1995, was released in the spring of 1999. Even with its price tag of $70, Col Solare won't make anyone rich. It will, however, add more buzz to Washington State.

Oregon

If Washington State is the Bordeaux of the New World with its distinctive Cabernet Sauvignon and Merlot, then Oregon is the Burgundy with its Pinot Noir. A few times I have alluded to Oregon's rise in the wine world since Robert Drouhin, a famous French negociant specializing in Burgundy wines, bought property in Oregon back in the 1980s. What I neglected to mention until now is that Oregon, like Washington State, came into the spotlight when one of its Pinot Noirs wowed the French in a tasting in 1979. The wine with the "wow" was an Eyrie Vineyard Pinot Noir.

For the record, Eyrie Vineyard Pinot Noir was made by a former Californian, David Lett, who decided that Oregon provided more desirable growing conditions for Pinot Noir.

Oregon's main wine-growing regions, which also happen to be recognized AVAs, include:

- Willamette Valley
- Umpqua Valley
- Rogue River Valley

The top red wine labels, primarily Pinot Noir, to look for from Oregon include:

- Domaine Drouhin
- Ponzi Vineyards
- Rex Hill Vineyards
- Sokol Blosser Winery
- Erath Vineyards
- Tualatin
- Elk Cove
- Eyrie Vineyards
- Firesteed
- Aldesheim
- Archery Summit
- Beaux Frères
- Bethel Heights Vineyards
- Chehalem Vineyards
- Cooper Mountain Vineyards
- Cristom Vineyards
- Evesham Wood Vineyard
- Eola Hills

- Bridgeview
- Henry Estate
- Lange
- Montinore Vineyards
- Willamette Valley Vineyards
- Oak Knoll

Vintages are more important to Pinot Noir, which can be a difficult grape to grow and make into wine in the first place. It requires a tremendous amount of skill, both in the vineyard as well as in the actual winemaking. Good recent vintages to look for are 1993, 1994, 1996, 1997, and 1998.

Compared to French Burgundy, Pinot Noir from Oregon is said not to have the same ability to age. In general, it's a good idea to drink Pinot Noir from Oregon during its youth to fully appreciate the fresh-picked–berry flavors of the Pacific Northwest. The better-made wines, however, such as those from Domaine Drouhin, Eyrie Vineyards, Ponzi, and Sokol-Blosser, have a tendency to last.

New York State and Long Island

For good red wines from New York, I'm going to direct you straight to Long Island. Of all of New York's wine-growing areas, Long Island has had the greatest success with red wines. Bordeaux varieties such as Cabernet Sauvignon, Merlot, Cabernet Franc, and Petit Verdot are grown on the Island, but the real superstar is Merlot.

The eastern end of Long Island has two of its own specially designated AVAs:

- The Hamptons
- North Fork of Long Island

Look for Merlot and other red varietals and Bordeaux blends from these Long Island wineries:

- Bedell Cellars
- Bridgehampton
- Gristina
- Hargrave Vineyard
- Pelligrini Vineyards
- Pindar Vineyards
- Palmer Vineyards
- Paumanok Vineyards
- Peconic Bay Vineyards

Just the facts

- California wine country offers the biggest selection of red grape varietals and styles made in America.
- Zinfandel *is* a red grape, and it definitely is worth exploring.
- Most American red wines are ready to drink upon release, but there are reds, especially California Cabernet Sauvignons, worthy of cellar aging and collecting.
- California makes some great Merlot but also look to Washington State and Long Island, New York.
- Bordeaux blends from California, Washington State, Oregon, and New York State (particularly Long Island) rival those of France.
- Some major European winemakers are either partnering with American wine producers or buying U.S. vineyards outright to produce great wines.

- Syrah will be the next big red grape in America.

- The American wine industry is a baby next to its European counterparts, and it will continue to evolve.

GET THE SCOOP ON...

Italian reds for every occasion ▪ Bold reds from Spain ▪ Surprise values from Portugal ▪ Shiraz from Down Under ▪ The Bordeaux of the Southern hemisphere ▪ Malbec from Argentina ▪ An unusually good grape from South Africa

Old- and New-World Reds

Consider Chapter 7, "Old- and New-World Whites," as an aperitif to whet your appetite for what is to follow in reds. White wines can be very enjoyable and thirst-quenching, especially during warmer weather, but good reds with all their layers of flavors are for savoring.

Now the plot thickens. Practically every "Old-World" and "New-World" region in this chapter brings at least one native grape to the table to produce their signature wine. They may very well also produce other international varietals, a growing trend in the wine world, but their reputation is built on their native grape and style.

As you learned in Chapter 7, wine from Europe is considered to be "Old World." Wine from everywhere else is considered to be "New World." Because France and the United States are covered separately in this book, these are the wine regions you'll find on the following pages:

TABLE 10.1: OLD AND NEW WORLD

"Old World"	"New World"
Italy	Australia
Spain	Chile
Portugal	Argentina
	South Africa

New Zealand is considered part of the "New World," but in terms of selecting the best wines from this country and the ones you are most likely to find in the United States, stick to the whites, especially Sauvignon Blanc. Be advised, however, that New Zealand is working hard on its reds, especially Pinot Noirs. These will be the ones to watch in the near future.

From Italy with love

Like Italy's food, which I adore, Italian red wine is something you can really sink your teeth into. Whether you are having a little pannini sandwich or a pizza or you are enjoying a plate of pasta or lobster risotto, there is a wine for you. Vines cover practically every inch of this Mediterranean boot. It's no wonder that Italy is the number one wine producer in the world.

The Italians take special care with their red wines. Look at the table on the following page to pick out the major red-wine–growing regions and the reds for which they are known.

Italy's notable native red-grape varieties are:

▪ Nebbiolo

▪ Barbera

▪ Dolcetto

▪ Sangiovese

TABLE 10.2: ITALIAN REGIONS AND THEIR REDS

Region	Wine
Tuscany	Chianti (as in Sangiovese), Brunello di Montalcino
Piedmont	Barbera, Dolcetto, Nebbiolo
Veneto	Bardolino, Valpolicella
Abruzzo	Montepulciano d'Abruzzo
Apulia	Salice Salentino
Lombardy (specifically the district)	Grumello, Inferno, Valtellina Sassella, Valgella
Friuli	Merlot, Cabernet Sauvignon, Cabernet Franc
Trentino-Alto Adige	Cabernet Sauvignon, Merlot

Italy also dabbles in these international varieties:

- Cabernet Sauvignon
- Merlot
- Cabernet Franc

Quality control, Italian style

Italy uses two special designations, similar to the AOC laws, to control the quality of its wines. These designations are:

> Denominazione di Origine Controllata (DOC)
>
> Denominazione di Origine Controllata Garantita (DOCG)

The "G" for "guaranteed" is the highest designation a wine can receive.

For a wine to be eligible for DOC or DOCG designation, it must conform to the rules and regulations governing the following:

1. The grape varietal that can be used to make different styles of wine

2. The grape blend—how much of a certain grape must be included in a given wine

3. Acceptable grape yields—the maximum amount of wine that can be made from a vineyard

4. The geographical boundaries between individual wine regions

5. The minimum aging requirements for different wines

6. The minimum alcohol content for some wines

Ironically, the very laws that were intended to safeguard the quality of Italian wines threatened to pigeonhole the category into a status quo, "same old, same old" situation. A new generation of Italian winemakers started to question the rules, especially after seeing and tasting the new and different styles that were coming out of California, where winemakers are not bound by ironclad tradition. They started to experiment on their own with different grape varietals, different blends, and different aging techniques such as using the smaller French oak barrels instead of the industrial-size tanks.

Because these winemakers dared to be different and ventured to use "New-World" techniques, their wines could not be granted DOC or DOCG status even though technically many of them are of better quality, and their higher price tag reflects the special TLC they receive. By Italian law, they must be labeled *vino da tavola,* or table wine. Unlike other Italian wines that are named for their place of origin or their grape varietal, these Super-Tuscan "vino da tavola" wines carry proprietary names. Some of the better-known ones are:

- Cabreo Il Borgo

- Excelsus

- Fontalloro

- Flaccianello

- Ornellaia

- Sassicaia

- Solaia (Antinori)

- Sammarco

- Summus (Castello Banfi)

- Tignanello (Antinori)

Tuscany

This region in the heart of Italy makes some of the best and most expensive wines that the country has to offer. Chianti, Brunello di Montalcino, Vino Nobile di Montepulciano, and Carmignano make up Tuscany's roster of wines.

Chianti

Chianti is made from a minimum of 75 percent Sangiovese with the addition of other grapes including up to 10 percent of "nontraditional" grapes such as Cabernet Sauvignon, Merlot, or Syrah. Chianti ranges in style from light and fruity to more tannic and complex, and it makes an excellent accompaniment to food. Over the past several years, Chianti has made a huge comeback thanks to the proliferation of Italian restaurants, from the independent mom-and-pop restaurants to full-fledged casual-restaurant chains like The Olive Garden and California Pizza Kitchen.

There are three quality levels of Chianti, from the most basic and least expensive to the more expensive and age-worthy:

TABLE 10.3: TYPES OF CHIANTI

Quality	Name	Description
Good	Chianti	Light and fruity
Better	Chianti Classico	Must come from the more specific "Classico" appellation in the heart of Chianti
Best	Chianti Classico Riserva	Must come from the more specific "Classico" appellation in the heart of Chianti and undergo a minimum aging of 27 months

Top Chianti producers include:

- Antinori
- Badia a Coltibuono
- Brolio
- Castello Banfi
- Castello di Gabbiano
- Cecchi
- Felsina
- Marchesi de' Frescolbaldi
- Melini
- Nozzole
- Poggerino
- Ricasoli
- Ruffino
- San Felice

Brunello di Montalcino

Brunello de Montalcino is one of Italy's more expensive wines that is made from the Sangiovese grape. This Tuscan DOCG wine is intended to be aged anywhere from 5, 10, or even 20 years to enhance your drinking pleasure.

Look for some of these top Brunello di Montalcino producers:

- Altesino
- Barbi
- Biondi-Santi
- Carparzo
- Castello Banfi
- Col d'Orcia
- Poggio Antico

Vino Nobile di Montepulciano

Vino Nobile di Montepulciano is made primarily from the Sangiovese grape and also is expensive. This DOCG wine offers a little more fruit than the Brunello di Montalcino, which makes it a little more approachable, yet it is still full-flavored and robust.

Top producers of Vino Nobile di Montepulciano include:

- Avignonesi
- Boscarelli
- Fassati
- Poggio alla Sala

Carmignano

This DOCG wine is produced in an area only about 10 miles west of Florence. The Sangiovese grape forms the spine of this wine that is more tannic and less acidic than Chianti. Unlike Chianti, however, Carmignano uses up to 10 percent Cabernet Sauvignon in its blend. This adds a pleasant depth and complexity to the wine.

Moneysaver
If you don't want to pay the price for a Brunello di Montalcino, buy a Rosso di Montalcino instead. It's from the same area, but it comes from younger vines and is made in a fruitier style. It's not intended to be aged like the Brunello di Montalcino.

Reliable producers of Carmignano include:

- Ambra
- Artimino
- Poggiolo
- Villa Capezzana

As always, when you go to select a wine, make sure it comes from a reliable producer and then check the vintage. The most-recent better vintages to look for from Tuscany are 1990, 1993, 1995, 1997, and 1998.

Piedmont

This other major-league red wine region, which, incidentally, borders France, is home to two of Italy's most famous and generally expensive full-bodied wines:

- Barbaresco
- Barolo

Both wines, which are named for the villages within Piedmont where they are made, are produced from Italy's native Nebbiolo grape. They are similar in style, but Barolo is a bit more complex and "big," for lack of a better word, because it must undergo a little more aging than Barbaresco, which is stylistically lighter yet elegant by comparison.

Barbaresco and Barolo will both benefit from additional aging in your cellar. They can easily stand an additional 10 years of aging after their release and sometimes even more before you uncork them.

Top Barbaresco and Barolo producers include:

- Borgogno
- Fontanafredda
- Gaja

Moneysaver
If you don't want to spend the money on a Barbaresco or a Barolo, but you'd like to drink something that is comparable in style, try a Nebbiolo d'Alba that is made just outside the Barbaresco and Barolo areas. You will taste more fruit in the wine because it is not aged to the same degree.

- Pio Cesare
- Prunotto
- Renato Ratti
- Ceretto
- G. Conterno
- Conterno
- Michele Chiarlo
- Marchesi de Gresy
- Marchesi di Barolo
- Marcarini
- Giacosa
- Vietti

Fortunately, Piedmont produces other wonderful wines that are approachable practically upon release, and you can enjoy these while you wait for your Barolo and Barbaresco to mature. They often are a good value, though I'm watching the prices inch up as more wine drinkers discover them. Ranked from the lightest to the more full-bodied, they are:

- **Dolcetto**—This grape native to Italy is light-bodied and fruity. It often is described as the Beaujolais of Italy, though it is not as fruity as the French grape.

- **Barbera**—This deep-ruby-red grape is so prolific in Piedmont that it is known as a versatile everyday drinking wine.

- **Gattinara**—This small village in Piedmont, near Barbaresco and Barolo, produces delicious, easy-drinking reds from the Nebbiolo grape. The Nebbiolo grape is known locally as "Spanna," which is good for you to know in

Timesaver
For both Dolcetto and Barbera wines, seek out those from the Alba area. The label will read Dolcetto d'Alba or Barbera d'Alba. Barbera also is good from another areas known as Asti, (hence, Barbera d'Asti).

case you come across a little gem on the wine list or at your favorite wine shop.

In addition to many of the top Piedmont producers previously listed, one of my favorites is Travaglini.

Recent vintages to look for from Piedmont are 1990, 1993, 1995, 1996, 1997, and 1998.

Veneto: land of Valpolicella, Bardolino, and Amarone

Aside from Italy's popular, fizzy, sweet Lambrusco wines that so many Americans cut their wine teeth on before White Zinfandel was invented, the next step up is Valpolicella and Bardolino. It never occurred to me until I started to study wine that these two wines come from Veneto. It never really mattered because Valpolicella and Bardolino took on brand status—as did their white counterpart, Soave—in the same way that many casual wine drinkers today think of Chardonnay. You'd be surprised at how many people believe Chardonnay is a brand.

In any event, as wine consumers have become more sophisticated, wine producers from Veneto are doing their best to take their wines to the next level. Some boutique producers have picked out their top vineyards to produce single-vineyard Valpolicella, which is supposed to be a cut above and show more intensity. I'm not so convinced. When I'm looking for an inexpensive basic red to sit down with a pizza or something *pomodoro*, I still reach for one of these old faithfuls.

Three of the more familiar labels are:

- Bolla
- Folonari
- Santa Sofia

If you are looking for a more robust wine that packs a punch, try an Amarone. It is a special type of Valpolicella made from the ripest grapes on the vine. The grapes are picked and left to dry on a mat until they shrivel like raisins. The intensely sweet grapes are then crushed and made into wine. In the process, the winemaker allows most of the sugar to ferment and turn into alcohol. This means you end up with a dry wine that is higher in alcohol content than your average table wine. Instead of an average alcohol content of 12 percent, an Amarone has more like 14 to 16 percent. Even though it sounds like it has all the makings of a dessert wine, Amarone is a perfect choice for heavier dishes or strong cheeses.

Due to the specialized nature of Amarone, expect to pay $25 and up for a good bottle such as those made by:

- Allegrini
- Bertani
- Bolla
- Masi
- Tommasi

Other Italian reds

In addition to Tuscany, Piedmont, and Veneto, there are other Italian wine regions worth exploring for your red-wine–drinking pleasure.

- **Abruzzo**—This region, located at the calf of the boot on the Adriatic Sea, produces easy-drinking, affordable reds called Montepulciano d'Abruzzo. They are made from the Montepulciano grape.
- **Apulia**—Located on the heel of the boot, Apulia produces a red called Salice Salentino

that is a little rough around the edges but not
bad for a daily quaff.

- **Lombardy** (specifically the Valtellina district)—
  Some lightweight reds made from the
  Nebbiolo grape come from this northern
  region that borders on Switzerland. Individual
  villages to look for are Grumello, Inferno,
  Sassella, and Valgella.

- **Friuli**—Italy's northeasternmost region has
  had considerable success with these red international varieties: Merlot, Cabernet Sauvignon,
  and Cabernet Franc.

- **Trentino-Alto Adige**—This is another northeastern region, neighboring Friuli, that produces some excellent, food-friendly examples
  of Cabernet Sauvignon and Merlot.

Olé for Spanish reds

Over the past 10 to 15 years, Spain has aggressively
given itself a makeover to shake off its provincial
ways and to show the world that it is a significant
global player, alongside the rest of the European
Union. Madrid has undergone an incredible trans-
formation with new building and industry;
Barcelona has hosted the Olympics, a major coup;
and in the wine industry, state-of-the-art wineries
and techniques are becoming more common.

As a result, the red wines, like the whites, are
fresher and fruitier. The traditional heavily oxidized
monsters are mostly a thing of the past. In the
process, some new wine regions have emerged that
are creating exciting new Spanish styles, and some
of the long-established producers continue to
improve their wines. In addition to all the quality

enhancements, the good news is that Spanish wine still represents good price quality, whether you are buying a bottle for under $10 or you are splurging on a $30 to $40 bottle.

Spain's three major red-wine–growing regions are:

- Rioja
- Ribera del Duero
- Penedès

Throughout Spain's winemaking regions, you'll find wines made from these two native grapes:

- **Tempranillo**—This is Spain's version of Cabernet Sauvignon.
- **Garnacha**—We know it as Grenache. In Spain, however, it often is blended with Tempranillo to round out the wine and to add dimension.

You'll also see Cabernet Sauvignon and Merlot appearing more often out of Spain.

Historic Rioja

It's no coincidence that Spain's red-wine-making industry began in Rioja, close to the French border. When a root louse known as phylloxera (fil-LOX-er-ra) infested the vineyards of France, virtually eating its way across Bordeaux and other parts of Europe, some French winemakers crossed the border to set up shop in Rioja where the climate and growing conditions are similar. Although the native grape variety in Rioja is Tempranillo, not the Cabernet Sauvignon, Cabernet Franc, or Merlot of Bordeaux, to this day, you can still find wines from Rioja made in a Bordeaux style. There is fruit in the wine, but it is usually more subdued.

Bright Idea!
When I'm looking for a good value in reds, I usually scan the Spanish-wine section. I almost always find a reliable producer that has a wine with a few extra years of age on it, something that is more desirable in red wines. In 2000, for example, instead of settling for a 1998 Merlot or Cabernet, I can probably get a Spanish red from 1995 or 1996.

The top Rioja producers are:

- Bodegas Montecillo
- Compañia Vinicola del Norte de España (CUNE)
- La Rioja Alta
- Lopez de Heredia
- Marqués de Cáceres
- Marqués de Riscal
- Marqués de Murrieta
- Martínez Bujanda
- Muga

Age matters

A certain amount of additional age and quality go hand in hand with red Rioja wines. Important terms to look for on the label, from least to most expensive, that will help you make your selection are listed in the table below.

TABLE 10.3: SPANISH TERMS FOR LEVELS OF WINE QUALITY

Quality	Term	Description
Good	Crianza	The wine has undergone a total of two years of aging with a minimum of one year in an oak barrel.
Better	Reserva	The wine has undergone a total of three years of aging with a minimum of one year in oak.
Best	Gran Reserva	The wine has undergone a total of five years of aging with a minimum of two years in oak.

Unofficially...
Here are two important points about aging: Reserva and Gran Reserva wines are made only in the best years. The best Spanish-wine producers usually exceed the minimum requirements.

In addition to the level of quality (Crianza, Reserva, Gran Reserva) that will appear on some Spanish labels, other important elements to look for are:

Denominacíon de Origen—Region of origin

Producer

Cosecha (Spanish for "harvest" or vintage year)

Brand or proprietary name of the wine

Importer

Alcohol content

Ribera del Duero

Ribera del Duero has been producing red wine for centuries, but it's relatively new to Americans because not many different brands have been available. This is changing rapidly, however, because more bodegas (wineries) are springing up in the region, and more wines from the area are being exported. The red wines from the Tempranillo grape yield intense red color and highly concentrated fruit flavors with a good amount of tannin for balance.

Ribera del Duero is probably not the place to look for values, but there are some excellent wines to be had. Two of my favorite producers are:

- Vega Sicilia
- Pesquera

There are many other reliable producers on the market including:

- Balbas
- Boada
- Emilio Moro
- Fuentespina
- Ibernoble
- Mattaromera
- Melior

- Protos
- Valduero
- Viña Mayor

Like Rioja, Ribera del Duero uses the designations of age on its labels: Crianza, Reserva, and Gran Reserva. The only difference is that Ribera del Duero uses an additional designation to show that a wine is young, or "joven." These are wines that have not been aged in wood or that have been aged in the barrel for less than one year.

Penedès

Penedès, just south of Barcelona in the Cataloñia region, is famous for its state-of-the-art sparkling-wine facilities where wineries like Freixenet and Codorniu produce Cava. When it comes to red wine, however, Penedès is one of the more innovative regions of Spain. In addition to the native Tempranillo and Garnacha grapes, you see a lot more cutting-edge winemaking done with Cabernet Sauvignon.

My two favorite red-wine producers from Penedès are:

- Torres
- Jean León

The Torres family, in particular, produces a full range of Spanish wines, both red and white, for every pocketbook. The family is among the first to label some of their wines by varietal such as "Merlot." Worth a splurge, however, if you can find it, is the Torres Gran Coronas. This is its top-of-the-line bottling of Cabernet Sauvignon with a distinctive black label that goes for about $50.

In Spain, your better red-wine vintages are 1982, 1989, 1991, 1994, 1995, 1996, 1997, and 1998.

Unofficially...
Two up-and-coming red-wine regions in Spain are Priorato, which is near Penedès, and Navarra, which is next to Rioja. Priorato produces some very good Rhône-style reds. Navarra, better known for its refreshing rosé wine, also produces some good red wines from its native Garnacha grape, and it is beginning to use international varieties like Cabernet Sauvignon and Merlot.

Portugal sees red

Unless I'm in Portugal, it doesn't occur to me to look for a red Portuguese wine, but this is slowly changing. Like the rest of the Iberian Peninsula, Portugal is getting with the program to make wines that people outside of the country want to buy.

The major red-wine-growing regions of Portugal are:

■ **Dão**—The most famous region

■ **Douro**—A well-established region

■ **Bairrada**—An up-and-coming region

■ **Alentejo**—An up-and-coming region

For now, traditional grape varietals native to Portugal (normally blended) are your best bet. These are the same grapes used to produce Port, which attests to their quality. Don't be concerned with sweetness, however, because unlike Port, which is a fortified wine, Portugal's red table wines are fermented in a dry style. The most prominent grapes are:

■ Touriga Nacional (in Dão and in the Douro)

■ Touriga Francesa

■ Tinta Roriz

■ Tempranillo (in the Douro)

■ Baga (in Bairrada)

■ Castelão Frances (also known as Periquita in the south)

Winemakers are experimenting with international varieties such as Cabernet Sauvignon and Merlot, but these are not nearly mainstream yet.

When you select a Portuguese wine, you might come across some of the following terms:

Unofficially...
I've already mentioned the Rothschild family's investment in Chile with Los Vascos. More recently, Domaine Rothschild (Lafite) has invested in an old estate called Quinta do Carmo in southern Portugal's Alentejo area.

- **Garrafeira**—Technically, this means that the wine has undergone additional aging (two years in wood and one in the bottle). Some producers use the term to refer to their better bottlings.
- **Colheita**—This term means vintage.
- **Quinta**—This term means estate or vineyard.
- **Tinto**—This term means red.

Some top producers of Portuguese red wines include:

- Adega Cooperative de Borba
- Caves Aliança
- Caves Velhas
- Ferreira
- J.P. Vinhos
- Quinta do Carmo
- Ramos Pinto
- Sogrape

Australia

There is nothing discrete about Australia's red wines. They are big and juicy and are brimming over with fruit. It's relatively easy to select an Australian wine because producers put the name of the grape varietal on the label, just as we do in the United States.

As for where the red grapes grow, in Australia, it's really up to the winemakers. They can plant their red grapes wherever they can make them grow. Some areas do better than others, and this is why the appellations are beginning to take on a little more importance than they used to.

The top wine regions are listed in the following table.

TABLE 10.4: AUSTRALIAN WINE REGIONS

Region	Area	Types of Wine Produced
New South Wales	Hunter Valley	Shiraz and Cabernet Sauvignon
	Mudgee	
South Australia	Barossa Valley	Shiraz and Cabernet Sauvignon
	Coonawarra	World-class Cabernet Sauvignon
	Clare Valley	Shiraz
	McLaren Vale	
Victoria	Yarra Valley	Pinot Noir
	Goulburn Valley	Red Rhône varietals
	Rutherglen	
Western Australia	Margaret River	Bordeaux-style reds
	Pemberton	

Within these regions, the top appellations are considered to be:

- Barossa Valley

- Coonawarra

- Hunter Valley

- Margaret River

You've probably tasted many of the red varietals Australia produces even if the wines were not from Australia. You have probably had a Cabernet Sauvignon from California or a Pinot Noir from the Burgundy region of France. Still, Australia does put its own spin on the grape. Here is a taste profile of the main varieties:

- **Shiraz**—Australia is best known for this grape that is known as Syrah in other parts of the world, notably the Rhône Valley. Like the Rhône wines, the Australian version is big and saucy.

- **Cabernet Sauvignon**—Typically, the Australians make their Cabernet a lot like those of California. Again, it is heavy on the fruit but dry.

  The neat little twist here is that, many times, Australian winemakers will blend their Shiraz with Cabernet Sauvignon to create a wine that is uniquely Australian.

- **Grenache**—Australia blends with this Rhône-style grape.

- **Mourvèdre**—This Rhône grape is turning up in more Rhône-style blends from Australia.

- **Merlot**—It was only a matter of time until Merlot mania reached Australia. Expect to see more Merlot coming out of Australia, used as both a 100 percent varietal and as part of a blend.

- **Pinot Noir**—An up-and-coming grape for Australia, this is lighter and more elegant when done correctly.

Reliable producers of Australian red wines include:

- Château Reynella
- Hardy's
- Lindemans
- Orlando
- Penfolds
- Petaluma
- Rosemount Estate
- Rothbury
- Seaview
- Seppelt

- Tyrell's
- Wolf Blass
- Yalumba

As with its white wines, you can't go wrong with Australian vintages. Over the past 10 years, there has been such minimal variation from vintage to vintage that it's not really worth making yourself crazy for the everyday wines. The only exception would be for anyone who collects Australian wines because there are many age-worthy collectibles.

Chile

Unlike many of the other "Old-World" and "New-World" wine countries, Chile has not developed a reputation for its own native grape but for its easy adaptability at producing any number of international varieties. Chile is emerging as the Bordeaux of the Southern Hemisphere, thanks to the growing conditions, climate, and soil so conducive to varieties like Cabernet Sauvignon and Merlot. Foreign investment by high-profile French and American winemaking families hasn't hurt either.

The wine regions known best for their red wines are:

Unofficially...
Top winemakers from Bordeaux and California have been consulting with their Chilean counterparts to help make better-quality wine. It appears to be working.

TABLE 10.5: CHILEAN WINE REGIONS

Region	Types of Wine Produced
Maipo Valley	Cabernet Sauvignon
Rapel Valley and the subregion of Colchagua	Merlot and Cabernet Sauvignon
Maule and the subregion called Curicó Valley	Cabernet Sauvignon

Top producers from Chile make many wines in the $10-and-under category that are quite welcome for everyday consumption. Recently, we have begun to see some Chilean wineries push the envelope on winemaking practices and pricing as they release their "Super-Chileans" at over $50.

Two recent "Super-Chileans" introduced to the market are:

- Montes Alpha "M"
- Seña (made from the partnership between Robert Mondavi Winery in California and Errazuriz Winery of Chile)

Of course, they are made in limited supply, but if a $55 bottle from Chile flies, which was unheard of until recently (and insiders predict that they will), expect to see more expensive bottlings from Chile as well as less price resistance in the $12 to $15 range where you will certainly get a good bottle of red wine.

A sampling of reliable producers of Chilean red wine includes:

- Caliterra
- Carmen
- Carta Vieja
- Casa Lapostolle
- Concha y Toro (Beginning with the 1999 vintage, their most inexpensive wines will be marketed under the name "Frontera.")
- Montes
- Walnut Crest
- Undurraga
- Veremonte
- Viña Santa Carolina
- Santa Rita
- San Pedro

Argentina

Like any firstborn, there's no doubt that Chile broke significant ground in becoming a player in the international wine industry. Now it's Argentina's turn to tango, and it is doing so with the red grape Malbec.

Winemakers are exploring and experimenting within the different wine regions of Argentina to determine which grapes grow best. When it comes to red wine and specifically to Malbec, however, the place is Mendoza.

Even within Mendoza, winemakers are taking a "California" approach and comparing grape quality from one vineyard to the next. Trapiche, for example, the biggest winery in all of Argentina, recently introduced its own "super" wine (with a super $55 price tag) called Iscay. The wine was created by Bordeaux wine wizard Michel Rolland, who teamed up with Trapiche's winemaker Angel Mendoza to select the best of the best. They blended 50 percent Malbec from their Las Palmas vineyard with 50 percent Merlot from Trapiche's El Chiche vineyard. This might not mean a great deal to many wine drinkers yet, but this is how California got started. So, you can see where things are headed.

You don't have to pay more than $50 for a good bottle of red wine from Argentina. In fact, there are many in the $10-and-under category. The field broadens, of course, if you're willing to spend a bit more.

Some good red-wine producers from Argentina include:

- Alamos Ridge
- Bianchi
- Bodegas Esmerelda

- Bodega Norton
- Catena
- Etchart
- Finca Flichman
- Navarro Correas
- Trapiche
- Weinert

South Africa

Now that the political dust has settled, there couldn't be a better time to discover the wines of South Africa. The country produces many of the red varietals we know and love such as Cabernet Sauvignon, Merlot, and even Shiraz (which they refer to as Syrah). You might even find some good values in these wines, but for my money and occasional bouts with ABC (anything but Cabernet), pour me a Pinotage.

Pinotage is a grape variety widely grown in South Africa that perhaps is best described as the yin and the yang of grapes. It combines the elegance of Pinot Noir with the cruder Cinsault, and the combination works beautifully.

South Africa's wine country is fairly localized to the southern tip of the country.

The major regions are:

- **Stellenbosch**—This area is best known for its red wines including Pinotage. Many of South Africa's better-quality wineries are based here.

- **Constantia**—This area is known for Cabernet Sauvignon.

- **Paarl**—This area is known for good reds as well as late-harvest whites.

- **Robertson**

Reliable producers of South African reds, especially Pinotage, include:

- Backsberg Estate
- Beyerskloof
- Cheetah Valley
- Clos Malverne
- Kanonkop Estate

Good recent vintages for South African red wines are 1994, 1995, and 1996. Most South African reds are ready to be consumed upon release, and they are not the type of wine you would lay down in the wine cellar for major aging.

Just the facts

- If you have recently discovered Sangiovese, try Chianti from Italy.
- Barbaresco and Barolo are Italy's "big league" reds.
- Rioja offers one of the best values for older, smoother-tasting red wines.
- If you like red Bordeaux, try a red wine from Chile and save a few bucks.
- Argentina is making Malbec another red variety to watch and to add to your personal wine repertoire.
- Pinotage from South Africa offers a completely different and totally welcome red-wine flavor.

All Blush and Bubbles

PART IV

GET THE SCOOP ON...

The difference between rosé and blush wine ▪
How pink wines are made ▪ How Sutter Home
encouraged more people to pull corks ▪ The garden variety of grapes used to make rosé ▪ Where
the best rosés come from ▪ How to select and
enjoy rosé wine

Rosé or Blush Wine

W hat is the difference between a rosé and a blush wine? Wine wizards will tell you that, technically, a blush wine is paler in color than a rosé. Chances are, if the wine is labeled "blush," it is American because the term was first used on California pink wines. Blush wines are generally sweeter than those from Europe. "Rosé" is more likely to be European, although there are American winemakers who call their pink wine "rosé." Other paler rosé wines might be called "Vin Gris." Again, these usually come from Europe, notably the Loire Valley. I say pink is pink. Try a few different kinds, get to know what style you prefer, and enjoy it.

How and where rosés are made

There are two commonly used methods to make rosé wines. The first method, and the most important for our purposes in this chapter, is to crush red grapes and separate the red skins from the juice to extract a minimum amount of color. Keep in mind that the grape juice, even in red grapes, is actually white. It is the red skin that gives red wine its color.

243

The longer the winemaker allows the skins to remain in contact with the juice, the deeper the hue. The resulting pink grape juice is then fermented and vinified as if it were a white wine. This means that the grape juice, also known as "must," will be fermented on its own, away from the skins. In red-wine production, the grape juice is fermented with the skins for a longer period to extract the red color and the tannin and complexity that one expects from red wine.

The second method involves blending red and white wine to make rosé. The Champagne region in France is one of the few wine regions that permits this blending process. Rosé Champagnes will be covered more in Chapter 12, "Sparkle Plenty."

TABLE 11.1: THE RED GRAPES AND THEIR PINK ALIAS NAMES

Red Grape	Pink Alias Name
Zinfandel	White Zinfandel
Pinot Noir	Blanc de Pinot Noir, Blanc de Noir
Cabernet Sauvignon	Cabernet Blanc, Cabernet Blush
Grenache	White Grenache, Vin Gris
Merlot	Merlot Rosé
Barbera	Rosato

Places where rosé or blush wines are commonly made include:

- **France**—These wines are made in the Loire Valley (Rosé d'Anjou), Provence, Languedoc-Roussillon (sometimes referred to as the Midi), the southern Rhône Valley (Tavel), and Champagne (blanc de noir).

- **California**—These wines can be found in all winegrowing regions.

- **Spain**—Spain is developing an excellent reputation for rosé wines, especially those from Navarra which are known as rosado.
- **Italy**—Rosé wines are known as rosato.

Sutter Home's "overnight" success

One of every 10 bottles of table wine in the United States today is a white Zinfandel of some sort.

It all started in the 1970s with a then-little-known winery called Sutter Home. This winery was known for making robust-style red Zinfandels. (Remember that Zinfandel is a red grape. There is no such thing as a white Zinfandel grape.) At the time, red wine was not "in," and if most wine consumers were drinking red, it was not Zinfandel.

According to Sutter Home folklore, Louis "Bob" Trinchero was experimenting with ways to make his Amador County Reserve Zinfandel more robust when he decided to drain some grape juice from the vat to increase the concentration of the remaining grape juice with the red skins. He continued to ferment the concentrated vat of grape juice and skins into a heartier red Zinfandel. Meanwhile, he had this leftover grape juice. Just for fun, he fermented the pale pink juice like a dry French rosé and offered the wine as a curiosity to guests who visited the winery's tasting room. Although people were interested in this pink libation as a novelty, they thought the wine was too dry. The official story is that, in response, Trinchero started leaving a small amount of residual sugar in this "White Zinfandel" to add a hint of sweetness, which made it easier for many to enjoy. That's one version. But unofficially, I have heard that Trinchero had been making a limited quantity of white Zinfandel for a

Unofficially...
Originally, Bob Trinchero called his blush wine "Oeil de Pedrix," which means "Eye of the Partridge" in French. The Bureau of Alcohol, Tobacco, and Firearms, which regulates the wine business in the United States, nixed the name because it required an English translation on the label. Trinchero decided to keep it simple—White Zinfandel.

few years when, in a fluke of fermentation, which happens sometimes, the wine he produced came out a bit sweeter than he had intended.

Bob Trinchero added the word "blush" to the label because the term "rosé" was not en vogue in the United States, and the White Zinfandel flew out of his tasting room doors. Shortly thereafter, Bob and his brother, Roger, realized that they had backed into a major wine trend and made the conscious decision to increase production of Sutter Home White Zinfandel. From its original 220 cases made as a novelty, Sutter Home White Zinfandel today sells more than 4 million cases per year. After struggling as a mom-and-pop winery for more than 35 years, Sutter Home became an overnight success in the 1980s.

The brand's astounding success spawned a whole new category of American blush wines, much to the chagrin of the wine media and "serious" winemakers who looked down their noses at this light, refreshing, fruity, and yes, sweet, pink elixir. Many wineries, including a few "serious" ones, hopped on the bandwagon to produce blush wines made from the Zinfandel grape, but others sought to emulate the success with grapes like Cabernet Sauvignon, Grenache, and Merlot. After all, in addition to Beaujolais Nouveau, in terms of cash flow, white Zinfandel is relatively easy to produce, requires no aging to speak of, and provides a return on investment within a few weeks of the harvest. White Zinfandel has turned into a 21-million-case-per-year business, making white Zinfandel the number two "white wine" favorite of consumers behind Chardonnay.

Ironically, Sutter Home recently introduced a Merlot Rosé to capitalize on America's love affair with the Merlot grape and the winery's signature blush wine style for which it has become famous. This time, however, Sutter Home decided to go with the word "rosé" instead of "blush" on the label, probably in an effort to keep the Sutter Home White Zinfandel blush franchise at a reasonable distance from its new Merlot Rosé but also because it is supposed to be more European in style, down to the darker color.

Some major players that you can expect to see in the white Zinfandel blush market include:

- Sutter Home
- Beringer
- Glen Ellen
- Gallo
- Fetzer
- Robert Mondavi Winery
- Sebastiani (Vendange White Zinfandel)

You'd be surprised at how many California wineries make a blush, rosé, vin gris, or whatever they might call their pink wine, even if it's made in only limited quantities. Following is a sampling of some well-known wineries that produce pink wine, along with what they call it. Perhaps your favorite winery is on this selective list. If you don't see the pink wine on the market, chances are you'll find it in their tasting room if you get a chance to visit wine country.

TABLE 11.2: ROSÉ- OR BLUSH-PRODUCING WINERIES IN CALIFORNIA

Winery	Their Wine
Beaulieu Vineyards	Pinot Noir Vin Gris, Sangiovese Bianco
Bonny Doon	Vin Gris (Rhône style)
Cakebread	Rosé
Château Potelle	Rosé
Chimney Rock	Rosé of Pinot Noir
Cline Cellars	Vin Gris (Rhône style)
Corbett Canyon Vineyards	White Zinfandel
Creston Vineyards Winery	White Zinfandel
Deer Valley Vineyards	White Zinfandel
Delicato Vineyards	White Zinfandel
DeLoach Vineyards	White Zinfandel
Emerald Bay Winery	White Zinfandel
Heitz Wine Cellars	Grignolino Rosé
Louis Martini Winery	White Zinfandel
McDowell Valley Vineyards	Grenache Rosé
Mirassou Vineyards	White Zinfandel
The Monterey Vineyard	White Zinfandel
Parducci Wine Cellars	White Zinfandel
J. Pedroncelli Winery	White Zinfandel and Zinfandel Rosé
Joseph Phelps Vineyards	Grenache Rosé (Rhône style)
R.H. Phillips Vineyard	White Zinfandel
Sanford Winery	Pinot Noir Vin Gris
Simi Winery	Rosé of Cabernet Sauvignon
Stone Creek Wines	White Zinfandel
F. Teldeschi Winery	White Zinfandel

French rosé

Rosé wines in France generally are dry as opposed to American blush wines, particularly white Zinfandel, which is on the sweet side. They can be produced from a wide variety of grapes and are usually simple wines, though it is possible to find a more distinctive rosé made from grapes like Pinot Noir or Cabernet Sauvignon. As a general rule, the younger the rosé, the better, so drink them while they're young without any pomp or circumstance, well chilled.

In France, you will find the finest rosés produced in the areas discussed in the following sections.

Loire Valley

The most famous of the Loire Valley's rosé wines is Rosé d'Anjou. It is made from grapes such as Gamay and Malbec as well as other local red varietals. Compared to other French rosé wine, Rosé d'Anjou is considered to be "off-dry," which means it has at least a hint of sweetness, more like an American blush wine.

A drier rosé from the Loire Valley is Rosé de Loire, which must contain at least 30 percent Cabernet Franc in its blend with other local grapes.

Another drier-style rosé from the Loire is called Cabernet d'Anjou. It is a wine made from Cabernet Franc grapes that also has a slightly higher alcohol content.

Sancerre, the well-known dry white-wine–producing area of the Loire Valley, also produces some very tasty rosés. Some reliable rosé labels to look for from the Loire Valley include:

- Vinival Rosé d'Anjou
- Remy Pannier Cabernet Franc Rosé Vin de Pays
- Domaine Sautereau Sancerre Rosé
- Les Champ Clos Sancerre Rosé
- La Poussie Sancerre Rosé

Provence

The hot, Mediterranean climate of the French Riviera lends itself to the production and enthusiastic consumption of Provence rosé wines. They are the perfect match for the Mediterranean cuisine by the sea that includes garlicky mussels and bouillabaisse, a regional specialty. About half of the wines made in Provence are rosés. Among the better-known classic southern French grapes used to produce Provence rosés are Grenache, Cinsault, Carignane, and Mourvèdre, but we're beginning to see more winemakers using Syrah and Cabernet Sauvignon in their blends.

Main appellations in Provence include:

- Côtes de Provence
- Côtes d'Aix-en-Provence
- Bandol
- Coteaux Varois
- Coteaux des Baux

Look for some of the following rosé labels from Provence:

- Commanderie de la Bargemonne
- Domaine de Blanquefort
- Domaine Fabre Cordier
- Domaines Ott
- Domaines Bunan
- Château Calissane
- Château Revelette
- Château Routas
- Château Vignelaure
- Domaine Richeaume

Languedoc-Roussillon

This region also is sometimes referred to as the Midi, and it is a well-known producer of good-value reds, though it also makes some light, crisp rosé wines to enjoy on a hot summer day. Again, the grape varieties are pretty much native to southern France and include Carignane, Grenache, Cinsault, Syrah, and Mourvèdre.

Appellations to look for include:

- Corbières
- Coteaux du Languedoc
- Côtes du Rousillon
- Minervois
- Saint-Chinian

Some labels to look for in the Languedoc's main appellations are:

- Domaine Salvat
- Les Clos de Paulilles
- Château de Cazeneuve
- Domaine Georges Bertrand
- Domaine de Fontsainte (Gris de Gris)

Some key producers sell their wines under the more general Vin de Pays d'Oc label rather than the higher AOC designation. If you know the producer, this is not a problem at all.

Examples include:

- **Georges Duboeuf**—The Beaujolais king produces some reliable and inexpensive rosé Vin de Pays d'Oc.
- **St.-Martín Val d'Orbieu**—Look for the Rosé de Syrah.

- **Fortant de France**—This producer has a full line of wine from the Languedoc-Rousillon. Try either the Syrah Rosé or the Merlot Rosé, both Vin de Pays d'Oc.

Rhône Valley (Tavel)

Tavel is the most famous rosé appellation in the southern Rhône Valley, which produces the dry rosé for which it is named. Grenache is the main grape used to make Tavel, but like other wines made in the Rhône Valley, several different grapes are permitted in the blend. Another area of the Rhône that makes some good rosés—and good-value wines in general—is the Côtes du Luberon. This little area is sandwiched between Provence and the Rhône Valley.

Top Tavel producers to look for include:

- Paul Jaboulet (L'Espiègle)
- E. Guigal
- M. Chapoutier

Spanish rosado

The major wine regions of Spain that produce rosé wines are Navarra and Rioja. Navarra and Rioja are neighboring regions located in the northeast section of Spain, close to the southern border of France. In both districts, Grenache, known as "Garnacha" in Spain, produces the lion's share of the rosado wines made although some Tempranillo is used. Winemakers, however, are beginning to experiment more with Cabernet Sauvignon and Merlot, especially in Navarra. As with all rosé wines, it is best to consume them while they are young.

Look for the following rosados from Navarra:

- Bodegas Julian Chivite
- Bodegas Ochoa

- Palacio de la Vega

- Vinicola Navarra

- Bodegas Nekeas

- Bodega Romero

Some very reputable Rioja producers also market a fuller-bodied rosé compared to those you will find in France. They include:

- R. Lopez de Heredia Vinña Tondonia

- Marqués de Cáceras

- Bodegas Martinez Bujanda

- Bodegas Montecillo

- Bodegas Sierra Cantabria

- Marques del Puerto

- Viña Valoria

- Bodegas Muga

- Bodegas Corral

Other rosados from Spain to look for include:

- René Barbier (from Penedès)

- Vallformosa (from Penedès)

- Castillo Perelada (made from Cabernet Sauvignon)

Italian rosato

As in California, rosé wines are made throughout Italy, but some of the better ones come from Tuscany.

Italy does not have the same reputation for rosé wines as France does for its Tavel or Rosé d'Anjou or even America's white Zinfandel.

What the Italians do have is a tradition of winemaking that goes back for so many centuries that their rosés are simply taken for granted as just

Unofficially...
About half of Navarra's wine production is rosado, so you could say they know what they're doing. The style is dry.

another wine. The emphasis in Italy is really on the reds. For you, the consumer, this means you can get some good bargains if you come across an Italian rosato that you enjoy.

Try one of the following from Tuscany:

- Capezzana Rosato di Carmignano
- Il Poggioliono
- Antinori
- Michele Satta
- Fattoria di San Donato

Other rosato wines you might want to try include:

- Salice Salentino Rosato
- Dr. Cosimo Taurino

How to select and serve pink wines

Armed with the information you now have about the major winemaking regions that produce pink wine, select a style you like. By this, I'm really referring to the level of sweetness that you're interested in. The truth is that most people who drink white Zinfandel like to say that they prefer dry wine. Realistically, white Zinfandel is, at the very least, slightly sweet. It happens to go very nicely with simple food; it's perfect for a picnic or just having on hand in the fridge. Besides, you can't beat the $5 price tag that some of the major wineries offer.

Ironically, since the beginning of the white Zinfandel phenomenon, I've noticed people getting restless. They started with Sutter Home, and many of them are still enjoying their white Zinfandel. Now that they have become more comfortable with white Zinfandel, however, they are interested in expanding their horizons and paying a comparable price for a Beringer White Zinfandel. Others will even go to the next level and trade up to something like a DeLoach, which upscale restaurants are likely to carry. This is the way of the world.

If dry is your style, lean to France. Care for a more full-bodied flavor? Go to the Rhône Valley within France or even farther south to Spain or Italy.

Whatever you do with pink wine, don't get caught up with vintages unless someone is trying to sell you a very old rosé. For the most part, you want to select the youngest vintage you can find and drink it now or certainly within the next year or two if you really want to stretch it.

Serve your rosé, blush, or vin gris well-chilled, just as you would a white wine. Pull the cork and enjoy!

Just the facts

- Blush wines from California generally are sweeter than rosés from Europe.

- Blush wines are a good stepping-stone from white to red, but they aren't necessarily just for beginners.

- White Zinfandel is made from the Zinfandel grape, which happens to be red.

- White Zinfandel is the number two "white wine" behind Chardonnay.

- Some well-known, top-quality wineries in California and Europe produce blush or rosé wines.

- Rosé wines are best consumed young, and they taste best when well-chilled.

GET THE SCOOP ON...

The difference between Champagne and
sparkling wine ▪ What to use for mimosas and
with wedding cake ▪ Chilling a bottle in a hurry
▪ Opening a bottle of bubbly properly ▪
Selecting Champagne for your taste and budget

Sparkle Plenty

I love Champagne. I love everything about it,
from the gentle jet stream of tiny, delicate bubbles that dance in the glass to the tall, slender
flute in which it is served. Best of all, there is always
a celebratory mood that comes with popping a cork
of Champagne. I enjoy it so much that I look for
reasons to celebrate. It could be a family gathering,
the end of a hectic workweek, the completion of a
project, or a romantic dinner with my husband without the kids.

It amazes me that many Americans don't share
my enthusiasm for Champagne. I finally figured out
why a few years ago when I brought a new colleague
from the office to a Champagne tasting. In the taxi
on the way to the tasting, she confided that she
really didn't like Champagne. When she took her
first taste at the restaurant, however, I noticed a surprised look on her face and then her eyes lit up. She
discreetly nudged me with her elbow and said under
her breath, "That's good stuff." That's exactly what
it was. This was the good stuff, not the insipid, sweet,
bubbly plonk so often poured at a wedding to toast
the happy couple.

Though I do have Champagne taste and I'm talking about the true Champagne from France, I don't always have a Champagne budget. That doesn't stop me, however, and it shouldn't stop you because there are wonderful sparkling wines from around the world for virtually every taste and price point. Some of the finest sparkling wines come from our own backyard in California, but you'd be surprised by the discoveries you will make if you try sparklers from other parts of the United States as well as regions such as Spain, Italy, and Australia. You'll even find good sparkling wines from other parts of France outside the Champagne region. These, however, cannot be labeled Champagne by law. Instead, they must be called sparkling wine or Crémant.

Champagne versus sparkling wine

There is a difference between Champagne and sparkling wine, even though many people refer to all bubbly as Champagne. Champagne must come from the region of Champagne in France that is located about 90 miles northeast of Paris. It's less than two hours away by car or train, which is about what it takes to travel from San Francisco to the Napa Valley.

If you were to look at a map, you'd notice that Champagne is the northern most winegrowing region in France. The cool climate combined with the chalky soil, for which Champagne is known, produces grapes with crisp acidity.

In the region of Champagne, only these three types of grapes may be used to produce Champagne:

- **Pinot Noir**—This red grape contributes body and fullness to the wine.

- **Pinot Meunier**—This red grape adds a fresh, supple quality to the wine.

- **Chardonnay**—This white grape makes the wine lighter and provides elements of finesse and elegance.

There are four main wine regions within Champagne:

- Montagne de Reims
- Vallée de la Marne
- Côte des Blancs
- Côte des Bar

Of the 312 villages, or crus, in Champagne, 16 stand out for quality. According to French law, they receive quality ratings from 80 to 100 percent. The following 17 crus, located in Montagne de Reims (where Pinot Noir is grown) and the Côtes de Blancs (known for Chardonnay), are top-rated.

TABLE 12.1: TOP CRUS OF CHAMPAGNE

Montagne de Reims	Côte des Blancs
Ambonnay	Avize
Aÿ	Chouilly
Beaumont-sur-Vesle	Cramant
Bouzy	Le Mesnilsur-Oger
Louvois	Oger
Mailly-Champagne	Oiry
Puisieulx	
Sillery	
Tours-sur-Marne	
Verzenay	
Verzy	

How Champagne is made

A special process known as "méthode champenoise" produces Champagne.

Unofficially...
Crémant is the term now used to describe the best sparkling wines made in France outside the Champagne region. Crémant used to connote a slightly less fizzy sparkler, but because the term "méthode champenoise" was outlawed by the European Union, this term often replaces it.

1. The grapes are picked by hand—not by mechanical harvesting—during the harvest, which takes place in September and October.

2. The grapes are quickly and gently pressed to extract the white juice from the red skins to produce a white wine. (Even Champagne is referred to as a white wine.) To make rosé Champagne, the winemaker has the option of allowing the red skins to come in contact with the white grape juice, as you would do in any rosé winemaking, or he could mix some red and white wine together. For more information about making rosé wine, refer to Chapter 11, "Rosé or Blush Wine."

   For their product to be labeled Champagne, winemakers are allowed to press the grapes only twice. The first pressing, which yields the very best juice, is called the cuvée. The cuvée is used to produce the most expensive Champagne, which also is known as tête de Champagne, prestige cuvée, or luxury Champagne.

3. The second pressing is called the taille and is used in the blend to produce vintage and non-vintage Champagne.

4. The grape juice (also known as must) is placed into vats for the first fermentation, and it turns into still wine.

5. In January or February following the harvest, the winemaker does the "assemblage." He or she literally assembles a blend of still wines from the current harvest. If the wine is so extraordinary that it will be used to make a vintage Champagne, all the wines assembled will come from that vintage. If the wine is

considered to be of regular quality, it will be used for a nonvintage Champagne. To make nonvintage Champagne, the winemaker will blend still wines from the current vintage or harvest along with still wines from previous years. As many as 40 different wines could be assembled to create the blend. The purpose of blending the older wines with the new is to maintain the Champagne house's style. It's a form of quality control that enables them to produce a consistently good style.

6. After the final blend is created, the winemaker adds a little cane sugar and yeast to the still wine. The wine is bottled, temporarily capped with a metal bottle cap like those used to close some soft drink and beer bottles, and stored on its side in the cool, dark cellar "sur lie," which is French for "on the lees." The sugar and yeast interact to cause a second fermentation inside the bottle, which produces carbon dioxide. This explains where the bubbles come from.

    The lees are sediment made up primarily of dead yeast cells, and they are a natural by-product of fermentation. The mingling of the wine with the lees adds complexity to the resulting wine. Nonvintage Champagne must be aged at least one year in the bottle before it can be sold. Vintage Champagne must be aged a minimum of three years. The better houses age their wines longer before release.

7. The next step is to remove the lees, or sediment, without removing the bubbles. This is accomplished through riddling, which is known as "remuage" in French, and disgorgement, which is "dégorgement" in French.

Bright Idea!
In case you're ever stuck for cocktail conversation, you might be interested to know that there are about 49 million bubbles in the average Champagne bottle. This is the number that a wine-loving engineer named Bill Lembeck calculated.

Riddling is the gradual process by which the sediment is physically moved from the side of the bottle to the neck. The bottles are placed head first and tilted slightly downward into an A-frame wine rack. Traditionally, each day, a winery worker called a riddler, or "remueur," would slightly turn each bottle and point it slightly downward to move the sediment toward the neck of the bottle. After about six weeks of this methodical twisting, the bottle would gradually turn upside down, and the sediment would be trapped in the neck of the bottle. Today, this process is done mechanically and takes a fraction of the time.

8. The final step is the disgorgement of the sediment. The upside-down bottle is placed into a brine solution to freeze the sediment in the neck of the bottle. The temporary cork is removed, and the carbon dioxide propels the sediment out of the bottle.

    Before the bottle is closed again with the permanent cork, the winemaker adds a small amount of wine and sugar, known as *dosage*, to add the desired degree of sweetness to the wine.

    The degree of sweetness from the driest to the sweetest is as follows in the table on the next page.

9. After the *dosage* has been added, the wine is recorked and labeled.

As you can see, the méthode champenoise process is extensive and laborious. The best sparkling-wine producers outside the Champagne region use the méthode champenoise process. They used to include this term on the label, which was a buzzword

TABLE 12.2: LEVELS OF CHAMPAGNE SWEETNESS

Level	Name	Description
driest	extra-brut	This bone-dry style is made without the addition of dosage.
	brut	You will encounter this very dry style at wine shops and in restaurants more often than the extra-brut.
	extra-dry	This style is slightly sweet.
	sec	Ironically, this word for dry actually means medium-sweet.
sweetest	demi-sec	This style is sweet.

for consumers to look for. The European Union, however, clamped down and outlawed use of the term "méthode champenoise" outside the Champagne region.

To help you select a good sparkler, today you can look for one of the following terms on the label to find out if it was made by the méthode champenoise process:

- méthode traditionnelle

- méthode classique

- méthode traditionnelle classique

- fermentation en bouteille selon la méthode champenoise

- fermented in this bottle

- método tradicional (in Spanish)

In essence, no matter what country the sparkling wine is from, if the label indicates (in the native language) that the wine was made by the "traditional method" or was "fermented in this bottle," it's méthode champenoise.

Less-expensive sparkling wines are made by a bulk method known as the Charmat process. Instead of the wine fermenting in its own bottle, the whole batch of wine ferments in large tanks. There is a considerable difference in the methods, which is why you can get a sparkling wine made using the bulk method for under $5. Even then, it has to say on the label that the wine is made by the bulk or Charmat process.

What determines style?

Champagne houses are known to produce a certain "style" of wine. Their nonvintage wines, especially, are more typical of their style. When I reach for a bottle of Taittinger, one of my absolute favorites, I know I'm going to have a light- to medium-bodied Champagne. I'll drink it as an aperitif by itself, with hors d'oeuvres, or as a dynamite accompaniment to crisp Peking Duck. If I select a Veuve Clicquot, another bubbly that I adore, I know I'm in for a fuller, richer-bodied wine that I most likely will enjoy with a meal, something like grilled veal chops and risotto or lobster.

Champagne style is determined by a variety of factors. One factor is the blend of the grape varieties. You already know that the winemaker has three grapes at his or her disposal: the white grape, Chardonnay, and two red grapes, Pinot Noir and Pinot Meunier. White grapes produce lighter-style wines than reds, so if the winemaker is heavy-handed with the Chardonnay, expect a lighter-style wine. The opposite is true if he leans toward the reds.

Two stylistic buzzwords that you might see on a label are:

> **Blanc de blancs**—This term signifies a white wine made from white grapes—100 percent

Chardonnay. Expect this Champagne to be light and elegant.

Blanc de noirs—This term lets you know that you have a white wine made from black grapes, in this case, Pinot Noir and/or Pinot Meunier. Because of the exclusive use of red grapes, you'll have a fuller-bodied wine.

In general, vintage-dated Champagnes, especially those that are considered to be the Champagne house's best, or tête de cuvée, will be fuller-bodied and more complex. In part, this is because of the quality and intensity of the grapes, but it also is because these wines undergo more aging and are released when they are more mature.

On the next page is a table of some of the more popular Champagnes on the market and where they fall as far as style, from the lightest and most delicate to the fullest and richest.

How to read a Champagne label

In the middle of the 18th century, Champagne producers began labeling their wine, but these labels were merely small bits of paper pasted on bottles with a few handwritten comments. Over the years, labeling has become more important.

The following information is optional, but it most likely will be found on the top-quality Champagnes:

1. Vintage year, known in French as "millésime"—This will appear on Champagne only if the wine is exclusively made from the grapes of one harvest. The absence of a vintage date on this label indicates that this is a nonvintage Champagne. This means it is made from a

TABLE 12.3: CHAMPAGNES AND THEIR STYLES

Light and delicate	Light to medium	Medium	Medium to full	Full and rich
Abelé	Ayala	Charles Heidsieck	Paul Bara	Bollinger
Batiste-Pertois	Billecart-Salmon	Delamotte	Heidsieck Monopole	Drappier
Besserat de Bellefon	Deutz	Jacquart	Henriot	Gosset
Bricout	Laurent-Perrier	Mïet et Chandon	Louis Roederer	Alfred Gratien
Castellane	G.H. Mumm	Joseph Perrier	Salon	Krug
A. Charbaut et Fils	Perrier-Jouët	Philipponnat	J. Sélosse	Veuve Clicquot
Jacquesson	Pommery	Piper-Heidsieck		
Lanson	Ruinart	Pol Roger		
Taillevent	Taittinger			
	De Venoge			
	Nicolas Feuillatte			

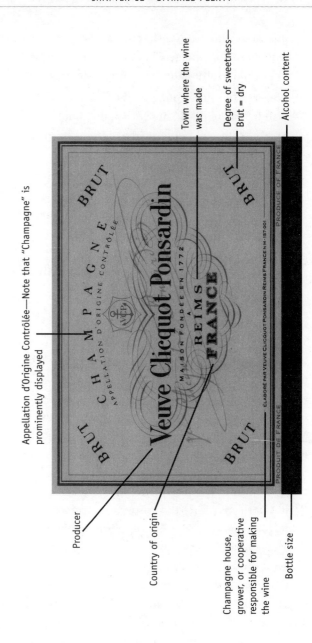

Appellation d'Origine Contrôlée—Note that "Champagne" is prominently displayed

Town where the wine was made

Degree of sweetness—Brut = dry

Alcohol content

Producer

Country of origin

Champagne house, grower, or cooperative responsible for making the wine

Bottle size

Note: The absence of a vintage date indicates that this is a nonvintage champagne. This means that it is made from a blend of wine from different harvests or vintages. Nonvintage champagne is good to give an idea of a champagne house's typical style.

Timesaver
It's great to know how to read a Champagne label, but the key elements to look for are:

1. The name "Champagne" standing alone

2. The words "Produce of France"

3. The location of the producer in the Champagne region

4. The degree of dryness such as brut (dry)

blend of wine from different harvests or vintages. Nonvintage Champagne gives an idea of a Champagne House's typical style.

2. Reference to the grape variety used—This will be Blanc de Blancs for Champagnes made from 100 percent Chardonnay grapes and Blanc de Noirs for wines made from 100 percent Pinot Noir and/or Pinot Meunier grapes.

3. Reference to the cru—Grand Cru or Premier Cru refers to the best-rated villages of the Champagne region. The 17 grand crus were mentioned previously in this chapter, but there are 41 premier crus as well.

How to select Champagne

To its detriment, Champagne has developed a reputation as a special-occasion indulgence rather than the affordable luxury that it is. As a result, people who are not regular Champagne drinkers have a tendency to save the bottle. And save it. And save it. My advice? Don't. Unlike collectible classics such as fine Bordeaux, Burgundy, and California Cabernet Sauvignon, Champagne does not require aging. It is ready to drink upon its release to the market, and most Americans prefer the crisp, fresh, fruity taste of a youthful sparkler. The British traditionally prefer their Champagne with a little more age, which gives the wine a more oxidized taste.

Once you decide you are in the mood for Champagne, you need to narrow down the criteria and focus on what kind. Consider the following: Do you prefer a light-, medium-, or full-bodied bubbly? Do you plan to have Champagne by itself, with a meal, or with dessert? Are you planning to serve it at brunch and mix it with orange juice to make mimosas? The answers to these questions will help you decide what level of dryness or sweetness would be most appropriate.

Brut and extra-dry, for example, two of the dryer styles, are good as an aperitif or to complement a meal. Sec and demi-sec, the two sweeter styles, pair best with wedding cake, dessert, or rich foods such as foie gras or Stilton cheese. Champagne, in general, is an excellent accompaniment to Asian and Pacific Rim cuisine, spicy foods, and fried foods. In the case of mimosas, you might not want to use Champagne at all and opt for a less-expensive sparkling wine.

How much do you want to spend? You know you're in for a little indulgence when you buy Champagne because you have to drop $25 to $30 for a basic nonvintage bottle, but you can do damage control in a few different ways. The first thing you can do is select from these three categories:

- **Nonvintage Champagne**—This is the least expensive Champagne. It is made from a blend of different years and is the most typical of the producer's style.

- **Vintage Champagne**—Made in the better years, vintage Champagne is made exclusively from the grapes of the vintage named on the label. It undergoes more aging than nonvintage Champagne. ∎

- **Prestige cuvée**—Also known as tête de cuvée or luxury Champagne, this wine not only carries the vintage year on the bottle, but it is made only from the first pressing of the producer's very best grapes. It also undergoes more aging than vintage Champagne. These

Unofficially...
Not every year is a vintage year in Champagne. Producers decide for themselves whether a harvest is good enough to merit the production of vintage Champagne. If they decide the harvest is worthy, the individual Champagne producer declares it a vintage year.

include the likes of Dom Pérignon, Cristal, Taittinger Comtes de Champagne, and La Grande Dame. If you want to enjoy the very best, or if you want to impress, and money is no object, go for it!

The second strategy you can use if you're trying to get the best value is to seek out reputable but lesser-known Champagne producers. Two reliable producers that I have found to be excellent values are Nicolas Feuillatte and Charbaut et Fils. If you scan the Champagne section in your wine shop regularly and develop a rapport with your wine merchant, you can uncover value discoveries of your own.

Another option is to sidestep the Champagne issue ever so slightly and move into French sparkling wines, particularly those of the Loire Valley. In addition to the name of the producer, which is very important in selecting a good sparkling wine, look for buzzwords on the label that let you know you are selecting a sparkling wine from the Loire Valley. The buzzwords include "Brut Saumur," "Saumur Crémant" "Brut Méthode Traditionnelle," "Vouvray Brut," or "Crémant de Loire." You can get some very tasty and interesting sparklers for $10 to $15. Some of the most reliable producers from the Loire Valley area are:

- Bouvet

- Gratien & Meyer

- Langlois-Château

Sparkling alternatives

There are times when even the most reasonably priced Champagnes cost more than you want to spend. Go to Plan B, which is to select a sparkling wine made using the méthode champenoise process. Your best bet for excellent price and value in sparkling wine is to look to a number of possibilities from California or a few from Washington State, notably Chateau Ste. Michelle.

United States

California has made quantum leaps in making sparkling wine over the past 25 to 30 years. It's no coincidence that California started making better sparkling wine when some major French Champagne producers and Spanish cava makers started to buy property in California to see what they could do with sparklers. Here are some notable examples of French and Spanish ownership and the bubbly they produce.

TABLE 12.4: FRENCH AND SPANISH WINERIES IN CALIFORNIA

French Owner	California Sparkling Wine
Moët et Chandon	Domaine Chandon, super-premium Etoile, Pacific Echo (formerly known as Scharffenberger)
Taittinger	Domaine Carneros
Roederer	Roederer Estate
	Maison Deutz*
Champagne Mumm	Mumm Cuvée Napa
	superpremium DVX

Spanish Owner	California Sparkling Wine
Freixenet	Gloria Ferrer
Codorniu	Codorniu Napa

*Maison Deutz originally was owned by the Champagne house Deutz Champagne in partnership with Beringer Vineyards until Roederer bought out the company. Beringer still runs the show in California.

California sparkling wines with French pedigree usually cost a few dollars less than their Champagne counterparts, and they are getting better and better with each harvest. You can get good nonvintage California sparklers for $10 to $20, and you certainly can pay more as you get into vintage sparklers and special bottlings, though it still will be a deal compared to Champagne.

For Francophiles, it might be comforting to find American sparkling counterparts, but there are some excellent American-owned wineries in California that I consider to be benchmarks in sparkling wine quality. Three wineries that stand out in my mind are Iron Horse (Sonoma), especially the Wedding Cuvée and one of its rare rosé sparklers; J, from the Jordan Winery (Sonoma), which is so well-known for its French-style Chardonnay and Cabernet that the quality-driven Jordan family created a sparkler with finesse that was matched only by its stylish bottle; and Schramsberg Vineyards (Napa), one of the oldest wineries in California wine country that has a long tradition of producing some of the finest sparkling wines in the country.

The following are some of the top California labels to look for, along with the special designation some use for their top-of-the line cuvées in parentheses:

- Domaine Carneros (Le Rêve)
- Mumm Cuvée Napa (DVX)
- Roederer Estate
- S. Anderson
- Domaine Chandon (Étoile)
- Gloria Ferrer
- Schramsberg (J. Schram)
- Iron Horse
- Korbel

- Pacific Echo (made by Scharffenberger)
- Tribaut

Bright Idea!
Korbel is an excellent value, especially in the $10 range, but it has good entries at higher price points, up into the $20 range as well.

Washington State broke through the clutter of the American sparkling wine market when Château Ste. Michelle pointed out to the world that its winery sits at the same latitude as the region of Champagne. Château Ste. Michelle reasoned that, because it shared the latitude and had similar climatic conditions as Champagne, its sparkling wines were as good as Champagne's. There's a modicum of truth to this. The truth is that Château Ste. Michelle does make a very good sparkling wine that is priced well below Champagne. It provides excellent value for the quality.

New York State is another big producer of sparkling wine, from both the Finger Lakes and the North Fork of Long Island. You won't find any major bargains here, but there are some good sparklers made in New York. Look for some of these labels:

- Lenz
- Riverview
- Pugliese
- SagPond
- Fox Run
- Great Western

Spain

Long before American méthode champenoise was such a big deal, many consumers turned to Spain as an affordable alternative to Champagne. Using the same traditional method but different grapes, cava, the Spanish sparkling wine made in the traditional method, continues to offer some of the most popular great values. A few boutique wineries such as

Juve y Camps are emphasizing greater finesse and elegance in the style. The result is a more expensive sparkling wine—considerably more than many consumers are accustomed to paying for Spanish sparklers—but it still represents a good value for the higher quality. Of course, only you can decide if it's worth the price to you.

The majority of Spanish cava is produced in Penedés near Barcelona. One of the two big names in cava is Freixenet, known especially for Cordon Negro, which comes in a black ("negro") bottle. The other big name is Codorniu. The price of entry for a bottle of dry cava brut from either maker is about $8. It will be a little less at discount and a little more without one, depending on where you shop.

Other Spanish sparklers to look for include:

- Segura Viudas
- Paul Cheneau
- Castellblanch
- P. Lopart
- Juve y Camps
- Marques de Monistrol

Italy

Italy is another winemaking region that has produced sparkling wine ("spumante" means sparkling in Italian) for years, but many people protest that it's too sweet. Yes, there are many good sweet sparklers from Italy, and if you're looking for a good partner for tiramisu, this is the place.

I also thought that Italian sparklers started and ended with sweet wine, but a few years ago, one of my best friends who loves all things Italian opened an Italian sparkling wine to have with dinner. I politely took a sip, expecting soda-pop sweetness, but was pleasantly surprised by the crisp, toasty flavor. Another pleasant surprise was when she shared the price tag of this elegant-looking bottle of Zardetto—about $10. What a deal! I immediately went out and bought a case to have on hand for occasions when I want bubbles but not necessarily Champagne. Since then, I've looked at Italian wines differently.

Dry Italian sparkling labels to look for include:

- Zardetto
- Zonin
- Ferrari
- Fontannafredda
- Marchesi de'Frescolbaldi
- Ca' del Bosco

Australia

I suggest Australia as a sparkling wine alternative for the more adventurous. Over the past 15 years, I've watched the Australian wine category grow in the United States from very humble beginnings and then take off in every price and style. I'm beginning to see more sparklers from Down Under hit the market. They are all over the board in price ($8 to $35), grape varieties, and styles. You'll find Australian sparkling wines made from many different grapes including the red grapes Pinot Noir, Shiraz, and Cabernet Sauvignon as well as the white grape Chardonnay.

Some popular Aussie sparkling wines include:

- Rosemount
- Hardys
- Yalumba

- Seppelt

- Seaview

- Wyndham Estate

- Taltarni

- Château Reynella

- Orlando

Storing and serving Champagne

Champagne or sparkling wine is best stored in a cool, dark place away from heat, light, vibrations, and severe temperature swings. Do you need a special cellar? No. I like to keep a bottle lying down on the bottom shelf of the fridge and a few more in my wine rack.

Before you serve Champagne or sparkling wine, be sure the bottle is well-chilled to about 42 to 47 degrees Fahrenheit. If you need to chill a bottle of bubbly in a hurry, resist all temptation to stick the bottle in your freezer. You don't want the bottle to freeze and explode. The quickest method is to place the bottle in a bucket filled with ice, cold water, and salt for about 30 minutes. The salt in the solution lowers the freezing temperature, speeding up the process.

The best stemware to use for Champagne and sparkling wine is the tall flute or tulip glass. On occasion, I still see restaurants and hotels that should know better serving Champagne in the old-fashioned, saucer-shaped glass that is better left for ice cream or fruit salad.

The tall, slender glassware allows the tiny bubbles to rise in a continuous stream. This is important because the bubbles tell you a lot about the quality of the Champagne or sparkling wine. The best

Champagnes and sparkling wines have smaller bubbles, and they last longer in the glass.

How to open Champagne and sparkling wine

Believe it or not, the pressure per square inch (PSI) in a bottle of Champagne is roughly equivalent to that of a tire on an 18-wheeler. When you open a bottle, always point it away from yourself and others to avoid serious eye injury. Then follow these steps:

1. Remove the foil.

2. Keep one hand on top of the cork at all times. Untwist and loosen the wire muzzle that covers the cork.

3. Take a clean dish towel or cloth napkin and put it on top of the cork so you can grip the cork more easily. This also works as a safety precaution in the event the cork pops before you open the bottle. The napkin will catch the cork before it hurts someone.

4. Gently remove the cork by turning it in one direction and the bottle in the other. The goal is to ease the cork out, letting a little carbon dioxide escape so the cork doesn't shoot out. Contrary to popular belief, if you have opened the bottle correctly, you should hear a light, pleasing fizz rather than a loud pop, and the Champagne should not foam out of the bottle.

5. Never use a corkscrew to open a bottle of Champagne or sparkling wine.

Just the facts

■ The Champagne region in France produces the best sparkling wine in the world.

- There are different quality levels of Champagne that make it an affordable luxury for most wine drinkers.

- The best sparkling wines use the same production method as that used in Champagne called méthode champenoise.

- Champagne is expensive because of the labor-intensive méthode champenoise, the limited area in which it can be produced, and the law of supply and demand.

- The quality of the bubbles tells you a lot about the bubbly.

- Most Champagnes and sparkling wines are best when consumed young.

- If you open a bottle of Champagne or sparkling wine properly, the cork will ease out gently rather than pop.

- You can find many excellent sparkling-wine values from other winegrowing regions outside Champagne.

GET THE SCOOP ON...
The approachability of Port ▪ When and how to
decant ▪ Port versus Port-style wines ▪ Wines to
fill a sweet tooth ▪ Postprandials that will make
you feel warm all over

After-Dinner Delights

Chapter 13

For people who look forward to a meal because of the dessert in store, you can make the postprandial experience all the merrier with a glass of dessert wine. There are many different kinds from which to choose, but Port stands out as a dessert wine definitely on the rise with most American wine drinkers. One of the main reasons for this is the availability of Port by the glass on so many wine lists today. You can spend as little as $5 for a basic Ruby Port or more than $50 for a special Vintage Port. This enables you to sample a Port without having to invest in the price of a full bottle, which can run into hundreds of dollars.

Port from Oporto

Port is the fortified wine that comes from the Douro region of northern Portugal, specifically the town of Oporto. True Port from Portugal is labeled "Oporto" to distinguish it from Port-style wines made in other countries such as the United States, Australia, and South Africa. Port almost always is a red wine. White Port sometimes is produced and usually is blended with the red, though Europeans tend to drink White Port as an aperitif.

According to wine lore, Port was created in the late 1600s when the French and the British were engaged in trade wars. France cut off the Bordeaux supply so the Brits could not get their fill of "Claret," as they called the French red wine, so they turned to the Portuguese, with whom they had a better political relationship. To preserve the wine for the long voyage, the Portuguese shippers "fortified" the wine by adding brandy to the casks. In the process, they unknowingly created one of the richest, most aromatic wines that soon would become a favorite of the British, the French (long after the trade wars ended), and ultimately, the Americans.

Port is made by adding neutral grape brandy to wine during fermentation. The brandy serves to stop the fermentation, creating a wine that is typically sweeter and higher in alcohol. The level of sweetness is determined by the Port producer's house style. While table wines range from 8.5 to 13 percent in alcohol content, Port registers more like 20 percent because of the addition of the brandy.

Wood Port

Wood Ports are aged in wood (namely barrels) and are the least expensive. They are ready to drink upon their release to the market. Because they are filtered during production, Wood Ports do not throw sediments and do not require decanting.

Here's a more detailed rundown of the kinds of Port you will find within this category:

- **Ruby Port**—This ruby-red Port is the most basic and least expensive made from a blend of nonvintage wines. It is bottled young (after only two to three years of aging in wooden casks), which contributes to its fruity flavor.

- **Tawny Port**—Tawny is lighter in color than Ruby Port and has a more subdued flavor.

- **Aged Tawny Port** (with an indication of age)— Unlike the regular Tawny, Aged Tawny Port must spend more time in wood (at least six years). It not only takes on a browner color, but it also loses the burst of fruit and replaces that flavor with more nuttiness and complexity. Although Aged Tawny Ports are made from blends of better-quality wines, they are labeled 10, 20, 30, or 40 years old to indicate the average number of years of the blend used.

- **Colheita Port**—This is an Aged Tawny Port except that the wine is made from a single vintage rather than a blend of wines, and it is aged at least seven years in wood.

- **Vintage Character Port**—This is not a Vintage Port at all; rather, it is a souped-up Ruby with more wood age that shows off some good fruit flavors.

- **Late-Bottled Vintage (LBV)**—LBV is another type of super-Ruby Port that is made from the more concentrated wines of a single vintage such as a Vintage Port as opposed to a blend. It is aged in wooden cask for four to six years. Some Port producers filter the wine before bottling, which means there is no need to decant and the LBV is ready for consumption upon release. Others opt to bottle the LBV without filtration, like a Vintage Port, which means it will throw a sediment and therefore needs to be decanted before drinking. Unfiltered LBV will benefit from further aging in the bottle like Vintage Port. This "poor man's Vintage Port" is ready to drink sooner

Timesaver
Some of the best Port houses do not use the term "Vintage Character" on their label, preferring to use a proprietary name instead. Among those who do not are : Fonseca Bin 27, Graham Six Grapes, Sandeman Founder's Reserve, Noval LB, Cockburn Special Reserve, Ramos-Pinto's Quinta da Urtiga, Warre's Warrior, Quinta do Infantado Estate Reserve, Dow's A.J.S., and Taylor's First Estate.

Watch Out!
Don't be fooled
into thinking
that a Port is
Vintage Port just
because it carries
a vintage date,
describes how
old the wine is,
or even uses the
term "Vintage"
as in "Late-
Bottled Vintage."
All Vintage Port
must be bottled
in Portugal with
the word
"Vintage," the
name of the pro-
ducer, and the
year of harvest
and bottling
stated on the
front label.

than true Vintage Port, and in fact, it tastes best when consumed four to six years after the year of bottling. A true Vintage Port needs 10 to 15 years of age, and the better ones may last 50 or more years.

Vintage Port

The different Ports that fall within this category might spend some time in wood, but they develop further with bottle aging. Because Vintage Ports are bottled without filtration, sediment will form in the bottle, and they need to be decanted.

They don't make Ports any better or more expensive than Vintage Port, which is made in only the very best years from a single harvest. It can be blended from various vineyards or from a "Single Quinta," or "Single Estate," in which wine is used from one particular estate to produce the Vintage Port. The wine spends only two to three years in wood before it is bottled unfiltered and left to mature in the bottle. It will develop good complexity in the space of 10 to 15 years, and the very best vintages are extremely long-lived. This is why Vintage Port is such a highly coveted collectible. It also goes back to the law of supply and demand. Vintage Port amounts to only 2 percent of Portugal's total Port production.

As in the French region of Champagne, it is up to Port producers to declare a vintage in an extraordinary year. Port producers must submit a sample to the government to get approval. Vintage years come about three times in a decade. Recent top vintages include 1983, 1985, 1991, and 1992. If you can find them, excellent older vintages are 1955, 1963, 1966, 1970, and 1977.

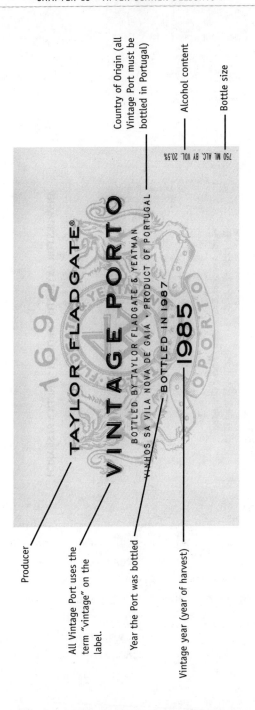

Producer

All Vintage Port uses the term "vintage" on the label.

Year the Port was bottled

Vintage year (year of harvest)

Country of Origin (all Vintage Port must be bottled in Portugal)

Alcohol content

Bottle size

TAYLOR FLADGATE®

VINTAGE PORTO

BOTTLED BY TAYLOR FLADGATE & YEATMAN

VINHOS SA VILA NOVA DE GAIA • PRODUCT OF PORTUGAL

BOTTLED IN 1987

1985

1692

750 ML ALC. BY VOL. 20.5%

The best way to buy Port is to look for a reliable producer. Regardless of the vintage or style, these are among the best:

- Cockburn
- Croft & Co.
- Dow
- Fonseca
- W. & J. Graham & Co.
- Niepoort & Co. Ltd.
- Quinta do Noval
- Sandeman
- Taylor Fladgate
- Warre & Co.

Other excellent shippers include:

- Calem
- Churchill
- Delaforce
- Ferreira
- Osborne
- Ramos Pinto
- Smith Woodhouse

In an ideal world, you would enjoy a bottle of great Port in the company of good friends while lazing around a fireplace. If that's not going to happen and you hesitate to open a bottle for fear that the leftover Port will go bad, don't worry about it. Once opened, Port will last for up to one month when recorked tightly and stored in the refrigerator. In all honesty, however, I would open a more ordinary Port if I knew I wasn't going to finish it within a week. I'd save the special Vintage Port for an evening with friends with the full expectation that there would be nothing left to save.

How to decant Port

Though there is romance associated with the decanting of any wine, it is only necessary when the wine throws sediment, as in the case of Vintage Port and some Late-Bottled Vintage Ports. Ideally, you should leave the bottle standing upright overnight, or at least for a few hours, to allow the sediment to drop to the bottom of the bottle.

To decant a bottle, you'll need a decanter or carafe, a candle, and matches. Be sure the decanter or carafe is absolutely clean because you probably don't use it on a daily basis. Then follow these simple steps to decant Vintage Port:

1. Remove the capsule from the neck of the bottle.

2. Extract the cork.

3. Wipe the lip of the bottle with a clean napkin.

4. Light a candle so you can distinguish the Port from the sediment as you transfer the Port to your decanter or carafe.

5. Hold the decanter or carafe firmly in one hand.

6. With your other hand, gently pour the Port into the decanter while holding both the bottle and the decanter in front of the candle at such an angle that you can see the Port pass through the neck of the bottle.

7. Pour in one uninterrupted motion until you see the sediment reach the shoulder of the bottle and then stop.

8. Repeat step 6, making sure to stop each time you see more sediment reach the shoulder of the bottle. Continue this procedure until all of the Port has been transferred sediment-free from the original bottle to the decanter or carafe.

If you are fortunate enough to get your hands on a bottle that is 30 or more years old, the cork will be very difficult to remove by conventional means. You might need a special wine tschotchke called Porto tongs to remove the cork. They look something like the old-fashioned pliers that dentists used to use to extract teeth in the pioneer days of the old Wild West. To use the Porto tongs, follow these directions:

1. Heat the Porto tongs until they are red hot.

2. Clamp the Porto tongs around the neck of the bottle below the cork for about 10 seconds.

3. Remove the Porto tongs and pour cool water on the neck of the bottle. The upper part of the top containing the cork should come off in one neat piece.

Port-style alternatives

If you enjoy Port and are feeling adventurous, you might want to consider a Port-style wine from Australia or South Africa. The grapes used are different from those in Porto from Portugal, but there are stylistic similarities, and quite often, you can find one you enjoy for a reasonable price.

From Australia, look to some of the major wine producers for Port-style wines as well:

- Hardys
- Wyndham Estate
- Rosemount

From South Africa, you might want to consult your wine merchant about:

- Boland Wynkelder
- Cheetah Valley
- KWV
- Rooiberg

Sauternes and Barsac

Some of the best dessert wine in the world is made in the Bordeaux region of France, particularly the wine regions of Sauternes and Barsac. Only sweet white wine is produced in these two neighboring communes. It's interesting to note that all Barsac wines are Sauternes, but the wine producer has the option of using the more specific commune name Barsac. Wine wizards claim to be able to distinguish the nuances between the areas—and maybe a few of them can—but I stick by my advice and recommend that you try a few different wines to determine which one you enjoy most.

These sweet, delectable dessert wines from France are made by allowing the grapes to remain on the vine until they become overripe and begin to raisinate. In ideal climatic conditions, the grapes will be attacked by the beneficial mold *Botrytis cinerea,* also known as noble rot. The mold acts to further concentrate the juice within the grape and adds an element of complexity. When these raisin-like grapes are pressed, the juice contains so much natural sugar that it cannot possibly all be fermented into alcohol. The result? A sweet, honeyed nectar of the Gods.

For the winemakers, it's a major crapshoot to produce these wines. They put themselves at risk by leaving the grapes on the vine beyond the normal

Watch Out!
Sauterne, without the "s" on the end, is not the same as Sauternes. The one without the final "s" is an inexpensive sweet wine from the United States or another part of Europe that tastes nothing like the genuine article.

harvest. For that to work in their favor, first, the weather has to cooperate. Second, the noble rot must occur. Third, they must be willing to send their grape-picking crews out to the vineyard several times to comb the vines for grapes as they are ready. This adds up to an expensive gamble that has the potential to pay off in spades in a very good year. Mother Nature, however, only cooperates an average of three or four times per decade to provide the ideal conditions. Even then, the crop can be limited at best.

The three white-grape varieties used in Sauternes and Barsac are:

■ **Sémillon**—This variety accounts for the majority of the grapes planted in this area and usually accounts for 80 percent of the blend used in the finished wine. Of the three grapes, Sémillon is most susceptible to noble rot, which is a good thing.

■ **Sauvignon Blanc**—This crisper grape contributes freshness and acidity to the wines.

■ **Muscadelle**—Compared to the other two grapes planted, Muscadelle is in the minority. When used, however, it adds good aroma to the wine.

If money is no object when selecting a Sauternes or Barsac, it's a no-brainer to go back to the Official Classification of 1855. In addition to classifying the best Château of the Médoc, the wine brokers also rated their top Sauterneses. At the time of the classification, dessert wines were very fashionable.

TABLE 13.1 THE OFFICIAL CLASSIFICATION OF 1855 FOR SAUTERNES AND BARSAC

Vineyard	Commune (Modern Name)
Great First Growth—"Grand Premier Cru"	
Château d'Yquem	Sauternes
First Growths—"Premier Crus"	
Château La Tour Blanche	Bommes (Sauternes)
Château Lafaurie- Peyraguey	Bommes (Sauternes)
Clos Haut-Peyraguey (known today as Château Clos Haut-Peyraguey)	Bommes (Sauternes)
Château de Rayne-Vigneau	Bommes (Sauternes)
Château Suduiraut	Preignac (Sauternes)
Château Coutet	Barsac
Château Climens	Barsac
Château Guiraud	Sauternes
Château Rieussec	Fargues (Sauternes)
Château Rabaud-Promis	Bommes (Sauternes)
Château Sigalas-Rabaud	Bommes (Sauternes)
Second Growths—"Deuxiemes Crus"	
Château Myrat (known today as Château de Myrat)	Barsac
Château Doisy Daëne	Barsac
Château Doisy-Dubroca	Barsac
Château Doisy-Védrines	Barsac
Château D'Arche	Sauternes
Château Filhot	Sauternes
Château Broustet	Barsac
Château Nairac	Barsac
Château Caillou	Barsac
Château Suau	Barsac
Château de Mallee	Preignac (Sauternes)
Château Romer (known today as Château Romer du Hayot)	Fargues (Sauternes)
Château Lamothe	Sauternes

Few will argue with the reliability of the Classification of 1855 for the selection of excellent Sauternes and Barsacs, but there are a few others you should know about that are not included in the classification. Incidentally, they fetch a price comparable to the classified wines. They are:

- Château de Fargues (owned by Château d'Yquem)

- Château Gilette

- Château Raymond-Lafon

Moneysaver
Sauternes is so rich that you are likely to be satisfied with just a small glass, with or without dessert. Instead of investing in a full bottle (750 ml), look for a half-bottle size (375 ml), which is more common in dessert wine. Expect to pay a little more than half the full-bottle cost.

The price of entry into the classified Sauternes/Barsac category is $30 or so for recent vintages, and it escalates as you encounter great-celebrated older vintages, which incidentally are long-lived.

If you're in the mood for a Sauternes or Barsac from France but you're not in the mood to part with $30, you can look to a lesser-known appellation such as Ste.-Croix-du-Mont, Loupiac, or Cadillac as an alternative.

Otherwise, go with a regional wine labeled "Sauternes" or "Barsac." Look for a wine from a reliable producer—the reliable producer is key—that is not necessarily Château Anything. All the label has to tell you is that it is a wine from Sauternes or Barsac and that it is from a reliable producer. You will not get the same depth and complexity of a classified Château, but you're not going to spend as much either. It may very well fill your sweet tooth at the moment, as long as you understand that you get what you pay for. B&G and Baron Philippe de Rothschild are both reliable producers of regional Sauternes.

In terms of vintages, I usually advise not to make yourself crazy over them, but when it comes to Sauternes and Barsac, they really do mean something. It does take a special combination of climatic conditions and nerve on the producer's part to make the best Sauternes and Barsacs.

The best recent vintages to look for are 1990, 1995, 1996, and 1997.

From earlier years, look for 1967, 1975, 1976, 1983, 1986, and 1988.

Other dessert wines from France

You can get some other very good dessert wines from other areas of France. In the Loire Valley, for example, you've got Vouvray, which is well-known for its dessert wines made from 100 percent Chenin Blanc grapes. These grapes are attacked by noble rot just like the grapes in Sauternes and Barsac.

From the Rhône Valley, which is practically synonymous with big, earthy red wines, look for a sweet white dessert wine from an appellation called Beaumes-de-Venise. This southern Rhône wine is made from the Muscat a Petits Grains. Unlike other French dessert wines in which the grapes are botrytis affected, the winemaker stops the fermentation by adding a neutral spirit, leaving behind residual sugar that gives you sweetness. Top Rhône producers including Chapoutier, Jaboulet, and Delas make a Beaumes-de-Venise wine.

Germany's signature

German winemakers desperately want their wines to be considered a mainstream, versatile, dry alternative to France, California, Italy and anyone else who makes wines we like to drink in America. Although this is becoming more and more possible if you make a small effort to get to know Germany better (see Chapter 5, "Noble German Whites"), don't overlook the obvious. The Germans truly have the Midas touch when it comes to making dessert wine.

To get a grip on dessert wine from Germany, here are some basics you need to know to make your selection:

1. In general, you're looking at Germany's better-quality wines that are considered to be "Qualitätswein mit Prädikat," abbreviated QmP. This term must be included on the wine label.

2. You're interested in the ripeness level of the grapes. Generally speaking, the riper the grapes, the sweeter the fruit and the richer the wine will be.

3. The easiest part is that you are looking at the Riesling grape, the signature item or house specialty of Germany.

4. You're going to need to narrow down your selection by region. The top ones to look for in German dessert wines are:

   ■ Mosel-Saar-Ruwer

   ■ Rheinhessen

   ■ Rheingau

   ■ Pfalz

5. The reputation of the producer or shipper is an important consideration.

If you have read Chapter 5, you know that the ripeness levels of the grapes picked at harvest, from the least to the most ripe, are:

■ **Kabinett**—This is the lightest and least expensive style of German wine and one that is not associated with the great German dessert wines.

- **Spätlese**—In German, spätlese means "late picking" to indicate that the grapes were picked after the normal harvest so they are a little riper.

- **Auslese**—Bunches of grapes that were left on the vines later in the harvest are picked out to make Auslese wines. It is safe to say that you are getting into more expensive, sweeter wine at this level.

- **Beerenauslese**—Individual berries or grapes are picked off the vine later in the harvest.

- **Trockenbeerenauslese**—Individual berries are left on the vine even longer until the grapes begin to shrivel like raisins.

- **Eiswein**—The English translation, "ice wine," perfectly describes how this dessert wine is made. Grapes are left on the vine to freeze and then are pressed immediately after being picked. German law mandates that the grapes used to make Eiswein must be at least of the Beerenauslese ripeness level.

Though sweet-style wines can be made from grapes at any level of ripeness, the dessert wine category realistically begins at Beerenauslese and includes Trockenbeerenauslese and Eiswein.

Some of the best wines in the world are German dessert wines. It is not uncommon to see the very best ones—recent vintages, mind you—with a price tag from $100 to $400. If you can find them at all, they probably are on the auction block. But don't despair. You can get an excellent bottle of German dessert wine at retail in the $20 to $40 range, and from time to time, you can discover some great values in the $10 to $15 range if you dedicate yourself to looking.

Unofficially...
As in Sauternes and Barsac, in Germany, the grapes are left on the vine in hope that *Botrytis cinerea*, or noble rot, will attack the grapes to help produce a delectable dessert wine. In German, this beneficial mold is called "Edelfäule."

Look for some of these top dessert wine producers from Germany:

- Egon Müller
- C. von Schubert
- Gunderloch
- Robert Weil
- Dr. Loosen
- Selbach-Oster
- Dr. von Bassermann-Jordan
- Dr. Bürklin-Wolf
- Lingenfelder
- J.J. Prüm
- H. Dönnhoff
- Schloss Johannisberg
- Muller-Catoir
- Kurt Darting
- Dr. Pauly-Bergweiler
- Georg Breur

Late harvest wines from the United States

It wasn't until the 1970s that California began making dessert wines regularly from *Botrytis*-affected grapes as they do in France and Germany. Winemakers, however, were not allowed to use the German words like Beerenauslese and Trockenbeerenauslese on their wine labels to convey the level of sweetness. The solution was to call the wines "late harvest," but even then winemakers had to come up with special designations to convey the style of the wine. They decided to follow the same guidelines used by the Germans but to Americanize the names. Here is a list of the American terms and the German style they emulate.

Late Harvest =	Auslese
Select Late Harvest =	Beerenauslese
Special Select Late Harvest =	Trockenbeerenauslese
Ice Wine =	Eiswein

These styles are not arbitrarily selected. In California, as in Germany, the grapes must have a minimum level of sugar to produce a certain style of wine. With that in mind, a California wine labeled "late harvest" will be sweeter than an ordinary table wine you might have with your main course, but it will not be as rich as a "select late harvest" wine.

Practically anything goes in California, so late harvest wines can be produced from a variety of grape varieties. Among them are:

- Riesling (the most common grape used)
- White Riesling
- Gewürztraminer
- Sémillon
- Chenin Blanc
- Viognier
- Pinot Gris
- Muscat
- Sauvignon Blanc
- Zinfandel (one of the few red grapes used for late harvest wines in California)

Some top late harvest wine producers from California include:

- Beringer Vineyards
- Bonny Doon Vineyard

- Chalk Hill Estate
- Chappellet
- Château St. Jean
- Far Niente (Dolce)
- Ferrari-Carano Vineyards & Winery
- Frog's Leap Winery
- Geyser Peak Winery
- Grgich Hills
- Jekel
- Joseph Phelps Vineyards
- Long Vineyards
- Markham Vineyards
- Quady
- Robert Pecota Winery
- Rosenblum Cellars
- Trefethen Vineyards

The Pacific Northwest and New York State also produce some very enjoyable dessert wines. Unlike California, where anything goes with the grape varieties, these areas specialize in but are not limited to the more traditional varieties like Riesling, Sémillon, and Gewürztraminer.

From Washington State, look for:

- Château Ste. Michelle
- Columbia Crest
- Covey Run
- Hogue
- Kiona

From Oregon, some of the familiar faces to emerge are:

- Amity
- Elk Cove
- Eola Hills
- Erath
- Tualatin
- Willamette Valley

In New York State, you'll find some good dessert wine from both the Fingerlakes and Long Island. From the Fingerlakes, look for:

- Dr. Konstantin Frank
- Fox Run
- Hermann J. Wiemer

From Long Island, look for:

- Bedell
- Palmer

Other dessert wine options

You also can turn to many other parts of the globe for dessert wine. In addition to the mainstays from France, Germany, and California, you can find some delicious wines and many good buys from Australia and Italy. A third option, which I find intriguing because it's off the beaten path, is Hungary.

Australian "stickies"

Long before Australia became known for excellently priced and valued Chardonnays and Shiraz wines, its wine industry produced primarily sweet wines that the Aussies call "stickies."

As in Germany, the most popular sticky is made from the Riesling grape. But as in California, you also are likely to find late harvest wines made from Sémillon and occasionally other grape varieties as well.

It's an easy transition for someone who enjoys California dessert wines to try stickies from Australia because the wines are labeled by grape varietal. The Australians also indicate on the label that the wine is late harvest. Best of all, if you discover that you enjoy stickies, you are likely to enjoy the reasonable price, too. They can be found for as little as $10, and the price rises into the $50 range.

Some reliable producers of Australian stickies include*:

- Cranswick Estate
- Peter Lehmann
- Lindemans
- Seppellt
- Yalumba

Italian Vin Santo

The most popular Italian dessert wine for sipping and for dunking biscotti, those irresistible Italian biscuits, is Vin Santo.

Vin Santo is a white, sweet Italian wine made primarily in Tuscany but also in Trentino and Veneto. The two main grapes used are Trebbiano and Malvasia.

Unlike the other classic dessert-winemaking regions that leave the grapes on the vine in the hope that they'll be attacked by noble rot, in Italy, they pick the grapes and lay them out to dry on mats like raisins. As the grapes shrivel, the juice becomes sweeter and more concentrated. The grapes are pressed and then fermented in small barrels. Though many different styles are produced, the ones most commonly seen in the United States are the dessert variety.

*Note that Australian Port producers were listed earlier in this chapter with other Port houses.

Here is a sampling of good Vin Santo producers:

- Antinori
- Badia a Coltibuono
- Brolio
- Capezzana
- Lungarotti
- Marchesi de' Frescobaldi

Hungarian Tokay

The wine has been around forever, but I must admit that this is a rather new discovery for me. It comes from a wine region in northeastern Hungary known as Takaj-Hegyalja. The actual wine is not labeled "Tokay" but "Tokaji." Different styles are produced, but the mother lode is in the sweetest style labeled "Tokaji Aszú," which is made from grapes affected by *Botrytis cinerea,* the noble rot that keeps coming up in this chapter.

If you want to know just how sweet the wine is, you'll have to check the label to see how many "puttonyos" were added to the dry wine during production. Hungarian Tokays on the market generally have anywhere from three to six puttonyos. I love to say, "puttonyos" (poo-TOE-nyos). Puttonyos is the Hungarian term to convey the level of sweetness in the wine. To help put it in perspective, six puttonyos is similar in ripeness to a Trockenbeerenauslese from Germany.

There is only a handful of top Hungarian Tokay producers:

- Château Pajzos
- Disznoko
- Oremus
- The Royal Tokaji Wine Company

The best-quality Tokay is not cheap by any standard. It will cost you in the hundreds, that is, if you can find it at all. The price for a good-quality Tokay begins at about $30 and quickly escalates, but it often is well worth it.

Just the facts

- Port is the hottest category of dessert wines today, available for virtually every taste and budget.

- Many restaurants carry good selections of Port and other dessert wines by the glass so you can sample the elixir before investing in a bottle at home.

- You only need to decant Ports that throw sediment.

- Sauternes produces the world-class dessert wine Château d'Yquem, among others.

- German dessert wines are highly coveted auction collectibles.

- California, Australia, South Africa and Hungary, among others, all produce excellent dessert wines.

Buying and Ordering Wine

GET THE SCOOP ON...
The risk you take when you order the
house wine ▪ When to order by the glass or by
the bottle ▪ Versatile food-friendly reds and
whites ▪ When and how to send back wine

PART V

Demystifying the Wine List

Chapter 14

Perhaps the biggest barriers between you and a good glass of wine at a restaurant are the wine list and having to ask the server which wines are available by the glass. It can be frustrating to people who are not totally comfortable with wine, and it can be maddening at times even for those who are.

For many people, the problem with ordering wine at a restaurant is the potential embarrassment factor, especially if you fumble with the wine list or look like you don't know what you're doing. Many people also are afraid of making the "wrong" choice.

This is especially a problem if you are romancing a date, trying to impress business clients, or hosting a dinner party at a restaurant. No matter the circumstance, the wine list can add an element of stress to a meal that is supposed to "restore." After all, that's where the word "restaurant" comes from.

The best way to meet the challenge is to learn your way around a wine list and to be familiar with the ritual of wine service. Don't be afraid to ask some questions. If you follow this advice, you will be able to order wine with confidence wherever you go.

A note about restaurant markups

Generally, restaurants mark up their wines to two to three times their cost. There are some who take a higher markup, more typical of hotel pricing and others who are extremely competitive.

Moneysaver
The best strategy to maximize value when you order from the wine list, whether you are buying by the bottle or by the glass, is to avoid buying both the cheapest wine and the most-expensive wine on the list.

Although this is the general rule, many restaurants use what they call a sliding-scale markup. This means that the lower-end wines will be priced on the higher end of the scale, while some of the higher-end wines might be priced at only 50 percent over the restaurateur's cost. In real-life terms, a wine that costs a restaurateur $7 per bottle might appear on the list for $21, while a wine such as a good white Burgundy that costs $75 will list for only $150, a relative bargain.

Restaurateurs are fond of saying that you can put only money in the bank and not percentages, which explains their sliding-scale markup in a nutshell. For more expensive bottles that typically don't move as quickly, they would rather take a smaller percentage markup to move the wine and make the dollars.

When it comes to wines by the glass, restaurants typically serve a 5-ounce or 6-ounce pour. So, for a regular-size 750-ml bottle, which is equivalent to 25.4 ounces, the restaurateur gets roughly four to five glasses of wine out of a bottle. If a bottle is priced at $24 on the wine list, the restaurateur takes the bottle price, divides it by the number of glasses in the bottle, and then usually tacks on a dollar or so. Consider the extra dollar a service charge since you don't have to buy the whole bottle. Unlike bottle sales, where customers take responsibility for the full bottle whether they consume one glass or the whole thing, the restaurateur has to cover his costs in offering wines by the glass. These costs include spillage, pillage, and spoilage. Spoilage is a real concern with wines that might not sell well.

Here are two examples of how a restaurant comes up with its wine-by-the-glass price.

Sample Pricing Formula for a 5-Ounce Glass of Wine:

$24 bottle ÷ 5 servings = $4.80 + $1 = $5.80 per glass

(Usually, the price will be rounded up to $6 per glass.)

Sample Pricing Formula for a 6-Ounce Glass of Wine:

$24 bottle ÷ 4 servings = $6 + $1 = $7

(Depending on the restaurant, this wine by the glass is likely to be priced at $6.50 to $7.)

Some restaurateurs bypass this formula altogether and price the glass at whatever it cost them to buy the bottle.

Some people express outrage at the prices restaurants charge on a wine list, often with good reason. In all fairness to restaurants, however, they have to buy the wine, store it properly, use the proper stemware, and invest their time and money to train their staff to suggest and serve wine properly. The issue of storage alone, in terms of space and proper refrigeration, is certainly one good reason for a wine's markup. It becomes an even bigger factor, however, at some top wine destination restaurants where they buy wine and cellar it until it is ready to drink. At that time, they add the wine to the list. Few restaurants have the storage capabilities or the money to tie up wine that they do not plan to put on their wine list for sale immediately.

The best way around restaurant wine markups is to bring your own bottle (BYOB). There are two cases in which you can BYOB:

1. The restaurant does not own a liquor license and encourages its customers to bring their own. My husband and I love these places, which typically are mom-and-pop establishments that shower their attention on the food. We like to bring a great bottle of wine to go with dinner and then leave extremely satisfied by the dining-out experience and the money saved by not having to pay the restaurant markup. BYOB restaurants usually do not charge a corkage fee, a service charge for opening and serving you the wine.

2. The restaurant permits you to bring your own wine subject to a corkage fee. I've seen this done by serious wine aficionados who bring in rare wines to be enjoyed with a special meal. If you want to bring your own wine to a restaurant, be sure to ask the maitre d' or owner first and find out what the corkage fee is. A standard corkage fee of $10 to $15 is added to the check for each of the personal bottles you bring. You have to understand that wine is a moneymaker for restaurants, and they'd really prefer you not bring your own. If you think you're going to save money by bringing in a bottle that's not special, you more than likely would be better off ordering from the restaurant's wine list.

I've found that the best way to find BYOB restaurants is through word of mouth, though a few years ago I came across a book for the New York, New Jersey, and Philadelphia areas called *Bring Your Own*

Restaurant Guide by Henry Nunez. The book could use an update, but it's a good start. Your local wine merchant also could be a good source for BYOB restaurants. Another more national source for BYOBs is the Zagat Survey for various American cities. Though Tim and Nina Zagat do not list BYOBs as a separate category, if a restaurant allows you to bring your own wine, it will be noted in the description.

Different types of wine lists

Wine lists come in many forms. The most traditional is a separate menu that the server presents when you sit down or when you ask for it. Many restaurants that offer a more limited selection include the wines right on the food menu. This makes it very easy for the guest and the server. Other mid-scale theme restaurants feature all the beverages on a separate menu that might already be on your table when you sit down or that might be presented to you with your food menu.

Wine-by-the-glass offerings might be part of the wine list, or they might be featured on a blackboard like a dinner special. They also might be featured on a table tent. In a worst-case scenario, the server might recite the wines by the glass to you. I usually find this to be counterproductive. Whenever I ask the server about wines by the glass, I always ask to see the list so I can avoid the recital. About 50 percent of the time, they'll come back with a list, which makes it easier to select a wine.

In finer restaurants, you'll usually see even more wines listed separately with the dessert menu. This is where you'll find liquid after-dinner delights such as Port, Sauternes, late harvest Rieslings, and Vin Santo. Many restaurants today offer dessert wines by the glass or by the half bottle (375 ml).

Bright Idea
Sometimes, the menu includes wine suggestions from the chef. I've even seen this on dessert menus. More often than not, it's a safe bet, so try it!

The extended wine list

You've probably heard about the speakeasies that existed during Prohibition such as the famous 21 Club in New York, where you had to knock on the door and tell Jack and Charlie the secret password to get in. This is similar to the extended wine list. It's a list, separate from the restaurant's main wine list and the dessert wine list, that features more expensive collectibles and rarities. You'll find an extended wine list, sometimes called the reserve wine list, at top wine destinations. You just have to know to ask for it. It doesn't cost anything to look, and there are even some good buys to be found. For a list of America's top wine destinations, refer to Appendix B, "Resource Guide," at the end of the book.

House wine and wines by the glass

When you just want a glass of wine and you don't feel like dealing with the list or the server, the easiest thing to do is to ask for the house red or white. It's a good restaurant, you figure, so how bad could a glass of the house wine be? Unfortunately, you'd be surprised.

In all but the most dedicated wine destinations, the house wine is the cheapest deal that the restaurant could find to pour. If the wine is pleasant for you to drink, consider yourself ahead of the game. Though it might be the cheapest glass on the menu, it is by no means the best value. You almost always are better off making your selection from a restaurant's wine-by-the-glass offerings, even if it means spending an extra dollar or two.

When it comes to saving a few dollars, if you and a friend are having a few glasses of wine together—even if you're at a bar—consider ordering a bottle instead. Once you've consumed two glasses apiece, you've paid as much as the bottle price. Of course, this works only if you are enjoying the same wine.

Flights

One of the more fun ways to enjoy wine at a restaurant is when it is served in flights. A flight is a sampling of three or four wines by the glass, usually grouped together by themes such as "Big California Cabernets." You get 2 ounces of each wine, served to you on a circle sheet placemat so you can keep track of which wine is which. The idea is to taste the wines, with or without food, to see what you like best.

If you go out with a group of friends and select different flights, you've got a serious tasting going on without the hassle of buying full-size bottles and planning a formal tasting. It couldn't be easier. For a list of destinations that offer flights of wine, refer to Appendix B, "Resource Guide" at the back of the book. Enjoy your flight!

How to read a wine list

No matter what type of wine list you peruse, you always should find the following basic information to facilitate your selection:

1. The name of the wine

2. The type of wine, such as Chardonnay, Cabernet Sauvignon, Barolo, Red Bordeaux, or even more specifically, Margaux

3. The name of the producer, such as Castello Banfi or Joseph Drouhin

4. The vintage (except for nonvintage Champagne, nonvintage Port, and a few other exceptions)

5. The price

Unofficially...
Two interesting types of flights you might consider are:

Horizontal flight—You sample several of the same wine from different producers but all from the same vintage.

Vertical flight—You sample three of the same wine from the same producer but from a range of vintages.

Some restaurants, especially national chains, are reluctant to include the vintage year on the wine list because of availability. Simply put, the year on the wine list might not be the same as the wine currently in stock. In many cases this is not the end of the world, but when you are looking at more expensive wines from all regions, such as Burgundy, Bordeaux, and California Cabernets, the vintage is important.

Other restaurants that do not consider wine a priority neglect to include the name of the producer or shipper. This is vital information you need to know to make an informed wine selection. If you don't see the vintage or the producer's name, ask for more details before ordering.

Wine lists by region versus varietal

Traditionally, wine lists have been organized by country or by wine region. The main wine regions featured tend to be France (with a separate section for Champagne), California, Italy, Spain, and Germany. As awareness has grown about other great wine regions such as Australia, South America, New Zealand, and South Africa, restaurateurs have begun adding the individual regions to the list or simply grouping them all under the category "New World Wines."

California has really made an impact on the way wine is marketed, and this is reflected on many contemporary wine lists in the United States. Instead of dividing the world of wine, some restaurateurs list all their Chardonnays together whether they are from California, Burgundy, or Argentina. The same is true for Cabernet Sauvignon, Merlot, and Pinot Noir.

In daily practice, I'm seeing restaurateurs use a little of both. They might feature "Chardonnay" as a category because it is such a buzzword for all wine drinkers, yet they might categorize all other varietals as "White Wine." They might create a separate category for California's pricey blends, or they might feature them as "Bordeaux Blends" near the French Bordeaux section. In this same vein, it is popular to break out Italy's designer blends from their traditional wines and place them into a category known as "Super Tuscans." This "super" title, along with the "super" prices, sends a strong message to anyone reading the list that these are not ordinary table wines.

Progressive wine lists

In an attempt to make the wine list more accessible to customers and more food-friendly, a variety of different restaurants are using a progressive wine list. This means that the wines are listed in order from the lightest-style wine, intended to match well with the restaurant's lighter dishes, to the fullest-bodied wines that complement the more robust or complicated dishes. The idea has been used on restaurant wine lists sporadically throughout the years, but Tim Hanni of Wine Logic, Inc., formerly of Beringer, formalized and popularized this form of wine list organization by promoting The Beringer Progressive Wine List system during his tenure at the winery.

You should recognize whether or not the list is progressive because, in most cases, it will say so right on the list. On the wine list of Legal Sea Foods, the popular mid-scale seafood chain based in Boston, under each wine list heading you'll see "Wines are listed in ascending order according to body and flavor intensity." In this particular case, Legal Sea Foods has separate categories for "American

Chardonnay," "Imported Chardonnay," "American White," which includes all other varietals, and "Imported White." The red wines get the same treatment, except they do not create a special category for any one American red varietal. They all are listed under "American Red."

Ascending order works like this in terms of basic style. In the whites, you'll have:

> Light, off-dry white, and blush wines
>
> Light, dry white wines
>
> Fruity and light white wines
>
> Fruity and medium-bodied white wines with some oak
>
> Fruity and full-bodied white wines with more oak
>
> Full-bodied oaked white wines

In red wines, you typically see:

> Light, fruity reds
>
> Light- to medium-bodied reds with some fruit and a hint of tannin
>
> Medium-bodied reds with light tannin
>
> Full-bodied reds with medium tannin
>
> Full-bodied monsters with a mouthful of tannin (great with full-bodied food)

Some restaurants include a mission statement on their wine lists that describes how the list is organized. Others prefer to let the servers inform you so they can "connect" with the customer.

That's the other side of the progressive wine list. In addition to making it easier for customers to understand, it also is supposed to make it easier for servers to assist guests and to make informed recommendations. It's empowering—no matter which side of the table you're on.

How to order wine

A variety of considerations comes into play when you prepare to order wine at a restaurant. If you are a foodie, you probably selected the restaurant with a general idea of what you want to eat. You might want to look at the menu and decide on your food before you make your wine selection.

If you are more interested in the wine experience, sit down and ask for the wine list immediately. After you have made your wine selection or selections, look over the menu and come up with something to complement your wine.

Regardless of your approach, the biggest question to ask yourself and those at your table is, What are you in the mood for?

The beauty of ordering wine at a restaurant is that there are so many choices. If one person is having the proverbial steak and another has ordered the Dover sole, the option of ordering wines by the glass ensures that both parties can have a wine that truly complements their food. In most cases, you can still agree on a good bottle that will do justice to both if you consider the "weight" of the food and the type of sauce.

Wine is a wonderful thing in that it allows you to get creative and take a gourmet approach to matching it with food—but you don't have to. Just as in cooking, sometimes you just want to put the food on the table. You don't want to fuss over it. The same is true for wine. Sometimes you don't want to make a megillah over your selection. You just want a glass or a bottle of wine. Your best strategy is to select something—red, white, rosé, or sparkling—that you know you like. How bad could it be?

As simple as it seems, the act of ordering wine can be a little intimidating, especially if you are venturing into unfamiliar territory. You can ask the server for your wine by name, but if the list includes bin numbers, which many of them do, give that number to the server as well. In the majority of restaurants that sell wine, except true wine destinations, the truth is that the server is more uncomfortable selling and serving wine than you are buying it. By providing the bin number, you increase your chances of getting the correct bottle of wine the first time.

Need help navigating the list?

Maybe you've just been handed a wine list that's as thick as the Yellow Pages, as is the case at Bern's Steak House in Tampa, Florida. Perhaps you're looking at a more limited list at your local Outback Steakhouse, and you could really use a little more information to make your selection such as the vintage or a description of what the wine tastes like. Maybe you're just in the mood to try something different for a change, but you could use a little nudge from a reliable source. In any of these scenarios, you should be able to ask someone for a little help.

Sommelier, cellarmaster, or server?

Top-notch wine destinations will have a wine specialist on staff known as the sommelier (so-mel-YAY) or cellarmaster. This person knows the list like the back of his or her hand because he or she creates it, maintains it, educates the waitstaff, and consults with the chef about food and wine pairings. Thankfully, these days you don't often see the stuffy white-gloved, tuxedo-clad sommelier wearing a tastevin around the neck. If that's not intimidation, I don't know what is.

In the absence of a sommelier or cellarmaster, restaurants that are serious about selling wine take the time and effort to educate their servers about wine and wine service. This type of restaurant doesn't have to be the most expensive. It could be a mid-scale chain or your local neighborhood cafe. You will know right away because the servers assume you will be starting off with a glass of wine or will be ordering a bottle rather than saying, Can I get you some drinks from the bar? They are eager to share their recommendations and feel confident making food and wine suggestions whether they are working with a progressive wine list or a traditional one.

This is the same type of server who can entice you to try one of the chef's "Specials of the Day" even if you entered the restaurant already knowing what you wanted. You get the feeling that they know what they're talking about and that they get to taste the food and the wine themselves. You trust the server to take care of you. This has all the makings of a win-win situation.

Whether you are dealing with a sommelier, a cellarmaster, or a well-informed server, take advantage of the situation and ask for a little help or advice. It's not a sign of weakness, and it doesn't cost you any more. To help make sure you get a bottle of wine you will enjoy, at least try to let the person know whether you are looking for a red, white, or rosé and the basic style such as a dry or fruity wine. Give an indication of complexity if you can, such as light-bodied and easy to drink or full-bodied and more robust. You could even get more specific and ask for a Chardonnay from a particular country or region.

Better yet, if you're in the mood to experiment with, say, Rhône varietals, this is the perfect time to consult with the wine maven at the restaurant. Even if you are an experienced taster, these specialists taste on a daily basis and are on the cutting edge of new releases.

In terms of cost, you probably have a price range in mind for what you want to spend on a bottle of wine at a restaurant. You can either specify your price range to the sommelier or server, or if you feel uncomfortable verbalizing this in front of your party, simply point to a wine on the list and say, I'm looking for a wine along these lines. That should get your message across.

Flying solo

The polar opposite of the enthusiastic server who truly enjoys learning about wine and food is the server who is really an actor or actress who is just waiting tables until his or her ship comes in. Consider yourself sunk.

These are the servers who deflate your inquiries about the day's specials by telling you they don't eat meat of any kind. And if you even suggest that they tell you what Chardonnays they have or ask for a recommendation, they inform you that they don't drink wine.

Your best bet is to walk out of the place before ordering and don't return to that restaurant again. Sometimes it's not that convenient, however, especially if you are out on a busy night with friends and you know you can't get a table elsewhere. You might decide to make the best of a bad situation. It's time to fly solo. Trust your own instincts.

The most basic wine list survival technique for safety

Whether you are faced with an ill-informed server or a know-it-all that you'd rather not consult for your wine selection, here is a foolproof strategy you can use to order wine:

1. **Region:** To keep things simple, stick with American wines, especially those from California. For the sake of simplicity, I single out California because of its presence on most restaurants' wine lists. Also, it is almost impossible to get a flawed bottle of wine from California. The quality is high, and the labels are in English. If you want to get fancy, you can always look for a wine from Napa or Sonoma, two of the better-known premier winegrowing areas in the state.

2. **Vintage:** Because of California's near-perfect growing conditions, vintage is not as big an issue for everyday wine drinkers. As a general rule, order a white wine within two to three years of the vintage date. If you're having dinner in 2001, choose a white wine such as a Chardonnay made in 1998 or 1999. For reds, order a wine within four to 10 years after the vintage date. Again, if you're having dinner in 2001, you might want a Cabernet Sauvignon vintage dated between 1991 and 1997.

3. **Varietal:** The old adage, "White with fish and fowl, red with red meat," is helpful, but again, consider the balance of matching lighter wine with lighter food and heavier wine with heavier dishes. In whites, Chardonnay is generally a crowd-pleaser as is Cabernet Sauvignon or Merlot in reds.

4. **Producer or Winery:** Go with a well-known winery rather than a boutique winery unless you are familiar with the quality.

How the wine savvy cut to the chase

For the more adventurous, follow these steps in selecting wine at a restaurant:

1. Take your time. Don't let the server give you the rush act. Just tell him or her, I love your list. I just need a few moments, thank you.

2. Determine whether you want a red, white or rosé. Usually, a selection of red or white cuts the list in half. Rosé leaves you with a handful of choices at best.

3. Quickly comb the wine list to determine what the restaurant specializes in. If you see the house specialty leans toward South America, consider a wine from Chile or Argentina.

4. Admire the trophy wines, but mentally cross them off your list. They're not worth the money.

5. Determine what you want to spend on a bottle of wine. If you don't want to go more than $30, ignore those bottles.

6. Unless you're in a situation such as a business dinner or the perfect date, when it's best to stick with a sure thing, look for the unexpected and obscure. Dining out is a perfect time to experiment.

7. Narrow down your choices and then call over the server or sommelier. Get the scoop on the wines, what he or she recommends, and why.

8. Give it a shot. You never know what you will like until you try it.

If you do like it, be sure to write down the name of the wine so you can buy it at your local wine shop or ask your retailer to order it, assuming it is available.

Getting a grip on the wine ritual

Another source of discomfort for some guests, who might want to order a bottle of wine but opt for a glass as an easy out, is the "wine ritual." It needn't be a big deal, but there are a few points of etiquette with which you need to be familiar.

Restaurant staff works on the assumption that the person doing the entertaining at the table is the host, is paying the bill, and is ordering the wine. The server brings the wine list to the host, unless the host chooses to give the wine list to someone else at the table to make the selection.

In the case of a man and a woman dining together, whether for personal pleasure or an obvious business meeting, I'm sorry to report that old habits die hard. Servers have a tendency to give the wine list to *him* rather than to *her*. A woman's best strategy for nipping this potentially embarrassing moment in the bud is to let the manager or maitre d' know ahead of time that she will be hosting a dinner. Plan B is the direct approach. Ask the captain or server as soon as you and your party are seated to see the wine list.

Here's a walk-through:

- **Selection**—Select your wine and order by giving the server, captain, or sommelier the name and/or bin number.

- **Presentation**—When the server brings the wine to the table and presents it to you, check to see that the wine is the one you ordered and that the vintage corresponds to the one on the wine list. If either one is wrong, let the server know. He or she will go back for the correct bottle. If the vintage does not agree with the one on the list, the server might tell you that they ran out of the other vintage and that this is what is in stock. For many everyday wines, this is not a tragedy though it is an annoyance. For older wines and wines from areas of the world where there is a huge difference between one year and another, however, it's best to refuse the wine.

■ **Cork Presentation**—After the server opens the wine, he or she will present you with the cork. Don't sniff it unless you want to know what a cork smells like. You might be a little suspicious of the wine if you find that the cork is dried out, which is an indicator that it has been stored standing up and not on its side. In truth, the whole cork presentation is a throwback to the early days before major wine labeling when the name of the winery or château was ingrained on the side of the cork. It proved the integrity of the wine in the bottle. Just smile at the server and ask him or her to pour you a taste because this is what you've been waiting for.

■ **Taste Test**—The server will fill your glass only about $1/3$ of the way to allow you to swirl the wine and release the aroma. In truth, you don't even need to take a sip of the wine to decide whether it's good or not. You can merely put your nose in the glass and take a whiff. If you like what you smell or taste, nod your approval to the server. He or she will pour for the rest of the table before returning to fill your glass about half full.

When to send wine back and how to do it

The server has opened the bottle of wine and has poured you a taste, but it just doesn't seem right. Should you send it back?

It depends.

The number one reason in my book for sending a wine back is if the wine is corked (meaning it smells or tastes like cork or the mold that might form on a cork, which is rather unpleasant) or if the wine has oxidized. When a wine has oxidized, air has seeped through the cork and into the wine, making the wine taste like Madeira or Sherry (hence the term "madeirized"). This also can happen to a wine if it is stored improperly such as in that cute little rack over the grill in the open kitchen.

If either is the case, do not hesitate to tell the server that the bottle is corked or that the bottle is bad. There is no need to make a scene. Do it quietly. Most restaurants will whisk the bottle away without question, especially if it's a bottle under $50 on the list. The last thing a restaurateur needs to do is scrutinize the judgment of the host and embarrass him or her in front of the table. When you hit the $50 mark and above, however, it's not uncommon for the sommelier, captain, or even the chef/owner to come over and personally taste the "bad" bottle.

Any restaurant worth its salt will take back a corked bottle. Some have an even more liberal policy and will take back a bottle even if it is not corked. To them, it's better than inflaming a guest, and

Unofficially...
When you order a bottle of wine for the table, the correct pour is $1/3$ to $1/2$ full to allow you to swirl the wine and enjoy the aroma. When you order a wine by the glass, however, you should expect the glass to be $3/4$ of the way full.

besides, they can use the wine for staff tastings. Any wine that has turned or spoiled should be sent back, just as you'd send back an overcooked or under-cooked steak.

Do not abuse the situation, however. It is inap-propriate to return a bottle simply because you don't like it. The only exception to this rule is if the server recommends a wine so highly that he or she gives you his personal guarantee: "If you don't like it, *I'll* drink it." In that case, pour him a glass.

Just the facts

- Never buy the cheapest or most expensive wines on the list.

- Different types of wine lists are available at many restaurants. In addition to the regular list, there also might be a list of wines by the glass and a dessert-wine list.

- A progressive wine list makes it easier to match wine and food without having to be a wine con-noisseur or gourmet.

- House wines are cheaper but usually represent the worst value.

- Wine flights are a fun way to taste different types of wine with a minimal investment.

- If a wine is bad, send it back.

GET THE SCOOP ON...
Special features to look for in a wine shop ▪
Retail markups and sales strategies ▪ Going
steady with your wine merchant ▪ How to buy
and sell at auction ▪ Buying direct from the
winery ▪ Legal mumbo jumbo

How to Find a Good Wine Merchant

Chapter 15

There are liquor stores that happen to sell wine in virtually every little hamlet of the United States where it is legal to do so, and then there are wine merchants. These are the retailers who, regardless of whether they handle spirits and beer in their stores, have a special passion for wine. You can just tell from the moment you enter the store and sometimes even before.

Some fine-wine merchants dress their windows with the same attention to detail as Macy's or The Gap, and they often tie into the same seasonal and special holiday themes as their fashion counterparts except that wine merchants showcase wine.

Get past the window and walk through the door. In the best shops, you'll find a virtual Willy Wonka's Chocolate Factory of wine with a staff on hand that is eager to assist you. Even smaller stores will offer a wide selection of wines in a variety of price ranges to accommodate anyone from the novice to the connoisseur. Your mission is to identify a shop where you'd like to shop on a regular basis.

Unofficially...
One of the more
creative displays
I've seen in a
while featured a
full window of
Veuve Clicquot
Champagne with
its orange and
black label in a
sophisticated
Monster Mash
scene for
Halloween.

What to look for in the store and in the people

You should look for many of the same things in a good wine shop that you would look for in any other retail situation. There are, however, a few other ways that a retailer can send a strong wine message. With a little careful observation, you separate the wine merchants from the liquor store owners. Here are some signs to look for in a serious wine merchant:

1. The store is well-lighted, neat, and clean.

2. There are wide aisles for easy shopping, and if space permits there are shopping carts so you don't have to break your arms carrying heavy bottles.

3. The room temperature is reasonable and constant. You certainly don't want to buy your wine from someone running a Turkish bath, but a few overzealous wine merchants keep their stores at a chilly 62 degrees all year round "for the sake of the wine." Personally, I don't find a meat locker conducive to browsing, which is part of the fun, unless you're dealing with older, rarer wines, in which case the cooler temperature is greatly appreciated.

4. Wine is everywhere you turn but with a sense of order. It is neatly stacked either on its side in wine racks or in case stackings.

5. You notice a wide variety of wines from many different wine regions and in a range of prices.

6. You see salespeople helping other customers make their wine selections, and you observe good rapport.

7. If the store sells specialty food, it cross-merchandises wine with food.

8. The store features temperature-controlled storage for its better wines. If the wine merchant is courting serious wine consumers, he may have private lockers on the premises that he might rent out to hold special cases.

9. There are wine publications at the register, or a separate section is devoted to wine magazines and books. It also might sell wine accessories. (Not all retailers are permitted to sell magazines, books, or wine accessories due to strict prohibitive state laws.)

10. Where legal, the wine shop features weekly in-store wine tastings for you to sample wines. If in-store wine tastings are prohibited, better wine shops arrange special wine dinners at restaurants in town, and you can participate for a fee.

11. The wine shop communicates with its customers through informative newsletters and/or Web sites.

12. You might see a few stray wine glasses from time to time. Though this might appear to conflict with the "neat and clean" rule, these stray wine glasses tell me that the staff is tasting the wines. This means they should be able to make informed recommendations.

If your wine merchant meets these 12 criteria, you've hit a home run. You're still way ahead of the game, however, if you find a conveniently located wine shop where you know you can browse a good selection of everyday and special occasion wines, the staff is friendly and knowledgeable, and the prices are reasonable.

Building a relationship with your wine merchant

Once you've decided where you want to shop for wine, get to know the wine merchant. Remember, at a good store, you'll often find the owner working the floor alongside his or her salespeople. In the better stores, you'll find a crew of knowledgeable wine mavens.

If the wine merchant is any good, the first and most basic things he or she will ask you about are your level of knowledge and your budget. If you are a wine novice, be honest. Tell the wine merchant that you are getting into wine and you are not very knowledgeable. Tell him you plan to be a regular customer, and you want to spend $12 to $15 on a regular basis. I use this price range because you can get a much broader range of styles from virtually every winemaking country.

A good wine merchant will help you select wines that provide a good example of what the varietal should taste like or what typical Burgundy or Rioja tastes like. One top wine merchant explained to me, "I'm going to try to give you an education. It's difficult for me to give you $6 bottles of wine every day." That is, if you are interested in developing your palate and expanding your own personal wine repertoire.

This same retailer will send a customer home with a lean Chablis and the recommendation to have it with fish in a cream sauce and a Kendall-Jackson Chardonnay, which is fruity and completely different from the Chablis. As you would with your hair stylist or your corner grocer, go back and let the retailer know what you did and didn't like and why. He or she will get a handle on the types of wine you prefer, and voilà, you'll get more personal wine

Bright Idea!
If you want to get some quality time from your wine merchant, shop at a time when the store is not busy so your wine merchant can focus on your needs. Rather than going on a Friday after work or on a Saturday afternoon, consider going early in the week.

recommendations. We're talking about an ongoing dialogue with your wine merchant every two or three weeks. If you find that your wine merchant is recommending more "misses" than "hits," find another wine merchant who will listen better.

There's no need to take copious notes, though many people are fond of saving the labels from their favorites and jotting down their impressions.

On the other hand, if you are more comfortable with the $5 or $6 wine, say so. There are plenty of inexpensive bottles on the wine shelves, and your wine merchant should be able to help you find a few you will enjoy. You can always trade up to higher-quality, expensive wines, but you don't have to. If more people took a casual approach to wine, we would be a step closer to being a wine-drinking country.

No matter how high or low your level of knowledge or experience with wine, the important things to remember are:

- Do not be intimidated.

- Trust your palate and don't make excuses.

In addition to seeking out a one-on-one relationship with your wine merchant, you can get an inside track on making some informed wine selections by taking advantage of the store's special features. These may include the following:

- **In-store wine tastings.** They aren't necessarily fancy, but they don't have to be. The best way to select a wine is to have the opportunity to taste it first. In states where this is legal, the store will usually hold a weekly wine tasting. Depending on the state and the store, the tasting might be complimentary or you may

> 66
> You should be able to tell if they're selling you the bullshit of the week.
> —An anonymous retailer on building relationships with wine merchants
> 99

have to pay a nominal fee, which usually is worth it so you don't get stuck with wine you don't like. Keep in mind that you're tasting the wine by itself. If you like the wine on its own, it's an easy buying decision for you to make. Some wines will not taste good to you without food, but what a difference it will be when you get them home for dinner. You can ask your wine merchant about suggested wine and food pairings, or you'll just know from experience after you have participated in a few wine tastings.

- **Store newsletters.** You can really get a handle on what's coming into the shop by reading the store's newsletters. The staff will often help write it and include their personal tasting notes, which are especially helpful if you find that you enjoy wines they recommend. Newsletters also keep you abreast of special events and sales.

- **Store catalogs.** If at no other time of the year, great wine merchants will create a catalog for the holidays to feature their gift baskets and special offerings. They make wine shopping easy. Sherry-Lehmann in New York publishes one of the best wine catalogs I've seen. It is beautiful to look at, fun to read, and filled with more goodies than Bacchus could ever have hoped for. By all means, find out if your wine merchant publishes a catalog and put yourself on the mailing list.

- **Store Web site.** More and more retailers are entering cyberspace as another means to communicate with their customers. On the better sites, you can read current or past newsletters online, check their calendar for special events, ask wine-related questions, compare tasting notes, and even order wine online. For a list of retail Web sites, please turn to Appendix E, "Wine on the Web," at the end of the book.

■ **Wine clubs.** These come in a variety of forms. By joining the store's wine club, you usually are added to the mailing list for the store's newsletters, catalogs, and special sales. You might be issued an identification card that entitles you to a discount when you present it at the time of purchase, just like at a grocery store. The wine store might even offer a special deal in which you join a "Wine of the Month" club and get a predetermined assortment of wine sent to you each month. This would be similar to Harry & David's "Fruit of the Month" club. To find out what type of wine club your wine merchant offers, simply ask for details.

Returning bad bottles

As in a restaurant situation, the only time to return a bottle of wine is if the wine is corked, meaning the wine smells like cork or Madeira when you open it. Although corked wines do not present a health hazard as would spoiled chicken or beef, the smell overpowers the wine and detracts from the experience. Part of the problem with real corks is that they are natural products made from the spongy bark of cork trees, mostly from Portugal and Spain. On occasion, they could be flawed, and this affects the wine. This is why you're beginning to see some fine wines using synthetic corks.

A good wine merchant will take back a bad (as in corked or spoiled) bottle if you bring your original

Unofficially...
Even at some of the better stores, on occasion, you will pick up a bottle that is sticky or that exhibits other signs of potential leakage stemming from poor storage. There might be wine residue on the outside of the bottle's neck, or more obviously, you might see a slightly pushed out cork. Avoid buying these bottles and bring them to the attention of your wine merchant.

receipt and the remaining wine. This is especially true if you have an established relationship with the wine merchant. After all, the retailer wants to keep you as a customer. Keep in mind that the meaning of "bad" is corked or spoiled. It does not mean that you tried a wine and didn't like it so you thought it was bad.

Top retailers tell me that, on average, more than 50 percent of the bottles returned to them are not necessarily bad. The customer merely didn't like the wine. The typical scenario unfolds like this:

A friend recommends a special wine: "Go and buy that Barolo. It's really a great wine." The customer splurges on the great Barolo for $30 when he really wanted to spend $12 to $15. To the customer, the wine didn't taste like $30. In fact, he didn't even like it. For all that money spent, it had to be "bad." He marches back to the wine merchant and demands a refund. Unfortunately, this happens more often than you think, and it puts everyone in an awkward situation. It also does nothing to further your wine education.

This is not to say, however, that you should never return a bottle of wine. If you do, it is best to return the bottle as soon as you discover the defect so the wine merchant can see it for himself—certainly within the next day or two. Don't wait until the following week when the opened wine will have turned anyway. Also, it's bad form to return an empty or near-empty bottle.

A note about retail markups

On average, most independent wine merchants work on a 30 percent markup. This might sound like a lot, but you are paying a premium for the wine merchant's expertise and the services his store offers. Store often feature some well-known wine brands as loss leaders at only a 10 to 15 percent markup. This gives the independent merchant a vehicle for competitive-price advertising, it gets people into the store, and it may make you think twice about buying wine from the local warehouse club or discounter that typically works on a 10 percent markup.

Why should you ever go into a store knowing that you are going to pay more? Here's a line-by-line comparison:

- A wine merchant has a staff of knowledgeable people and a well-chosen selection of wines. An ordinary discount price club or grocery store does not have wine specialists, with very few exceptions.

- Because the wine merchant employs "wine people" who check in wine all day as opposed to a receiver who checks in soccer balls and frozen peas alongside the wine, the chances are better that the wines will not be lying on the loading dock in subzero or tropical temperatures.

- If you don't find the wine you are looking for and the wine is available, an independent merchant will special order your wine. At the discount price club or grocery store, what you see is what you get.

- Through his own relationships with wineries and his distributors, an independent wine merchant may carry wines that are difficult to obtain elsewhere. Warehouse clubs and grocery stores may have some special bottles, but it's not the same.

- When you pay for your purchase at an independent wine merchant's store, you get a bag or a box to carry your wines home. The staff often gift wraps your bottle or at least supplies you with a little gift bag so you can do it yourself. They'll even help you to your car if you want. On occasion you'll get a box from a warehouse club, but most of the time, you'll find yourself with a shopping cart filled with clanging bottles that you must somehow nest into your trunk so they don't break.

Watch Out!
In some states, the liquor store within a warehouse club like PriceCostco is not operated by the same company. It is leased to an outside vendor. This is why you can return a $1,500 laptop and get your cash back without their blinking an eye, but they might balk at refunding a questionable $15 wine.

- If you get a bad bottle, a wine merchant is more likely to take it back without a hassle, assuming you have the receipt. The warehouse club, on the other hand, might not be as forgiving.

As you can see, there's a definite trade-off. You will get a better price deal at a warehouse club, an aggressive wine discounter, or a grocery store working on high volume. This pays off for two types of buyers. The first type is people who buy in volume, especially the 1.5 liter bottles of popular mainstream brands. They make perfect house wines. The other type is the more experienced buyer who knows a good deal on Tête de Cuvée Champagne (such as Taittinger Comtes de Champagne or Far Niente Cabernet Sauvignon) when he sees one. In the case of more expensive purchases, I would buy a bottle and try it before committing to a case. If you wait too long, however, they sell out. If you fit into either of these categories, I'd stock up on your house wine along with your cases of toilet paper and industrial-sized ketchup. After all, it's the American way.

Buying strategies

The buying strategy you use to select your wines will depend on what you want to get out of the deal. Are you looking for everyday wines for your personal enjoyment? Or, are you building a more serious collection? What do you like and how much do you want to spend? How price sensitive are you?

Cheaper by the dozen

The most obvious buying strategy if price is a top consideration is to buy your everyday commodity wines at a warehouse club or from an aggressive discounter.

Another good strategy is to buy in bulk wherever you shop. In many stores, if you buy by the case, which is 12 bottles, you will get a 10 to 15 percent discount. In almost all cases, the discount applies to a case of the same type of wine, not a mixed case. It all adds up.

Wine futures

With the feeding frenzy of trading happening on Wall Street, wine futures seem to be a lot sexier than investing in pork bellies. Sexier, yes, but to what purpose?

Wine futures traditionally have been offered on first-growth Bordeaux and Burgundy gems where there is an international market and definitely a greater demand than supply. The whole idea of buying futures is to ensure that you get your supply of top Château wines come hell or high water. The only thing is that you have to put your money up long before the harvest and then wait for your wine to be released and sent to you (actually to your wine merchant) in "the future." By buying a future vintage of Château Very Expensive, you take a gamble that the harvest is going to be wonderful and that your wines will be wonderful as well. You also believe deep in your heart that you're getting a good deal because you came in on the ground floor. In a good harvest and especially in a stellar one, once the wines are officially released to market, the price sky-rockets.

People who bought Bordeaux futures in 1982 did well. Unfortunately, people who bought in 1991, 1992, 1993, and 1994 did not make the same financial killing. You could have bought these wines four years later for less than the price of the futures.

In the 1980s, California entered the futures game. Robert Mondavi Winery was among the first to enter the fray because of Robert Mondavi's personal conviction that the finest California Cabernet Sauvignons can sit on the table alongside first-growth Bordeaux.

Some insiders dismiss the idea of California futures strictly as a means to better cash flow. Due to the current supply-and-demand situation that exists for the finest California Cabernets, however, it is worth getting your name on your favorite wine producer's mailing list if you can so you can consider whether this is the buying strategy for you.

For collectors of a particular French château or California producer, buying wine futures is the best way to be assured of a regular supply.

The pros and cons of buying direct

Before we get into the nitty-gritty of buying your wine directly from the source, you must understand that, traditionally, there is a three-tier system that governs wine sales in the United States:

1. The winery produces the wine.

2. A distributor sells the wine to retailers.

3. The retailers or wine merchants sell the wine to consumers.

Technically, a wine cannot be sold in a given market unless a distributor is handling the product; however, there are exceptions. There are two ways you can buy direct:

1. Buy direct from the winery.
2. Buy online.

People frequently travel to wine country, taste wines at a winery, and like them so much that they buy some to take home. If they really go nuts, they sign up to be on the winery's mailing list and begin a relationship in which they buy wines directly from the winery. This is especially true for smaller wineries that might not have a distributor in certain markets. Even if some of the smaller wineries do have a distributor, the winery often complains that its wines are getting lost in a sea of bigger brands and therefore its wines are not promoted and marketed as aggressively as they could be.

The other way to buy direct is to buy online. It's a matter of convenience, much as Amazon.com has been for books. For people who know what they want, it's perfect.

It's not that perfect for the government, however, which feels that it's missing out on tax dollars that would have been spent at retail stores, the wine distributors who are being cut out of the middle, and the upset retailers who believe *they* should get the business.

All this direct buying has led to a closer look at U.S. interstate shipping laws. Some states allow you to ship wine in and out of state, and others don't.

Recent legislation has given anti-interstate wine-shipment laws some teeth, making violations a felony in some cases. The whole idea of making violations a felony is to deter wineries from even thinking about interstate shipping because they could risk losing their license to make wine altogether—an automatic end to their business.

How to start a wine collection

The best way to start a wine collection is to begin at the level at which you are most familiar. If you drink Chardonnays in the $5 to $10 range, begin by buying wines from these categories from all winegrowing regions. If you prefer the $12 to $15 range, seek out wines in this range and so on. The point is that, with some time, you will get some good wine tasting under your belt, and you will learn to be more discriminating between styles of wine, which inevitably will make you less price resistant.

In terms of money, it goes without saying that deep pockets can buy you an instant wine collection, but people who do not have as much to spend on wine need not worry. Set aside a weekly or monthly budget for wine and stick with it.

Once you get bitten by the wine bug, you might want to get a little more serious about collecting. In addition to buying wine for your everyday consumption, you might begin to buy more special wines that will improve with age. Typically, these are big reds like the better Bordeaux, Burgundy, Cabernet Sauvignon, Rhône wines, Brunellos, Riojas, and of course, Vintage Port. There also are some white wines that will evolve beautifully with age such as the better White Burgundy, big California Chardonnays, some Rieslings from Germany and Alsace, and dessert wines including Sauternes and late harvest wines.

You have two choices here:

1. Follow your heart and your taste buds and buy wines that you personally enjoy. As a wine drinker, you will watch them develop and evolve over the years.

2. Buy only blue-chip, famous-name wines that should appreciate with time, both in the bottle and in price. Your price of entry will be higher, but it's the safest wine investment you can make if your goal is to sell it down the road for a profit. If this is the case, you had better be absolutely certain that the wines are kept in primo condition. Otherwise, you will have a lot of bad expensive wines in your cellar. For more information about how to store your wines, see Chapter 17, "Essential Tools and Tricks."

Buying at auction

One of the best ways to buy more mature, ready-to-drink wine is at auction. Auctions can be an excellent source of fine collectibles below retail prices if you can find the wines on the market at all. But just as buying clothing at popular discount outlet centers does not guarantee you a bargain, you really have to go into an auction knowing something about the merchandise and the going price on the market.

Wine auctions have only become popular since the 1980s. Up to that time they weren't legal in many states, including New York. They have gained a following, however, first from serious wine collectors and then from restaurateurs and retailers who also wanted to find good mature wines that they could offer to round out their wine list or to add to their retail shelves. Until recently, they could be a

Bright Idea
When you collect wine, it always is best to buy by the case so you can taste the wine in several stages of its development. You might pull a cork early on and decide that it needs more time. You then might go back to it a year or more later and decide that all the elements are in perfect harmony. The worst-case scenario is when you pull a cork and decide that the wine is over the hill. It's like putting the steak back on the grill and letting it get overdone.

little overwhelming for regular folks who want to start a wine collection because the lots typically are big and the smaller ones generally carry a stratospheric price tag.

A good friend of mine who collects wine recently went to a more accessible auction operated by Christie's in New York. The auction was done in conjunction with one of New York's top wine merchants, Zachys of Scarsdale, New York. They auctioned off about 30 lots of wine that day. The wines were broken down by theme so you could bid on a lot consisting of one bottle or even two cases. There was a "horizontal" lot, for example, which consisted of four different 1994 California Cabernet Sauvignons. There also was a "vertical" lot of Château Latour—1982, 1988, 1989, and 1990.

My friend personally snapped up two cases of 1990 Burgundy for $700, or $30 per bottle. "I'm talking premier cru Beaune," he boasted. "If you bought these at retail, you'd be shelling out $90, $100, or even $120 a bottle." At the same auction, he bought a bottle of 1990 Château Latour for $325. At a normal auction, this bottle would easily fetch a price in the mid- to high-$400 range.

"What about the additional cost of buying at auction?" I asked. Yes, you pay state tax and a 10 to 15 percent commission on the final gavel price. At the end of the day, my friend spent $5,000 and said, "I don't regret a single purchase." His secret? He went prepared.

Auction strategies

Here's what you have to know to buy or sell at auction:

- Get your hands on an auction catalog. You can buy one from the auction house in advance, usually for $10 to $25. Study the catalog so you know before you get to the sale what lots you plan to bid on. If you don't have a game plan, you are likely to get caught up in the bidding frenzy and overpay. This is not the time or the place to make an impulse buy.

- Look for the following key information about the wines for sale in the auction catalog:

  1. The condition of the wine.

  2. The condition of the label if you are look-ing at a special "artist series" such as those that appear on the famous Château Mouton-Rothschild.

  3. A "cork" report. Along with this, look for information about the wine levels, referred to as "ullage." The ullage refers to the air space between the wine and the bottom of the cork. A small amount of evaporation is inevitable in older wines, but beware if the levels are suspiciously low. This is a sign that the wine might have turned. You don't want to pay big bucks for an oxi-dized wine, but if you still feel compelled to bid on that bottle, make sure you don't overpay.

  4. How and where the wine has been stored. This is referred to as the wine's "prove-nance." In an ideal world, you want to buy a wine that has had few owners so it hasn't been transported all over creation. You also want it to come from a temperature- and humidity-controlled cellar.

  5. The auction house's anticipated price range of how much the individual lots will

Unofficially...
Wine is grouped into "lots" for sale at auction. A lot might con-tain one bottle or several. The exact contents will be described in the auction catalog.

sell for. This gives you a reference point for your own bids.

■ Do your homework. This is the time to compare notes with the experts from top wine publications, wine merchants, and even competing auction houses that deal with wine. Also consult with vintage charts because, when it comes to buying more mature wines, vintage does matter. An excellent source of wine auction information, including an ongoing price index of wines sold at auction, is *Wine Spectator* and its excellent Web site, www.winespectator.com.

■ Find out whether the auction house is offering a presale tasting. For serious buyers, it is well worth the tasting fee to be able to taste for yourself before you commit to buying. Of course, with many rarities, this it is not always possible, but it never hurts to ask.

■ At the auction house, you register for a paddle with a major credit card, and you usually need to supply a bank reference.

■ When it's time to bid, all you have to do is raise your paddle.

■ If, for whatever reason, a wine fails to attract a bid at the low end of the price range in the catalog, the wine might not be sold. As a seller, you make an agreement with the auction house ahead of time as to the lowest price you will accept. If this price is not met, the wine is "passed." This is auction talk for no sale.

■ If you make a mistake such as bidding on the wrong lot, your best bet is to let the auctioneer

Bright Idea
Auctions are exciting to attend, especially if you are bidding. If you want to ensure that you will not go crazy, however, you can place your bid by mail or fax it before the auction. Just let the auction house know your top bid for any one lot.

know immediately. Better auction houses will try to work with you because they don't want you to be forced into buying something you didn't want in the first place.

If you're a novice, attend a few auctions just to observe and learn the drill. Make a mental note of the regulars who attend. They will stand out. When you do start bidding, use some of these strategies:

- Sit at the back of the room where you can observe all the bidding action.

- Don't challenge the high rollers. Price is no object to them, and they will bid whatever it takes to get what they want.

- If the auction house is offering one or more identical lots for sale in both the morning and afternoon sessions on the same day, make your bids at the later session. The early bird may catch the worm, but he probably will have to pay top dollar for it. You are more likely to get a bargain in the afternoon. In addition, by the afternoon, many bidders might have exhausted their resources.

Special tips for selling at auction

Here are some things you need to know if you want to sell your wine at auction:

- The biggest issue to the auction house is how and where your wine has been kept.

- The auction house will inspect your cellar and the condition of the wines.

- Most auction houses won't bother with lots that are not worth at least $1,000. It's not worth their time.

Timesaver
Keep individual photos of your wines on file to illustrate their condition. This can make it easier for you to get an auction house to take your collection on consignment, and it most certainly helps for insurance purposes.

- To facilitate a potential sale, create your own personal wine list that includes the following pertinent information:

  1. Type of wine

  2. Name of wine producer

  3. Vintage

  4. When you bought the wine and from where

  5. How long you have owned the wine

  6. The conditions under which the wine has been stored

  7. Wine levels or "ullage"

- After an auction house agrees to sell your wine, you need to agree on a reserve level. This is the lowest bid you will accept on your wine. You don't want to give the wine away, but you don't want to put a ridiculously high price tag on your minimum unless you plan to drink it yourself.

- Expect to pay these standard fees:

  1. Consignment fee to the auction house (10 to 20 percent of the final bidding price)

  2. Insurance fee

  3. Shipping and handling fees

Wine auction houses and retailers

In most states, individuals are not permitted to sell their wine to other individuals, but an increasing number now sell to retail stores or via auction. Due to the patchwork quilt of laws governing wine, call your state's local Alcoholic Beverage Control (ABC) office to get specific information about local laws or consult with one of the well-known, reputable auction houses or wine merchants in the following table.

TABLE 15.1: WINE AUCTION HOUSES BY STATE

State	Auction House
California	Butterfield & Butterfield Auction House (415-861-7500)
	Christie's Los Angeles (310-385-2600)
New York	Sotheby's Auction House (212-606-7000)
	Sotheby's runs wine auctions with:
	Morrell & Company (212-688-9370)
	Sherry-Lehmann (212-838-7500 or 212-606-7207)
	Christie's Auction House (212-636-2000)
	Christie's runs wine auctions with:
	Acker, Merrall & Condit (212-787-1700)
	Zachys (914-723-0241)
	Phillips International Auctioneers (212-570-4830 or 800-825-2781)
Illinois	The Chicago Wine Company (847-647-8789)
	Davis & Company (312-587-9500)
	John Hart Fine Wine Limited (312-944-5385)

Many fine-wine retail merchants buy and sell from private wine cellars. Check with your local merchant. Many are listed in Appendix B, "Resource Guide," at the back of this book.

Wine advisers

Just as there are personal trainers and career coaches, today there is an emerging field of professionals called "Wine Advisers." These are people who presumably will help you collect the right wines at the right price.

If you feel you need someone to act as your personal wine adviser, I still maintain that you are better off finding a good professional wine merchant.

Bright Idea
Sotheby's, one of the top auction houses, has partnered with Amazon.com to enable you to get in on the bidding action from the comfort of your home through its subsidiary, Livebid.com. It makes the process very easy and accessible, and it looks like the beginning of a new trend.

Build a relationship with the merchant and talk wine. If you need some special attention, whether it's a little hand-holding at a wine auction or orchestrating an important wine dinner, you could perhaps make some special arrangements with the retailer or consult with another trusted wine professional. In either case, some type of fee will be involved for his or her services. They may charge you by the hour or by the project, or in the case of auction purchases, they may ask for a 5 to 10 percent commission on the wine purchased.

Perhaps you know a restaurateur who attends auctions regularly, or you have become acquainted with a wine educator. The important thing is to consult with someone who has a proven wine background, not just someone who likes wine, was told he has a good palate, and decided to call himself a "Wine Adviser." Because it's not a regulated business, here are some questions to ask:

1. How long have you been in the wine business?

2. In what capacity have you been affiliated with wine?

3. What types of wine do you drink?

4. What wines do you collect? Is the wine you collect worth more than the price you originally paid?

5. What is the most money that you personally have ever paid for a bottle or lot of wine? You want to do business with someone who puts his money where his mouth is.

6. What is the most that you have ever spent on behalf of any one client? Ideally, you should deal with a wine adviser who has made purchases above what you plan on spending so he doesn't look at you like the gravy train.

7. Should I buy at auction? Any wine adviser worth his salt will be able to recommend auctions and show you the ropes. He should be able to advise you when it's best to bid and when it's best to fold.

If you are looking for a wine adviser to help you build your wine collection through auction sales, you should expect that he or she will do the homework on the wines slated for sale and their condition.

Just the facts

- The most important things to look for in a wine merchant are selection, knowledgeable staff, service, and competitive prices.

- A good wine merchant is a good listener who will make wine recommendations based on what you like.

- There are many extras you can take advantage of in a wine shop including in-store tastings, special wine events, and informative newsletters.

- It's better not to buy wine on a blind recommendation.

- You can save money by buying wine by the case.

- Wine can be a good investment, but there are no guarantees. You're better off if you enjoy drinking it and sharing it with friends.

- Auctions are a good source of mature, ready-to-drink wines.

- Know your local wine laws before you buy direct. The government is cracking down on direct shipments.

Entertaining with Wine

Chapter 16

GET THE SCOOP ON...
How to select wines for any party ▪ Estimating
how much wine you'll need ▪ Dealing with
caterers ▪ Throwing a wine-tasting party ▪
Champagne cocktails and palatable punches

PART VI

Crowd Pleasers

No matter what the occasion for entertaining, the object is the same. You want everybody, or at least most everybody, happy with your wine selection. In the case of a special event or a big party, the goal is not necessarily to provide the best wine experience everyone has ever had in their lives. But you don't want your guests to go home after the party and ask each other, What was that dreadful stuff they served?

There are some variations on this pleasing theme, depending more specifically on the purpose behind your entertaining.

Business entertaining

In the case of business entertaining, you might be wining and dining a client, making an impression on a prospective client to attract new business, celebrating a new partnership, or even closing a deal.

As the host, you want to make your guest happy. You've gone out of your way to select a good restaurant. Now it's time to select a good wine to complement the meal and, more importantly, to make your guest feel special.

Let me backtrack for a moment. Those of us in the wine and food industry commonly seek out restaurants that are known to have a good wine list. This means more than just a wine list with a good, solid selection of wines by the bottle. For lunch meetings when we are entertaining, it also is especially important for the restaurant to offer premium wines by the glass. The "house red" and "house white" simply won't do.

One important criterion for me personally when I entertain a professional "wine" person, whether he or she is the winemaker, importer, or marketer, is that the restaurant sells that person's wine. If I'm unsure, I will call the restaurant ahead of time and ask, or I might even ask for them to fax me the wine list. In cases when the wine is a top priority, you might ask the maitre d' or proprietor about bringing your own wine (assuming they don't carry it), subject to a corkage fee of $10 to $15 per bottle. In most business entertaining, unless you have a very specific bottle of wine in mind, you can almost always find a suitable alternative at a restaurant that has a good wine list.

At lunchtime in many of the top "expense account" wine destinations, you still will quite often see a bottle of wine on the table, but many businesspeople prefer to limit their lunchtime consumption to ordering by the glass so they don't feel sleepy in the middle of the afternoon.

For diners who look at a bottle of wine and say with exasperation, I could never finish a bottle or A bottle is too much, here's an interesting aside: A 750-ml bottle of wine contains 25.4 ounces. If you go

Bright Idea!
For business entertaining, become a "regular" at one or a handful of restaurants. Keep a current copy of the menu and wine list at your office so you can pinpoint or narrow down your wine selection before you sit down. It will keep you from fumbling and wasting time at the table.

to practically any fast-food outlet or any deli that sells fountain drinks, you will find that their "Biggie" size, so popular today, amounts to 26 ounces. People routinely gulp down this oversized drink on their own, yet they are reluctant to share a bottle of wine among two to four people, which comes out to one to two glasses per person.

I'm not urging you to go out and order a bottle of wine if all you really want is a glass. I'm just showing you that it's really not as much as you might think.

Business protocol for wine

Protocol is especially important in a business situation. By making the restaurant reservation, you assume the position of host. You confirm your role as host by the way you interact with the restaurant's maitre d' and with the server when you ask for the wine list. From that point on, the server looks to you for the selection, presents you with the bottle, and pours you a taste for your approval.

If your client is a wine geek or an enthusiastic consumer, you might turn the wine list over to him or her and give carte blanche to make a selection. This is one sure way to please your client, but it can be risky business unless you have an unlimited expense account.

The other sure-fire way to please your client is if you follow a few basics of wine and food pairing:

1. Ask your client whether he or she prefers red or white. The answer to this question eliminates half of the list.

2. Select a lighter-style wine with lighter-style food.

3. Select a fuller-bodied wine with heavier food.

4. Select a wine from an area considered to be the restaurant's specialty. A fine Italian restaurant, for example, presumably carries a good selection of fine Italian wines.

5. Select a recognizable name, whether it is the winery or the producer. Few people who drink California wine are not familiar with names like Mondavi, Beringer, and Kendall-Jackson, and few people who drink French Champagnes are unfamiliar with Möet-Chandon White Star or Dom Pérignon. These are by no means the only good wines on a given wine list, but they certainly represent a small sampling of the bread-and-butter wines that even the most casual wine-consuming clients will recognize and appreciate.

Price as a consideration

Unless fiscal responsibility is the theme of your business meeting, don't select a wine from a lesser-known producer in a lesser-known wine region to get a "value" wine. Save this approach for your personal night out. Don't order the cheapest wine on the list. You get what you pay for, and you will look cheap.

If you are reading the list from right to left and you notice that most bottles fall in the $30 to $40 range, select a bottle that is at least within this range. Go to the next price level or beyond if you are looking to impress.

When you sit down with a client, if it is clear that he or she is interested in a glass of wine, the server will give you a separate list, will point out the selections on the food menu, or will recite your options. A definite benefit to wines by the glass is that you and your clients can make your own selections. You don't have to worry about making the "right" choice.

Dinner party

Regardless of whether you are more comfortable making reservations or you feel creative enough to cook at home, a dinner party affords you the opportunity to pull out all the wine stops.

If you select one of your favorite restaurants as the venue for your dinner party, it almost always is a less formal situation than business entertaining. Let the evening unfold. Consider who it is you are entertaining. Do you have a table peppered with wine mavens with whom you will consult informally about the table selections? For groups such as these, the wine selection and banter that goes with it are part of the fun. If you are the resident wine wizard, just try to gauge the mood of the table. Unless anyone objects, start with a crisp white aperitif to get the juices going. Then move into red.

To add a little drama to the evening, you can order a larger-format bottle such as a magnum (equivalent to two bottles) or even a Jeroboam (equivalent to six bottles) for larger parties. As one restaurateur I know likes to say, "When these large bottles come out on the floor, it's a show stopper."

This same dinner party at home presents a more controlled situation. You're the one planning the menu, deciding on the number of courses, and ultimately selecting the wine. Again, you want to follow the natural progression with your wines, from lightest bodied to fullest flavored. You want the wine to enhance the food, not overpower it. You also want the wine to stand up to the food, however, or else you might as well drink water.

Bright Idea
If your client is unsure about his or her wine selection, decide for yourself quickly and speak up. It's even better if you order one of the "better" (translation: more expensive) glasses of wine so your client will feel comfortable doing the same. It sets the tone for your meeting.

Part of the benefit of entertaining at home is that it's more personal. You serve foods that you personally enjoy and that are special to you. It only makes sense for you to take a similar approach to selecting wines for entertaining at home.

People enjoy trying new wines, especially when the host is "into wine." For more tips about selecting wine for a dinner party, see the section called "Wine with Food" in Chapter 1, "Wine—What Are You Saving It For?"

Brunch

Whether you are meeting a group of friends at a restaurant or having them over for brunch, simple is best. You can just whip up an Italian fritatta, serve some fresh-baked muffins, slice up some fruit, and you're there. Brunch is not brunch, however, without Bloody Marys and Mimosas. The Mimosa, of course, is the traditional brunch drink made by mixing Champagne or sparkling wine with orange juice.

Bright Idea
If you're going to mix Champagne or sparkling wine with orange juice to prepare Mimosas, do yourself a favor and buy fresh juice—not the concentrate. It makes a difference.

As a Champagne purist, I will not mix good Champagne with anything. I know people who will use only French Champagne, and good stuff at that, and they claim they can tell the difference. I tend to doubt it.

My personal preference is to use less-expensive Champagne or, even better, sparkling wines that fit into the $10-and-under category such as some of those from Spain, Italy, and California. There are plenty on the market that I am happy to enjoy by themselves if I'm in the mood for bubbly, but they really do add a perfect taste dimension and a little zing to a Mimosa.

Banquets: weddings, anniversaries, bar mitzvahs and bat mitzvahs

These are Kodak moments—those special parties where everything is supposed to be magical and perfect. There is no margin for error here.

You probably are dealing with the catering department of a hotel, restaurant, catering hall, country club, or temple that should know something about food and beverage. Alternatively, you may be dealing with an outside caterer who will handle the food portion of your party but not get involved with the bar. When it comes to the selection and service of beverages, including wine, you're on your own.

Where do you begin?

Dealing with banquet directors

When you are dealing with a banquet director, it's good to have an idea of what type of food and wine you want to serve at your party, but I think it's best to go with an open mind.

A good banquet director will immediately ask you about:

- The type of event or party you are planning: wedding, anniversary party, office holiday party, and so on.

- The style of the party and the level of formality: reception, hors d'oeuvres, sit-down dinner, or buffet.

- What you plan to spend. A caterer will need a price range to know what he or she has to work with in terms of the level of food, beverage, and service.

Before you sit down to meet with a banquet director, prepare the following information:

1. The date and time you would like to hold the party.

2. How many guests you expect to host. You should estimate a range such as 175 to 200.

3. What type of cocktail hour will you hold? How long will it last (an hour or an hour and a half)? Do you prefer a Champagne reception, wine only, or a full bar?

4. During the cocktail hour, will drinks be available only at the bar? Will cocktail servers roam the floor taking orders from guests? Will cocktail servers pass Champagne and/or wine?

5. What type of food will be served during the cocktail hour? Are you content with a few simple trays of assorted cheeses, crackers, and fresh fruit? Do you prefer hot and cold hors d'oeuvres passed butler style? Or, will you go all out and have buffet stations?

6. Do you expect to serve Champagne or sparkling wine just for the toast? Will it be available at the bar? Do you want to serve Champagne or sparkling wine with dinner?

Think about what type of wine you'd like to serve with dinner. Have a red and a white style in mind. Wait until you see the banquet director to look at the wine list and discuss your wine options.

You know that you have x dollars to spend on this party. Keep in mind that a party is not just food and beverage. There are other considerations such as music, flowers, and other decorations, not to mention tax and gratuity. It all adds up.

Catering wine options

When it's time to select the wines for your special event, you have more choices than you may know about. Standard procedure is for the caterer to try to sell you certain food and beverage packages, almost like the old Chinese menus in which you pick a selection from column A and another selection from column B.

The standard catering-wine list is a limited list of wines featuring the hotel's house wine and a small selection of basic, food-friendly wine types that probably include Beaujolais, Merlot, Chardonnay, and White Zinfandel. You will not be familiar with many of the brands, and they want it that way. More and more, wine companies are producing lines of wine that you'll never see on a retail shelf. That way, when you buy the wine from the caterer, you cannot compare the price of the wine to what you'd pay your wine merchant. Wines such as Burlwood and Copperidge, for example, are moderately priced labels from E & J Gallo Winery that you will see only in restaurants and hotels.

One catering wine that I never hesitate to recommend is Whispering Peak Vineyards from California. It happens to be the house wine at the Grand Canyon in the hotel El Tovar, which is operated by the Federal Parks Commission, and it is available at many other hotels nationwide. The wines, which include Chardonnay, Cabernet Sauvignon, Merlot, and Pinot Noir, are consistently good, and the label is smart looking, a plus for anyone serving wines to company.

These "standards" provide a good starting point, and some of them might suit you just fine. If they don't, however, there's nothing wrong with asking

Bright Idea
When you meet with the catering director, make it clear immediately that you consider the wine to be an integral part of your party. This will alert the caterer to take more care with the wine selection rather than leaving it for the last minute and sticking you with the hotel's house wine.

to make some alterations to either your food menu or your wine selections. If you're working from a standard menu that includes the hotel's house wine, for example, and you'd really be much happier with one of its premium offerings, discuss this with the catering director and figure out how much more it will cost per person.

If you don't like what you find on the hotel's catering wine list, ask to see the wine lists that the hotel uses at its own restaurants. These will offer more variety and, generally, a better selection of premium wines that the hotel already keeps on hand. They won't mind selling it to you.

It is possible in many instances for serious customers to taste the food and wine before committing to a menu. If you are unfamiliar with the wine or are waffling with your selection, ask your catering director about setting up a tasting.

Perhaps you have something special in mind that you want to serve at your party, and it's not on the hotel wine list. Ask the banquet director if the wine can be special-ordered for your party. As long as he can order it from his wine distributor, he most likely will sell it to you at the standard hotel markup of three times his cost.

Your other option is to bring in your own wine subject to a corkage fee. The corkage fee is the service charge that the catering facility adds to your bill for opening and serving the wines. The standard corkage fee is $10 to $15 per bottle. On occasion, a hotel might tell you that the fee is $20 to $25. For many caterers, this is not set in stone. Your best bet is to negotiate the corkage fee down.

Just so you're fully prepared, you need to know that the hotel probably will charge tax and gratuity

Watch Out!
If you order wine from the hotel's wine list and don't use it all, the hotel should take back the unopened bottles. If you special-order wines and have leftovers, you're stuck paying for it. To protect yourself, negotiate with the catering director to sell you all special-ordered wine at his cost.

on top of the corkage fee. If you're talking about bringing in two cases of wine (or a total of 24 bottles) with a $15 corkage fee, that's $360 plus tax and gratuity on this amount.

Wine service at banquets

Selecting the actual wines that will be poured at your event is one thing, but deciding how you want them served is another. In catering, you can't assume that they are going to serve the way you want them to unless you specifically ask or at least double-check with your catering director.

Take the example of a formal wedding for which you expect 175 to 200 guests. You have selected wines that you know they will enjoy, but you want to make sure your guests receive attentive service and don't have to spend the better part of the evening waiting for a glass of wine or Champagne.

Some specific questions to ask are:

- How many bars will be set up for my party?

- How many cocktail servers will be working the party?

- How many bartenders will be working the party?

- Who will be serving wine during the dinner?

The catering director might respond by telling you that they use one bar per 200 guests and that this is "standard." It might be the standard that some caterers use to operate the average party, but it is a good idea to build a little cushion into your budget to enable you to buy better service. Ask for an additional bar and an additional bartender and/or cocktail server. Make sure there are enough banquet servers on staff during the dinner so there are servers dedicated to serving wine at the tables instead of having the food server do double duty, which happens all the time. The additional staff will help make sure that your party runs seamlessly.

As a rule of thumb, caterers will set up one or two bars per 200 people. You might want two or sometimes even three, depending on your crowd. They usually will staff one bartender per bar. You might prefer to have two bartenders taking care of each bar. For dinner service, a caterer will probably assign one server for every 15 guests. You might ask for additional servers to lower the ratio to one server for every 10 guests. This will raise the level of service.

You can hire an extra cocktail server to pass Champagne and white wine. This adds to guest convenience and takes the pressure off the bar. To enhance wine service at dinner, consider designating a few of your servers as wine stewards for the evening. Their only job will be to serve wine to your guests. This will help ensure that your guests get to enjoy their wine with their food.

Sometimes, in the interest of speeding up service, a catering staff will pre-open several bottles of wine before they are needed. At the end of the evening, you end up with a lot of partially filled bottles. If you are trying to save money and you know that you are able to return unopened bottles to the catering department at the end of the party, you need to discuss with your catering director ahead of time what is an acceptable amount of pre-opened bottles. If you direct the staff to open bottles only as needed, however, you need to realize that this will slow down wine service.

Another tip for enhancing wine service is to be sure all tables are preset with one Champagne flute, one red-wine glass, and one white-wine glass.

In cases in which you want to be assured that your guests do not have to look for a server to pour wine, consider presetting the tables with a bottle of red and a bottle of white (in an ice bucket). It might not be as stylish as having a server pour for everyone, but sometimes it is a more practical solution.

What to buy for an event and how much

When it comes to throwing a party, no matter how many people are involved, the most commonly asked questions are:

- What kind of wine should I buy?
- Should I serve red, white or rosé?
- Do I need to serve any alcohol besides wine?
- How much wine do I need to buy?

For people who are dealing with a qualified catering director or a food and beverage professional, I advise that you leave such questions in his or her hands. These professionals deal with big parties day in and day out. In 95 percent of the cases, they are right on the money. You can help them help you, however, by giving input about the type of crowd you expect.

When my husband and I were married, I'll never forget our first meeting with our catering director. He was a true professional and knew his stuff cold. Yet when it came to talking about Champagne and the Champagne toast, his initial advice was, "People don't drink Champagne. They just toast with it."

"Not this group," we explained. Our group included a fair number of restaurant, hotel, and wine people, not to mention "regular" people who love good food and drink. "This is a Champagne crowd," we told him. We selected some premium wines from their list, but we brought in our Champagne (Taittinger) and didn't have to worry about leftovers. There were none.

Similarly, while I was updating the banquet service guidelines for this book, whenever I asked my catering friends about how much and what kind of wine to select for a party, they inevitably asked about the type of crowd we were talking about. "If you mean doctors and lawyers," they'd say, "you're talking more and better wines." As a group, these professionals are more likely to be really into wine. On the flip side, you might be entertaining a large group but know that they will have a glass of wine and then switch to Diet Coke.

In terms of color, banquet directors find on average that their customers drink 60 percent whites and 40 percent reds. Rosé and blush wines are not widely used for catering meals, though you are more likely to find White Zinfandel at the bar during the cocktail hour. The general feeling is that White Zinfandel drinkers most often will switch over to a white wine, like a Chardonnay, during a party without any difficulty. As for grape variety, Merlot is the current "in" red grape, and Chardonnay continues to dominate the white wine category.

I'm sorry to report that Champagne is relegated to the ceremonial toast at most catering functions, though a Champagne crowd will have a glass with a first course. On rare occasions, and I'd venture to say in some hard-core, wine-savvy groups, Champagne could be served as a "regular" wine throughout the meal.

Because of the cameo appearance that Champagne often makes, banquet directors use these rules of thumb for how much to buy and serve:

- For a toast: one bottle for every eight guests (That's about 3 ounces each if you fill the glass halfway, which is more than enough for a toast.)
- For a cocktail reception: one bottle for every three to four guests
- For dinner: one bottle for every two to three guests

When you are entertaining, is it necessary to serve any alcohol other than wine? If you want to keep the party simple, do a few things, and do them right. I'd say stick to wine, especially if you're working with an outside caterer, not necessarily a hotel. If you've got the hotel at your disposal along with easy access to a full bar, however, you might as well take advantage of it and be an accommodating host.

The issue of how much wine you'll need to buy is important any time you're hosting a special event, but it takes on greater importance if you are throwing a party on your own. I've seen many cases in which the host hires a wonderful caterer who will prepare and serve the food but will not touch the bar other than to recommend some bartenders you might hire.

Here are two other formulas that will come in handy for cocktail receptions:

Wine-only—If you are having a "wine-only" reception and pouring 6-ounce glasses of wine, expect to serve 1.5 to 2 drinks per person during the first hour and an additional 1 to 1.25 drinks per person for the second hour.

Full bar—If you are offering a "full bar" including wine during a reception, expect that 30 to 35 percent of your guests will drink wine.

To come up with the magic number of how much wine you need for a full-bar reception, follow these simple steps:

1. Take the number of guests expected at the party and multiply by 35 percent to get the number of wine drinkers.

2. Then multiply the number of wine drinkers by 12 ounces (for two glasses) to get the number of ounces you'll need.

3. Take the total number of ounces and divide by 25.4 ounces (the number of ounces in a regular-size bottle of wine) to find out the total number of bottles needed.

4. Take the total number of bottles and divide by 12 (the number of bottles in a case) to determine how many cases you'll need.

For example, let's take a cocktail reception for 200 guests:

Step 1: 35 percent × 200 guests = 70 wine drinkers

Step 2: 70 wine drinkers × 12 ounces = 840 ounces

Step 3: 840 ounces ÷ 25.4 = 33 bottles

Step 4: 33 bottles ÷ 12 = 2.75 cases

For a cocktail hour that is going to be more like two hours and be accompanied by a full assortment of appetizers and hors d'oeuvres, you can easily round up your estimate to three cases. Then, if you like, you can determine how much red and how much white to buy by using the 60/40 formula (60 percent white to 40 percent red).

Technically, if formulas are precise, you'd need 1.8 cases of white wine and 1.2 cases of red. To keep it simple, just go with two cases of white to one case of red.

If you are serving wine just for dinner, figure on 12 to 16 ounces per person. If you are planning a cocktail hour or a Champagne reception preceding the dinner, however, allow for 9 to 14 ounces of wine per person. In both cases, all you have to do is multiply the number of guests by the anticipated number of ounces needed per person to come up with the total amount of wine you'll need. Then divide your total ounces by the number of bottles in a case, and voilà, you get your case figure.

For simple home entertaining, whether you've invited over a few neighbors or have a house full of guests for cocktails or dinner, some of the best advice I've seen recently came from the back of a wine bottle.

Throughout this book, I have urged you to read not only the front label but also the back label because you never know what extra information a winery might supply. I took my own advice recently and scrutinized the back label of Vendange Chardonnay, a very popular, very affordable Chardonnay made by Sebastiani. (Note: The Sebastiani name doesn't appear on the label, but that's what it is.) At a discount outlet or a Price Club, you can buy a 1.5-liter "crowd pleaser" size for about $10.

Anyway, the back label of this Vendange Chardonnay explains that "Vendange" (Von-DONJ) means "grape harvest" in French. It also gives you an idea of the taste profile within the bottle—hints of apples and French oak. It tells you how to serve the wine—chilled—and suggests foods that go well with it—poultry, seafood, and pasta dishes.

Unofficially...
Even though there is a trend toward red wines at cocktail receptions, people have a natural tendency to reach for white wines because they like to start with something lighter. Equally important, they are reluctant to mingle and risk being bumped into during the course of cocktail conversation. Simply put, they don't want to wear red wine.

What I really like about this back label, however, is that it tells you, "This bottle contains 10 five-ounce glasses of wine." It goes on to give you its shelf life once opened: "If recorked securely, it may be enjoyed up to a week." You can't ask for much more helpful information than that.

The mechanics of setting up wine service at home

It doesn't take rocket science to set up a good party; it just takes good organizational skills. Here's what you need to do:

- Order your wines early to make sure you get what you want.

- Pick them up at least a few days before your party so there's no last-minute rush to get the wine.

On the day of the party, have the following tools on hand:

- A knife or razor blade to open the cases of wine

- Two to three corkscrews per bar or wine station

- Wine tubs in which to chill wine

- Ice

- Clean cloth napkins

- Ample clean stemware

The key to any good party is ice, especially when you're serving white or blush wines. You also can often rent wine glasses from your wine merchant, food caterer, or local party store.

Whether you are serving a large party of people or giving them a wine memento to take home, you should know that many different bottle sizes are

Moneysaver
Remember to buy by the case to save money. When you're buying in bulk for a larger party, also ask the wine merchant if he or she will take back unopened bottles when the party is over. If you've built a relationship with the merchant as suggested in Chapter 15, "How to Find a Good Wine Merchant," this should not be a problem.

available. The following are for Champagne and sparkling wine.

TABLE 16.1: SIZES OF WINE BOTTLES

Size	Number of Bottles	Milliliters/ Liters	Ounces
Split	1/4	187 ml	6.3 oz.
Half-bottle	1/2	375 ml	12.7 oz.
Bottle	1	750 ml	25.4 oz.
Magnum	2	1.5 liters	50.7 oz.
Jeroboam	4	3.0 liters	101.4 oz.
Rehoboam	6	4.5 liters	156.0 oz.
Methusehal	8	6.0 liters	202.8 oz.
Salmanazar	12	9.0 liters	307.2 oz.
Balthazar	16	12.0 liters	416.0 oz.
Nebuchadnezzar	20	15.0 liters	520.0 oz.
Sovereign	36	27 liters	936.0 oz.

Entertaining recipes

Red, white, and rosé are usually all you'll ever need to entertain guests, but sometimes you'll want to offer something a little out of the ordinary. Here are some recipes that will make it look as if you fussed, even if you really didn't.

My favorite bartender, Dale DeGroff, who was at the legendary Rainbow Room until it closed to the public recently, created these three special Champagne cocktails. Fortunately, he's still in town behind the "stick," as he likes to call the bar, at his own place called Blackbird in midtown, mixing these and many others.

Ritz Cocktail

Dale DeGroff's tribute to the Ritz Cocktails of Paris and Madrid.

Watch Out!
Half-bottles (375 ml) age quicker than standard bottles because they contain more oxygen per milliliter of wine than a standard (750 ml) size. The neck of both bottles is the same size, so there is the same amount of air space between the top of the wine and the cork, which affects the wine. For the same reason, large-format bottles have a tendency to mature slower than the standard 750 ml.

1 ounce Cognac
$^1/_2$ ounce Cointreau
$^1/_4$ ounce Maraschino Liqueur
$^1/_3$ ounce fresh lemon juice
Champagne
Stir in a mixing glass all ingredients except the Champagne. Strain into a Martini glass and fill with Champagne. Garnish with burnt orange peel.

Champagne Mango

1 $^1/_2$ ounce mango purée (sweetened with simple syrup—see recipe below)
4 ounces Champagne
Dash of Maraschino Liqueur
Prepare in a cocktail mixing glass and pour into Champagne flute. Top with Maraschino Liqueur. Garnish with lichee.

Champagne Passion

1 ounce passion fruit purée
$^1/_2$ ounce Alize Liqueur
Champagne
Pour passion fruit purée into a cocktail mixing glass and then slowly add Champagne while stirring gently. Float Alize Liqueur on top.

Other favorite recipes perfect for entertaining include:

Mimosa

2 ounces chilled fresh orange juice
4 ounces chilled Champagne or sparkling wine
Pour orange juice into a Champagne flute. Top with Champagne. Garnish with an orange slice.

Kir Royale

4 ounces chilled Champagne or sparkling wine
$^1/_2$ ounce Crème de Cassis
Pour Crème de Cassis into a Champagne flute. Top with Champagne.

Kir

4 ounces chilled dry white wine

¹/₂ ounce Crème de Cassis

Pour Crème de Cassis into a wine glass. Top with chilled dry white wine.

Bellini

2 ounces peach purée

6 ounces chilled Champagne or sparkling wine

¹/₄ ounce peach liqueur

Pour the peach puree into a Champagne flute. Add the Champagne. Drizzle peach liqueur over the top of the drink.

French 75

Juice of 1 lemon

1 ounce simple bar syrup (see recipe below)

1 ¹/₂ ounces Brandy

2 ounces chilled Champagne or sparkling wine

Shake the lemon juice, simple syrup, and Brandy with ice. Strain into a highball glass. Top off with chilled Champagne.

Simple Bar Syrup

Makes 1 quart

3 cups sugar

2 ¹/₂ cups water

Combine the sugar and water in a large saucepan. Cook over high heat for three to four minutes or until the sugar dissolves, stirring constantly. Bring to a full boil. Remove from heat. Set aside to cool completely.

(Note: If you store simple bar sugar in an airtight container in your refrigerator, it will last for one week.)

Timesaver
If it's too much of a hassle to make the simple bar sugar in a saucepan, you can put the ingredients in a bar shaker and shake well. Be sure to shake up the sugar each time before using.

Champagne Cocktail

1 sugar cube

2 dashes Angostura Bitters

5 ounces chilled Champagne or sparkling wine

Place sugar cube in a Champagne flute and shake two dashes of Angostura Bitters on the cube. Fill the rest of the glass with chilled Champagne. Garnish with a twist of lemon.

Champagne Punch

1 bottle Champagne or sparkling wine

4 ounces Brandy

2 ounces Curaçao

1 ounce Grand Marnier

1 ounce Grenadine

1 Tablespoon simple sugar

Mix together ingredients in a pitcher or bowl. Add a small block of ice. Slice orange, lemons, and pineapple and add to the bowl. Garnish with fresh sprig of mint. Serve in a stem glass or punch cup.

Organizing a wine-tasting party

There are many different ways to organize a wine-tasting party. Depending on the group, you can assemble a serious tasting in which you select a theme such as Chardonnays from all over the world.

Start small by limiting the group to six or eight friends to keep the tasting manageable. To make sure there is enough wine for tasting and socializing afterward, have two bottles of wine per person. You might supply it, or you might ask your friends to bring a bottle of chilled Chardonnay from the country of their choice.

For a more formal tasting, set your dining room table with a plain white tablecloth and place a tasting sheet place mat down at each place setting.

Place a clean wine glass on each circle of the circle sheet.

In the meantime, take the chilled wines that are to be used for the tasting and wrap them in aluminum foil, even covering the capsule at the neck. You should do this because more experienced tasters might pick up a clue as to the contents of the bottle. The idea is to taste the wines "blind" so that no one has preconceived notions of what he or she is tasting.

Assign each wine a number, again using the 1 to 6 example. When you pour the wines during the tasting for your guests, you will pour bottle number 1 into the wine glass that sits on the number 1 position on your circle sheet.

Assuming that you know the wines to be tasted ahead of time and that you want to get a little fancy, make a copy of the label on a piece of paper and provide room below the label for your guests to make their own tasting notes.

Go through the five S's of tasting as described in Chapter 3, "How to Taste Wine": see, swirl, smell, sip, and savor. Write down your first impressions of the wine, what it reminded you of, and how long the taste lingered in your mouth. Make sure everyone has enough time to taste the wines and then compare notes with each other.

If you're feeling especially geeky, try to guess where the wine came from, from what winery, and if you think you're really good, what vintage it is. In tastings such as these, I always like to know the suggested retail price because, at the end of the day, after you taste a wine and you decide whether you like it or not, the price helps you decide how it will fit into your own wine-drinking repertoire.

Bright Idea
If you plan to taste six wines, create your own circle sheets by tracing the bottom of the glass on a piece of white paper. Number the circles on the circle sheet from 1 to 6 to correspond to the numbers you will be assigning to the wines.

Unofficially...
When we taste wines professionally, we usually are asked to refrain from wearing a scent and from smoking. That way, we can taste the wine without smelling someone's perfume, cigarettes, or cigars. For a "serious" home tasting, you might want to do the same, at least for the "serious" part of the tasting.

Maybe because I already get the opportunity to do serious tastings, I really enjoy people who put together less cerebral wine tastings. For the last several years, we have visited a couple who has thrown a wine-tasting party during homecoming where we went to college. Each year they select a different theme. Last year's theme was "The Italian Famiglia."

Essentially, we come equipped with two bottles. (It doesn't matter if they are red, white, or rosé.) The host, who happens to be a professional computer wizard, checks it into his computer system, assigns it a number, and wraps it in aluminum foil so it will be "blind." The wines are indiscriminately placed throughout the house with an assortment of goodies to eat. You might take a few notes in the beginning of the evening, but truth be told, you just start making mental notes of whether you liked the wine and you rate it on a scale from 1 to 20.

For people diligent enough to take notes and turn in ratings, they come up with the evening's top scorer and the loser. The person who brought the top wine gets a prize, and the loser gets a gag gift. It's not very serious, but it's light years away from the days when we used to consume beer kegs—and it's a lot more fun.

Just the facts

- You need to let the catering director know up front that wine is important to your party. Otherwise, it will receive very low priority.

- There's no reason for you to get stuck with a hotel's unimaginative catering wine list.

- Serving wine from oversized bottles, such as Champagne from double magnums, adds drama to an event.

- You can enhance wine service at your party by requesting extra bartenders or servers. It will cost a few bucks more, but it often is worth it.

- There are easy formulas for deciding how much and what kind of wine to buy for your party. The most important factor, however, is to know your crowd.

How to Serve and Store Wine

PART VII

Chapter 17

GET THE SCOOP ON...
Corkscrews and other wine accouterment ▪ How to open wine and Champagne properly ▪ What temperature to store and serve wines— really ▪ When, what, and how to decant ▪ How to save the leftovers

Essential Tools and Tricks

After you've selected your wine, you're only halfway there. You still need to know how to serve and store it properly, whether you plan on opening it for dinner tonight or laying it down in your cellar for some special occasion in the future.

One of the best things about enjoying wine is that you get to decide how casual or how fussy you want to make the experience. It's a lot like going out to eat. You can go out and grab a quick bite at the local coffee shop, or you can make reservations at a gourmet restaurant and dine. You're fulfilling the basic need for food in both cases, and physically, you're going through the same motions.

It's the same thing with wine. At its most basic level, if you're having a white wine, you serve it chilled. If you're having a red, you keep it at room temperature. You grab a corkscrew, open the bottle, pour it into some wine glasses, and enjoy.

I don't want to spoil it for the minimalists, but there are some essential tools and a few tricks worth knowing to make a good thing better.

Extracting the cork

No matter your level of wine expertise, you have to begin with the cork. Ironically, twist-off caps like the ones used for beer bottles would be the easiest, most effective means of closing a bottle of wine. We talk about twist-off tops a lot in the trade and the wine press as a good alternative to bad corks, but few premium winemakers want to risk parting from the perceived higher level of quality associated with a cork-finished product. This leaves you needing to know how to select and handle a corkscrew.

Outside of my wine friends and a handful of friends who are not in the business but drink wine as part of their lifestyle, I find that most people shy away from opening a bottle. They simply aren't comfortable using the corkscrew. It's no big deal, however, if you have the right tools.

Double-winged opener

Ironically, one of the most popular household corkscrews, the metal double-winged opener, is not really the best to use. It was probably one of the first user-friendly corkscrews on the market years ago. All you have to do is place the corkscrew on top of the bottle and screw the auger (sometimes referred to as the "worm") into the cork, which raises the wings. When you push the wings down, the cork is extracted. I grew up with this type of corkscrew at my parent's home, and I know first-hand that the auger often mangles the cork, leaving shreds of cork in your wine. If you insist on using this type of corkscrew, at least avoid using it on older bottles in which the cork is probably more fragile. It won't stand a chance against the blunt auger.

Waiter's corkscrew

My corkscrew of choice is the waiter's corkscrew. It folds flat like a Swiss Army knife and contains three simple elements that pull out when needed: a knife, an auger, and a lever (which also doubles as a soft drink or beer opener).

Follow these simple steps to properly open a bottle of wine with a waiter's corkscrew:

1. Remove the capsule. This is the covering over the neck and cork on top of the bottle. You can use the blade to cut underneath the protruding lip of the bottle, or you can remove the capsule entirely if you prefer. Some wine capsules are still made of lead, especially the older ones and some imports, and you don't want the wine coming into contact with the lead. Fold the knife back into the corkscrew.

2. Take a clean, damp napkin or cloth and wipe the top of the cork just in case there is a little dirt or mold. This is normal and won't affect the wine.

3. Pull out the lever and the auger until they are fully extended. Your waiter's corkscrew should now look like a "T." Place one hand on the bottle and, with your other hand, insert the tip of the auger into the center of the cork and screw it in clockwise as deeply as possible. It's okay if the auger goes completely through the wine cork. It won't hurt anything.

4. Gently fold down the lever. You want to line up the notch at the bottom of the lever with the top lip of the bottle. To do this, gently push

Bright Idea
If you're dealing with an extra long cork, you might want to extract the cork only halfway as directed in step 5 and then screw the auger deeper into the cork as in step 3 before extracting the cork. This should prevent you from breaking the cork.

the side of the corkscrew opposite the lever down until the notch lines up with the top lip of the bottle. Place the notch of the lever securely on the top lip of the bottle.

5. Place one hand around the neck of the bottle at the bottom of the lever for support and your other hand firmly on top of the corkscrew and lift. The lifting action eases out the cork.

6. Before serving the wine, take a clean damp cloth or a napkin and wipe the lip of the bottle, both inside and out, in case there is any cork residue or tartrates. Tartrates are harmless crystals that sometimes are found at the bottom of a cork.

Pulltap's

Recently, I discovered a more clever version of the waiter's corkscrew called Pulltap's. This product is marketed by Bermar America, which is based in Malvern, Pennsylvania. It looks exactly like a waiter's corkscrew with the exception of one important modification: the lever has two notches instead of just one. The second notch allows you to ease the cork out part way with the top lever. Then, without having to turn the corkscrew into the cork further, you can merely use the bottom notch to remove the cork. A regular waiter's corkscrew costs $5 to $6, and a Pulltap's will run about $12.

Screwpull

Another popular household corkscrew that does the job well and is extremely easy to use is the Screwpull. It looks more like the double-winged model, except it is made of heavy-duty plastic and doesn't have wings. There is no need for wings because the plastic base of the Screwpull is designed to anchor onto the top lip of the bottle for leverage. (This is what the lever of the waiter's corkscrew does.) After you remove the capsule from the wine bottle and clean off the top of the cork, follow these simple steps:

Watch Out!
If you come across a stubborn cork that doesn't look like it's going to budge, don't try to force it with the Screwpull. The plastic, as heavy duty as it is, will break.

1. Place the base of the Screwpull on top of the bottle.

2. Turn the handle clockwise to insert the extra-long, Teflon-coated auger into the cork.

3. Continue turning the handle clockwise until the cork is extracted.

4. Don't forget to take a clean, damp cloth or napkin to wipe inside the lip and the outside neck of the bottle.

5. To remove the cork from the Screwpull, simply hold onto the cork with one hand while you turn the handle counterclockwise.

The Screwpull is really a neat little invention. It is available in personal household models for $20 to $25 in fine wine shops, gourmet food and kitchen shops, and wine catalogs.

Ah-So

At times, a corkscrew with an auger simply will not do the job as well as a two-pronged corkscrew known as the Ah-So. The idea is to slide the prongs between the bottle and the cork so that the prongs can grasp the cork in a vice grip and extract it without damage. Cases in which double-pronged corkscrews are particularly handy include:

- Super–tight-fitting corks

- Old corks

- Damaged corks

On the other hand, if you've got a cork with any play at all, this is not the right time to use an Ah-So because you'll probably end up pushing the cork down into the bottle of wine.

To use the Ah-So, after you remove the capsule from the wine bottle and clean off the top of the cork, follow these simple steps:

1. Hold the bottle in one hand. Slide the slightly longer prong into the space between the bottle and the cork, following with the shorter side.

2. Grip the handle of the Ah-So firmly and, using a back and forth motion, gently push the corkscrew into the bottle until the base of the Ah-So touches the top of the cork.

3. Twist the handle counterclockwise while pulling the cork gently.

4. Don't forget to take a clean, damp cloth or napkin to wipe the inside lip and the outside neck of the bottle.

The Ah-So cork extractor is available at many fine wine shops and specialty stores for about $8 to $10.

Troubleshooting cork catastrophes

"Cork situations" happen to everybody at one time or another, and they can be embarrassing, especially if you're entertaining guests. Here are three typical scenarios:

1. You're opening a bottle of wine, and the cork breaks in half. Half remains in the neck of the bottle.

   If your cork breaks in half, your best tool is the waiter's corkscrew. Instead of placing the auger directly on top of the remaining cork, insert it at a slight angle. When the auger is through the cork, use the fulcrum against the bottle top as leverage to extract the cork. For full details on how to use a waiter's corkscrew, refer to the step-by-step process described earlier in this chapter.

2. As you insert the corkscrew, the entire cork proceeds to drop into the wine.

   If the whole cork (or even chunks of it) gets pushed into your bottle of wine, you can try to pour carefully around it, or you can buy a special wine tchotchke known as a cork retriever. It's a very clever device made of three pieces of sturdy wire designed to act like a slender claw. The wire is attached to a handle to make your fishing expedition a little easier. The best place to buy a cork retriever is through wine-accessory catalogs, and they cost about $10.

3. As you turn the corkscrew, the auger mangles the cork and sends a layer of cork flakes into your wine.

   The case of the mangled cork is perhaps the messiest. It's not harmful, but drinking wine with cork crumbles is right up there with getting sand in your spinach salad. You might opt to pull out a decanter or a carafe and bone up on your decanting skills to eliminate the cork. To make sure you get rid of it all, consider using cheesecloth or a coffee filter.

Serving temperature

Perhaps casual wine drinkers don't think much about proper serving temperature beyond the basics of chilling whites and rosés and serving reds at room temperature. What happens most often, however, is that whites and rosés are served icy cold, and red wines usually are served too warm.

With an inexpensive picnic wine, you probably want to chill down your white wine or blush alongside your beer and bottled water because the object is refreshment, pure and simple.

If you're getting into more complex wines, such as some of the better Chardonnays, White Burgundy, or a really good Riesling, you don't want to numb the flavors by overchilling the wine.

A similar thing happens to red wines if you serve them too warm. The higher temperature throws off the balance by masking the fruit and increasing your perception of the alcohol. If you're supposed to serve wine at "room temperature," how could it be too warm, you might wonder? The "room temperature" guideline began in Europe where room temperature tends to be in the mid-60s, a little chilly by our standards. Today, many Americans keep their thermostats at 70 degrees Fahrenheit and many even higher. Those couple degrees make a world of difference in the way the wine tastes.

Here are some basic serving temperature guidelines:

TABLE 17.1: WINE SERVING TEMPERATURES

Wine Type	Temperature
Picnic wines such as white Zinfandels, Chenin Blancs, and inexpensive white blends	45°to 50°F
Basic whites such as Sauvignon Blancs and Rieslings	45° to 55°F
Champagnes and sparkling wines	42° to 47°F
Light reds such as Beaujolais, Pinot Noir, Sangiovese, and inexpensive red blends	55° to 60°F
Big reds such as Cabernet Sauvignon, Rhône, Burgundy and Bordeaux	60° to 65°F

If you need to chill any type of white wine in a hurry, including rosé and Champagne, put the wine in a bucket with a mixture of ice and cold water. It's quicker than putting a bottle of wine "on ice," and it is also quicker than putting a bottle in your refrigerator. It will take you two hours to chill your wine in a refrigerator, for example, whereas it will take only 30 minutes in an ice bucket mixed with cold water and ice. Resist all temptation to stick the bottle in your freezer because nine times out of ten you will forget, and the bottle might freeze and explode.

You have control over the wine's temperature when you are serving at home, but you don't when you order wine at a restaurant. There are still things you can do, however, to make sure you can enjoy wines served at the proper temperature in a restaurant situation.

Bright Idea
One of the sharpest wine saleswomen I know told me about this 15-minute rule: Take white and rosé or blush wines out of the fridge 15 minutes before serving them so they aren't too cold. Put red wine in the fridge for 15 minutes before serving it to cool it off just a bit.

TABLE 17.2: WINE-SERVING TEMPERATURE IN A RESTAURANT

Situation	Solution
The white or rosé wine is too cold.	Ask the server to leave it on the table and out of the ice bucket.
The white or rosé wine is too warm.	Ask the server to leave the bottle of wine in the ice bucket with some cold water for a "few moments" while you look over the menu.
The red wine is too warm.	Ask the server for a bucket with some cool water. Place the bottle of red wine in the bucket for 10 to 15 minutes.
The red wine is too cool.	This is unusual, but if it happens to you, pour the wine into the glass and pick it up by the bowl rather than by the stem. This allows the heat of your hands to warm up the wine.

Proper stemware

I thought I knew how wine was supposed to be served until I went to school in Madrid and saw the locals order a glass of wine at their local bar and receive a "copita." In my language, we call this a juice glass. I have to admit that I was bummed because I thought everyone drank from fancy wine glasses. What's up with that?

What I learned is that people might drink from a variety of different glasses, but there is a basic standard that all serious wine drinkers prefer. They want to drink from a glass with these attributes:

1. It should be a clear glass so they can see the wine.

2. It should be unadorned glass without special etching or design, again for better viewing of the wine.

3. They want a stem so that they don't have to cup the bowl of the glass and warm the wine unnecessarily.

4. Ideally, the glass will have a thin wall to minimize the space between the wine and one's palate.

5. The top lip should be cut and polished rather than have a "rolled rim."

You can get suitable glassware from a variety of stores for as little as $5 per stem, but the price goes up invariably with the quality of the stemware.

One brand of glassware that has caught the attention of the wine trade is Riedel from Austria. The company has been around since 1756, but it turned the American wine-consuming public on its ears in the 1980s. The point of difference between Riedel crystal and its competitors is that Riedel designs its glassware to enhance the taste of the wine. The glasses are literally designed—from the shape of the bowl to the size of the glass to the size of the opening—to deliver the wine directly to the appropriate sensor area. Theoretically, by drinking a fruit-filled Cabernet Sauvignon from a glass created by Riedel, you should be able to have the element of fruit delivered unadulterated to the "sweet" sensors at the front of your mouth. (See Chapter 3, "How to Taste Wine," for more details about the mechanics of tasting wine.)

The price obviously escalates as you reach high-fashion crystal such as Orrefors, Waterford, and others. Rather than going for etched crystal on the bowl of the glass, the trend is to buy the crystal with the most imaginative stems, which doesn't interfere with viewing the wine. A great and colorful example of this is the "clown" line from Orrefors of Sweden. This line contains a whimsical use of color and shapes at the base of a Champagne flute.

As for the wine glasses themselves, you want them to be thin-walled to minimize the distance between you and your wine. This might not be conducive to dishwasher cleaning, but it certainly is conducive to selecting a top-quality wine vessel.

In terms of actual size, you want the following for everyday wine consumption (most Riedel glasses hold more wine than those listed below, but the proper pour size remains the same):

TABLE 17.3: WINE GLASS CAPACITY AND "PROPER POUR"

Type of Glass	Capacity	Proper Pour
White Wine	8 to 10 ounces	3 to 4 ounces
Red Wine	10 to 12 ounces	4 to 5 ounces
Champagne	8 to 10 ounces	4 to 5 ounces
Port or Dessert	5 to 7 ounces	2 to 3 ounces

Note! ➜

In general terms, red wine glasses should be larger than white wine glasses to give you room to swirl and enjoy the nose and flavor of the wine. White wine glasses should be medium-sized and port or dessert wine glasses are smaller yet to allow you to concentrate on the fruit of the wine. Champagne is served in a flute rather than a coupe to allow you to enjoy the dancing bubbles.

White wine glass.

Red wine glass.

Champagne glass.

Port wine glass.

In fine-dining situations in which wine is an important centerpiece, you might see wine glasses that look like they could double as goldfish bowls. The large, special stemware is intended to allow you to swirl the wine to your heart's content to fully release the bouquet for your smelling and sipping enjoyment.

How to decant wine

Though there is a certain romance associated with the decanting of any wine, it is only necessary when the wine throws a sediment, as in the case of old collectible Bordeaux, California Cabernets, Vintage Port, and some Late-Bottled Vintage Ports. Yet there are many in the wine business who believe that young wines can also benefit from decanting and aeration.

Ideally, you should leave the bottle standing upright overnight, or at least for a few hours, to allow the sediment to drop to the bottom of the bottle.

To decant a bottle, you need a decanter or carafe, a candle, and matches. Be sure the decanter or carafe is absolutely clean because you probably don't use it on a daily basis. Follow these simple steps to decant your wine:

1. Remove the capsule from the neck of the bottle.

2. Extract the cork.

3. Wipe the lip of the bottle with a clean napkin.

4. Light a candle so you can distinguish the wine from the sediment as you transfer the wine to your decanter or carafe.

Bright Idea
If you have the storage capacity at home, it's nice to have the different-size wine glasses for the different styles of wine. If space is an issue, however, you can buy one 10-ounce all-purpose wine glass. I'd still find room for some Champagne flutes, though.

5. Hold the decanter or carafe firmly in one hand.

6. With your other hand, gently pour the wine into the decanter while holding both the bottle and the decanter in front of the candle at such an angle that you can see the wine pass through the neck of the bottle.

7. Pour in one uninterrupted motion until you see the sediment reach the shoulder of the bottle and then stop.

8. Repeat step 6, making sure to stop each time you see more sediment reach the shoulder of the bottle. Continue this procedure until all of the wine has been transferred sediment-free from the original bottle to the decanter or carafe.

For advice on opening and decanting Vintage Port, please refer to Chapter 13, "After-Dinner Delights."

Break open the bubbly

Believe it or not, the pressure per square inch (PSI) in a bottle of Champagne is roughly equivalent to that of a tire on an 18-wheeler. When you open a bottle, always point it away from yourself and others to avoid serious eye injury, then follow these steps:

1. Remove the foil.

2. Keep one hand on top of the cork at all times. Untwist and loosen the wire muzzle that covers the cork.

3. Take a clean dish towel or cloth napkin and put it on top of the cork so you can grip the cork more easily. This also works as a safety precaution in the event the cork pops before

you open the bottle. The napkin will catch the cork before it hurts someone.

4. Gently remove the cork by turning it in one direction and the bottle in the other. The goal is to ease the cork out, letting a little carbon dioxide escape so the cork doesn't shoot out. Contrary to popular belief, if you have opened the bottle correctly, you should hear a light, pleasing fizz rather than a loud pop, and the Champagne should not foam out of the bottle.

Never use a corkscrew to open a bottle of Champagne or sparkling wine.

The best stemware to use for Champagne or sparkling wine is the tall flute or tulip glass. The tall, slender glassware allows the tiny bubbles to rise in a continuous stream. This is important because the bubbles tell you a lot about the quality of the Champagne or sparkling wine. The best Champagnes and sparkling wines have smaller bubbles that last longer in the glass.

How to save leftovers

Wine is one area in which many people do not welcome leftovers. They are afraid that the leftover wine will spoil almost instantly. The truth is, if you leave wine exposed to air for an extended period of time, it will oxidize and lose its freshness. If you take the proper steps to store whatever is left after you open a bottle, however, it doesn't have to be that way.

The most basic and low-tech method of saving wine leftovers is to merely put the cork back in the bottle as soon as you are done with it and return it to the fridge. I even put my opened red wines back in the refrigerator for safekeeping. I find that both

Bright Idea
If you find the Champagne cork to be a little stubborn or if your hands are not the strongest in the world, you might find a Champagne key to be a worthwhile investment. It's a pliers-type device that helps you grab and turn the cork with ease. It costs $15 to $20 in a good wine shop or wine catalog.

reds and whites stored this way after their initial opening will last between three and five days.

For Champagne and sparkling wine, you can buy special Champagne stoppers at your local wine shop or through a wine catalog for about $10. Unlike the regular rubber stopper I use to recork my still wines, the Champagne stopper features a longer stopper that fits down into the neck of the bottle. It also has two wings that actually grip onto the protruding lip of the bottle. This keeps the cork from popping off again and will keep the bubbly sparkling for two to three days.

For dessert wines with a higher alcohol content, such as Port, you can keep an opened bottle for up to one month when recorked tightly and stored in the refrigerator.

Two other easy and affordable tools for saving your leftovers for about one week are Vacu-Vin and Private Preserve.

Vacu-Vin

Vacu-Vin is an inexpensive device that consists of a pump that looks a little like a corkscrew without the auger and a pair of rubber stoppers. When you want to put away your leftover wine, you just follow these simple steps:

1. Insert the rubber stopper into the top of the bottle.

2. Place the pump over the stopper and pump the handle three or four times. The pump removes virtually all the air from the bottle, and the rubber stopper keeps a firm seal. When you remove the rubber stopper the next time you open the bottle, you will hear a light pop that lets you know the pump did its job.

Bright Idea!
To store my left-over wine at home, I use the rubber stoppers that come with the Vacu-Vin device instead of putting the original cork back in the wine. I believe the rubber stopper seals the wine better than the cork, which has a hole in it once you've used the corkscrew.

Vacu-Vin costs about $15 at better wine shops and in wine catalogs.

Private Preserve

Private Preserve is a handy canister of inert nitrogen that you can spray into the bottle before you recork it. Every canister comes with a skinny straw attachment, which you attach to the nozzle. The nitrogen acts as a gaseous blanket to protect your leftover wine from oxygen. A single canister costs only about $10 and will preserve about 120 bottles. Private Preserve also is available at better wine shops and in wine catalogs.

Cruvinet

More extensive and expensive wine-preservation systems are certainly available, but you probably don't need them. If you like to keep a selection of wines by the glass on hand, however, like some of the better restaurants and wine bars, you could buy a smaller version of a Cruvinet or a Winekeeper System. These are commercial-quality nitrogen preservation systems that also can be quite attractive. They often are featured in specialty wine catalogs.

Le Verre de Vin

Another professional wine-preservation device is called Le Verre de Vin. It's a vacuum-based system that mounts on the wall and that looks like a dustbuster in the shape of a wine bottle. When you want to put away your leftover wine, you just insert a rubber stopper like those used by Vacu-Vin, hold the bottle up to the Verre de Vin, and apply gentle upward pressure. A green light on the Verre de Vin illuminates when you've fully sealed the bottle. According to professionals who use the device, the wine can last for up to 21 days. The device can even handle Champagne and sparkling wine. Because this is a professional system, it is more costly—about $3,500. To some serious wine consumers, however, it could be worth it. Unlike the other systems mentioned, Le Verre de Vin is currently available only through Bermar America, which is based in Narbeth, Pennsylvania, and can be reached at (610)889-4900.

Storing wine at home

Most of the time, you're going to buy wine to open for dinner tonight, or you might stock up for the next few weeks. Even though you're not a collector, you still need to know how to store wine properly when you get it home. It's just like any other shopping expedition. You put your milk in the fridge and your ice cream in the freezer, and you leave your tomatoes out on the counter because you know they won't taste as good if you store them in your refrigerator. Why should wine be any different?

Ideal wine cellar conditions are a stable optimum temperature of 55 degrees Fahrenheit. Chances are, these conditions do not exist in your house or apartment. I know they certainly do not exist in mine. Your best bet for storing wines at home is to look for an area that meets these criteria as closely as possible:

- Identify the coolest place in your house or basement. If a place exists that's between 50 and 65 degrees, that's great. A tad higher is not going to make a difference if you are a casual consumer who just wants to keep some ready-to-drink bottles on hand.

- Avoid placing your wine rack near a cooling or heating vent.

- Store wine bottles on their sides to keep the cork moist. The general belief is that, if you store your bottles standing up and the wine is not in constant contact with the cork, the cork will dry out and air will seep in to oxidize the wine.

- Keep your wines in a dark place away from bright light and away from major vibrations such as those from your family home-entertainment center.

- Humidity, according to the experts, should be in the 70- to 80-percent range. Humidity is especially important for collectors who are laying down their wines for years of aging because a dry cellar will dry out the corks and could potentially expose the wine to air. A cellar that is overly humid will develop mold on the bottles. This mold damages the labels and simply doesn't look good. Although humidity can have an effect on "real collections," it should not be a major concern for the casual consumer.

If you started to pick up a few special bottles here and there during your travels to wine country and now you find that you can't stop buying, face it, you're becoming a collector. You're going to want to protect your investment. It's only natural.

Here are some ways to do this:

- Convert a closet or dedicate a room to becoming your "home cellar."

- Buy special refrigeration units especially for your wine.

Watch Out!
The biggest danger to your wine is exposure to major temperature swings. Your home might be perfectly air conditioned or heated while you are at home, but if you shut it down while you are at work or away on holiday, you might leave your wines at risk.

- Rent a locker at your local fine wine merchant.
- Rent warehouse space through your local wine merchant.

If you're going the do-it-yourself closet conversion route, plenty of kits are available through wine catalogs and on the Web. For a small conversion, you're probably looking at about $1,000. For people who prefer a stand-alone unit, there are some beautiful temperature- and humidity-controlled cooling units that become furniture in your home. Depending on the size and the style, these units cost a little more than converting a closet, at the very least, and the sky is the limit, at the very most.

During the latest round of good economic times, there began a trend to building wine cellars into the design of new construction. In cases where wine cellars were not part of the original plan, more and more serious wine consumers are having one custom-built.

Maybe you're not living in your dream house yet, and you don't want to invest in converting or buying a special cooling unit. The next best thing is to rent space at your wine merchant's store or at a warehouse that stores wines properly.

Begin with your wine merchant, especially if you are a new collector and just want to put a few special cases away in a temperature-controlled locker. You might treat this transaction as you would a safety deposit box at your local bank. You can rent different-size boxes to keep your valuables, depending on how much stuff you have to store. The same is true at a wine shop. You often can rent a locker to store as little as a few cases or as many as a dozen or more. It all depends on the amount of space the retailer sets aside for customers' wines. Some of the

Watch Out!
No matter what type of cooling unit you use for your home cellar, remember that you need to vent the warm air that the cooling unit produces— outside of the cellar and away from the wine.

better wine merchants also offer off-site warehouse storage where you can keep the bulk of your wines.

Alternatively, there are storage facilities that specialize in wine storage. Check your telephone directory, scour the classifieds in wine publications, or surf the Web to get more information. You can contact them directly. The price for renting lockers or storing wine off-site can be as little as $1 per case per month to as much as $10 per case per month.

On the plus side, if you store your wines with a professional wine merchant or a special facility, you can feel comfortable that your investment is being taken care of. The biggest drawback is the same whether you are keeping your valuables in a bank vault or your wine in storage: you need to plan ahead to get to your stuff. This means you cannot go to your wine cellar spontaneously to retrieve your well-aged Barolo for your last-minute dinner party. For many people, however, this is a small price to pay for peace of mind.

Just the facts

- Invest in a good corkscrew, learn how to use it properly, and you'll never go thirsty again.

- There is such thing as serving white wine too cold and red wine too warm.

- A properly designed wine glass can actually change the way a wine tastes—for the better.

- When you properly open a bottle of Champagne, you should let a little carbon dioxide ease out of the bottle so it doesn't pop, and the cork does not shoot across the room.

- If you recork wine and put it back in the fridge after you open it, the wine will last for three to five days with no problems.

- Store wines on their side in a cool environment and guard against major temperature swings.

Glossary

Abruzzo (a-BRUTZ-so) An Italian wine region known for the red wine Montepulciano d'Abruzzo and the white wine Trebbiano d'Abruzzo. In English, the region often is referred to as Abruzzi.

acid One of the four taste sensations of wine. Sometimes acid is described as tart, sour, or acidic. You taste acid most on the sides of your tongue.

aftertaste The taste that remains in your mouth after you swallow a sip of wine. Sometimes this also is referred to as the finish.

Aged Tawny Port with an Indication of Age A Tawny Port that spends more time aging in wood, which gives it a more nutty flavor. This Port is labeled with an average age of the wines used to create the blend such as 10, 20, 30, or 40 years old.

aging The process by which wines develop and improve in a barrel, tank, or bottle. Some wines will improve with additional aging; others are meant to be consumed upon release.

Albariño (al-ba-REE-nyo)   A white, trendy grape from Spain.

alcoholic   When a wine is described as being alcoholic, the alcohol overpowers the balance of the wine and gives off a burning sensation in your mouth.

Alexander Valley   An important American Viticultural Area (AVA) in northern Sonoma, California.

Aloxe Corton (ah-LOHKS cor-TONE)   A famous village in the Côte de Beaune region of Burgundy, France.

Alsace (al-ZAS)   A French wine region bordering Germany that is best known for its crisp white wines and light-bodied reds.

Amarone (ah-ma-ROW-ney)   A full-bodied red wine from the Veneto region of Italy. The grapes are dried on a mat until they shrivel like raisins and then are crushed and made into wine. This heavy-duty red has a high alcohol concentration of 14 or 15 percent.

AOC   Appellation d'Origine Contrôlée. This is the system used by the French for quality control of their wines. It refers to where the wine is made whether it is the region, village, or even the specific vineyard.

AP Nr   This abbreviation appears on German Qualitätswein labels along with a serial number that proves the wine was tasted by a government panel for quality-control purposes.

aperitif (ah-pair-eh-TEEF)   A wine or other beverage consumed before the meal.

aroma   Technically, aroma refers to the way the grapes smell. Bouquet refers to how the wine smells.

Though professional wine tasters may split hairs over the two, these terms often are used interchangeably.

Auslese (ows-LAYZ-eh)   A term used in German winemaking for a level of ripeness. In German, it translates to "picked out," which refers to the grapes left on the vine longer to ripen and thus become sweeter. Auslese wines are sweeter than Kabinett and Spätlese but less so than Beerenauslese and Trockenbeerenauslese.

AVA   American Viticultural Area. A federally recognized American appellation such as Napa Valley.

balanced   A term used in wine tasting to describe a harmonious melding of the wine's basic components—sweet (sugar), sour (acid), and bitter (tannin and alcohol).

Balthazar (balt-a-CZAR)   A large-format Champagne bottle that holds the equivalent of 16 regular-size (750 ml) bottles.

Barbaresco (bar-ba-RES-co)   One of the biggest, most age-worthy red wines from the Piedmont region of Italy. Like Barolo, it is made from the Nebbiolo grape, but it is generally has more finesse.

Barolo (bah-RO-low)   One of the biggest, most age-worthy red wines from the Piedmont region of Italy. It is made from the Nebbiolo grape.

Barossa Valley (ba-RO-sa VAL-ley)   An important wine appellation in Australia.

barrel aging   Some wines are placed in small oak barrels before they are bottled. For white wines such as Chardonnay, it adds an element of complexity. For sturdy red wines, it helps mellow the wine and minimize its bite.

barrel fermentation   When you see this term on a wine label, it tells you that the wine—red or white—was aged in small oak barrels as part of its production. This is supposed to impart a more complex flavor to the wine.

barrique (bah-REEK)   The French word for barrel.

Barsac (BAR-zahk)   The famous region next to Sauternes in France that is known for its world-class dessert wine.

Beaujolais (bo-jo-LAY)   A wine region in Southern France known for its light, fruity red wines.

Beaujolais Nouveau (bo-jo-LAY new-VO)   The first "new" Beaujolais released from the harvest. This Beaujolais is especially light and fruity because it is harvested, produced, and shipped for sale to retailers and restaurants within weeks of picking the grapes. The official release date is the third Thursday in November, just in time for Thanksgiving.

Beaujolais-Village (bo-jo-LAY vee-LAJ)   This Beaujolais comes from any number of designated villages in the region. In terms of quality, Beaujolais-Village is better than Beaujolais Nouveau and "regular" Beaujolais, but it is not as good as those from one of the region's top 10 crus, which incidentally do not use the term "Beaujolais" on the label. Instead, they use only the name of the specific cru (village) from which it originates.

Beaune (bone)   A prestigious region in the Côte d'Or of Burgundy, France, known especially for its wonderful red wines.

Beerenauslese (bear-en-OUSE-lez-sah)   A term used in German winemaking for a level of ripeness. In German, it literally means that the individual berries or grapes were picked off the vine later. This level of ripeness, used to make wonderful dessert wines, is below only Trockenbeerenauslese.

bitter   One of the four taste sensations of wine, it is sometimes described as tannic or astringent. Bitterness is detected on the back of the tongue.

Blanc de blancs (blahnk du blahnk)   A white wine made from white grapes.

Blanc de noir (BLAHNK du nwahr)   A white wine made from red grapes.

blush wine   This term usually describes a white wine made from red grapes and is most commonly associated with White Zinfandel. Blush wine generally is sweeter and pinker than rosé wine from France and other regions.

body   This term is used to describe the weight of the wine or its perceived viscosity.

botrytis cinerea (bo-TRY-tis cin-eh-RAY-ah)   A "good" mold that forms on grapes and shrivels them, leaving a more sugar-concentrated grape that is perfect for producing rich dessert wines or late harvest wines. Botrytis cinerea is known as Edelfäule in Germany, pourriture noble in France, and noble rot in the U.S.

bouquet   Describes how the wine smells. Aroma, on the other hand, technically refers to the way the grapes smell. Though professional wine tasters might split hairs over the two, these terms often are used interchangeably.

Bourgogne (bor-GO-nyah)   The French word for Burgundy. It often is found on their labels.

brix (bricks)   The winemaker's scale of measurement to gauge the amount of sugar in the unfermented grape juice.

Brunello di Montalcino (brew-NELL-oh dee mon-tahl-CHEE-no) One of Italy's biggest and best red wines from the Tuscany region. It is made from the Brunello grape, which is something like the Sangiovese.

brut (broot) A term in French that describes the driest Champagne and sparkling wines.

Cabernet Franc (cab-er-NAY frahnk) A red grape from the Bordeaux region and the Loire Valley, both in France.

Cabernet Sauvignon (cab-er-NAY sav-en-NYON) A red grape used to make some of the best wines from Bordeaux, France; California; and other countries.

Carbonic Maceration (car-BON-ick MASS-er-a-shun) This winemaking technique is used to create a fruitier-style wine, as in Beaujolais and other areas. Whole bunches of grapes are put into tanks, usually made of stainless steel, that contain carbon dioxide instead of crushing the grapes in an open tank, which allows more contact with air.

Carmignano (car-me-NYAHN-o) An important red wine region in central Italy near Florence that produces wines primarily from the Sangiovese grape.

cask A wooden container or barrel used to store and age wines.

Catelonia (cat-eh-LONE-ee-ah) A major winemaking region in Spain, located in the northeastern part of the country near Barcelona. It includes Penedès and Priorato.

cava (KAH-vah) The Spanish term for sparkling wine made from the traditional Champagne method, méthode champenoise.

cellarmaster The American term for sommelier, the person at a restaurant who is responsible for maintaining the wine cellar and helping guests with their wine selection.

Chablis (chab-LEE) The northernmost winemaking region in France that produces crisp white wines from the Chardonnay grape known as Chablis.

Chambertin (sham-bear-TEEN) One of the most famous French vineyards in the world. It is located in the Côte d'Or region of Burgundy, which is known for its red wine.

Chambolle-Musigny (shom-BOW moo-sig-NEE) A village in the Côte de Nuits in Burgundy, France, that produces velvety red wines from the Pinot Noir grape.

Champagne (sham-PAIN) The region of France that produces the world's best sparkling wine made in the traditional Champagne method, also known as méthode champenoise.

Chardonnay (SHAR-do-nay) The best known, most popular, and most expensive white grape grown in Burgundy, France; California; and virtually all other parts of the winemaking world.

charmat An inexpensive way to produce sparkling wine by using large tanks to ferment the wine instead of the individual bottle.

Chassagne-Montrachet (shah-SAG moan-ra-SHAY) A top wine-producing village in the Beaune region of the Côte d'Or in Burgundy, France. It is known best for its Chardonnay.

château (shah-TOE) In France, a château refers to the vineyard and the house attached to it.

château bottled A wine bottled on the property that produced it, especially in Bordeaux, France.

Château Lafite-Rotshchild (shah-TOE la-FEET ROTHS-child)   A first-growth Bordeaux from the Médoc district. The winery is well-known for its wine and for the famous artist series labels that the Baroness Philippine de Rothschild commissions each year just as her father, the Baron Philippe, did before her since the end of World War II.

Château La Tâche (shah-TOE la tash)   One of the top vineyards of Burgundy famous for its red wine made from Pinot Noir.

Château Latour (shat-TOE la-TOOR)   A first growth Bordeaux from the Médoc district.

Château Pétrus (shat-TOE PEH-troos)   The top vineyard of Pomerol in Bordeaux, France.

Château Margaux (shat-TOE mar-GO)   One of the most famous first growths of the Médoc region of Bordeaux, France.

Château d'Yquem (shat-TOE d'ee-KEM)   The highest-rated dessert wine in the world. It hails from the Sauternes region of Bordeaux, France.

Châteauneuf-du-Pape (shat-toe-NOOF du pop)   A robust red wine from the Rhône Valley in Southern France.

Chenin Blanc (SHEN-in Blahnk)   A white grape grown in the Loire Valley, France; California; and other parts of the world.

Chianti (key-ON-tee)   A red wine from Tuscany in Italy that is made primarily from the Sangiovese grape.

Chianti Classico (key-ON-tee CLASS-ee-co)   A step above Chianti in quality and price.

Chianti Classico Riserva (key-ON-tee CLASS-ee-co REE-serve-ah)   The best-quality and level Chianti you can buy.

Cinsault (san-SO) A red grape grown in France, especially the Midi region and the Rhône Valley, as well as South Africa.

Claret (clar-AY) An old British term for Bordeaux. It sometimes is still used today to refer to a red wine.

Classification of 1855 The famous ranking of the best Bordeaux in the world. Sometimes it is referred to as the Official Classification of 1855.

Classified Growth Refers to the top chateau wines of Bordeaux, France. Sometimes they are referred to as Classified Château.

clean This term used in wine tasting refers to a wine that both looks good in terms of color and appearance (clear) and is palatable without any noticeable flaw.

colheita (col-hee-ta) The Portuguese term for vintage.

Colheita Port (col-HEE-ta port) An aged Tawny Port that has been made from a single vintage rather than a blend of wines. Colheita Port must be aged for at least seven years in wood.

Coonawarra (COON-a-war-ra) An important appellation in Australia that is known especially for its red wines.

cosecha (co-SAYCH-ah) The Spanish term for harvest or vintage.

Côte de Beaune (coat de BONE) An important wine region in the southern part of the Côte d'Or in Burgundy, France, that is known for its white wines.

Côte de Nuits (coat de New-EES) An important wine region in the northern part of the Côte d'Or in Burgundy, France, that is known especially for its red wines.

Côte d'Or (coat DOOR) Meaning "golden slope" in French, this refers to one of its best wine regions in Burgundy.

Côte Rôtie (coat row-TEE) A red wine from the northern part of the Rhône Valley in France.

Côtes-du-Rhône (coat du RONE) All of the wines produced in the Rhône Valley of France are referred to as Côtes-du-Rhône. Some are marketed under a more specific area within the Côtes-du-Rhône such as Côte Rôtie.

Crianza (cree-AHN-za) This Spanish term refers to aging. Specifically, a Crianza wine must be aged for a minimum of one year in oak and one year in the bottle. Aside from Spanish wines labeled "joven" for young or "sin crianza" for without age, this is the most basic level.

crisp This wine tasting term refers to a white wine that is a little tart or that has good acid balance.

Crozes-Hermitage (crows er-mee-TAJ) A popular red wine from the northern Rhône Valley region of France.

cru (crew) This term is French for "growth," but it actually refers to a vineyard. A crus vineyard generally is believed to be of better quality than most.

Cru Beaujolais (crew bo-jo-LAY) The best-quality Beaujolais you can buy. It comes from one of the top 10 Beaujolais districts within the region.

Cru Bourgeois (crew boo-JWAH) Wines from Bordeaux, France, that are not considered to be one of the top five growths can be given this designation to show that the wine has been recognized for its quality.

Cru classé (crew class-SAY) This French term means "classed growth" and refers to the top chateau wines from the Bordeaux region.

crush The crush is the harvest time when the grapes are picked and crushed to make wine. The crush in California, for example, takes place in September and October.

cuvée (que-VAY) The French term for "blend." It most commonly is used when speaking of Champagne or sparkling wine blends, but it sometimes also can be used to describe the mixture of the grapes used in any wine blend.

decant (de-CANT) The process of transferring the contents of a wine bottle into a decanter or carafe for the purpose of removing the sediment from the wine.

degorgement (day-gorj-MOAN) The step in the méthode champenoise process in which the bottle top is frozen and the sediment is expelled from the bottle.

delicate A term used by wine tasters to describe a wine that is light-bodied and often times elegant as opposed to big and robust.

demi-sec (DE-mee seck) This term literally means "half-dry," but it refers to a wine, usually Champagne or sparkling wine, that is off-dry or slightly sweet.

Denominazione di Origine Controllata (dee-nom-in-ah-zee-YONE-ay dee oh-ree-JEE-nay con-troll-LAH-tah) Abbreviated DOC, this is the Italian equivalent of the French AOC laws intended to protect the integrity of the wine and to assure quality control.

Denominazione di Origine Controllata Garantita (dee-nom-in-ah-zee-YONE-ay dee oh-ree-JEE-nay con-troll-LAH-tah gar-en-TEET-ah) Abbreviated DOCG, this is the Italian government's highest level of DOC with the additional "G" for "garantita," or guaranteed quality.

Dolcetto (dole-CHET-to) A red wine from Piedmont, Italy, that is made from the Dolcetto grape, which produces a light, fruity wine similar to that of Beaujolais from France, though perhaps drier.

domaine (doe-MAIN) The French word for estate. It often is used in Burgundian wine, though you will see the term used for wines from other countries.

Domaine Romanée-Conti (doe-MAIN ro-man-EE CONE-tee) Wine wizards commonly use the abbreviation DRC to refer to this grand cru vineyard of the Côte de Nuits in Burgundy that produces extraordinary reds.

dosage (doe-SAJ) A mixture of wine and sugar that is added to Champagne to determine how dry or how sweet the finished product will be.

double magnum A large-format bottle of wine that holds the equivalent of two regular 750 ml bottles.

dry wine A tasting term that refers to a wine that is definitely not sweet or even sour (acidic).

earthy A commonly used descriptor for wines that taste like the "terroir" (in French) or soil. It very often but not always is a compliment to the wine and the winemaking practice.

Edelfäule (eh-dell-FOY-luh) "Noble rot" in German. See botrytis cinerea.

Eiswein (ICE-vine) The German word for "ice wine." It describes an actual sweet dessert wine that is made by pressing frozen grapes.

elegant How wine tasters often describe well-balanced wines that tend to display subtle flavorful characteristics.

enology (eh-NO-lo-gee) The study of wine. It often is spelled "oenology."

Erzeugerabfüllung (AIR-tsu-gare-ahb-foo-lung) In German, this means "estate-bottled."

estate-bottled The vineyard owner bottles the wine from his or her own vineyard in his or her own wine cellars. The term is intended to denote authenticity and quality.

extra dry Champagne or sparkling wine that is not as dry as brut but is drier than demi-sec.

fat In wine-tasting terms, a wine described as fat is one that is extremely full-bodied but out of balance.

fermentation The process by which grape juice or must is turned into wine.

finesse How a wine taster describes a wine with elegance, balance, subtle flavors, and class beyond the taster's expectations.

finish Sometimes referred to as aftertaste, this is the taste that remains in your mouth after you swallow a sip of wine.

first growth The highest-ranked chateau wines from Bordeaux according to the Official Médoc Classification of 1855.

flinty A wine-tasting term often used to describe a white wine with a minerally or austere taste.

fortified wine   A wine such as Port in which neutral grape brandy is added to boost the alcohol content. The alcohol content in a fortified wine will get up to 14 to 16 percent, whereas a normal table wine will range from 8.5 to 13.5 percent.

fruity   Describes a wine in which you can easily taste the flavor of the grape such as Beaujolais from France or Dolcetto from Italy.

Fumé Blanc   Another word for Sauvignon Blanc in California.

Gamay (gam-AY)   The red grape variety used to produce Beaujolais in France and, to a lesser degree, in California.

Garnacha (gar-knotch-chah)   A red grape grown in Spain. It is called Grenache in other countries.

Garrafiera (gar-ah-fee-YER-a)   If you see this term on a Portuguese label, it is an indication that the wine has some additional age.

Gattinara (gat-tee-NAR-rah)   A red wine made in the Nebbiolo area of Piedmont, Italy. It often is a bargain compared with Barolo and Barbaresco.

generic wine   Can be used to refer to wine that "borrows" wine terms from other countries such as a California wine taking on the name Chablis to market a white wine. Sometimes "generic wine" refers to the name a wine marketer makes up to sell the wine.

Gevrey Chambertin (jeh-VRAY sham-ber-TAN) The name of a village and, incidentally, a very good red wine from the Côte de Nuits area of Burgundy, France.

Gewürztraminer (geh-VERZ-trah-mee-ner)   "Gewurz" means "spicy" in German, and it describes the pungent floral nose of this grape. Gewürztraminer is found in Alsace, Germany, and California.

Gran Cru (gran crew)   The highest rank of quality that a Burgundy wine can achieve.

Grand Cru Classé (gran crew class-SAY)   The top Bordeaux in the classification.

Gran Reserva (grahn reh-ZER-vah)   Meaning "grand reserve" in Spanish, this indicates the age of the bottle of wine. A wine labeled "Gran Reserva" must have gone through a total of five years of aging with two of those being spent in wooden barrel.

Graves (grahv)   Dry white wine from the Graves area of Bordeaux, France.

Grenache (gre-NOSH)   A red wine grape grown in Spain and the Rhône Valley in Southern France. In Spain, it is called Garnacha.

Halbtrocken (hab-TROCK-en)   Meaning "half dry" in German, this describes a wine that is off-dry or a bit sweet.

Herbaceous (herb-A-shus)   A wine-tasting term that refers to wine that smells and tastes extremely vegetal. You are likely to find an herbaceous wine in some Sauvignon Blancs from the Loire Valley in France, California, or New Zealand.

Hermitage (erm-ee-TAJ)   One of the best red wines made in the northern Rhône Valley, France. A good example also is made in Australia.

Hunter Valley   The top-rated Australian appellation, it is well-known for its Chardonnay.

inferno   A red wine made from the Nebbiolo grape in the Lombardy region of Italy. It usually represents a good value.

Jeroboam (ger-oh-BOAM)   Large-format wine bottle that holds the equivalent of six regular 750 ml bottles.

jug wine Inexpensive wine traditionally sold in wine jugs in sizes ranging from 1.5 to 3 liters and sometimes even 5 liters today (bag in the box).

Kabinett (cab-ee-NET) A term used in German winemaking to express a level of ripeness of the grapes in Qualitätswein mit Prädikat (QmP). Kabinett is the lowest level and often the lightest, driest German wine made.

Kir (keer) A popular aperitif made from a combination of white wine with crème de Cassis, a black currant liqueur. When used in Champagne or sparkling wine, it makes a Kir Royale.

Languedoc-Roussillon (lan-gweh-DOC roo-see-YOHN) A wine region in Southern France that hugs the Mediterranean coast like a crescent. Also known as the Midi, this region produces a high volume of wine, which means it offers good value.

late-bottled vintage Port Often abbreviated and referred to as LBV, this ruby Port is made from more concentrated wines of a single vintage, such as Vintage Port, as opposed to a blend of wines. Unlike regular ruby Port, LBV is aged for four to six years in a wooden cask instead of only two to three years. It is ready to drink upon release.

late harvest Term used primarily in California to describe dessert wines made from either grapes left on the vine to ripen more fully or those affected by noble rot.

lees The sediment that settles at the bottom of the fermentation tank or barrel during the winemaking process.

legs An unusual wine-tasting term that refers to what happens after you swirl the wine in your glass. The wine at first coats the inside of the glass. Then you'll begin to notice long drops descending like rain drops on a windowpane. In wine, however, the legs, or "tears" as they sometimes are called, give you an idea of how alcoholic a wine is. A wine with more alcohol generally has bigger legs.

light   The word that wine tasters use to describe a wine that is not full-bodied.

Loire Valley (lo-WAHR VAL-lee)   A winemaking region in France that is well known for its white wines, rosé wines, and some lighter reds.

long-vatted   To make rich-colored red wines, the grapes are fermented while in contact with their (red) skins for an extended period of time, which is what long-vatted refers to.

Mâcon (ma-CONE)   An important white-wine–growing region in the southern area of Burgundy, France.

Mâcon-Villages (ma-CONE vee-LAJ)   A commune within the Mâcon region of Burgundy, France, where better white wines are made.

maderized (MEH-deh-rized)   The term used to describe a wine that has been oxidized or that simply is over the hill and smells like Madeira.

magnum   A large-format bottle that holds the equivalent of two regular 750 ml bottles of wine or 1.5 liters.

Malbec (mal-BECK)   A red wine variety that is considered to be the specialty of Argentina, although it grows in other wine regions as well. This also refers to a grape used as a softening agent when blended with Cabernet Sauvignon, Merlot, and sometimes Cabernet Franc in Bordeaux.

malolactic fermentation   Technically, this is a secondary fermentation in which the harsh acid of the fruit (grapes) is transformed into milder acid. You usually hear about malolactic fermentation in red wines such as Beaujolais, but it also can be found in some white whites such as California Chardonnays. In either case, it adds a flavor dimension to the wine, making it richer.

Margaret River An important appellation in Australia.

Margaux (mar-GO) A highly celebrated red-wine-growing region in the Médoc area of Bordeaux, France. It is home to first-growth Château Margaux among other wonderful wines.

Médoc (meh-DOCK) A famous wine-growing region in Bordeaux known for its world-class red chateau wines.

Merlot (mare-LO) A food-friendly red grape variety used as part of a blend in Bordeaux along with Cabernet Sauvignon and Cabernet Franc. It also is bottled as a 100 percent varietal in California and elsewhere.

Méthode champenoise (METH-ode SHAMP-en-nwaz) The traditional method by which Champagne and some sparkling wines are made.

Methuselah (meth-OOS-eh-lah) A large-format bottle that holds the equivalent of eight regular 750 ml bottles.

Meursault (mare-SO) An important wine-growing region in the Côte de Beaune region of Burgundy, France. It is known best for its excellent white wines made from Chardonnay, though it also produces some good reds from Pinot Noir.

microclimate Refers to an area where there's a climate within a climate. You might find a warm wine-growing area, for example, but there may be a region within the area that is noticeably cooler.

Midi (See Languedoc-Rousillon.)

Millésime (MEE-leh-zeem) French for "vintage."

Mise En Bouteille (MEEZ en boo-tay) French for "bottled."

Montrachet (MOAN-ro-shay) Famous grand cru vineyard in the Côte de Beaune area of the Côte d'Or in Burgundy that produces a heavenly white wine from Chardonnay.

Mosel-Saar-Ruwer (MO-zil czar ROO-ver) An important wine-growing region in Germany.

Mourvèdre (moor-VEY-dre) A red grape grown in the Rhône Valley of France and in other parts of Southern France.

Müller-Thurgau (MEW-lare THUR-gow) The second most important grape in Germany behind Riesling, it often is used to make wine blends. It also is widely used in New Zealand.

Muscadet (MUSK-ah-day) A light, dry white wine from the Loire Valley of France that is produced from the grape of the same name.

must Another word for unfermented grape juice.

Nahe (NAH-he) An important wine-growing region in Germany.

Napa Valley One of California's most important wine-growing areas north of San Francisco.

Navarra (na-VAR-ra) An important wine-growing region in Spain that is known especially for its rosé wines, although it also produces some good reds. In English, it is referred to as Navarre.

Nebbiolo (neb-ee-OO-lo)   An native red grape that is important to Italy's wine production. It is used to produce the top wines of Piedmont such as Barbaresco and Barolo.

Négociant (ne-GO-see-ahn)   French for "shipper."

noble rot   A "good" mold that forms on grapes and shrivels them, leaving a more sugar-concentrated grape that is perfect for producing rich dessert wines or late harvest wines. See Botrytis cinerea.

nonvintage Champagne   Champagne made from a blend of different vintages. No vintage appears on the label.

nose   Can be used as a noun by wine tasters to describe the smell of the wine—its bouquet or aroma. The term also be can used as a verb, "to nose" the wine, which is the act of smelling it.

Nuits-Saint-Georges (new-EE san george)   A famous village in the Côte de Nuits region of Burgundy, France. It produces world-class red wines from Pinot Noir.

oak   The actual container in which the wine is sometimes fermented and/or aged.

oaky   The description for a wine that tastes as though it spent some time during the winemaking process in oak barrels or wood of some sort.

oenophile (EN-oh-feel)   A wine lover. Sometimes spelled, "enophile."

Oporto (oh-PORT-oh)   The official name for Port wine from Portugal.

over the hill   Term used to describe a wine that is past its prime and will not taste as good as it might have, had it been consumed earlier.

oxidized The term used to describe a wine that tastes like it has been exposed to air for too long. A wine that smells or tastes oxidized sometimes is said to taste like Madera, sometimes referred to as maderized.

Pauillac (poi-YAK) A village in the Médoc area of Bordeaux that is well-known for its red wines.

Penedès (pen-eh-DESS) An important wine-growing area in Spain near Barcelona that is well-known for its sparkling wine production, known as Cava, as well as innovative red wine making.

Petit Château (puh-TEET shat-TOE) Lesser-known vineyards in Bordeaux, France, that produce decent wine at a good value.

Petite Sirah (puh-TEET see-RAH) An important red-wine grape grown in the Rhône Valley of France, parts of California, and elsewhere.

Pfalz (faults) An important wine-growing region in Germany.

Phylloxera (fil-LOX-ser-rah) A plant louse that attacks the roots of grapevines and destroys vineyards. Chile is one of the few winemaking countries that have never been affected by this pest.

Piedmont (PEED-mont) One of Italy's most important wine-growing regions that is known especially for its red wines.

Pinotage (PEE-no-taj) A red grape that is a combination of Pinot Noir and Cinsault. It grows in South Africa.

Pinot Blanc (PEE-no blahnk) A white grape that is grown in the Loire Valley of France.

Pinot Grigio (PEE-no GREE-gee-oh) A popular white grape grown in Italy that produces the crisp white wine of the same name. In France, they call the grape Pinot Gris.

Pinot Meunier (PEE-no MOO-nyay)   A red grape used widely in Champagne production.

Pinot Noir (PEE-no nwahr)   This red grape is sometimes called the "headache grape" by winemakers because it is difficult to grow anywhere but in cooler climates that are perfectly suited to it. Virtually all red wines from Burgundy are made from the Pinot Noir grape.

plonk (plohnk)   A slang term for wine that is less than good.

Pomerol (PALM-er-rall)   The top red-wine–growing district in Bordeaux. It is home to Château Pétrus, one of the world's most expensive wines.

Pommard (po-MAR)   An important winemaking village in the Côte d'Beaune area of Burgundy, France, that is famous for its red wine.

Port   The sweet, red, fortified wine from Portugal that is officially known as Oporto.

Pouilly-Fuissé (poo-WEE fwee-SAY)   A popular dry white wine made in the Mâconnais area of Burgundy from the Chardonnay grape.

Pouilly-Fumê (poo-WEE foom-AY)   A popular dry white wine made in the Loire Valley of France from the Sauvignon Blanc grape.

Premier Cru (pre-MYAY crew)   A term that means "first growth" in French. In terms of ranking, Grand Cru is higher than Premier Cru.

proprietary name   A brand name created by a producer to exclusively market his or her wine. One of the best known proprietary names is Mouton-Cadet, the inexpensive line of Bordeaux wine produced by

Baron Philippe de Rothschild. Proprietary names sometimes are used by producers to market their top-of-the-line wines such as Tignanello, the "Super-Tuscan" wine produced by Piero Antinori. Because Tignanello did not conform to DOC or DOCG standards, Antinori decided to give the wine its own identity.

Puligny-Montrachet (poo-li-NYEE MOAN-row-shay) One of the most famous dry white wine producing villages in the Côte de Beaune region of Burgundy, France. The wines are made of Chardonnay.

Puttonyos (POO-tone-yose) A Hungarian term used to express the level of sweetness in Hungary's Tokay dessert wine. It works on a scale of three to six puttonyos, with three being the least amount of sweetness and six the most.

Qualitätswein (QUAL-ee-tates-vine) This term means "quality wine" in German.

Qualitätswein mit Prädikat (QUAL-ee-tates-vine mit PRED-ee-cat) German for "quality wine with distinction."

quinta (KEEN-tah) Portuguese for "vineyard" or "estate."

reserva (ray-SERV-ah) The Spanish word for "reserve," which indicates that a wine has spent additional time aging.

residual sugar An indicator of how sweet a wine is.

Rheingau (RINE-gow) One of the most important white-wine–growing regions in Germany.

Rheinhessen (RINE-hess-en) An important white-wine–growing region in Germany.

Ribera del Duero (Ree-BEAR-ah del DWER-oh) Important wine-growing region in the northwestern part of Spain.

riddling (RID-ling)   During the méthode champenoise process, the bottles of wine are placed in special racks head first. A worker called a "riddler," who has since been replaced by a machine, twists all the bottles slightly on a daily basis until the bottles are upside down to move the sediment down to the cork. The process of turning the bottles is called riddling.

Riesling (REECE-ling)   A noble white grape variety that grows well in Germany, California, and Alsace, France.

Rioja (ree-OH-ha)   A top-quality red-wine making region in Spain.

riserva (REE-SERV-ah)   Italian for "reserve," this term means the wine was subjected to additional aging.

rosado (ro-SAHD-doe)   Spanish for "rosé."

rosato (ro-SAH-to)   Italian for "rosé."

Rosé (row-SAY)   Pink wine. This term sometimes is used interchangeably with blush, except that rosé from France is usually drier than blush wines from California.

Ruby Port   Young, fruity Port that is made from a blend of nonvintage wines.

Salmanazar (sol-man-ah-CZAR)   A large-format bottle that is the equivalent to 12 regular 750 ml bottles of wine.

Sancerre (sahn-SARE)   A dry white wine made in the Loire Valley of France using the Sauvignon Blanc grape.

Sangiovese (san-gee-oh-VAY-she)   A native red grape of Tuscany, Italy, that is used as the backbone of Chianti, which also is grown in parts of California.

Sauterne (saw-TURN) Though this term is pronounced the same as the world-famous dessert wine that takes its name from the French region, "Sauternes," this term without the "s" on the end is more likely to be a cheap generic dessert wine from other winemaking regions.

Sauternes (saw-TURN) The world-famous white dessert wine from the village by the same name in Bordeaux, France.

Sauvignon Blanc (SAV-in-nyon blahnk) A white grape found in many different wine regions especially the Loire Valley, Graves, and Sauternes regions in France. In California and Washington State, where the grape also flourishes, it is known as Fumé Blanc.

sediment The dregs of the wine that most reds and some whites throw during the maturation process.

Sémillon (SEM-me-yohn) A white grape grown mostly in the Graves and Sauternes regions of Bordeaux, France. You also can find it in other wine-growing regions such as Australia, where it often is blended with Chardonnay, and Chile.

Shiraz (SHE-roz) A hearty red grape widely planted in Australia that is known in other parts of the world as Syrah.

short-vatted Wines that are short-vatted are produced by separating the grape juice from the red skins before too much color is extracted. This process is used to produce blancs de noir Champagne or sparkling wine as well as some rosé wines.

sommelier (so-mel-YAY) French for "wine steward." See cellarmaster.

Sonoma (suh-NO-mah)   One of California's most important wine-growing areas located north of San Francisco.

Spätlese (SCHPATE-lay-suh)   A term used in German winemaking to express a level of ripeness in Qualitätswein mit Prädikat (QmP) wines. In German, it translates to "late," which refers to grapes that were left on the vine after the regular harvest. Spätlese is the level above Kabinett.

stainless-steel fermentation   This refers to fermentation that takes place in a temperature-controlled metal tank as opposed to a cement or wooden barrel. Stainless-steel fermentation produces a fresher and fruitier style of wine in which you can taste the flavor of the grape varietal.

still wine   Nonsparkling wine.

St.-Émilion (sahnt eh-meel-ee-YOHN)   A district in the Bordeaux region of France known for its wonderful red wines.

St.-Estèphe (sahnt es-TEFF)   An important red wine village and district of the Médoc in Bordeaux, France.

St.-Julien (sahnt CHEW-lee-en)   An important red wine village and district of the Médoc in Bordeaux, France.

sulfites (sull-FIGHTS)   A certain amount of sulfites occurs naturally during the winemaking process, but it is common to add sulfer to wine to prevent the growth of harmful bacteria and to prevent spoilage.

sulfur   See Sulfites.

Sur Lie (soor LEE)   French for "on the lees," this refers to wine resting on its own sediment. This adds complexity and body to the wine that often is found in Champagne and some Chardonnay from California and France.

Süss Reserve (soos reh-SERVE) The process by which unfermented grape juice is added to German wine after fermentation to add sweetness to the finished product.

Syrah (see-RAH) A red wine grape grown primarily in the Rhône Valley, France, in some of California, and in Australia, where it is called Shiraz.

Tafelwein (TOFF-el-vine) German for "table wine."

tannin (TA-nin) Describes the bitter sensation you might feel especially when drinking a red wine. It is similar to drinking a cup of strong tea that makes your mouth pucker.

Tawny Port Lighter in color than Ruby Port, this Port also has a more subdued flavor.

tears See Legs.

Tempranillo (temp-pra-KNEE-yo) The most important red wine grape of Spain.

terroir (terr-ROHR) In French, it means "soil" and refers to the inherent character of the earth that influences the taste of the wine.

Tête de Cuvée (tett day coo-VAY) Top-of-the-line Champagne.

tinta (TEEN-ta) The Spanish and the Portuguese refer to their red wines generically as "tinta."

Trebbiano (rreb-bee-ON-oh) An important native white grape of Italy.

Trocken (TROCK-en) German for "dry."

Trockenbeerenauslese (Trohck-ehn-BEER-ehn-ows-LEHS-eh)   Sometimes abbreviated by wine wizards as TBA, Trockenbeerenauslese is a term used in German winemaking to express a level of ripeness. Trockenbeerenauslese is when the individual berries are left on the vine long after the normal harvest so the berries get unbelievably sweet. These grapes inevitably make some of the best dessert wine in the world.

Tuscany (TUSK-an-ee)   Important red-wine-growing region of Italy.

unfermented grape juice   Grape juice before it is turned into wine. Unfermented grape juice also is sometimes referred to as "must."

varietal grape   Varieties such as Chardonnay are called varietals.

varietal wine   Wine that is labeled by its primary grape variety.

Veneto (ven-EE-to)   An important wine-growing area of Italy that produces Veronese wines.

village wine   Wine that comes from a specific village, especially in Burgundy, France.

Vinho Verde (VEE-no VUR-day)   This means "Green wine" in Portuguese and refers to Portuguese white wine that is intended to be consumed young.

Vino Nobile di Montepulciano (VEE-no no-BEE-le dee MOANT-te-pool-chi-an-oh)   A major red wine produced in Tuscany, Italy.

vintage   The year the grapes are harvested.

vintage Port   Port made only in the best years from a single harvest and intended to mature in the bottle with age.

Viognier (vee-oh-NYAY)   A white grape grown primarily in the Rhône Valley but now also in parts of California.

Vitis Labrusca (VEE-tis la-BREW-sca)   A Native American grape species responsible for grapes such as the grapey-tasting Concord of New York state. You don't see wines made from Vitis Labrusca as much today, though there still are some on the market.

Vitis Vinifera (VEE-tis vin-IF-er-ah)   European grape varieties such as Chardonnay, Cabernet Sauvignon, Merlot, and most of the other popular grape varieties come from this species.

Volnay (voll-NAY)   A village in the Côte de Beaune region of Burgundy, France.

Vougeot (voo-JO)   A village in the Côte de Nuits region of Burgundy, France.

Vouvray (voo-VRAY)   A white wine from the Loire Valley in France that is made from Chenin Blanc.

white Zinfandel   A wildly popular pink wine that originated in California and is made from the red Zinfandel grape.

wood Port   This term encompasses a basic category of Port that is aged in wooden barrels and is ready to drink upon its release.

Zinfandel (ZIN-fan-dell)   A red grape that was once thought to be native to the United States, until recent DNA fingerprinting showed its true ties to Europe. This grape produces wines ranging from a light, fruity style to a full-bodied delicious monster.

Resource Guide

Champagne destinations

Between my own personal travels and my friends at the Champagne Wines Information Bureau in New York, I've compiled a solid base of Champagne destinations for you to try when you are in any of the following cities. Many of these bubbly spots are as elegant as the Champagne you will enjoy while visiting them, but to be safe, you might want to call ahead because some of them are extremely comfortable and casual.

Arizona

Different Point of View
Pointe-Hilton at Tapatio Cliffs
Phoenix, AZ
602-866-7500

Windows on the Green
The Phoenician Resort
Scottsdale, AZ
602-423-2530

California (Northern)

Bix Restaurant & Lounge
San Francisco, CA
415-433-6300

Bubble Lounge
San Francisco, CA
415-434-4204

Chemin de Fer
Eureka, CA
707-441-9292

Greystone Restaurant
(The Culinary Institute of America's dining room,
housed in a former monastic winery)
St. Helena, CA
707-967-1010

Harry Denton's Starlight Room
(Rooftop nightclub)
Sir Francis Drake Hotel
San Francisco, CA
415-395-8595

Jack's
San Francisco, CA
415-421-7355

La Colonial
San Francisco, CA
415-931-3600

Lobby Lounge
The Ritz-Carlton San Francisco
San Francisco, CA
415-296-7465

Rubicon
Sacramento, CA
415-434-4100

Trader Vic's
Emeryville, CA
510-653-3400

Tra Vigne
St. Helena, CA
707-963-4444

California (Southern)
Bar Marmot
(Hotel bar in a renovated 1920s Hollywood landmark)

The Château Marmot
Hollywood, CA
323-656-1010

C Bar & Restaurant
Beverly Hills, CA
323-782-8157

Les Deux Café
Los Angeles, CA
323-465-0509

Lucques
Los Angeles, CA
323-655-6227

The Peninsula Beverly Hills
Beverly Hills, CA
310-551-2888

Polo Lounge
Beverly Hills Hotel & Bungalows
Beverly Hills, CA
310-276-2251

The Ritz-Carlton Laguna Niguel
Dana Point, CA
714-240-2000

Sky Bar
The Mondrian Hotel
Los Angeles, CA
323-848-6025

Florida
Jimmy'z at the Forge
Miami Beach, FL
305-604-9798

Smith & Wollensky
Miami Beach, FL
305-673-2800

Georgia
Bone's
Atlanta, GA
404-237-2663

The Dining Room
The Ritz-Carlton Buckhead
Atlanta, GA
404-237-2700

Illinois
Ambria
Chicago, IL
773-472-5959

Bistro 110
Chicago, IL
312-266-3110

Narcisse Champagne Salon & Caviar Bar
Chicago, IL
312-787-2675

Park Avenue Café
Chicago, IL
312-944-4414

Pops for Champagne
Chicago, IL
773-472-1000

Kentucky
Lilly's Restaurant
Louisville, KY
502-451-0447

The Oakroom
The Seelback Hilton
Louisville
502-585-3200

Louisiana
Brennan's Restaurant
New Orleans, LA
504-525-9711

The Grill Room
Windsor Court Hotel
New Orleans, LA
504-522-1992

Massachusetts
Biba Restaurant
Boston, MA
617-426-7878

Blantyre
Lenox, MA
413-637-3556

The Dining Room
The Ritz-Carlton Boston
Boston, MA
617-536-5700

Michigan

The Rattlesnake Club
Detroit, MI
313-567-4400

Nevada

Bellagio Resort & Casino
Las Vegas, NV
888-987-6667

New York

Asia de Cuba
New York, NY
212-726-7755

Blackbird
New York, NY
212-692-9292

Bond Street
New York, NY
212-777-2500

Bubble Lounge
New York, NY
212-431-3433

Caviarteria
Delmonico Hotel
New York, NY
212-759-7410

Champagne's
New York, NY
212-639-9460

Clementine
New York, NY
212-253-0003

Flute
New York, NY
212-265-5169

Harry Cipriani
New York, NY
212-753-5566

Harry Cipriani—Downtown
New York, NY
212-343-0999

Mercer Kitchen
The Mercer Hotel
New York, NY
212-966-5454

Monzú
New York, NY
212-343-0333

Petrossian
New York, NY
212-245-2214

SoHo Kitchen & Bar
New York, NY
212-925-1866

Torch
New York, NY
212-288-5151

Vandam
New York, NY
212-352-9090

Wall Street Kitchen & Bar
New York, NY
212-797-7070

Windows on the World
New York, NY
212-524-7000

Ohio
The Refectory
Columbia, OH
614-451-9774

Sammy's
Cleveland, OH
216-532-5560

Pennsylvania
La Bec-Fin
Philadelphia, PA
215-567-1000

Striped Bass
Philadelphia, PA
215-732-4444

South Carolina
Cedar Grove Plantation
Edgefield, SC
803-637-3056

Texas
Brennan's Restaurant
Houston, TX
713-522-9711

The French Room
Adolphus Hotel
Dallas, TX
214-742-8200

Wonderful wine lists

Wine Spectator, the number one wine publication in
the United States, reviews wine lists from restaurants

all over the world and each year recognizes the very best. Here are some of my personal favorites:

California

The Carnelian Room
San Francisco, CA

Patina
Los Angeles, CA

Peppone
West Los Angeles, CA

Rubicon
San Francisco, CA

The Sardine Factory
Monterey, CA

Top O' the Cove
La Jolla, CA

Valentino
Santa Monica, CA

The Winesellar & Brasserie
San Diego, CA

District of Columbia

Seasons
The Four Seasons Hotel in Georgetown
Washington, DC

Illinois

Carlos' Restaurant
Highland Park, IL

Charlie Trotter's
Chicago, IL

The Dining Room
The Ritz-Carlton Chicago
Chicago, IL

Italian Village Restaurant
Chicago, IL

Louisiana
Brennan's
New Orleans

Emeril's
New Orleans

Massachusetts
The Dining Room
The Ritz-Carlton Boston
Boston, MA

Olives
Cambridge, MA

New Jersey
The Manor
West Orange, NJ

Park and Orchard
East Rutherford, NJ

New York
Felidia Ristorante
New York, NY

The Four Seasons
New York, NY

Le Cirque 2000
New York, NY

Montrachet
New York, NY

Smith & Wollensky
New York, NY

Sparks Steak House
New York, NY

Windows on the World
New York, NY

North Carolina
The Angus Barn
Raleigh, NC

Ohio
The Refectory
Columbus, OH

Tennessee
The Wild Boar Restaurant
Nashville, TN

Texas
The Mansion on Turtle Creek
Dallas, TX

Vermont
The Hermitage Inn
Wilmington, VT

Washington State
Canlis
Seattle, WA

Wisconsin
Pizza Man
Milwaukee, WI

Fine wine merchants
Whether you purchase wine for everyday enjoyment or are interested in collecting, your best bet is to hook up with a fine wine merchant who will advise, educate, and serve you well. Here are some of the top wine merchants in the country, listed by state. Many of them have more than one retail outlet where legal. Hopefully, one of them will have a store near you.

Alaska
Brown Jug
Anchorage, AK

Oaken Keg Spirits Shop
Anchorage, AK

Arkansas
Popatop Wine Merchant
Little Rock, AR

Arizona
AJ's Purveyor of Fine Foods
Scottsdale, AZ

California
Beltramo's
Menlo Park, CA

Beverages, & More!
Concord, CA

Dean & DeLuca
St. Helena, CA

Draeger's
Menlo Park, CA

Duke of Bourbon
Canoga Park, CA

Hi-Time Cellars
Costa Mesa, CA

Jon's Market
Los Angeles, CA

The Jug Shop
San Francisco, CA

K&L Wine Merchants
Redwood City, CA

Lucky Stores
San Leandro, CA

Mr. Liquor
San Francisco, CA

Raley's
West Sacramento, CA

Ralph's Grocery Company
Compton, CA

Red Carpet Wine & Spirits Merchants
Glendale, CA

John Walker & Company
San Francisco, CA

The Wine Club
San Francisco, CA

The Wine House
Los Angeles, CA

The Wine Merchant
Beverly Hills, CA

Trader Joe's
Pasadena, CA

Vons
Arcadia, CA

Wally's
Los Angeles, CA

Wine Exchange
Orange, CA

Colorado
Applejack Liquors
Wheatridge, CO

Argonaut Liquors
Denver, CO

Boulder Liquor Mart
Boulder, CO

County Line Liquor
Littleton, CO

West Vail Liquor Mart
Vail, CO

Connecticut

Crazy Bruce's White House Liquors
West Hartford, CT

Elmer's Townline Liquor
Norwalk, CT

Harry's
Danbury, CT

Liquor Depot
New Britain, CT

M&R Liquors
Manchester, CT

Warehouse Wines & Liquors
Stamford, CT

Delaware

Kreston Liquor Mart
Wilmington, DE

Liquor World
Claymont, DE

District of Columbia

Calvert Woodley
Washington, DC

Giant Foods
Washington, DC

MacArthur Liquors
Washington, DC

Schneider's of Capitol Hill
Washington, DC

Florida
ABC Fine Wine & Spirits
Orlando, FL

B-21
Tarpon Springs, FL

Big Daddy's
Ft. Lauderdale, FL

Crown Liquors & Wine Merchants
Coral Gables, FL

Foremost Sunset Corners
Miami, FL

Gooding's
Apopka, FL

Kash n' Karry
Tampa, FL

Laurenzo Brothers
North Miami Beach, FL

Pantry Liquors
Miami, FL

Georgia
Beverage Warehouse
Roswell, GA

Green's Package Stores
Atlanta, GA

Jax Package Store
Atlanta, GA

Mink's Package Store
Marietta, GA

Pearson's Wine of Atlanta
Atlanta, GA

Tower Liquor
Doraville, GA

Hawaii
Vintage Wine Cellar
Honolulu, HW

Illinois
DiCarlo's Armanetti
Willowbrook, IL

Gold Standard
(Superstores operate under the name Binny's)
Chicago, IL

Malloy's SavWay Liquors
Oak Brook, IL

Sam's Wines & Spirits
Chicago, IL

Schaefer's
Skokie, IL

Wine Discount Center
Addison, IL

Zimmerman's
Chicago, IL

Indiana
21st Amendment
Indianapolis, IN

Belmont Beverage Stores of Indiana
Fort Wayne, IN

Marsh Supermarkets
Indianapolis, IN

Kansas
Lukas Liquor Superstore
Overland Park, KS

Kentucky
Cork n' Bottle
Covington, KY

Liquor Outlet/The Party Source
Louisville, KY

Shopper's Village Liquors
Lexington, KY

Louisiana
Hokus-Pokus Liquors
Alexandria, LA

Martin Wine Cellar
New Orleans, LA

Thrifty Discount Liquor
Bossier City, LA

Maine
RSVP Discount Beverage
Portland, ME

Maryland
Mayflower Wine at Sutton Place
Bethesda, MD

Massachusetts
Atlas Liquors
Medford, MA

Big Y Wines and Liquors
Springfield, MA

Brookline Liquor
Brookline, MA

Kappy's Liquor
Everett, MA

V. Cirace & Son
Boston, MA

Yankee Spirits
Sturbridge, MA

Michigan
Merchant of Vino
Farmington Hills, MI

Minneapolis
Chicago Lake Liquors
Minneapolis, MN

Haskell's
Minneapolis, MN

MGM Liquor Stores
St. Paul, MN

Surdyk's
Minneapolis, MN

Missouri
Berbiglia's
Kansas City, MO

Brown Derby
Springfield, MO

Gomer's Fine Wines
Kansas City, MO

Schnuck Markets
St. Louis, MO

Nevada
Ben's Discount Liquors
Reno, NV

Lee's Discount Liquor
Las Vegas, NV

The Wine Cellar Tasting Room
Rio Suite Hotel & Casino
Las Vegas, NV

New Hampshire
New Hampshire State Liquor Commission
(Note: New Hampshire is a control state, which means all of its wine shops are strictly controlled by the state government. This state takes great care in wine selection and merchandising.)

New Jersey
A&P Supermarkets
Montvale, NJ

Bottle King
Livingston, NJ

Home Wine & Liquors
Hackensack, NJ

Liquor Locker
Edison, NJ

Shoppers of Madison and Livingston
Madison, NJ

The Super Cellars
Paterson, NJ

Wine & Spirit World
Fort Lee, NJ and Ho-Ho-Kus, NJ

New York
67 Wine & Spirits
New York, NY

Astor Place
New York, NY

Century Liquor
Rochester, NY

Crazy Billy's
Deer Park, NY

Crossroads
New York, NY

Garnet Wines
New York, NY

House of Bacchus
Rochester, NY

Liquor Square
Syracuse, NY

Morrell & Company
New York, NY

Northside Liquor and Wine
Ithaca, NY

Park Avenue Liquor Shop
New York, NY

PJ's Warehouse
New York, NY

Pop's Wines & Spirits
Island Park, NY

Premier Liquors
Kenmore, NY

Rochambeau Wines and Liquors
Dobbs Ferry, NY

Sherry-Lehmann
New York, NY

Viscount Liquor
Wappingers Falls, NY

The Wine Connection
Pound Ridge, NY

Zachys
Scarsdale, NY

North Carolina
Harris Teeter's
Matthews, NC

North Dakota
Happy Harry's
Grand Forks, ND

Ohio
Arrow Wine
Dayton, OH

The West Point Market
Akron, OH

Oklahoma
Byron's
Oklahoma City, OK

Fikes Center Liquor Mart
Tulsa, OK

Pennsylvania
Pennsylvania Liquor Control Board
(Note: Pennsylvania is a control state, which means all of its wine shops are strictly controlled by the state government. This state takes great care in wine selection and merchandising.)

Rhode Island
Gasbarro
Providence, RI

Town Wine & Spirits
Rumford, RI

South Carolina

Green's Beverage Stores
Columbia, SC

Owens' Liquors
Myrtle Beach, SC

Tennessee

Buster's
Memphis, TN

Frugal MacDoogal's
Nashville, TN

Kirby Wines & Liquors
Memphis, TN

Mt. Moriah
Memphis, TN

Texas

Centennial Liquor Stores
Dallas, TX

Don & Ben's
San Antonio, TX

Feldman's Valley Wide
Harlingen, TX

Gabriel's
San Antonio, TX

H.E.B. Grocery Company
San Antonio, TX

Majestic Liquors
Fort Worth, TX

Marty's
Dallas, TX

Red Coleman's
Dallas, TX

Reuben's Wine & Spirits
Austin, TX

Rice Epicurean Markets
Houston, TX

Richard's Liquors & Fine Wines
Houston, TX

Sigel's Liquor Stores
Dallas, TX

Spec's Liquor Stores
Dallas, TX

Twin Liquors
Austin, TX

Western Beverages
San Antonio, TX

Virginia
Arrowine
Arlington, VA

Wisconsin
Club Liquors
Menasha, WI

Love's One-Stop Liquor
Milwaukee, WI

Ray's Liquor
Milwaukee, WI

Wyoming
The Liquor Store
Jackson Hole, WY

Town & Country Supermarket Liquors
Cheyenne, WY

Recommended Reading

The best way to keep abreast of wine trends, new wine releases, food and wine pairing, and insider news is to subscribe to at least one major wine publication. If you develop a special interest in a certain area or wine region, there also are many good books you can read.

Publications

- *Wine Spectator*—This is the number one wine publication in America. If you have time to read only one wine publication, this should be it. In addition to the semimonthly magazine, *Wine Spectator* publishes special editions dedicated to exploring wine country called *Wine Country Guide to California*. The publisher, M. Shanken Communications, also publishes other books about wines. *Wine Spectator* is available on the newsstands and by mail order.

- *Wine Advocate*—Robert Parker, Jr., one of the most highly respected palates in the industry, writes this bimonthly newsletter that is available by mail-order subscription.

- *International Wine Cellar*—Former *Food & Wine* columnist Steve Tanzer covers the globe, including lesser-known wine regions, in his newsletter, to assess and recommend wines as well as to interview top wine personalities.

- *Wine & Spirits*—In addition to wine reviews and tasting notes, you'll find good coverage on spirits.

- *Wine Enthusiast*—This large-format–wine magazine combines tasting notes and ratings with interviews with winemakers from around the world. Perhaps equally, if not better, well-known is this company's attractive catalog of wine accouterments.

Books

Bespaloff, Alex, et al. *The New Frank Schoonmaker Encyclopedia of Wine.* William Morrow & Company, October 1988.

Casas, Penelope. *Foods and Wines of Spain.* Random House, October 1982.

Coates, Clive. *Côte d'Or: A Celebration of the Great Wines of Burgundy.* University of California Press, September 1997.

Friedrich, Jacqueline. *A Wine and Food Guide to the Loire.* Henry Holt, March 1998.

Halliday, James. *The Wine Companion, Australia & New Zealand: 1999 edition.* HarperCollins Australia, November 1998.

Johnson, Hugh. *Hugh Johnson's Pocket Encyclopedia of Wine 1999.* Simon & Schuster, November 1998.

Johnson, Linda and Michael Broadbent. *The Wine Collector's Handbook: Storing and Enjoying Wine at Home.* The Lyons Press, January 1998.

Laube, James. *Wine Spectator's California Wine.* Wine Spectator Press, September 1999.

McCarthy, Ed and Mary Ewing-Mulligan. *Wine for Dummies.* Harper Audio, November 1996.

Norman, Remington, et al. *The Great Domaines of Burgundy: A Guide to the Finest Wine Producers of the Côte d'Or.* Henry Hold & Company, Inc., November 1996.

Parker, Robert M. Jr. *Bordeaux: A Comprehensive Guide to the Wines Produced from 1961 to 1997.* Simon & Schuster, October 1998.

Parker, Robert M. Jr. *Wines of the Rhône Valley.* Simon & Schuster, May 1997.

Robinson, Jancis (Editor). *The Oxford Companion to Wine.* Oxford University Press (Trade), November 1994.

Roby, Norman S. and Charles E. Olken. *Connoisseur's Handbook of the Wines of California and the Pacific Northwest.* Knopf, October 1998.

Spence, Godfrey. *The Port Companion: A Connoisseur's Guide.* IDG Books Worldwide, September 1997.

Stevenson, Tom. *New Sotheby's Wine Encyclopedia.* DK Publishing, October 1997.

Zraly, Kevin and Felicia M. Sherbert. (editor). *The Windows on the World Complete Wine Course Millennium Edition.* Sterling Publishing Co., Inc., August 1999.

Entertainment Wine Service Cheat Sheets

Y ou're having a cozy soiree at home for some friends, you're throwing the wedding of your daughter's life and inviting 500 of your closest friends and relatives, or you just like to party.

The age-old question is, How much wine should I get?

When you're in the hands of an able banquet director or caterer, it's usually not an issue. If you're on your own, however, you can use this handy set of Entertainment Wine Service Cheat Sheets to help you decide how much wine to buy as well as how much red and how much white you'll need.

The cheat sheets that follow cover:

- How much Champagne do you need for a Champagne toast?

- How much Champagne do you need for a cocktail reception?

- How much Champagne do you need if you are serving bubbly with your dinner instead of still wine?

- How much red and white wine do you need if you are hosting a standard one-hour cocktail reception with a full bar? (This way, you don't have to figure out how many of your guests will drink wine. We do that for you.)

- How much wine do you need if you are serving dinner only with no prior cocktail reception?

- How much red wine and white wine do you need for the preceding wine-only dinner without a cocktail reception?

- How much wine do you need if you host a one-hour, one-and-a-half hour, or two-hour reception?

- How much red and white wine do you need if you host a one-hour, one-and-a-half hour, or two-hour reception?

- How much red and white wine do you need for the basic one-hour reception, converted to cases?

Please note that all numbers are rounded.

Finally, remember that these are guidelines based on the average party. If you know your guests enjoy red wine only, minimize or eliminate the white wine. In the same vein, if you know your guests either are nondrinkers or really enjoy their wine, go with the appropriate lower or upper estimate.

Above all, enjoy your party. Remember not to overserve your guests and include an interesting selection of soft drinks for people who do not want to partake. You want everyone to get home safely.

TABLE D.1: CHAMPAGNE TOAST

Number of Guests	Total Bottles
6	$3/4$
8	1
12	$1^1/_2$
16	2
24	3
36	$4^1/_2$
48	$5^1/_2$
50	6
75	9
100	12
125	15
150	$17^1/_2$
175	$20^1/_2$
200	$23^1/_2$
225	$26^1/_2$
250	$29^1/_2$
275	$32^1/_2$
300	$35^1/_2$
325	$38^1/_2$
350	$41^1/_2$
400	47
500	59

TABLE D.2: COCKTAIL RECEPTION

Number of Guests	Total Bottles
6	$1^1/_2$–2
8	2–3
12	3–4
16	4–5
24	6–8
36	9–12
48	12–16
50	$12^1/_2$–17
75	19–25
100	25–33
125	31–42
150	38–50
175	49–58
200	50–67
225	56–75
250	63–84
275	69–92
300	75–100
325	81–108
350	88–117
400	100–133
500	125–167

TABLE D.3: CHAMPAGNE WITH DINNER

Number of Guests	Total Bottles
6	2–3
8	3–4
12	4–6
16	5–8
24	8–12
36	12–18
48	16–24
50	17–25
75	25–38
100	33–50
125	42–63
150	50–75
175	58–88
200	67–100
225	75–113
250	83–125
275	92–138
300	100–150
325	108–163
350	117–175
400	133–200
500	167–250

TABLE D.4: ONE-HOUR RECEPTION WITH FULL BAR

Number of Guests	Total Bottles	
	Red	White
6	$^1/_2$	$^1/_2$
8	$^1/_2$	1
12	1	1
16	1	$1^1/_2$
24	$1^1/_2$	$2^1/_2$
36	$2^1/_2$	$3^1/_2$
48	3	5
50	$3^1/_2$	5
75	5	$7^1/_2$
100	$6^1/_2$	10
125	$8^1/_2$	$12^1/_2$
150	10	15
175	$11^1/_2$	$17^1/_2$
200	13	20
225	15	$22^1/_2$
250	$16^1/_2$	25
275	18	$27^1/_2$
300	20	30
325	$21^1/_2$	32
350	23	$34^1/_2$
400	$26^1/_2$	$39^1/_2$
500	33	$49^1/_2$

TABLE D.5: WINE FOR DINNER
ONLY (NO RECEPTION)

Number of Guests	Total Bottles	
	Red	White
6	$1^1/_2$	2
8	2	$2^1/_2$
12	3	4
16	$3^1/_2$	$5^1/_2$
24	$5^1/_2$	8
36	8	12
48	$10^1/_2$	16
50	11	17
75	17	25
100	22	$33^1/_2$
125	28	$41^1/_2$
150	33	50
175	$38^1/_2$	58
200	44	$66^1/_2$
225	50	$74^1/_2$
250	$55^1/_2$	83
275	61	91
300	66	$99^1/_2$
325	72	$107^1/_2$
350	77	116
400	88	$132^1/_2$
500	$110^1/_2$	$165^1/_2$

TABLE D.6: WINE FOR DINNER ONLY (NO RECEPTION)

Number of Guests	Total Bottles of Wine	Number of Cases
6	3–4	$^1/_4$–$^1/_3$
8	4–5	$^1/_3$–$^1/_2$
12	6–8	$^1/_2$–$^2/_3$
16	8–10	$^2/_3$–$^5/_6$
24	12–15	1–1$^1/_4$
36	17–23	1$^1/_2$–2
48	23–30	2–2$^1/_2$
50	24–32	2–3
75	36–48	3–4
100	48–63	4–5$^1/_4$
125	59–80	5–7
150	71–95	6–8
175	83–110	7–9
200	95–126	8–10$^1/_2$
225	107–142	9–12
250	119–158	10–13
275	130–174	11–14$^1/_2$
300	142–189	12–16
325	154–205	13–17
350	166–220	14–18
400	189–252	16–21
500	237–315	20–26

TABLE D.7: NUMBER OF BOTTLES NEEDED FOR ONE-, ONE-AND-A-HALF-, AND TWO-HOUR RECEPTIONS

	One-Hour Reception	One-and-a-Half Hour Reception	Two-Hour Reception
Number of Guests	Total Bottles	Total Bottles	Total Bottles
6	2–3	3–4	4–5
8	3–4	4–5	5–6
12	4–6	6–8	7–9
16	6–8	8–10	10–12
24	8–12	12–16	14–18
36	12–17	18–23	21–27
48	16–24	24–30	28–37
50	18–24	24–31	30–39
75	27–36	36–47	44–58
100	36–48	48–62	59–77
125	44–60	60–78	74–96
150	53–71	71–93	89–115
175	62–83	82–109	106–135
200	71–95	94–125	118–154
225	80–106	106–140	133–173
250	89–115	118–155	148–192
275	98–130	130–171	162–211
300	107–142	142–187	177–230
325	115–154	154–202	192–250
350	124–166	166–218	207–269
400	142–189	189–249	236–307
500	177–236	236–311	296–384

TABLE D.8: NUMBER OF BOTTLES OF RED AND WHITE WINE NEEDED FOR ONE, ONE-AND-A-HALF, AND TWO-HOUR RECEPTIONS

Number of Guests	One-Hour Reception		One-and-a-Half-Hour Reception		Two-Hour Reception	
	Red	White	Red	White	Red	White
6	1	2	2	2	2	3
8	2	2	2	3	2	4
12	2	3	3	4	3	5
16	3	4	4	6	5	7
24	4	6	6	9	7	10
36	6	9	8	13	10	15
48	8	12	11	16	13	20
50	8	12	11	17	14	21
75	12	19	17	25	21	31
100	17	25	22	33	27	41
125	21	32	28	42	34	51
150	25	37	33	50	41	62
175	29	44	38	58	48	73
200	33	50	44	66	55	82
225	37	56	49	74	61	92
250	41	62	55	82	68	102
275	46	69	60	90	75	112
300	50	75	66	99	82	122
325	54	81	71	107	89	133
350	58	87	77	115	95	143
400	66	100	88	132	107	163
500	83	124	110	164	136	204

TABLE D.9: NUMBER OF CASES OF RED AND WHITE WINE NEEDED FOR A ONE-HOUR RECEPTION

Number of Guests	Red	White
50	8 bottles	1 case
100	$1^1/_2$ cases	2 cases
150	2 cases	3 cases
200	$2^1/_2$ cases	4 cases
250	$3^1/_2$ cases	5 cases
300	4 cases	6 cases
350	5 cases	7 cases
400	$5^1/_2$ cases	8 cases
450	6 cases	9 cases
500	7 cases	10 cases
750	10 cases	15 cases
1,000	14 cases	20 cases
2,000	27 cases	40 cases

Wine on the Web

Plugging into the cyber wine world

One of the best ways to stay totally plugged into the wine world is to surf the Web. It's amazing what you can find online these days. In wine alone, you can learn about wine regions, track down hard-to-find wines, compare tasting notes with other winos, arrange to buy or sell some collectibles, or arrange a trip to wine country. This only begins to scratch the surface. For those who prefer to have an idea of where they want to go before they begin, here's a list of some cool wine Web sites. I could create an entire phone book with Web sites related to wine, but due to space limitations, I'll just get you started.

Some general rules or pointers that I've learned by doing:

1. Speed matters. The faster your modem, the quicker and therefore easier your search will be. If you are lucky enough to be hooked up to a cable modem or a T line, you can bop in and out of sites like no one's business. However, if your computer is a few years older, and has less memory (less than 64 MB of RAM), you may

wait all day to navigate—at least that's how it feels. I've been using my "state of the art" computer to write this book, but I learned the hard way that 32 MB of RAM with a 28K modem is not what it used to be three years ago, so I've been surfing on my new state-of-the art computer with 256 MB of RAM, a 56K modem, and a cable modem line that works like greased lightning.

2. You don't always have to "know" the address of the Web site. Often, you just take an educated guess based on the name of the company or winery. For instance, the retailer "Duke of Bourbon" in Canoga Park, California, happens to have a Web site by the same name except that when you type in keys of a Web address you are not supposed to use spaces between words, so it is www.dukeofbourbon.com.

3. Generally, if your computer is not responding, be sure that you have the prefix www. (for worldwide web) and don't forget the suffix **.com** for most addresses or .org for an organization, **.edu** for a school or university, and **.gov** for a government agency. Some of the newer computers will allow you to simply type the main address, such as dukeofbourbon and they will search the Web to find out if it is a regular .com or .edu, and so on. If yours does not search the Web, be sure to use the full address, starting with http://www. dukeofbourbon.com/.

General Web sites

An excellent starting point is the 4anything network. You can get right into the wine area by using these addresses:

www.4wine.com

www.4champagne.com

www.4winecountry.com

www.4NapaValley.com

www.4foods.com

www.4gourmets.com

Publications

www.winespectator.com (*Wine Spectator's* Web site)

www.wine-advocate.com (Robert Parker's *The Wine Advocate*)

www.wine101.com

www.epicurious.com

www.food&wine.com

Wineries

www.cuvaison.com (Cuvaison Winery in California)

www.dchandon.com (Domaine Chandon Winery for sparkling wine in California)

www.domainecarneros.com (Domaine Carneros Winery for sparkling wine in California)

www.frederickwildman.com (Frederick Wildman & Sons Ltd. Importer)

www.jwine.com (J sparkling wine from Jordan Winery in California)

www.lindeman.com (Lindeman Winery in Australia)

www.mumm.com (Mumm Cuvee Napa for sparkling wine in California) www.niebaum-coppola.com (Niebaum-Coppola Estate in California)

www.penfolds.com (Penfolds Winery in Australia)

www.perrier-jouet-usa.com (Perrier-Joüet Champagne house in France)

www.ridge.com (Ridge Vineyards in California)

www.robertmondavi.com (Robert Mondavi Winery in California)

www.stsupery.com (St. Supery Winery in California

www.veuve-clicquot.fr.com (Veuve Clicquot Champagne house and wine importer in France)

www.vinonet.com (database of top German wineries)

www.vinosearch.com (database of 1,000 wineries; search by winery or by region)

www.vineyardbrands.com (Vineyard Brands importer)

Trade organizations

www.agriline.it/wol/wol_eng/default.htm (Wine Trade Bureau of Italy—Enoteca)

www.bordeaux.com (Bordeaux Bureau)

www.champagnes.com (Champagne Wines Information Bureau)

www.napavintners.com (Napa Valley Vintners Association)

www.nywine.com (New York Wine Growers Association)

www.nzwine.com (New Zealand Wine Commission's Web site)

www.sonomawine.com (Sonoma County Wineries)

www.wineandfoodassociates.com (information on Spanish wine)

www.wineaustralia.com (Australian Wine Bureau)

www.wine.co.za (Wines of South Africa)

www.wines-france.com (Food & Wine From France)

www.winesofchile (Chilean Wines)

Retailers

This list includes those that handle auctions.

www.dukeofbourbon.com (Duke of Bourbon—retailer in Canoga Park, CA)

www.winebid.com (online auction house)

www.zachys.com (Zachys—retailer in Scarsdale, NY)

www.AuctionVine.com (Morrell & Company's Web site for auctioning)

www.phillips-auctions.com (Phillips and Park Avenue Liquor Shop—auction)

www.magnumwines.com (auction)

www.sothebys.com (Sothebys, the New York-based auction house)

www.butterfields.com (Butterfields, the San Francisco-based auction house).

www.cellar.com (Schneider's of Capitol Hill, Washington, DC-based retailer) www.hitimewine.com (Hi-Time, the California-based retailer)

www.redcarpetwine.com (Red Carpet, the California-based retailer)

www.WineSellar.com (The WineSellar & Brasserie restaurant known for its award-winning wine list and retail shop)

www.virtualvin.com (find and buy wine on the Web)

www.winesociety.com (offers the world's widest selection of hard-to-find wines at unbeatable prices)

Other notable wine sites

www.winebrats.org (organization of "younger generation" winemakers who organize wine raves as part of their mission to bring wine down to Earth)

www.evinopolis.com (wine theme park in London)

www.wineparty.com (advice and software on how to organize your own wine tasting)

Wine systems & wine accessories

www.bermar.com (wine storage systems and accessories)

www.customwinecellars.com (wine cellars)

www.koolspace.com (wine cooling systems)

www.riedel.com (Riedel glassware)

www.vintagecellars.com (wine storage systems)

www.wineenthusiast.com (wine accessories and publications)

A

ABC (anything but
Chardonnay) wines,
17–19
Abruzzo, 217, 225, 399
Accessories, wine, 377–83,
474
Acid, 10, 399
Acidic foods, 10
Acidic wines, 49
Aconcagua Valley, 148
Advisers, wine, 343–45
After-dinner wines. *See*
Dessert wines
Aftertaste, 399, 411
Aged Tawny Ports, 281,
399
Aging, defined, 399
Ah-So corkscrews, 381–82
Albariño, 57, 135, 400
Alcoholic Beverage
Control (ABC),
342–43
Alcoholic content, 29, 30,
38, 400
Alentejo, 231
Alexander Valley, 115–16,
202, 400
Aloxe-Corton, 33, 167
Alsace, 32, 75–77, 400
Alto-Adige, 133, 217, 226
Alvarinho, 37, 57
Amador County, 119,
205
Amarone, 224–25, 400
Amazon.com, 343
America. *See* United States

American Viticultural
Areas (AVAs),
113–16, 201, 401
Anniversaries, 355–61
AOC (Appellation
d'Origine
Contrôlée), 38,
74–75, 116, 172, 400
Aperitifs, 78, 400
AP Nr, 400
Appellation d'Origine
Contrôlée (AOC), 38,
74–75, 116, 172, 400
Apulia, 217, 225–26
Argentina, 36
red wines, 237–38
white wines, 147–48,
150–52
Aroma, 54–55, 400–401
Arroyo Seco, 202
Astringent foods, 11
Auctions, 337–43
bidding at, 340–41
catalog for, 339–40
selling at, 341–43
Web sites, 473–74
Auslese, 35, 100–101, 293,
295, 401
Australia, 36
dessert wines, 297–98
Port-style wines, 286
red wines, 232–35
sparkling wines, 275–76
white wines, 137–45
appellations,
142–44
vintages, 145
Auxey, 169

B

Bairrada, 231
Balanced, defined, 401
Balthazar, 367, 401
Banquets, 355–61
  catering wine options,
   357–59
  directors, dealing with,
   355–56
  wine service at, 359–61
Barbaresco, 36, 222–23,
  401
Barbeques, 12–13
Barbera, 8, 36, 62–63, 195,
  217, 223, 244
Bardolino, 36, 217, 224–25
Bar mitzvahs, 355–61
Barolo, 36, 222–23, 330,
  401
Barossa Valley, 140, 143,
  233, 401
Barrel aging, defined, 401
Barrel fermentation, 61,
  123, 402
Barrique, defined, 402
Barsac, 32, 34, 179,
  287–91, 402
  classification of 1855
   and, 288, 289–90
Bar syrup, simple, 369
Bat mitzvahs, 355–61
Beaujolais, 32, 33, 160–62,
  193, 402
  grape varietals used, 64
  quality levels of, 160–61
  vineyards, 162
  vintages, best, 162
Beaujolais Nouveau, 160,
  402
Beaujolais-Village, 161,
  402
Beaume-de-Venise, 33, 59,
  91, 291
Beaune (village), 88, 168,
  169, 402

Beerenauslese, 35, 101,
  293, 295, 402–3
Bellini, recipe for, 369
Beringer Vineyards, 117,
  193, 198, 247, 271,
  311
Bermar America, 380, 394,
  474
Bitter foods, 10–11
Bitterness, 50, 403
Blanc de blancs, 264–65,
  403
Blanc de noir, 265, 403
Blends, 26–28, 56
Bloody Marys, 354
Blush wines, 23–24,
  243–55, 403. *See also*
  Rosés
Body of a wine, 29–30, 403
Books, recommended,
  454–55
Bordeaux, 26, 32, 34, 65,
  69
  dessert wines, 287–91
  red wines, 159, 172–84
   buying strategies,
    180–81
   classification of
    1855, 176–79
   Cru Bourgeois,
    179–80, 408
   grape varietals,
    173–74
   quality levels,
    175–76
   regions, 174–75,
    184
   vintages, best, 184
  white wines, 79–81
Botrytis cinerea, 101,
  287–88, 293, 299,
  403, 418
Bottle sizes, 38, 366–67
Bottling, 38
Bouquet, 54–55, 400–401,
  403

Bourgogne, 403. *See also*
Burgundy
Breast cancer, 43–44
Brix, 403
Brotherhood Winery, 129
Brunches, 354
Brunello, 63, 217, 404
Brunello di Montalcino,
36, 63, 217, 220–21
Brut, 263, 268, 269, 404
Burgundy, 32–33, 78. *See
also* Beaujolais
red wines, 159–72
best of, 164–69
quality levels,
160–61, 163–64
vintages, best, 162,
171
shipping from, 170
white wines, 57, 81–90
Business entertaining,
349–53
price as consideration,
352–53
protocol for wine,
351–52
Buying strategies, 21–22,
333–36. *See also*
Auctions
for Bordeaux red wines,
180–81
buying direct, 334–36
by the case, 333, 337,
366
for special events,
361–66
wine futures, 333–34

C

Cabernet Franc, 8, 63,
173, 197–98, 404
Cabernet Sauvignon, 8,
25, 29, 35, 36, 37, 404
Australia, 234
Bordeaux, 173–74

California, 69, 115, 116,
192, 198–201, 203
Chile, 149
flavor profile of, 63–64
Long Island, 129
New Zealand, 146
South Africa, 152
Cain Five, 207
California, 31, 35, 131. *See
also specific regions and
wines*
auction houses, 343
champagne destinations
in, 430–32
dessert wines, 295–96
red wines, 192–207
grape varietals,
193–200
Meritage, 205–7
regions, 200–205
vintages, best, 207
retailers, 440–41
rosé wines, 244, 245–48
sparkling wines, 271–73
white wines, 112–24
grape varietals,
120–24
vintages, best, 124
wine lists, favorite, 437
Carafes, 389–90
Carbonic maceration,
404
Carignan, 64, 187
Carmignano, 221–22, 404
Carneros, 116, 193, 201
Casablanca Valley, 148,
150
Cask 23, 207
Catalogs, store, 328
Catelonia, 404
Catering, 357–59
Cava, 273–74, 404
Cellarmaster, 314–16,
404–5
Central Valley, 119, 195,
204–5

Chablis, 32, 68, 81, 82–85, 405
  quality levels of, 83–84
  vineyards, 84–85
Chablis Grand Cru, 83, 84
Chablis Premier Cru, 83, 84
Chambertin, 165, 169, 405
Chambolle-Musigny, 33, 166, 169, 170, 405
Champagne, 24, 33, 257–70, 405
  destinations, best, 429–36
  for entertaining, 362–63
  grape varietals, 258–59
  labels, 39–40, 265, 267, 268
  "méthode champ-enoise," 259–64, 416
  nonvintage, 260–61, 264, 265, 268, 269, 418
  opening bottle of, 277, 390–91
  recipes, for entertaining, 367–70
  romance and, 16–17
  selecting, 268–70
  sparkling wine versus, 258–59
  stemware for, 388, 391
  storing and serving, 276–77
  style of, 264–65, 266
  sweetness levels, 263
  top crus of, 259
  vintage, 260–61, 265, 269–70
Champagne Cocktail, 370
Champagne key, 391
Champagne Mango, 368
Champagne Passion, 368
Champagne Punch, 370

Chardonnay, 8, 17–18, 57–58, 405
  Australia, 138, 140, 141, 142–44
  Burgundy, 81, 82. See also Burgundy, white wines
  buying tips for, 58, 60
  California, 117, 121–22
  in champagne, 259
  Chile, 148, 149
  expanding you horizons, 68
  flavor profile of, 57–58
  New Zealand, 146
  South Africa, 152
Charmat, 264, 405
Chassagne-Montrachet, 33, 86, 87, 88, 169, 405
Château, defined, 405
Château Bottled, 38, 405
Château d'Yquem, 289, 290, 406
Château Haut-Brion Blanc, 80, 81, 177, 181, 182
Château Haut Graves, 81
Château Lafite-Rotshchild, 406
Château La Tâche, 406
Château Latour, 177, 406
Château Margaux, 176, 177, 180, 181, 406
Châteauneuf-du-Pape, 33, 91, 186, 187, 188, 406
Château Pétrus, 95, 182, 390, 406
Chateau Ste. Michelle, 125, 126, 208–9, 210, 271, 273, 296
Chenin Blanc, 8, 10, 58, 152, 291, 295, 406
Chianti, 36, 217, 219–20, 406
  quality levels of, 219–20

Chianti Classico, 36, 220, 406
Chianti Classico Riserva, 220, 406
Chile, 36
red wines, 235–36
white wines, 147–50
Chilling, 384, 385
Champagne or sparkling wine, 276
in a hurry, 276, 385
Christie's Auction House, 338, 343
Cinsault, 187, 190, 238, 407
Claret, 280, 407. *See also* Bordeaux
Clare Valley, 140, 233
Classification of 1855, 176–79, 288, 289–90, 407
Classified growth, 179, 407
Clean, defined, 407
Clos des Mouches, 88, 169
Clos de Vougeot, 166, 169, 170
Cocktail receptions, 363–65
Codorniu, 230, 271, 274
Colchagua, 149, 235
Colheita, 232, 407
Colheita Port, 281, 407
Colheita Ports Vintage Character Port, 281
Collecting wine. *See* Wine collection
Colors of wine, 23–24, 51–52, 53. *See also* Red wines; Rosés; White wines
Col Solare, 210
Columbia Valley, 126, 208
Condrieu, 90
Constantia, 152, 153, 238
Cookouts, 12–13
Coonawarra, 140, 143, 233, 407

Corkage fees, 358–59
Cork extraction, 378–83
troubleshooting, 382–83
extra long corks, 380
stubborn corks, 381, 391
Cork presentation, 320
Corkscrews, 378–82
Cornas, 33, 185, 186
Cosecha, 229, 407
Costs. *See* Price
Côte Châlonnaise, 33, 81, 89–90, 171–72
Côte de Beaune, 33, 400, 407
burgundies, 162, 167–69
white wines, 81, 82, 86–89
quality levels, 86–87
vineyards, 87–88
Côte de Nuits, 33, 407
burgundies, 162, 165–67, 169
white wines, 81, 82
Côte des Bar, 259
Côte des Blancs, 259
Côte d'Or, 82, 86, 162–69, 171, 408
Côte-Rôtie, 33, 185, 186, 188, 408
Côtes du Luberon, 91, 187, 252
Côtes du Rhône. *See* Rhône Valley
Côtes du Ventoux, 91, 187
Crémant, 259
Crianza, 228, 408
Crisp, defined, 408
Crozes-Hermitage, 33, 185, 186, 188, 408
Cru, defined, 408
Cru Beaujolais, 161–62, 408
Cru Bourgeois, 179–80, 408

Cru classé, defined, 409
Crush, defined, 409
Cruvinet, 393
Curicó Valley, 149, 150,
    235
Cuvée, 260, 269–70, 409

D
Dao, 231
Decanters, 389–90
Decanting, 389–90, 409
    Port, 285–86
Degorgement, defined,
    409
Delicate, defined, 409
Demi-sec, 263, 269, 409
Denominación de Origen
    (DO), 135–36
Denominación de Origen
    Calificada (DOCa),
    136
Denominazione di
    Origine Controllata
    (DOC), 134, 217–18,
    409
Denominazione di
    Origine Controllata
    Garantita (DOCG),
    134, 217–18, 410
Dessert wines, 15–16, 37,
    279–300. See also
    Port
    American, 294–97
    Australian, 297–98
    French, 20, 79, 287–91
        Barsac, 32, 34, 179,
            287–91, 402
        Sauternes, 32, 34,
            79, 179, 287–91
    German, 34, 106,
        291–94
    Hungarian, 299–300
    Italian, 298–99
Dietary Guidelines, U.S.,
    44, 158
Dining. See Restaurants;
    Wine lists

Dinner parties, 353–54
Dinners
    casual family, 12
    formal parties, 13–14
Discounters, 332, 333
DOC (Denominazione di
    Origine Controllata),
    134, 217–18, 409
DOCG (Denominazione
    di Origine
    Controllata
    Garantita), 134,
    217–18, 410
Dolcetto, 8, 36, 64, 217,
    223, 410
Domaine, defined, 410
Domaine Romané-Conti,
    168, 169, 170, 410
Dominus, 206, 390
Dosage, 262, 410
Double magnums, 5, 410
Double-winged openers,
    378–79
Douro, 231, 279
Dry Creek Valley, 116, 202
Dry kosher wines, 14–15
Dry wines, 24, 94, 106, 410

E
Earthy, defined, 410
Edelfäule, 101, 410. See
    also Botrytis cinerea
Edna Valley, 116, 204
Eiswein, 35, 101, 293, 295,
    411
Elegant, defined, 411
Elgin, 153
Enology, 411
Entertaining, 347–73
    banquets, 355–61
    brunches, 354
    business, 349–53
    buying tips for, 361–66
    dinner parties, 353–54
    at home, 366–70
        recipes, 367–70
    tasting party, 370–72

Erzeugerabfüllung, defined, 411
Estate-bottled, defined, 411
Extended wine lists, 308
Extra-dry, 263, 269, 411

F

Far Niente, 117, 198, 202
Fat, defined, 411
Fermentation, 25, 82, 96, 411
  barrel, 61, 123, 402
  champagne, 259–64
  malolactic, 415–16
  Port, 20, 280
  white Zinfandel, 245–46
Finesse, defined, 411
Finger Lakes, 129, 273, 297
Finish, defined, 411
First growth, defined, 411
Fixin, 165
Flagey-échézeaux, 166
Flavor profiles, 56–67
Flights, 309, 436–39
Flinty, defined, 411
Food and wine pairing, 6–16
  grape varietals, 8
  reactions between food flavors and wine styles, 9–11
Formal dinner parties, 13–14
Fortant de France, 15, 189, 252
Fortified wine, 412
Fourniéres, 167
France, 32–34. *See also specific regions and wines*
  Appellation d'Origine Contrôlée laws, 38, 74–75, 116, 172, 400
  champagne, 259–70
  dessert wines, 287–91
  quality classifications, 74–75, 163–64
  red wines, 157–90
  rosé wines, 244, 248–52
  white wines, 73–91
  wine labels, 38, 74–75, 172, 400
Freixenet, 230, 271, 274
French 75, recipe for, 369
French Colombard, 58
Friuli, 36, 133, 217, 226
Fruity wines, 24–25, 412
Full-bodied wines, 29–30
Fumé Blanc, 58, 412. *See also* Sauvignon Blanc

G

Gallo Winery, 120, 247, 357
Gamay, 8, 64, 193, 412
Garnacha, 412. *See also* Grenache
Garrafeira, 232, 412
Gattinara, 36, 223–24, 412
Generic wines, defined, 412
Geographical origin. *See* Regions
Georges Duboeuf, 251
German Wine Law (1971), 98–99
Germany, 34–35, 40. *See also specific regions and wines*
  categories of wine, 98–100
  dessert wines, 291–94
  white wines, 93–109
    selecting tips, 104–6
  wine labels, 102–4
Gevrey-Chambertin, 33, 165–66, 169, 412
Gewürztraminer, 8, 32, 35, 58–59, 68, 76, 94, 123–24, 295, 412
Gigondas, 33, 186, 188
Gippsland, 141

Gisborne, 146
Givry, 33, 171, 172
Glassware. *See* Stemware
Glossary of terms, 399–427
Goulburn Valley, 141, 233
Government warnings,
    38–39
Grand Cru, 76–77, 83, 87,
    164, 169, 176, 184,
    268, 413
Grande-Reserve, 77
Gran Reserva, 228, 413
Grape varietals, 8, 56–67,
    317, 426. *See also spe-*
    cific grapes
    Australian white,
        143–44
    blends versus, 26–28
    body and, 29–30
    Californian, 120–24
    champagne, 258–59
    flavor profiles, 56–67
    trends in, 18–19
    wine lists by, 310–13
Graves, 79–81, 174, 177,
    181–82, 413
Grenache, 8, 35, 64, 187,
    190, 195, 227, 234,
    244, 252, 412, 413
Grgich Hills, 117, 296
Griffith Irrigation Area,
    139
Grosslagen, 105–6

H

Halbtrocken, 413
Half-bottles, 367
Hamptons, the, 129, 212
Hawkes Bay, 146
Health effects, of wine,
    43–45, 158
Heart disease, 43, 158
Herbaceous, defined, 413
Hermitage, 33, 185, 186,
    188, 413
Hermitage Blanc, 33,
    90–91

Home entertaining,
    366–70
    recipes, 367–70
House wines, 5–6, 308. *See*
    also Table wines
    price points, 19
Howell Mountain, 201
Hudson River Valley, 129
Humidity, 395
Hungary, dessert wines,
    299–300
Hunter Valley, 139, 143,
    233, 413

I

"Ice wine" (Eiswein), 35,
    101, 293, 295, 411
Inferno, defined, 413
Insignia, 206
International Wine Cellar,
    454
Italy, 36. *See also specific*
    regions and wines
    dessert wines, 298–99
    quality control, 134,
        217–18, 410
    red wines, 216–26
    rosés, 245, 253–54
    sparkling wines, 274–75
    white wines, 132–34

J

Jeroboam, 367, 413
Johannisberg Riesling,
    125, 208
Jug wines, 414
    Californian, 119–20

K

Kabinett, 34, 100, 292, 414
Kendall-Jackson Vineyards,
    114–15, 149, 151,
    196
Kir, 414
    recipe for, 369

Kir Royale, recipe for, 368
Korbel, 273
Kosher wines, 14–15

L

Labels, 37–43
  American Viticultural
    Areas (AVAs),
    113–16, 201, 401
  Australian, 234
  back, 365–66
  champagne, 265, 267,
    268
  French: Appellation
    d'Origine Contrôlée,
    38, 74–75, 172, 400
  German, 102–4
  Ports, 281, 283
  required information
    on, 37–40
  Spanish, 135–36
  useful information on,
    40, 43
Lake County, 118, 203
La Moutonne, 84
Languedoc-Roussillon, 34,
    189, 190, 251–52, 414
Late-bottled vintage Port,
    281–82, 285, 414
Late harvest, defined, 414
Lees, 261–62, 414
Leftover wine, 4, 358
  saving, 391–94
Legs, defined, 414–15
Leonetti Cellars, 126, 209
Le Verre de Vin, 393–94
Light, defined, 415
Light-bodied wines, 29–30
Lirac, 34, 186, 188
Livermore Valley, 118, 204
Lodi-Woodbridge, 119,
    205
Loire Valley, 32, 415
  dessert wines, 291
  rosés, 249
  sparkling wines, 270
  white wines, 77–79

Lombardy, 217, 226
Long Island, 128, 129,
    212–13, 273, 297
Long-vatted, defined, 415
Los Carneros, 116, 193,
    201

M

Mâcconais, 33, 81, 82,
    85–86, 415
McLaren Vale, 140, 233
Maderized, defined, 415
Magazines, wine, 453–54,
    471
Magnums, 5, 13, 38, 367,
    415
  double, 5, 410
Maipo Valley, 149, 150,
    235
Malbec, 18, 36, 65, 173,
    196, 415
Malolactic fermentation,
    415–16
Malvasia, 135, 298
Margaret River, 142, 143,
    233, 416
Margaux, 34, 175–79, 181,
    416
Markup
  at restaurants, 304–7
  by retailers, 330–32
Marlborough, 146
Marlstone, 206
Marsannay, 169
Marsanne, 59, 90, 141
Martinborough, 146
Maule Valley, 149, 235
Medium-bodied wines,
    29–30
Médoc, 32, 34, 174, 175,
    177, 182, 184, 416
Mendocino County, 118,
    195, 203
Mendoza, 151, 237
Merchants. *See* Retailers
Mercurey, 33, 89, 171,
    172

Meritage wines, 63, 69, 198, 205–7
Merlot, 8, 21, 35, 36, 244, 247, 416
  Australia, 234
  Bordeaux, 173–74
  buying tips for, 196
  California, 194–95, 203, 207, 247
  expanding your horizons, 69
  flavor profile of, 65
  Long Island, 129, 213
  Spain, 230
  Washington State, 125, 208, 209
Merlot Rosé, 247
Méthode champenoise, 259–64, 416
Methuselah, 367, 416
Meursault, 33, 68, 86, 87, 416
Microclimate, defined, 416–17
Midi. *See* Languedoc-Roussillon
Millésime, 265, 268, 417
Mimosas, 268–69, 354
  recipe for, 368
Mise En Bouteille, 38, 417
Montagne de Reims, 259
Montagny, 33, 171
Montepulciano d'Abruzzo, 217, 225, 226, 399
Monterey County, 118, 199–200, 204
Monthélie, 169
Montrachet, 417
Mood, 5
Morey-Saint-Denis, 166
Mosel-Saar-Ruwer, 97, 104, 106, 107, 292, 417
Moulis, 34, 175
Mount Veeder, 116, 202
Mourvédre, 65, 187, 190, 234, 417
Mudgee, 139, 233

Müller-Thurgau, 94, 146, 417
Murray Darling, 139–40, 141
Murrumbidgee Irrigation Area, 139
Muscadelle, 288
Muscadet, 10, 77, 78, 79, 417
Muscat, 32, 59, 76, 295
"Must" (unfermented grape juice), 100, 417, 426

N

Nahe, 97, 104, 108, 417
Napa Valley, 31, 417
  red wines, 193, 194, 196–98, 199, 201, 203
  white wines, 115, 117
Navarra, 37, 135, 230, 252–53, 417
Nebbiolo, 8, 11, 65, 195, 223–24, 226, 418
Nebbiolo d'Alba, 222
Nebuchadnezzar, 367
Négociant, defined, 418
Nelson, 146
Newsletters, store, 328
New South Wales, 139–40, 145, 233
New York State, 35. *See also specific regions and wines*
  auction houses, 343
  champagne destinations, best, 434–36
  dessert wines, 296, 297
  red wines, 212–13
  retailers, 447–49
  sparkling wines, 273
  white wines, 112, 128–29
  wine lists, favorite, 438–39
New Zealand, 36, 145–47

Noble rot, 418. See also
    Botrytis cinerea
"Nose," 54–55, 403, 418
Nuits-Saint-Georges, 33,
    167, 169, 418

O

Oak, defined, 418
Oakville, 202
Oaky, defined, 418
Oenophile, 418
Off-dry wines, 26
Oporto, 279–87, 418
Opus One, 28, 198, 206
Ordering wine, 313–14
Oregon, 35
    dessert wines, 296–97
    red wines, 207–8,
        210–12
    white wines, 112,
        127–28
Over the hill, defined, 418
Oxidized, defined, 419

P

Paarl, 153, 238
Pacific Northwest. See also
    Oregon; Washington
    State
    dessert wines, 296–97
    red wines, 207–12
    white wines, 125–28
Padthaway, 141
Parties. See Entertaining
Paso Robles, 202
Pauillac, 34, 175, 177, 178,
    179, 419
Pemberton, 142, 233
Penedés, 227, 230, 274,
    419
Pernand-Vergelesses, 167
Pessac-Léognan, 32,
    80–81, 174, 177, 181
Petit Château, defined,
    419

Petite Sirah, 65, 69, 200,
    204, 419
Petit Verdot, 173, 196, 206
Pfalz, 97, 104, 108–9, 292,
    419
Phylloxera, 227, 419
Pickberry, 207
Piedmont, 217, 222–24,
    419
Piesporter Goldtröpfchen,
    104
Pink wines. See Rosés
Pinotage, 37, 238, 239, 419
Pinot Blanc, 8, 21, 32, 35,
    94, 124, 204, 419
    flavor profile of, 59–60
Pinot Grigio (Pinot Gris),
    8, 10, 18, 36, 60, 68,
    76, 94, 419–20
Pinot Meunier, 258, 420
Pinot Noir, 8, 10, 11, 35,
    66, 420
    Australia, 234
    Burgundy, 159, 163, 171
    California, 115, 193,
        200–201
    in champagne, 258
    expanding your
        horizon, 69
    flavor profile of, 66
    Oregon, 35, 210–12
Plonk, defined, 420
Pomerol, 32, 34, 174,
    182–83, 420
Pommard, 33, 168, 169,
    420
Port, 15, 279–87, 420
    alternatives to, 286–87
    decanting, 285–86
    labels, 281, 283
    process for, 280
    producers, 284
    stemware for, 388
    sweetness levels, 280
    types of, 280–82
    vintage, 282, 284–85,
        426

Porto tongs, 286
Portugal, 36, 37. *See also*
    specific regions and
    wines
    (Oporto) Port, 279–87,
    418
    red wines, 231–32
    white wines, 136–37
Pouilly-Fuissé, 68, 78, 86,
    420
Pouilly-Fumé, 32, 68,
    77–79, 420
Pouilly-Vinzelles, 86
Premier Cru, defined, 420
Premier Grand Cru, 176,
    183–84
Prestige cuvée. *See* Tête de
    Cuvée
Price, 19–22. *See also*
    Markup
    determining cost of pro-
    ducing wine, 19–21
    money-saving tips,
    21–22
Priorato, 230
Private Preserve, 393
Progressive wine lists,
    311–13
Proprietary name, 420–21
Provence, 62, 250
Publications, 453–54, 471
Puligny-Montrachet, 33,
    68, 86, 87–88, 421
Pulltap's, 380
Puttonyos, 299–300, 421

Q

Qualitätswein, defined,
    421
Qualitätswein bestimmter
    Anbaugebiete, 98, 99
Qualitätswein mit Prädikat
    (QmP), 98, 99–100,
    292, 414, 421
Quinta, 232, 421

R

Rapel Valley, 149, 150, 235
Reading, recommended,
    453–55
Recipes, for entertaining,
    367–70
Red grapes, 8. *See also*
    specific grapes
    blending for rosés,
    243–44
    flavor profiles of, 62–67
Red wines, 23–24, 51–52,
    155–239. *See also* Port;
    and specific regions and
    wines
    Argentina, 237–38
    Australia, 232–35
    California, 192–207
    Chile, 235–36
    expanding your
    horizons, 69
    French, 157–90
    Italy, 216–26
    New York State, 212–13
    Oregon, 207–8, 210–12
    Pacific Northwest,
    207–12
    Portugal, 231–32
    refrigerating, 6
    return to, 157–59
    serving temperature,
    383–85
    South Africa, 238–39
    South America, 235–38
    Spain, 226–30
    stemware for, 388
    United States, 191–214
    Washington State,
    207–10
Regions, 19, 22, 30–37, 38.
    See also specific regions
    wine lists by, 310–13
Rehoboam, 367
Reims, 259
Reserva, defined, 421

Réserve Personnelle, 77
Residual sugar, 421
Resources, 429–55, 469–74
Restaurants. *See also* Wine
    lists
    business entertaining at,
        350–53
    champagne destina-
        tions, 429–36
    dinner parties at, 353
    markup at, 304–7
    ordering wine, 313–14
    sending wine back,
        321–22
    wine lists, favorite,
        436–39
    "wine ritual," 319–21
    wine-serving tempera-
        ture in, 385
Retailers, 323–36
    building a relationship
        with, 326–27
    buying strategies,
        333–36
    list of, 439–51
    markup, 330–32
    returning bad bottles,
        329–30
    selling to, 342–43
    signs to look for, 324–25
    special features of,
        327–29
    Web sites, 473–74
Rheingau, 97, 104, 105,
    107–8, 292, 421
Rheinhessen, 97, 104, 106,
    108, 292, 421
Rhône Rangers, 27, 59,
    123
Rhône Valley, 11, 18, 27,
    33, 408
    dessert wines, 291
    red wines, 185–89
    rosés, 252
    white wines, 90–91

Ribera del Duero, 37, 227,
    229–30, 421
Richebourg, 166, 169
Riddling, 261–62, 422
Riedel glassware, 386–87,
    474
Riesling, 8, 10, 94, 95–97,
    422
    Alsace, 76
    Australia, 144
    California, 117, 124, 295
    dry, 10, 32, 96
    expanding your
        horizons, 68
    flavor profile of, 60,
        95–96
    Germany, 34, 94, 95–97,
        104
    money-saving tips, 105
    New Zealand, 146
    South Africa, 152
Rioja, 36, 135, 227–29,
    252–53, 422
Río Negro, 151
Riserva, defined, 422
Ritz Cocktail, recipe for,
    367–68
Riverina, 139
Robertson, 153, 238–39
Rogue River Valley, 127,
    211
Romance, champagne
    and, 16–17
Rosado, 245, 252–53, 422
Rosato, 244, 253–54, 422
Rosé d'Anjou, 63, 249
Rosemount Estate,
    142–43, 145, 234,
    275, 286
Rosés, 23–24, 51–52,
    243–55, 422
    blending process,
        243–44
    California, 244, 245–48
    France, 244, 248–52

Italy, 245, 253–54
selecting, 254–55
serving, 254–55
  temperature,
    383–85
Spain, 245, 252–53
Rosso di Montalcino, 63,
    221
Roussillon. *See* Languedoc-
    Roussillon
Rubicon, 28, 207
Ruby Ports, 280, 422
Rully, 33, 89, 171, 172
Russian River Valley, 115,
    202
Rutherford, 202
Rutherglen, 141, 233

S

St.-Émilion, 32, 34,
    62, 174, 182–84,
    424
St.-Estéphe, 34, 175, 178,
    179, 424
St.-Joseph, 33, 185, 186,
    188
St.-Julien, 34, 175, 177,
    178, 179, 424
St.-Martín Val d'Orbieu,
    15, 251
St.-Véran, 85, 86
Salice Salentino, 217,
    225–26, 254
Salmanazar, 367, 422
Salta, 151
Salty flavor, 50
Sancerre, 32, 77–79, 249,
    422
Sangiovese, 18, 27, 66, 69,
    132, 194, 422
San Joaquin Valley, 119,
    195, 204–5
San Luis Obispo County,
    119, 204
Santa Barbara County,
    119, 204

Santa Clara County, 118,
    204
Santenay, 169
Sauternes, 32, 34, 79, 179,
    287–91, 423
  classification of 1855,
    288, 289–90
Sauvignon Blanc, 8, 10,
    11, 52, 61, 288, 423
  Australia, 144
  California, 117, 122–23
  Chile, 148, 149
  expanding your
    horizons, 68
  flavor profile of, 60–61
  Long Island, 129
  New Zealand, 145–46
  South Africa, 152
Savigny Les Beaune, 167,
    169
Saving wines, 4–6
  leftover, 391–94
Savoring wine, 55–56
Scheurebe, 94
Screwpulls, 380–81
Sec, 263, 269
Sediment, 261–62, 285,
    389, 423
Selling
  at auctions, 341–43
  to retailers, 342–43
Sémillon, 8, 35, 36, 61–62,
    68, 80, 144, 149, 288,
    295, 423
Servers, 315–16
Serving temperature,
    383–85
  champagne, 276
  guidelines for, 384
Shiraz, 423. *See also* Syrah
Shopping. *See* Auctions;
    Buying strategies;
    Retailers
Short-vatted, defined, 423
Sicily, 133
Sierra Foothills, 119, 205
Silvaner, 94

Simple bar syrup, 369
Size of bottles, 38, 366–67
Smell of wine, 54–55. *See
    also* Aroma; Bouquet;
    "Nose"
Sommelier, 314–16, 423
Sonoma Valley, 115, 424
    red wines, 194–95, 198,
        201, 203
    white wines, 117–18
Sotheby's Auction House,
    343
Sour taste, 49
South Africa, 37
    Port-style wines, 287
    red wines, 238–39
    white wines, 152–53
South America, 36. *See also
    specific regions and
    wines*
    red wines, 235–38
    white wines, 147–52
South Australia, 140–41,
    145, 233
Sovereign, 367
Spain, 36–37. *See also spe-
    cific regions and wines*
    red wines, 226–30
    rosés, 245, 252–53
    sparkling wines, 273–74,
        404
    white wines, 134–36
"Spanna." *See* Nebbiolo
Sparkling wines, 24, 257,
    270–76
    Australia, 275–76
    California, 271–73
    champagne versus,
        258–59
    Charmat process, 264,
        405
    Italy, 274–75
    opening bottle of,
        277
    Spain, 273–74
    storing and serving,
        276–77

Spätburgunder, 97
Spätlese, 34, 100, 106, 293,
    424
Spices, 7
Split, 367
Spumante, 274–75
Stags Leap, 202
Stainless-steel
    fermentation, 424
Steen, 37, 58, 152. *See also*
    Chenin Blanc
Stellenbosch, 152, 153,
    238
Stemware, 386–89
    for champagne, 276–78
    sizes of, 387–88
    for wine tastings,
        54
Stickies, 297–98
Still wines, 424
Stoppers, 392
Stores. *See* Retailers
Storing, 394–97
    champagne, 276–77
    criteria for, 394–95
    leftovers, 391–94
Sulfites, 39–40, 424
"Super-Chileans," 235–36
Sur lie, 123, 261, 424–25
Süss Reserve, 99, 425
Sutter Home, 245–47
Swan District, 142
Sweet foods, 9–10
Sweet taste, 49
Sweet wines, 25, 49
Swirling wine, 53–54
Syrah, 8, 11, 35, 36, 65, 66,
    69, 138, 185–86, 187,
    190, 199–200, 208,
    209, 233, 425

T

Table wines
    Tafelwein, 98, 99, 425
    vino da tavola, 218–19
    Vins de Table, 75

Tafelwein, 98, 99, 425
Taille, 260
Takaj-Hegyalja, 299–300, 421
Tannin, 11, 50, 425
Taste sensations, 48–51
Taste test, 320–21
Tasting party, 370–72
Tastings, 47–69, 372
    five S's of, 52–56
    flavor profiles, 56–67
    in-store, 327
    at restaurants, 319–21
    wine glasses used for, 54
Tavel, 252
Tawny Ports, 281, 425
Tears. See Legs
Temelcula, 116
Temperature for serving, 383–85
    champagne, 276
Tempranillo, 8, 66, 227, 229, 231, 425
Terroir, 83, 163, 425
Tête de Cuvée, 269–70, 425
Texas, 112
Texture of wine, 51
Tinta, defined, 425
Tokay, 299–300, 421
Trade organizations, 472–73
Trebbiano, 62, 298, 425
Trefethen Vineyards, 117, 296
Trentino, 133, 217, 226
Trilogy, 28, 207
Trocken, 425
Trockenbeerenauslese, 35, 101, 293, 295, 426
Tupungato, 151
Tuscany, 217, 219–22, 426

U

Ugni Blanc, 62, 152
Umami, 48, 51

Umpqua Valley, 127, 211
Unfermented grape juice, 100, 417, 426
United States, 35. See also specific regions and wines
    American Viticultural Areas, 113–16, 201, 401
    dessert wines, 294–97
    red wines, 191–214
    sparkling wines, 271–73
    top five producing states, 112–13
    white wines, 111–30

V

Vacqueyras, 34, 186, 188
Vacu-Vin, 392–93
Valentine's Day, 16–17
Vallée de la Marne, 259
Valpolicella, 36, 217, 224–25
Varietals. See Grape varietals
Veneto, 133, 217, 224–25, 426
Verre de Vin, 393–94
Victoria, 141, 145, 233
Village wine, 426
Vineyards. See Wineries; and specific vineyards
Vinho Verde, 136–37, 426
Vino da tavola, 218–19
Vino Nobile di Montepulciano, 36, 221, 226, 426
Vin Santo, 16, 298–99
Vins Délimités de Qualité Supérieure (VDQS), 75
Vins de Pays, 75
Vins de Table, 75
Vintage, 38, 317, 426
Vintage Character Ports, 281

Vintage Ports, 282, 284–85, 426
Viognier, 8, 18, 62, 68, 90, 123, 295, 427
Vitis Labrusca, 111, 427
Vitis vinifera, 111, 129, 427
Volnay, 168, 169, 170, 427
Vosne-Romanée, 166, 169, 170
Vougeot, 166, 169, 427
Vouvray, 32, 77, 78–79, 427

W

Waiter's corkscrew, 379–80
Walker Bay, 153
Walla Walla Valley, 126, 208
Warehouse clubs, 332, 333
Warehouse storage, 396, 397
Washington State, 35
  dessert wines, 296
  red wines, 207–10
  white wines, 112, 125–27
  wine lists, favorite, 439
Web sites, 469–74
  retailer, 328–29
Weddings, 355–61
Weight of wine, 8
Western Australia, 141–42, 145, 233
Whispering Peak Vineyards, 357
White grapes, 8. *See also specific grapes*
  flavor profiles of, 57–62
White wines, 23–24, 51–52, 71–154. *See also specific regions and wines*
  Australia, 137–45
  expanding your horizons, 68
  France, 73–91
  Germany, 93–109

Italy, 132–34
New York State, 112, 128–29
New Zealand, 145–47
Oregon, 112, 127–28
Pacific Northwest, 125–28
Portugal, 136–37
serving temperature, 383–85
South Africa, 152–53
South America, 147–52
Spain, 134–36
stemware for, 388
United States, 111–30
Washington State, 112, 125–27
White Zinfandels, 8, 10, 16–17, 35, 94, 254–55, 362, 427
  flavor profile of, 67
  Sutter Home and, 245–47
Willamette Valley, 127, 211, 297
Wine accessories, 377–83, 474
Wine advisers, 343–45
Wine Advocate, 453–54, 471
Wine auctions. *See* Auctions
Wine cellars, 395–96
Wine clubs, 329
Wine collection, 336–37
  advisers for, 343–45
  storing, 396–97
Wine Enthusiast, 454
Wine futures, 333–34
Wine glasses, 54, 386–89
Winekeeper System, 393
Wine labels. *See* Labels
Wine lists, 303–22
  favorite, list of, 436–39
  ordering from, 313–14
  reading, 309–13
  seeking assistance with, 314–16

survival technique for
  safety, 317–18
types of, 307–9
Wine merchants. *See*
  Retailers
"Wine repertoire," 67–69
Wineries. *See also specific*
  wineries
  buying direct from,
    334–36
  Web sites, 471–72
"Wine ritual," 319–21
Wines by the glass, 308–9
  markup on, 304–5
Wine serving temperature,
  383–85
  champagne, 276
Wine Spectator, 436–37, 453,
  471
Wine & Spirits, 454

Wine-tasting party, 370–72
Wine tastings. *See* Tastings
Woodbridge, 119, 205
Wood Ports, 280, 427

Y
Yakima Valley, 126, 208
Yarra Valley, 141, 233

Z
Zinfandels, 8, 35, 244, 427.
  See also White
  Zinfandels
  California, 119, 196–97,
    202, 203, 204, 207,
    295
  expanding your
    horizons, 69

Get the inside scoop...with the *Unofficial Guides©*!

Health and Fitness

The Unofficial Guide to Cosmetic Surgery
ISBN: 0-02-862522-6 Price: $15.95

The Unofficial Guide to Having a Baby
ISBN: 0-02-862695-8 Price: $16.99

The Unofficial Guide to Living with Diabetes
ISBN: 0-02-862919-1 Price: $16.99

Career Planning

The Unofficial Guide to Acing the Interview
ISBN: 0-02-862924-8 Price: $16.99

Business and Personal Finance

The Unofficial Guide to Investing
ISBN: 0-02-862458-0 Price: $15.95

The Unofficial Guide to Starting a Small Business
ISBN: 0-02-862525-0 Price: $16.99

Home and Automotive

The Unofficial Guide to Buying a Home
ISBN: 0-02-862461-0 Price: $16.99

The Unofficial Guide to Buying or Leasing a Car
ISBN: 0-02-862524-2 Price: $15.95

Family and Relationships

The Unofficial Guide to Childcare
ISBN: 0-02-862457-2 Price: $15.95

The Unofficial Guide to Dating Again
ISBN: 0-02-862454-8 Price: $16.99

The Unofficial Guide to Divorce
ISBN: 0-02-862455-6 Price: $16.99

The Unofficial Guide to Eldercare
ISBN: 0-02-862456-4 Price: $15.95

The Unofficial Guide to Planning Your Wedding
ISBN: 0-02-862459-9 Price: $16.99

Hobbies and Recreation

The Unofficial Guide to Casino Gambling
ISBN: 0-02-862917-5 Price: $16.99

All books in the *Unofficial Guide©* series are available at your local bookseller.